LATE ROMAN TOWNS IN BRITAIN

In this book, Adam Rogers examines the late Roman phases of towns in Britain. Critically analysing the archaeological notion of decline, he focuses on public buildings, which played an important role, administrative and symbolic, within urban complexes. Arguing against the interpretation that many of these monumental civic buildings were in decline or abandoned in the later Roman period, he demonstrates that they remained purposeful spaces and important centres of urban life. Through a detailed assessment of the archaeology of late Roman towns, this book argues that the archaeological framework of decline does not permit an adequate and comprehensive understanding of the towns during this period. Moving beyond the idea of decline, this book emphasises a longer-term perspective for understanding the importance of towns in the later Roman period.

Adam Rogers is a British Academy Postdoctoral Fellow at the School of Archaeology and Ancient History, University of Leicester. He has published articles on the archaeology of the Roman and Late Iron Age periods, especially in the areas of settlement and landscape studies, religion and ritual, and historiography.

Late Roman Towns in Britain

Rethinking Change and Decline

ADAM ROGERS

University of Leicester

CAMBRIDGE
UNIVERSITY PRESS

CAMBRIDGE UNIVERSITY PRESS
Cambridge, New York, Melbourne, Madrid, Cape Town,
Singapore, São Paulo, Delhi, Mexico City

Cambridge University Press
32 Avenue of the Americas, New York NY 10013-2473, USA

Published in the United States of America by Cambridge University Press, New York

www.cambridge.org
Information on this title: www.cambridge.org/9781107698796

First published 2011
First paperback edition 2013

A catalogue record for this publication is available from the British Library

Library of Congress Cataloguing in Publication Data
Rogers, Adam, 1981–
Late Roman towns in Britain : rethinking change and decline / Adam Rogers.
    p.   cm.
Includes bibliographical references and index.
ISBN 978-1-107-00844-1 (hardback)
1. Cities and towns, Ancient – Great Britain.   2. Great Britain – History – Roman period,
55 B.C.–449 A.D.   3. Great Britain – Antiquities, Roman.   4. Romans – Great Britain.
5. Urbanization – Great Britain – History.   I. Title.
DA145.R733   2011
936.2′04 – dc22   2010046484

ISBN 978-1-107-00844-1 Hardback
ISBN 978-1-107-69879-6 Paperback

For my father
who would have loved to have seen this
work through to publication.

Contents

List of illustrations

List of tables

Preface and Acknowledgements

This book is about our understanding of Roman urbanism and settlement change. It focuses on an archaeological study of the late Roman phases of towns in Roman Britain through a critical examination of the term 'decline' and examines the way in which towns as sites and places continued into the later Roman period. The emphasis on decline is a theoretical approach like other interpretative theories within archaeology, but authors of late Roman studies have not always felt comfortable in engaging in such debates when analysing archaeological material. The structures and uses of public buildings within towns provide a detailed case study for redressing this situation: the monumental architecture was used traditionally to demonstrate romanisation and civilised living, which was then followed by decay and ruin when their appearances began to change. Public buildings were meaning laden with rich biographies that formed major parts of the significance of towns as places. The towns themselves were symbolic places with long histories within wider landscapes. This book discusses the varied evidence for the continuing use of public buildings and alternative ways of interpreting these material representations of action in the past. Themes here include structural changes to buildings, timber additions to buildings, industrial activity within them, and their continued focus for many other kinds of activities.

Integrated into this study is the importance of historiography, demonstrating that many traditions within Roman archaeology and history, including theories relating to urbanism, landscape, and decline, developed within specific social contexts of the modern world. As a case study this is demonstrated by an investigation of Edward Gibbon's *The Decline and Fall of the Roman Empire* (published between 1776 and 1788), the context in which it was written, its reception in later times, and its impact on archaeological interpretation. By taking a longer-term perspective, this book also argues that it is necessary to challenge our understanding of Roman towns as part of the reanalysis of their later phases. This is undertaken by an investigation of the settlement and landscape context in which Roman towns developed. Many of these landscapes were meaningful, monumentalised by both artificial and natural features and ritualised before the appearance of classical urbanism. When towns in the later Roman period are placed within this wider context of landscape use over time, alternative visions of their later phases can be sought.

This book draws on a large amount of archaeological material, both published and unpublished, and it would not have been possible without the assistance and kindness of a large number of people. Firstly I would like to thank Professor Richard Hingley, Dr Anna Leone, and Professor Colin Haselgrove (now at the University of Leicester), who were always helpful, insightful, and willing to give their time as my supervisors whilst I was a doctoral student at the University of Durham. I would also like to thank everyone else who has helped me along the way in the Department of Archaeology, Durham, and in the School of Archaeology and Ancient History at the University of Leicester, where I am currently a British Academy Postdoctoral Fellow. I am very grateful to everyone who has supported me and to the Arts and Humanities Research Council for funding my doctoral research whilst I was at Durham. The book would also not have been possible without the help and time of staff at Cambridge University Press and my two anonymous referees, to whom I am grateful.

I would like to thank the following people for their time, interest, and goodwill during the process of data collection and analysis: Jan Allen, Mark Atkinson, Nick Bateman, Mark Bennet, Paul Bennett, Heather Bird, Nick Boldrini, Paul Booth, Peter Boyd, Richard Buckley, Sue Byrne, Alice Cattermole, Elizabeth Chamberlin, Laura Coats, Nick Cooper, Carrie Cowan, Philip Crummy, Megan Dennis, Simon Esmonde Cleary, Chris Evans, Edith Evans, Neil Faulkner, Ian Friel, Michael Fulford, Andrew Gardner, Paula Gentil, Louisa Gidney, Francis Grew, Peter Guest, John Herridge, Tim Higgins, J. D. Hill, Neil Holbrook, Sue Hughes, Henry Hurst, Mick Jones, Richard Jones, Sara Lunt, John Magilton, Cath Malony, Jenny Mann, Tracy Matthews, David Mattingly, Judy Mills, Tom Moore, Anna Morris, Rosalind Niblett, John Paddock, John Peterson, Graham Piddock, Claire Pinder, Kate Pretty, Andy Pye, Richard Reece, Helen Rees, Verlie Riley, Peter Rowsome, Ian Scrivener-Lindley, Paul Sealey, Sarah Semple, John Shepherd, David Thorold, Penny Ward, Chris Wardle, Peter Weddel, Roger White, Mark Whyman, Steve Willis, Rob Witcher, and Peter Woodward.

CHAPTER 1

Introduction

This book considers late Roman urbanism in Britain, but its approach has consequences for work across the Empire on both the late Roman period and urbanism in general. Studies of late Roman urbanism have commonly been influenced by the theory of decline and fall (e.g., Faulkner 2000a; Haverfield 1912; Liebeschuetz 2000; B. Ward-Perkins 2005), while, in association with this, studies of the growth of towns and the nature of preceding settlement pattern have been directed by notions of 'romanisation' and 'civilisation' (e.g., Frere 1967; Haverfield 1912; Millett 1990; Wacher 1975). The result of this is that the archaeological analysis of late Roman towns, and perhaps Roman urbanism more generally, has not advanced to the same theoretical sophistication as some other areas of Romano-British studies such as rural settlement and identity.

   This investigation focuses on the area of public space and the use of public buildings within towns in Britain, with the 'official' or 'public' towns – the *coloniae, municipia,* and *civitas*-capitals (Figure 1.1) – providing a further focus. The public buildings are used to evaluate the usefulness of the theory of decline for understanding urbanism and social attitudes at this time. These structures were a significant aspect of towns and the way in which they were experienced; they were perceived and used in symbolic ways (Boman 2003). As will become apparent in later parts of the book, public buildings have been the subject of a considerable number of excavations and have often received greater attention than many other aspects of Roman urbanism, being used as indicators of levels of 'romanisation', of civilisation in the 'Golden Age', and subsequent decline in the later Roman period. That they have been examined predominantly through this framework of interpretation might explain why the study of public buildings has perhaps become less fashionable in Romano-British research today. Apart from the production of important excavation reports and the discussions they contain (e.g., Fulford and Timby 2000; Yule 2005), there have been relatively few recent studies of public buildings in Britain, especially from theoretical perspectives (with important exceptions, including Creighton 2006; Mattingly 2006a; and Revell 2009). This situation indicates the need for reanalysis and the opportunity to demonstrate the usefulness of theoretical approaches when one is tackling subjects relating to urbanism.

   In studying the later Roman period there is a danger of becoming preoccupied with end dates, which in the case of urbanism can be problematic, because it places too much restriction on the significance of the sites as places. With this in mind, attention will be given to the archaeological evidence of activity within towns in the late Roman period rather than attempting to fit it into a restrictive historical framework. Focus will be on the varied evidence relating to the use of spaces enclosed by public buildings and the significance of buildings as places. Whilst space is a more geographically definable entity, place is connected with human experience, feeling, and thought; its importance need not necessarily be governed by economic circumstances or linear concepts of time (E. Casey 1996: 24–5; Ingold 2000: 149; Taylor 1997: 193). The end date of Roman Britain itself is debatable; the significance of A.D. 410 as a point of change is uncertain and it seems probable that many people continued to consider themselves as 'Roman' well into the fifth century (Bartholomew 1982; Birley 2005: 461–2; Esmonde Cleary 1989, 2004; M. E. Jones 1996). A loose framework for the late Roman period will be taken as the late third, fourth, and early fifth centuries after the 'third century crisis' (Mitchell 2007: 55–62). This has traditionally formed a dividing point between the late Roman and earlier periods, but the impact of this period of 'crisis' in Britain has been subject to review (see Chapter 3). As a result, this book concentrates on exploring methods for understanding evidence of activity that adopt a more theoretically and methodologically rigorous procedure.

Studies of the late Roman phases of towns often differ widely in methodology from explorations of other periods. In a recent study on landscape, M. Johnson (2007: 147–8, 198–9) commented on the distinction that is often drawn between work on the 'irrational' landscapes of prehistory and the 'romanticism and empiricism' of studies of the medieval period. This argument is also relevant for Roman-period landscape and settlement studies in which work has not tended to embrace the 'unfamiliar' as it has for prehistoric periods. Studies of Late Antiquity have especially been unwilling to embrace theoretical developments. In this book I attempt to draw the different approaches together. An important part of this is an examination of our understanding of Roman urbanism itself in Britain and its relationship with pre-existing land use.

1.1 The towns of Roman Britain

According to many authors who have written on Roman Britain, we know what towns are and what they were in the Roman period.[1] Towns were autonomous communities at the centre of a *territorium* and were divided into smaller administrative areas known as *vici* (Mann 1996: 104–8). The town had a number of functions, including the collection of taxation, jurisdiction, and the provision of a station for the *cursus publicus* (ibid.). In Latin, the word *oppidum* was used for an urban nucleus but this term had no strict meaning and could be used to cover a number of different types of settlement (Purcell 1996a: 1069; 1996b: 335). Legal definitions of towns are recorded in classical texts – the town (*oppidum*) is categorised as a *colonia, municipium,* and the urban centre of the *civitas*[2] – and these have been the basis of nearly all discussions of towns in Roman Britain (e.g., Collingwood and Richmond 1969; Frere 1967; Haverfield 1912; Wacher 1975).[3] It could be argued that this status was more important than the physical condition of the settlements, which was not so easy to maintain, especially in the late Roman period.

[1] The term 'town' is used here rather than 'city', except where quotations have used the latter; both terms have modern connotations but the term 'town' is more usual when one is studying Romano-British urbanism.
[2] This reflects the divisions of *oppida* listed in the *lex Rubria* (49 B.C.) as *municipium, colonia,* and *praefectura* (Purcell 1996a: 1069). This was a statute by which a colony was founded at Carthage-Junonia by C. Sempronius Gracchus (Crawford 1996: 852).
[3] Wacher's hugely influential work was updated and republished in 1995 but with no changes in emphasis to its organisation or discussion.

FIGURE 1.1. Map of Britain with the location of the main towns within the study (drawn by A. C. Rogers).

Although the *coloniae* and probably *municipia* are attested historically in Britain, the nature and function of the *civitas*-capitals is more problematic,[4] and the highly centralised *civitas*-capital system based on pre-existing tribal groups, originating mainly from Haverfield's influential work (1924: 191–4), has come under some scrutiny (e.g., Laurence 2001). Studies on identity certainly indicate a much more fragmented and fluid situation in the late Iron Age, which may have been harder to resolve after the conquest (e.g., Moore 2006; cf. S. Jones 1997) than is often imagined. We need to adopt a more flexible way to interpret the roles of a wide variety of settlements that occurred within the

[4] Haverfield (1912, 1913, 1924) did not use the term *civitas*-capital but instead 'tribal' or 'cantonal capitals' and sometimes 'provincial towns'. Collingwood and Richmond (1969) and Rivet (1958) also use the term 'cantonal capital' whilst Richmond (1963) wrote of 'tribal capitals'. Haverfield's work on the tribal organisation of Britain was hugely influential and was consolidated in Romano-British studies with the use of the term *civitas*-capital from the 1960s onwards (e.g., Frere 1967; Wacher 1966, 1975).

civitates (cf. Millett 2001). 'Small towns' especially are likely to have a more significant role in administration and the economy than is currently understood (cf. A. Brown 1995; Burnham and Wacher 1990), and using categories based on size, with smaller sites being considered less important that larger ones (cf. Childe 1950; Hopkins 1978: 71), is generally simplistic. Certainly, relying on images of Roman Golden Age urbanism provides fewer opportunities for alternative viewpoints of towns and the variety of settlements. As well as these legal definitions, towns are also often defined by attributes such as size, public architecture, planning, and organisation (cf. R. White 2007: 177), and it is changes to these that encourage analyses of decline in the late Roman period.

Despite these external changes, the significance of towns as places and foci of activity continued. It has been argued that a loss of population in the early fifth century is an important indicator of an end of urban characteristics at some sites (e.g., Biddle 1984). Certainly there are now deserted sites such as Silchester (Fulford, Clarke, and Eckhardt 2006) and Wroxeter (White and Barker 1998), which indicate that urbanism eventually came to an end here. Falls in population on some sites from the fifth century may represent political and economic change (cf. Dark 1994),[5] but these sites retained their importance as places and they were foci of church construction in the medieval period (cf. Bell 2005). Roman-style urbanism did eventually come to an end at all of the town sites in Britain, as did the Roman Empire.[6] The towns had varying biographies and post-Roman histories but it is important not to view the eventual outcomes as providing evidence of support for decline in the later Roman period. This book concentrates on the actions and experiences of people in these places in the later Roman period for which there is considerable opportunity for reanalysis.

Urban settlements in the past are not now as easy to understand as researchers once thought, which means that the dichotomy between continuity versus 'decline' is not a simple one. Approaches more common in areas such as urban geography, phenomenology, and landscape studies (e.g., Edensor 2000; Hall 2006; Massey 2005; Simonsen 2003; Tilley 1994)[7] demonstrate that studies of Roman urbanism are in need of greater theoretical rigour, especially to aid in the understanding of urban behaviour and aspects of continuity, transformation, and change in urban sites. There is a considerable amount of literature on place and space and the city in humanistic geography, reacting against positivist spatial science. Studies of the city have, for instance, begun to look at the 'lived bodily experience of city life' (Edensor 2000); human action is an important part of these sites. Edensor's work *Moving through the City* (2000) explored the way in which people act upon the city, inscribing their presence through movement in a process of continual remaking through which the city is continually regenerated. The city and its architecture are the physically and symbolically bounded spaces or stages for movement and interaction and, for Edensor (ibid.: 123), these moving 'performative' processes ceaselessly reconstitute the symbolic values of sites. Within archaeology, phenomenology has mainly been applied to prehistory, with far fewer studies relating to the Roman period. This has created an

---

[5] In the case of Silchester, a possible forced abandonment of the settlement in post-Roman times has been argued because it formed a threat to the development of new power bases (Fulford et al. 2006).

[6] However, it could be argued that the Roman Empire continues to be influential in the world to this day.

[7] Phenomenology originates largely from philosophical works such as Heidegger's *Being and Time* (1988; first published in 1927 in German with the first English translation in 1962). Here phenomenology is the science of the being of entities. Heidegger's term *Dasein* states that the most important form of being is being-in-the-world.

unnecessary methodological divide, because phenomenology could also be of use for understanding past cultural meanings in Roman and later periods, especially for areas such as Britain where there are few written texts.

Simonsen (2003) writes of what she terms 'walking in the city', an act which 'spatialises' the city and turns it into a collection of narratives of meaningful individuals. For her, cities are constituted by people practising in place (Simonsen 1997: 161); they are collections of stories (Massey 2005: 130) that build up over time – as places they have a narrative and 'accretional' quality (Thomas 1996: 83). Likewise, for Pile (2005: 1), an important part of the city is the social processes, customs, and traditions of the inhabitants, and, returning to the Roman period, for Willis (2007a) towns can be seen in terms of landscape events in which visual and phenomenological aspects are important. These are now unavoidable aspects to tackle in urban studies of historical periods; towns are far from straightforward and knowable. This focus of study on urbanism marks a considerable contrast with the dominant economic and political explanations in the 1960s and 1970s, a time of considerable post-war urban planning and, consequently, much archaeological work within towns.

In connection with this, 'landscape' is now a complex and problematic term within archaeology and has been the subject of much debate (e.g., M. Johnson 2007; Tilley 1994). The rational and economic view of land derived from post-medieval Western Europe is not always helpful for considering the use and understanding of land in earlier periods. Landscapes should not only be studied by empirical means but also through theoretical approaches. The term 'place' instead puts greater emphasis on the way in which sites were constructed, experienced, and used over time (Cresswell 2004). 'Natural' elements could be as significant and meaningful within landscapes as artificial features, although the dichotomy between culture and nature would not have been as marked as it is today (e.g., Bradley 2000; Insoll 2007):[8] '"natural places," then, have an archaeology because they acquired a significance in the *minds* of people in the past' (Bradley 2000: 35).

Natural elements could also be meaningful – they were not simply mundane aspects of the landscape. It is important to recognise that these meanings could survive to be used and transformed in different periods. Some archaeological studies of landscapes, for example, are now emphasising that certain places were the focus of occupation and activity over long periods of time, arguing that there was a 'repetition at them of ritualised acts' (Gosden and Lock 1998: 6; see also Miles et al. 2003). Places were laden with meaning through continued activity and the way in which features of the landscape were experienced. Roman towns often developed in the context of these pre-existing places and topographies imbued with symbolism and religious significance. Many of the places in which Roman towns were located were already foci of activity, which included both man-made features such as earthworks and natural features such as rivers, wetlands, and woodland. Roman towns that do not appear to have been located on monumentalised sites were nonetheless influenced by places with existing activity and meaning. Actions were influenced by visible

[8] The term 'natural place' has recently been debated by Insoll (2007) as an inappropriate differentiation from 'man-made places' in prehistory because the use or experience of sites in any way will have made them, in some respects, humanly created. This is an important discussion that looks at the blurring between 'natural' places and human spaces. Insoll's study looks at sacred groves and temples or shrines in prehistoric Europe. As an analogy he also looked at sacred places in the Tongo Hills of northern Ghana and demonstrated that even the 'natural' shrines were human constructs because they were 'sustained' or even 'created' by sacrifices, prayers, offerings, and other activities.

aspects of the landscape, and historical and mythical knowledge of the past (Bradley 2002: 80–1; Gosden and Lock 1998: 6). The continued use of towns in the late Roman period was part of this chronological sequence of meaning on the sites, which was built up over time.

The foundation of Roman towns in Britain also had ritual elements (Creighton 2006; Niblett 2005a: 105; Woodward and Woodward 2004). Studies have drawn on knowledge of Roman town foundation elsewhere in the Empire (e.g., Rykwert 1976) but have also demonstrated that there would have been local influences, and that an understanding of the towns and their setting was affected by places that had pre-existing meaning. An examination of the long-term meanings attached to the sites of Roman towns and the way in which they were used as places can help us to move beyond notions of decline in the later Roman period, a time when there was less emphasis on Classical forms of monumentality.

1.2 Late Roman urbanism

It is impossible to analyse and understand archaeological evidence without at least some influence from the modern social context in which it is being undertaken, but historio-graphical studies make it clear that many major cultural influences have affected the way in which archaeology has been approached. Recent years have seen a number of publi-cations on the historiography of Roman archaeology in Britain and the English-speaking world and the formation of tradition (e.g., S. Dyson 2006; Hingley 2000, 2008; Todd 2004). However, there are a much larger number of publications on the decline and fall of civil-isations and empires (e.g., Heather 2006; Tainter 1988; Yoffee and Cowgill 1988). These are valuable in their evaluations of the potential external and internal threats to large-scale organisations, but they do not necessarily allow analysis of experience at local levels where change will have been variable and interpreted in different ways. It is important not to view these entities in isolation following predetermined life cycles of growth and decline. This is where an analysis of the archaeology at a local level can help us. Changes to the economy and bureaucracy, for example, will not have had the same impact or have been perceived in the same way across the whole Roman Empire.

The theory of 'decline and fall' used in late Roman archaeological interpretation, including urban studies, is very much socially constructed and value laden. Much of the data for public buildings within towns were excavated and published with preconceived notions of the nature of Roman towns and the ways in which they changed in the late Roman period. There is still considerable uncertainty about the nature and function of public buildings in Roman Britain and the way in which they were used in the late Roman period, which should be addressed in greater detail. Sir Mortimer Wheeler's Verulamium (the Roman town near the modern city of St Albans) excavations in the 1930s (Wheeler and Wheeler 1936) emphasised a vision of decay and degradation in the late Roman period, with little appreciation of the considerable amount of evidence of activity, and the resulting image of the town has been influential in late Roman studies. Most accounts of late urbanism have tended to compare the excavated evidence unfavourably with that of the so-called Golden Age and contrast it negatively with the 'romanisation' of the towns (e.g., Faulkner 2000a; 2004; Liebeschuetz 2000). As Christie (2006: 185) emphasises, however, the inevitable physical decay in later Roman times does not 'denote the end of a town, but rather a redefinition, an ideological modification to the previous conception of "towns" or urbanism'. Decline and fall is especially related to economic models of understanding settlement, development, and change.

By examining the context and origins of the concept of decline and fall, one finds it possible to move away from an uncritical acceptance of this interpretation of change and transformation, in both late Roman studies and studies of the post-conquest arrival of civilisation. Edward Gibbon's (1737–94) *The Decline and Fall of the Roman Empire* (published 1776–88) is a key example of how the context of a text and its reception can have an influence on later academic thought and endeavour.[9] Gibbon's work had a huge impact on antiquarian and early archaeological practice and theory. Gibbon's attitude to the Golden Age and to pre-conquest settlement, as well as his knowledge of structural remains in Rome, proved highly important in shaping approaches to the Roman Empire and its later phases.

Gibbon did not use the term 'romanisation', but his approach to the conquered West, his appreciation of the cultural superiority and civilisation of Rome, and his coverage of decline in the later Roman period were similar to those of later writers. These authors, influenced by Gibbon, used the term as a convenient summary of the processes that they perceived took place after Roman conquest (e.g., Haverfield 1912; cf. Rogers and Hingley 2010). The approach of Francis Haverfield (1860–1919) and others, working in the context of the British Empire and its imperial endeavours (which drew on contemporary under-standings of ancient Rome for guidance and support), influenced the development of the discipline of Roman archaeology for decades to come. This genealogy of imperialism has now been studied in some detail and its impact on Roman archaeology has been subjected to considerable critical review, highlighting the emphasis on Roman elite view-points and the simplistic understanding of provinces such as Britain that this provided (see especially Hingley 2000, 2008; Mattingly 1997a, 2004, 2006a; Webster and Cooper 1996). This book contributes to the debate on romanisation and imperialism, emphasising the pre-existing values attached to places in Britain, the nuanced experiences involved in urban development, and the continuation of activity within these places into the later Roman period.

The late Roman phase of towns was an important period of these places and was part of the long-term use of these sites. As activity at many of these sites in the late pre-Roman period need not be seen as inferior to Roman urbanism, the late Roman phase of towns was also a significant period that requires analysis. In the case of many towns, such as Canterbury, Lincoln, and Winchester, the sites have remained important to the present day, albeit in a form different from Roman urbanism and via different pathways and spatial mores. In all cases the settlements had complex biographies, often also with some form of continuation from pre-Roman times. A number of themes relating to Roman Britain in the later Roman period are examined in detail here, including structural changes to the urban public buildings, timber constructions within them, and industrial activity. The detailed examination of the use of public buildings complements other studies of towns that have focused on the monumentality of public buildings and the use of space in earlier periods (e.g., Boman 2003; Favro 1996; Revell 1999).

---

[9] Reception studies have been especially important in looking at the use of classical texts (Beard and Henderson 1995), but they are also crucial for studying later works.

Christie's (2006) analysis of late Roman Italy, emphasising the concept of transformation rather than decline, is useful here: The structures of late Roman townscapes remained much more than simply skeletons to the early medieval towns that followed. The 'physical parameters' of the public buildings 'remained visible and even active' well into the post-Roman period even if 'some components were in part robbed out or even razed' (ibid.: 270). The structures continued to have an impact on the experience of these places despite the fact that the towns were neither static nor resistant to change. Towns were continually evolving and adapting: some buildings were demolished, and the material reused, whilst in other cases structures were maintained and repaired and the buildings absorbed additional functions or changed use entirely. These complexities in place biography represent peoples' actions, needs, and desires in the past; there was no strict dichotomy between continuity and change. Edensor's (2005) innovative study of modern-day industrial ruins also demonstrates that the structures could remain valued and important within towns beyond their original use; they also entrapped meaning from the past that survived in the present. These studies suggest that although towns change and appear to deteriorate, they can still remain viable and functioning places with considerable importance and meaning.

Public buildings framed activity that allows the detailed study of continuity and change of use. On a larger scale, the town as a whole was a space that gathered people and controlled movement, interaction, and experience. Public activities such as street processions, ceremonies, and speeches would have taken place within the town and linked with the public buildings (Lavan 2003a: 181). These could have continued unaltered into the latest phases of the town when forms of monumental architecture had begun to decay (Roueché 1999).[10] Whether such rituals took place in Romano-British towns is uncertain without documentary evidence, but the idea raises complexities that require acknowledgement. Movement of people to, from, and around towns was an important element providing meaning and representing ongoing activity at sites (cf. Insoll 2007).

1.3 Implications for the Empire as a whole

Although there will have been many local factors, differences, and influences across the Empire, it is important not to consider Britain in isolation but to keep in mind the broader picture (cf. Swift 2000). The reconceptualisation of late urbanism in Roman Britain in this book will be of huge importance for considering towns elsewhere. Archaeological studies of the late Roman period in other areas such as France, Spain, Italy, and North Africa have tended to rely more on historical frameworks and accounts in documents, of, for example, 'barbarian' invasions, for understanding the late phases of towns. This is, in part, understandable, because many useful texts survive that refer to events in these areas of the Empire that do not exist for Britain. The available evidence can, however, sometimes

---

[10] The ritual of *Adventus*, for example, was the means by which powerful cities greeted incoming dignitaries; it had a strong relationship with the monuments within the town, including the gates, arches, statues, and colonnaded streets (Lavan 2003b: 330). Roueché (1999) has looked at inscriptions of acclamations within public spaces at Ephesos and Aphrodisias during Late Antiquity and demonstrated that certain places within the towns, outside the public buildings, were foci of public ceremony and that this continued into the later Roman period. It is uncertain whether this occurred in Britain, but similar rituals across the townscapes and hinterlands are possible.

be problematic and lead to an overreliance on historical frameworks without addressing the theoretical complexities and potential of the archaeological evidence, although there have been some important recent works that do address some of these issues (e.g., Christie 2006; Leone 2007).

Kulikowski's (2004) reanalysis of some of the urban excavations in Spain has demonstrated how unconvincing some of the dating used by the excavators has been because of their attempt to fit the evidence with historical events. The situation is changing across Europe, but there is still much to be done to raise awareness of the difficulties of interpreting the evidence. In other conquered parts of the Empire, as in Britain, the pre-Roman evidence associated with town sites is frequently viewed as inferior to what came after, and most accounts of Roman urbanism do not address pre-Roman activity or an understanding of the landscape in any detail (e.g., Bedon 1996; Keay 1988; Maurin 1992).

1.4 Some practical considerations

One major issue that has to be recognised when one is attempting a study of the public buildings of urban sites is that there are vast differences in the state of preservation of each of the buildings and the extent of the excavations that have been undertaken. In a number of cases, the buildings have also been subject to intervention in the eighteenth, nineteenth, and early twentieth centuries, which has led to the disturbance of stratigraphy and the loss of later phases (e.g., Silchester – see Fox and St. John Hope 1893; and Caerwent – see Ashby, Hudd, and Martin 1904). Another cause of disturbance is the robbing of stone walls and floors of buildings during later archaeological periods. Post-war development within modern towns provided an opportunity to uncover Roman period buildings, but often excavation took place rapidly and in difficult circumstances (e.g., Leicester; see Cooper and Buckley 2004). It is likely that the latest Roman phases will have been particularly affected by urban disturbance, because they were often of a less substantial nature than earlier ones. Finds assemblages and less substantial features such as late floor layers, hearths within buildings, or timber structural remains will have been lost more easily than the earlier stone buildings.

Many of the towns are densely occupied today, and often only very small and widely separated areas of buildings have been exposed at any one time. This can influence the extent to which the structural history of buildings and the distribution of activities within them can be reconstructed. At Canterbury, for example, the *forum–basilica* has only been uncovered in very small areas (Frere and Bennett 1987). The extent of the theatre that has been uncovered is also minimal (Bennett 1988) and the St. Margaret's Street bathhouse, although being the subject of a number of excavations, has had a relatively small area of the total structure uncovered (K. Blockley et al. 1995). At other major Roman towns such as London (Figure 1.2), Colchester, and Cirencester, our knowledge of the public buildings is still fairly limited. Excavations in Leicester have produced some important indications of the extent to which Roman levels were destroyed by later activity. The walls of the *forum–basilica* on the St. Nicholas Place site had been heavily robbed (Buckley 2000), whilst excavations at Causeway Lane revealed widespread destruction of stone metalled areas and walls as a result of later medieval ploughing; a section of metalling and wall was found preserved, having fallen into a pit (R. Buckley, personal communication). At Blue Boar Lane and St. Nicholas Circle there were rare finds of late Roman mud brick, which had apparently been used as late structural material (R. Buckley and N. Cooper, personal communication), suggesting that mud brick buildings may have been fairly widespread across the town at this time.

Similar kinds of evidence have also come from other towns. At Verulamium, Frere (1983) demonstrated that small areas of *opus signinum* floor were, as a result of plough damage, all that survived of large areas of late occupation, whilst at the Lion Walk site in Colchester a fragment of Roman stratigraphy that had collapsed into a robber trench dating to the twelfth century was the only evidence surviving of late Roman occupation in that area of the site (P. Crummy 1984). It does now seem certain that there will have been more timber structures within towns in the later Roman period that will not have survived later disturbance, as were identified at Wroxeter where there was only limited later activity on the site (Barker et al. 1997; see Niblett, with Manning and Saunders 2006: 101–3 for a discussion on Verulamium). This has important implications for any argument seeking to emphasise the reduction of activity within towns in the later Roman period, and building in timber at this time need not be considered in terms of decline.

An important related issue is that of 'dark earth' that occurs on many of the sites below the early medieval occupation. The term was devised in London during excavations in 1977, and it was around this time that its importance in considering late Roman and post-Roman activity on sites was suggested (Macphail 1981: 309; Roskams 1991: 64). Prior to this, the dark earth had been interpreted as flood silts (Kenyon 1959) or the result of market gardening (Sheldon 1978: 40). Roskams (1991: 64–5) has suggested that the dark earth is largely a product of imported, dumped earth that may or may not then have been reworked. Apart from studies such as those by Macphail (1981, 1983), constraints on time and money have often meant that dark earth has not been carefully studied, and in some cases it has been removed without analysis to access earlier levels (Roskams 1991: 64–5).

A more recent analysis of sites in London has argued convincingly that in a number of cases the dark earth is more likely to have resulted from the truncation or reworking of late Roman occupation and stratigraphic layers, including the continuing use of the buildings together with features such as timber and clay buildings on the sites (Yule 1990: 620; see Section 8.2). An analysis of the stratigraphy and material also indicates that the assumption that dark earth formation took place only after site abandonment is probably not the case (Yule 2005: 80). At the 15–23 Southwark Street site, for example, there had been considerable post-Roman disturbance, including the removal of much of the dark earth. What did survive, however, contained a number of late Roman coins and it had the appearance of reworked late Roman strata, indicating use of the building here (Cowan 1992: 59–60). Similarly, the Winchester Palace site in Southwark had dark earth that contained considerable evidence of activity, including coins and the debris from bone pin manufacture, which may have been taking place in the building in its latest phase (Yule 2005: 78–9). If dark earth can represent late activity in these structures, then it clearly has implications for understanding late Roman towns. It highlights the caution needed when one is making assumptions about the latest phases of use of public buildings and the date of abandonment.

Analysing the use of public buildings in the later Roman period necessitates an examination of excavated finds assemblages associated with them. There are now some challenging approaches to the use of archaeological records and finds distributions in archaeology (cf. Hingley and Willis 2007). Important studies have examined the distribution of finds on

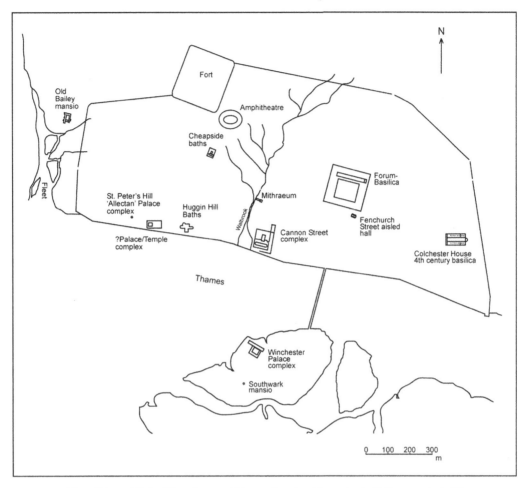

FIGURE 1.2. Plan of the public buildings known at Roman London (drawn by A. C. Rogers; adapted from Bateman 1998, Figure 2).

Iron Age sites in an attempt to identify the ways in which space was structured, an example being J. D. Hill's (1994) work on artefacts from pits and other contexts. There is also now a greater willingness to study the ritual deposition of objects in the Roman period and the complexity of the deposits found in the archaeological record and what they can tell us about attitudes towards landscape (e.g., Fulford 2001; Willis and Hingley 2007). Such detailed studies demand the comprehensive excavation and recording of sites, and it is often now difficult to carry out such analyses on earlier excavations.

Studies comparing assemblages of finds in an attempt to determine differing uses of sites have often used one of two techniques: an analysis of the quantities of different find types or a comparison of the percentages of each find type. J. Evans (1993), for example, compared the numbers of finds within structures in the Roman fort at Caernarfon to identify the way in which the use of the buildings changed over time. Cooper has explored the differences of finds assemblages from excavated sites across Leicester and the difference in proportion of finds within each period of the individual sites (Cooper 1999). One of the most methodologically rigorous attempts to examine site function through finds assemblages has been the study of objects from the legionary fortress in York, and its comparison with other military sites, using the multivariate technique of correspondence analysis (Cool and Baxter 2002; Cool, Lloyd-Morgan, and Hooley 1995). Gardner (2007) followed another approach by looking at the pattern of the distribution of finds across sites to identify separate aspects. Through this analysis he was able to argue that the traditional assumption of clear-cut 'civilian' and 'military' identities within forts was far too simplistic.

An important use of finds assemblages from late Roman contexts is their potential to show the continuing use of the buildings, and towns more generally, even when there is evidence of structural decay or when desertion of structures has been assumed. Site disturbance and the dumping of material can, however, cause problems for the analyst here. Much has been written on this subject and Allison's (1992, 2004) study of Pompeian houses has highlighted many causes of disturbance, even on a site that has traditionally been considered to be one of the perfect archaeological examples: the 'Pompeii Premise' (Binford 1981; Schiffer 1985).[11] In an attempt to deal with this problem at the Wroxeter baths-*basilica* excavations, the post-excavation analysis divided the finds into three categories according to whether they were objects from (A) floor surfaces, (B) pits and other features, or (C) dumps (Pretty 1997; R. White 1997: 371). Care must be taken, then, in analysing the context of the finds in an attempt to distinguish evidence of activities within buildings from debris dumped there from elsewhere. As well as contextual difficulties, the identification of objects from surviving pieces can be problematic and interpretations can be related to cultural biases (Allison et al. 2005: 3.1.2; Allason-Jones 2001).[12] Despite these difficulties, the examples discussed here highlight the potential in finds analysis, which can form an important and integral part of archaeological investigations.

1.5 Chapters of the book

Chapter 2 demonstrates the importance of historiographical studies within archaeology, looking at the key example of Edward Gibbon and his work *The Decline and Fall of the Roman Empire* as forming part of the context of the theory of decline dominant within late Roman archaeology. Next, Chapter 3 places the research into late Roman urbanism, and towns more generally, into its academic context by exploring the challenging nature of Roman urbanism and looking for new ways to interpret the late Roman data. This leads into Chapter 4, which examines the pre-Roman data at the sites of towns to analyse their significance as pre-existing places that had an influence on the nature of urbanism and the way in which the sites were perceived and experienced throughout the Roman period.

The book then moves on to examine the late Roman urban data, concentrating on public buildings. Chapter 5 examines interpretations of public buildings within towns and their structural state in the later Roman period. It argues that our understanding of these structures is sometimes less secure than is supposed, which means that it is even more difficult to make assumptions about their nature and use in the later Roman period. It also demonstrates that there is considerably more evidence of public buildings remaining in

---

[11] These disturbances included post-eruption clearance, post-eruption occupation, and robbing.
[12] Allason-Jones's (2001) study of the finds from the turrets along Hadrian's Wall has demonstrated that finds traditionally considered female, such as needles and nail-cleaners, were present in male-only contexts.

the later Roman period than has often been emphasised. Chapter 6 contributes further to our understanding of public buildings, with a discussion of the evidence of new buildings within towns in the late period; this is crucial for illustrating the positive continuation of some kind of urban authority and investment in new urban spaces whilst the 'old spaces' were undergoing changes, reflecting reordering priorities but continuing actions.

By considering the ways in which the buildings continued to be used, Chapter 7 demonstrates that the 'old spaces' remained important. It looks at the evidence of industrial activity within the buildings and the way in which this might be interpreted in the light of its spatial and social context. Chapter 8 then explores the evidence of timber structures and 'squatter occupation', demonstrating that these types of remains are important traces of more extensive late activity within the buildings, and across the towns in general. Chapter 9 concludes the study with further discussion of the significance and potential of the data available and their implications for understanding late Roman urbanism.

CHAPTER 2

Edward Gibbon: growth, the Golden Age, and decline and fall

Historiography is an important part of archaeological study because of what it can tell us about the development of interpretations of the past over time and what factors have influenced them. By analysing the origins of theoretical approaches, new directions can be proposed. Historiography can be useful in studies of Roman towns and the later Roman period. This is demonstrated here with a detailed examination of one important figure in the history of their investigation in Britain: Edward Gibbon. Hugely influential early archaeologists and ancient historians such as Theodor Mommsen (1817–1903), Camille Jullian (1859–1933), and Francis Haverfield (1860–1919) drew on Gibbon's approach to empire, civilisation, and decline even as they were influenced by the social and political milieux in which they themselves were working (cf. Freeman 2007; Hingley 2000; Rogers and Hingley 2010). Equally influential later writers on the archaeology of cities and civilisations such as Vere Gordon Childe (e.g., 1950), and Sir Mortimer Wheeler (e.g., 1943, 1966) were working very much within the established context of this previous work – and they went on to influence approaches in more recent times.

Gibbon's six-volume work *The Decline and Fall of the Roman Empire* (1776–88) is probably the most famous study, at least in Britain, of the late Roman period and of the Roman Empire as a whole. It has had an enormous impact on the way in which the later Roman period has been studied, with the image of decline and fall dominating many archaeological analyses. As a work of wider popular appeal, it has been influential in late-eighteenth-, nineteenth-, and early-twentieth-century society. What is less often acknowledged is that the text has also contributed towards informing views of the earlier Roman period and the period that preceded the conquest in parts of the Empire such as Britain, which is also addressed here.

Analysing Gibbon's writing has been a major area of academic pursuit, with focus especially on its influence on historical study, on themes such as Christianity and barbarism, and also as a work of English prose in its eighteenth-century setting (e.g., Jordan 1971; McKitterick and Quinault 1997a; Pocock 1999a, 1999b, 2003, 2005; Womersley 1988, 1997; V. Woolf 1943). However, its impact within archaeology and on the study of settlement, continuity, and change has not been subject to very much attention. The concept of decline and fall and the depictions of both the pre-conquest to Roman transition and of the Golden Age, as expressed within Gibbon's writing, were, in part, products of his (and contemporary society's) attitudes towards Roman civilisation and the Roman elite. They have influenced the way in which periods of change have been approached in archaeology.

Gibbon also influenced archaeological work more directly through his examination and descriptions of Rome and its structural remains.

This chapter considers Gibbon's attitude in *The Decline and Fall* to civilisation and barbarism, and to change and conquest, along with an examination of aspects of his character and upbringing that influenced his work. These elements contributed to the powerful images in his writing on decline and fall in the later Roman period. It is necessary, briefly, to examine the influences of the Enlightenment and the preceding civic humanist movement on Gibbon's work before moving on to his attitude to the physical remains of Rome and other towns, and his thoughts on pre-Roman settlement in the West. The chapter discusses his use of antiquarian research, together with the way in which his writing style emphasised both the splendour of the public buildings during the Golden Age and also their decline in the later Roman period and beyond. Central to Gibbon's narrative was the city, and especially Rome, around which all events revolved.[1] The chapter ends with a consideration of the way in which Gibbon's use of language depicted cities as physical representations of civilisation and how this differed from his descriptions of pre-Roman settlement, thus creating biases in archaeological study.

2.1 Reading Gibbon

The Decline and Fall was published in six volumes, with the first appearing in 1776, the next two in 1781, and the final three in 1788. The first three take the 'decline and fall' up to the end of the Western Empire, with the last three describing the Eastern Empire to the conquest of Constantinople by the Turks. The final chapter of the work, LXXXI, examines the state of Rome in the fourteenth century, whilst the earliest chapters of the first volume depict the Empire at the time between 'the death of Domitian to the accession of Commodus' when the 'human race was most happy and prosperous' and the 'golden age of Trajan and the Antonines' (*DF* I: 103–4). *The Decline and Fall* is not read so much today as an historical account of the later Roman Empire but more as a work of literature, and product of the eighteenth century, and it is often studied as such (e.g., Craddock 1989; Pocock 1999a; Womersley 1988). The work was particularly popular in the later nineteenth and early twentieth century – a period of intense interest in, and preoccupation with, imperialism – which was also the time at which Roman archaeology was developing into a discipline recognisable today. Here, the influence of Gibbon's work on studies of the Roman period and conceptualisations of the later Roman period are highlighted.

At the time when Gibbon was writing, the study of history was a hugely fashionable pursuit – especially the Roman period – and considered one of the highest forms of art (Ghosh 1997: 277) with the consequence that the eighteenth century saw a vast output of historical works (Dawson 1934: 159; McKitterick 1997: 164). Upon publication, Gibbon's first volume was an immediate success and hailed a masterpiece amongst followers of

---

[1] The references from Gibbon's *The Decline and Fall* are taken from the 1994 edited version of the work by David Womersley, published by Penguin in three volumes, each containing two of Gibbon's original volumes. The references in the text are presented as *DF* followed by the volume number and then the page number as it appears in the Penguin edition.

literature and fashion.[2] The first printing of 1,000 copies was sold out within a few weeks and led quickly to the production of second and third editions (Jordan 1976: 6). Gibbon became known as 'the Historian of the Roman Empire' (Pocock 1999a: 292). His work remained in print throughout the nineteenth century (as it still is today). The members of the committee of the 1894 Royal Historical Society's centenary celebrations of Gibbon's death included not only eminent historians, such as Theodor Mommsen (1864; 1996, new English edition), but also public figures such as the Prime Minister Lord Rosebery, who admired Gibbon's work greatly (McKitterick and Quinault 1997b: 9).

The image of Rome played an important part in the nineteenth- and early-twentieth-century social consciousness (Vance 1997), but because they had read Gibbon's work, people at the time were also aware of the fate of the Roman Empire and wished to avoid a similar course of events in the British Empire. Satirical works, such as the *Decline and Fall of the British Empire* by Elliott Mills (1905; from Hingley 2000: 31–2),[3] pretending to be a Japanese school textbook of the year 2005, show both the influence of the Roman Empire on contemporary thought and the role of Edward Gibbon in forming such views and opinions (ibid.; Vance 1997: 234). Another work, *The Decline and Fall of the British Empire* (Anon 1884), was said to have been written by an author called Edwarda Gibbon and published in New Zealand in the futuristic date of 2884 (Vance 1997: 234).[4] The Roman Empire was central to contemporary views of the greatness of the British Empire, but the reasons for Rome's decline, through Gibbon's work, were also often used to highlight its problems. Influential figures reading Gibbon at the time included Winston Churchill (Quinault 1997: 317–18), who was 'immediately dominated both by the story and the style' (Churchill 1941: 125);[5] it was mainly a work for the wealthy and educated (cf. McKitterick and Quinault 1997b: 1).

It is unlikely, then, that Gibbon would not have been read and drawn upon by Roman archaeologists in the nineteenth and early twentieth centuries, and the impact of this has remained into the present day. Haverfield clearly drew upon Gibbon and indeed refers to his use of ideas from the work (1912: 12). Others who drew upon Gibbon include John Collingwood Bruce, in his book *The Roman Wall* (1851), where he agrees with 'Gibbon's estimate of the character of the ancient Britons' (ibid.: 27). His description of visiting Hadrian's Wall mirrors Gibbon's first encounter with remains in Rome (see Section 2.4): 'The most ardent lover of the olden times cannot but startle as he treads the deserted streets, or enters the unbarred portals of BORCIVICUS, and other cities of the Wall' (ibid.: 31).

---

[2] With the publication of Gibbon's first volume, Horace Walpole (1717–97) proclaimed in a letter to the poet William Mason (1725–97), 'Lo, there is just appeared a truly classic work'; see W. Lewis, *Horace Walpole's Correspondence* (1955, Vol. 28, p. 243). Walpole, the fourth Earl of Orford, has often been taken as a significant indicator of the tastes and fashions of his day.

[3] This text was published anonymously in 1905 as *The Decline and Fall of the British Empire: a brief account of those causes which resulted in the destruction of our late ally, together with a comparison between the British and Roman Empires. Appointed for use in the National Schools of Japan. Tokio, 2005* (Oxford: Alden & Co.).

[4] In this work, many of the causes of decline of the British Empire were similar to those outlined by Gibbon in his work, such as town life, demoralising luxury, and physical inertia.

[5] Churchill read *The Decline and Fall* whilst he was a cavalry subaltern at Aldershot and when he was posted in Bangalore, India. His old headmaster at Harrow is purported to have said to him that 'Gibbon is the greatest of historians, read him all through'; and Churchill's own father, Lord Randolph, favoured Gibbon greatly and had memorised long passages when he was an undergraduate at Merton College, Oxford (Churchill 1941; Quinault 1997: 317–18).

2.2 Decline and fall

The concept of decline and fall, of course, was not Gibbon's invention; it was also prominent within ancient literature, in many cases representing the same biases towards contemporary concepts of 'civilisation' and the lives of the elite. The Greek poet Hesiod, writing around 700 B.C., describes in his *Opera et Dies* four races of people, each descending in quality, until the fourth, which was a race of iron; the Greeks saw a process of decline from earlier times. The concept of a Golden Age as an opposite to a decline to 'iron and rust' is also represented elsewhere: Cassius Dio, at the end of his description of the reign of Marcus Aurelius, wrote that his work 'now descends from a kingdom of gold to one of iron and rust, as affairs did for the Romans of that day' (LXXII.36.4). For Gibbon, as well, the 'golden age of Trajan and the Antonines had been preceded by an age of iron' (*DF* I: 104), indicating his view that what preceded and followed this period of the Empire was inferior.

Also influential on Gibbon were the writings of Tacitus, whose *Historiae* narrated the early greatness of the Empire and that allowed Gibbon, drawing on authors such as Cassius Dio, to begin his description of decline; he puts this at the end of the Antonine period with the death of Commodus in A.D. 192 (Pocock 2003: 17). The first-century B.C. work by Lucretius, *De rerum natura*, also explores the idea of decline and decay: 'the walls of the mighty world . . . shall be stormed all around, and shall collapse into crumbling ruin' (II.1144–6); the decay of the state is compared with the decay of the natural world. Cicero's *De republica* (published between 54 and 51 B.C.) contains similar sentiments, whilst Virgil's *Georgics* (published in 29 B.C.), drawing on Hesiod and Lucretius, describes an agricultural golden age that can then lead to decline (Johnston 1980). These written works projected a Roman elite viewpoint centred on Rome and are unlikely to represent the complexity of viewpoints across the Empire.

These ancient texts influenced the Renaissance humanist writers such as the fifteenth-century Leonardo Bruni, who described the decline of Rome beginning from the moment that the Republic ended, with the loss of liberty and virtue, and Flavio Biondo, who wrote of the moral decline of Rome (Pocock 2003: 166–78). Gibbon held these works in his library and would have read them in preparation for his writing (Figure 2.1; also see Keynes 1950).[6] Another work in his collection was by Thomas Hobbes (1588–1679), entitled *Leviathan* (1651; reprinted in 1946), which was a book on the natural condition of mankind. In times of war or insecurity, 'everyman is enemy to everyman' because of the fear of violent death (1946: 82); there is no place for culture or industry and the life of man is 'solitary, poor, nasty, brutish and short' (ibid.). These views are also reminiscent of Gibbon's writings on life in the Roman Empire in the later Roman period.

Gibbon's concept of decline was largely an elitist cultural creation reflecting his own attitudes and concepts of civilisation, which matched and developed those of society at the time. Gibbon and his contemporaries were reinventing Rome in a period of British

---

[6] An approximate catalogue of the books in Edward Gibbon's library at Bentinck Street was constructed by Geoffrey Keynes in the 1930s through an investigation of an extensive card-catalogue of Gibbon's Lausanne library (which is held in the British Museum), research in the London auction houses, and an earlier catalogue compiled in the nineteenth century (Keynes 1950: 1–2).

expansion and colonialism (cf. Hingley 2000: 29). Gibbon also owned a copy of the speeches of Aristides (Keynes 1950), an orator who spoke of the wonders of the Roman Empire in the age of the Antonines (Schiavone 2000).[7] Aristides' attitudes about cities and Roman life are reflected in Gibbon's writing, as is Strabo's view of agriculture versus the barbarity of pastoralism preceding urbanism (which mirrors the British aristocratic notion of farming and land ownership):[8] 'The spirit of improvement had passed the Alps' (*DF* I: 74) and '[the Romans] subdued and civilised so considerable a part of mankind' (*DF* III: 200). The influence of these views and Gibbon's text can also be seen in later works such as that by Francis Haverfield, who wrote on the 'romanisation' of Britain (e.g., Haverfield 1912), in a work which was also highly influential later (e.g., Frere 1967; Millett 1990).

The word 'civilisation' itself originated in the eighteenth century amongst political economists and was used to describe the progress of the enlightened society that could make things 'civil' (Burrow 1985: 81; Furet 1976: 209; see also discussions in Foucault, e.g., 1970).[9] By the 1800s it was seen as both a process and an achieved condition associated with social order, as well as refined manners and behaviour (Patterson 1997: 42). The idea of civilisation played a major part in the rise of the states of modern Western Europe and was also linked with colonial expansion (ibid.: 27, 30). Modern society was considered superior to previous states of human existence, and changes within the modern age were compared with, and projected back to, the Roman period. This, paradoxically, meant that the Roman period was being understood within the context of a society that was now very different. Gibbon's journey to Italy on his Grand Tour consisted, apart from his visit to Rome itself, not of travels to sites of Roman remains, but of a journey through the Renaissance and Baroque landscape and through the cities, palaces, and museums of art, fashion, and collections of Roman antiquities. Gibbon was 'voyaging through the history of taste' (Pocock 1999a: 276–9), seeing and constructing Rome through modern eyes. His *The Decline and Fall* represented 'Gibbon's Roman Empire' rather than that of the Roman period itself (Jordan 1971).

The Roman Empire described in *The Decline and Fall* was seen through Gibbon's eyes, but Gibbon did not create the social and intellectual milieu of his day single-handedly. Gibbon has been described as an historian of the Enlightenment and he was also in regular contact with a number of contemporary British historians, including David Hume, William Robertson, Adam Ferguson, and Adam Smith (Pocock 1999a). The Enlightenment was rooted in the belief in reason and commerce against religion (Collingwood 1946: 76; Pocock 1999b: 371). His 'dear friend Hume' (Gibbon 1966: 156) read and commented on parts of the *Decline and Fall*, and Gibbon, after reading Adam Smith's work, was increasingly aware of, and influenced by, economic and social factors; in Chapter two, for example, Gibbon defends luxury from an economic standpoint (*DF* I: 80; Burke 1976: 149). This emphasis on economics has also influenced intepretations within archaeology

---

[7] Examples are 'cities shine with radiance and grace' (Aristid. *Or.* XXVI.99) and 'the whole world has been adorned like a pleasure garden' (XXVI.99), whereas previously life was 'harsh, rustic, and little different from living on a mountain' (XXVI.101).

[8] Strabo writes this, for example: 'Formally the Allobroges kept up warfare with many myriads of men, whereas now they till the plains and the glens that are in the Alps, and all of them live in villages, except that the most notable of them, inhabitants of Vienna [formerly a village, but called, nevertheless, the 'metropolis' of the tribe], have built it up into a city' (IV.1.11).

[9] Much of Foucault's work (e.g., 1970) set out to analyse the way in which Western society has thought about and grouped things according to constructed concepts of civilisation.

FIGURE 2.1. Photograph of Bentinck Street, London; the site of Edward Gibbon's house and library is on the far right with the plaque on the wall (photograph by A. C. Rogers).

and has had an impact on the way in which change in the later Roman period has been conceived.

2.3 Gibbon's character and upbringing

Gibbon was influenced by the writings of the Roman elite and contemporary social attitudes to civilisation, but his own character and upbringing were also vital for the work that he undertook. His mother having died when he was ten years of age, Gibbon was brought up by a father preoccupied with class and society and able to live the life of a country gentleman as a result of the wealth made by his own father (Gibbon 1966: 24). Consequently, Gibbon greatly valued and appreciated the British aristocratic system and believed in the importance of birth and standing (Quennell 1945: 76). At school he was able to learn Latin and Greek and remarked that such schools 'deposit in the hands of a disciple the keys of two valuable chests' (Gibbon 1966: 38). Gibbon also described his interest in Roman history as a child: 'I was immersed in the passage of the Goths over the Danube when the summons of the dinner-bell reluctantly dragged me from my intellectual feast' (ibid.: 42). From an early age he believed in the importance of history and lived his life through books (Porter 1988: 44). At fifteen he was sent to Magdalen College, Oxford, where he was attracted by the 'size and beauty of the public edifices' and his 'vanity was flattered by the velvet Cap and silk gown which discriminate a Gentleman-Commoner from a plebeian student' (Gibbon 1966: 46). Gibbon records how he had imagined that 'the adjacent walks, had they been frequented by Plato's disciples, might have been compared to the Attic shade on the banks of the Ilissus' (ibid.: 47).

After being forced to leave Oxford because he had converted to Catholicism, he was sent to Lausanne in Switzerland by his father in the hope that he would revert to Anglicanism (Jordan 1976: 4). There, he was able to learn Latin and Greek with much greater proficiency; as a break from the Greek, Gibbon would withdraw 'to the free and familiar conversation of Virgil and Tacitus' (Gibbon 1966: 75). This increased his admiration for Rome, which culminated in his year-long trip to Italy. As an adult, Gibbon, through the wealth inherited from his father, was able to live a life of leisure and he valued external markers of class such as his membership in many of the London clubs (ibid.: 155; also see Brownley 1976: 21). Gibbon also believed in the virtues of the British parliamentary system and became a member of parliament himself (Gibbon 1966: 155–6). He despised and was suspicious of the masses and feared trouble and revolution. In Chapter VII of *The Decline and Fall*, Gibbon attributed the peace and prosperity of Europe in 1776 to a recognition of the 'superior prerogative of birth' (*DF* I: 188), advocating his preference for hereditary monarchy (cf. Bowersock 1976: 64). He compared this situation in Europe with Rome and saw the failure of the Antonine dynastic line as the beginning of the end (Pocock 2003: 451). Further comparisons include this comment to his friend Deyverdun: 'The decline of the two empires, Roman and British, proceed at equal pace' (Norton 1956: 218).[10] Gibbon's upbringing led him to value the British Empire and class system, and what it stood for, and thus comparisons with the Roman Empire, his other great interest, were inevitable. The term 'decline and fall' in this context is itself imperialist, further indicating the influences of the imperialism of Gibbon's day on his writing.

2.4 Gibbon and archaeology

Gibbon had always been interested in the surviving remains of Roman structures in Rome, and they were important in shaping his ideas: 'I can never forget nor express the strong emotions which agitated my mind as I first approached and entered the eternal City' (Gibbon 1966: 134). 'After a sleepless night [Gibbon] trod with a lofty step the ruins of the Forum; each memorable spot where Romulus stood, or Tully spoke, or Caesar fell was at once present to [his] eye' (ibid.). This was also the location in which Gibbon says that he first got the idea for writing his work: 'it was among the ruins of the Capitol, that I first conceived the idea' (*DF* VI: 1085). Gibbon took an interest in the remains themselves, not devoting himself entirely to the classical sources; indeed his first intention was not to write about the Roman Empire as a whole but simply the 'decay of the City' (1966: 136). At this time there were many antiquarian and archaeological studies connected with the Roman period and there was a surge in the popularity of classical antiquities, especially amongst the British aristocracy; in the words of Moatti (1989: 59), 'Rome and its remains were in everyone's heart'.[11] There was an emphasis placed on classics in education, with knowledge of Latin becoming a symbol of both erudition and class distinction (Farrell 2001: 97). On the Grand Tour, travellers equated themselves with the Roman elite (J. Black 1985: 235).

---

[10] Originally written in French: 'La decadence de Deux Empires, le Romain et le Britannique s'avancent à pas egaux'.

[11] Translated from the original French (Moatti 1989: 59): 'Rome et ses vestiges sont dans tous les cœurs'.

Stukeley's society, the *Equites Romani* (Society of the Roman Knights), was founded in 1722 and the Society of Dilettanti was founded in 1732. Members visited sites, compared findings, discussed future projects, adopted Roman names, and organised Roman-style banquets (Ayres 1997: 61, 92), as if continuing the Roman lifestyle and civilisation. Gibbon also founded the Roman Club in 1765 (ibid.: 61), which in his memoirs he terms a 'weekly convivial meeting' (G. B. Hill 1900: 169) although he does not record its activities.[12] These celebrations of Rome contrasted with depictions of pre-Roman Britain, such as in Philip James de Loutherbourg's etching, *The Britons* (1793), which illustrates a scythe-wheeled chariot and war gear next to a standing stone; Smiles (1994: 218–19) suggests that the words 'The Britons' in classical type cut across the image effectively imposes civilisation on these primitive peoples.

2.4.1 Gibbon and antiquarianism

Gibbon's interest in the city of Rome and its remains can be seen in the material that he read; he records how, through this, he began to 'collect the substance of my Roman decay' (1966: 146). In Lausanne in 1763, for instance, he read the fourth volume of Graevius' *Thesaurus antiquitatum Romanorum* (1694–9) containing Nardini's *Roma Antica* (1666), which describes all the Roman period remains in Rome (Ghosh 1997: 281).[13] Gibbon also read the works of the English antiquaries such as Whitaker, Gale, Stukeley, Camden, Dugdale, and Horsley (Womersley 1994: xii), and he drew upon and commented on many of their writings. More problematic was his use of the forged work of Richard of Cirencester (1335–1401) on the history of Roman Britain by Charles Bertrum (1723–65), which, although described by Gibbon as 'feeble' (*DF* II: 999, n. 111), was not challenged (Sweet 2004: 178).[14] Drawing on this bogus work, Gibbon wrote of the nine colonies in Britain 'of which London, Colchester, Lincoln, Chester, Gloucester, and Bath still remain considerable cities' (*DF* I: 64).

In his study of Roman roads Gibbon refers to the itineraries of 'Gale and Stukeley for Britain, and M. d'Anville for Gaul and Italy' (*DF* I: 77, n. 85). For Britain under the Empire he refers to 'our own antiquarians, Camden and Horsley' (*DF* I: 33, n. 8), valuing Camden especially highly: He was 'the British Strabo' and 'the father of our antiquities' (*DF* II: 997, n. 109; III: 22, n. 11). Gibbon was able to use the material critically: 'Dr. Stukely [*sic*]

---

[12] An edited list of the club's members is given in George Birkbeck Hill's edition of Gibbon's *Memoirs* (1900: 169), taken from Lord Sheffield's 1827 edition: Lord Mountstuart (now Marquis of Bute), Colonel Edmonstone, William Weddal, Rev. Mr. Palgrave, Earl of Berkley, Godfrey Clarke (Member for Derbyshire), Holroyd (Lord Sheffield), Major Ridley Thomas Charles Bigge, Sir William Guize, Sir John Aubrey, the late Earl of Abingdon, Hon. Peregrine Bertie, Rev. Mr. Cleaver, Hon. John Damer, Hon. George Damer (late Earl of Dorchester), Sir Thomas Gascoyne, Sir John Hort, and E. Gibbon.

[13] In his journal entry for 2nd October, 1763, Gibbon wrote 'J'ai lu Nardini . . . il est excellent' ('I have read Nardini . . . it is excellent'; see Bonnard 1945: 73) and for 29th October he refers to 'mon ami Nardini' ('my friend Nardini'; ibid.: 119). A number of entries in his journal start with 'J'ai lu Cluvier *Italia Antiqua*' ('I have read Cluvier's *Italia Antiqua*'), indicating that this too formed a major part of his knowledge of the Roman remains of Italy.

[14] Richard of Cirencester was a historical writer and monk. For uncertain motives, in 1757 Charles Bertrum published a work entitled *Rerum Gentium Historiae Antiquae Scriptores Tres*, part of which contained the forged work of Richard of Westminster that Stukeley equated with Richard of Cirencester. The writing included additions to the itineraries of Roman Britain amongst other falsities (Sweet 2004: 175–81).

in particular has devoted a large volume to the British emperor [Carausius]. I have used his materials, and rejected most of his fanciful conjections' (*DF* I: 366, n. 28). Gibbon also referred to antiquaries from other countries, including France, Germany, and Italy (*DF* III: 138, n. 55; III: 488, n. 113).

He was especially interested in antiquarian work carried out within towns, and large parts of the text are devoted to Rome, which is seen as reflecting the Roman Empire as a whole. In Chapters LXIX and LXXI Gibbon describes Rome in the twelfth and fourteenth centuries after its 'decline'. By the twelfth century 'Rome had been already stripped of her trophies' but there remained the 'venerable aspect of her ruins, and the memory of past greatness' (*DF* VI: 978–9). Gibbon refers to the remarks of Poggio Bracciolini, the Italian Rennaissance humanist (1380–1459), that the 'forum of the Roman people, where they assembled to enact their laws and elect their magistrates, is now enclosed for cultivation of pot-herbs, or thrown open for the reception of swine and buffaloes' (*DF* VI: 1063), and this echoes Gibbon's own comments about cattle now grazing within the amphitheatre at Lambesa in Algeria (*DF* IV: 645). By describing the Empire in ruins in this way Gibbon was demonstrating its decline but also, by contrast, emphasising the greatness of the Golden Age of Rome, an era he saw as comparable to his own time: one of increasing wealth and colonial exploits (Kelly 1997: 48).

Gibbon envisaged and described the decline of the Roman Empire through the physical destruction of its public buildings and monuments, but he also recognised the importance of the remains in providing access to the past grandeur of the Empire, similar access to that later valued by archaeological projects of the nineteenth and early twentieth centuries. He stated, for example, that 'the splendour of Verona can be traced in its remains' (*DF* I: 75), whilst in Volume III he lamented that 'the ruin of the fairest structures of antiquity still displays the ravages of those Barbarians' (*DF* III: 81). For Gibbon, they were 'Majestic ruins' (*DF* I: 70), and he was irritated that in medieval Rome 'the forms of ancient architecture were disregarded by a people insensible of their use and beauty [because of their barbarism]' (*DF* VI: 1072). This is linked to his understanding of and attitude to 'archaeological' investigation: 'the resurrection [of statues and other remains] was fortunately delayed till a safer and more enlightened age' (*DF* VI: 1082). The remains were thus interpreted through the 'enlightened' mindset with the resultant emphasis on the grandeur and monumental nature of buildings.

Apart from the work on prehistoric monuments, such as that by Stukeley and Aubrey, and interests in Celts and Druids (Morse 2005; Smiles 1994),[15] much of 'archaeology', especially for Gibbon, was concerned with the Roman period and he was well aware of activities at the time: '[T]he map, the description, the monuments of ancient Rome, have been elucidated by the diligence of the antiquarian and the student' (*DF* III: 1084). Other excavations included those at Pompeii, Herculaneum, and the Palace of Domitian (Matthews 1997: 27; Moatti 1989: 70–4; Parslow 1995). These excavations will have affected Gibbon's views regarding the splendour and comfort of the Roman Empire and its subsequent decline.

---

[15] In the mid- to later seventeenth century, Aubrey, for example, carried out much work documenting the megaliths around Britain, largely interpreting them as druid temples (Morse 2005: 36). Stukeley, in the early eighteenth century, saw prehistoric sites like Stonehenge as Celtic monuments (ibid.: 70).

2.4.2 *Gibbon's writing style*

Gibbon's language and unique style, such as the conversation he provides in his footnotes (Womersley 2002: 1–2), was also an important part of the work's popularity. He rewrote parts of the text numerous times to achieve his required effect. For Gibbon, history was a form of literature intended not only to instruct but also to entertain (Craddock 1989); the art of story telling, of narrative, was important and is one major reason why the work is still being read today. Gibbon knew his audience and wrote what they wanted to read; his writing was supporting social and political attitudes of the day. Consequently, situations, events, and descriptions will have been exaggerated, overdramatic, and idealised. Within *The Decline and Fall*, the language used to describe changes to the Empire and the fortunes of individuals was very much related to images of the structural decline of physical buildings that Gibbon had witnessed himself in Rome, and the words 'decay' and 'ruin' appear frequently. He speaks of the 'ruin of the Pagan religion' (*DF* III: 90), the 'decay of taste and genius' (*DF* VI: 391), the 'Ruin of Abundantius' and 'the destruction of Timasius', figures of the late Empire (*DF* III: 242), and the 'Desolation of Africa' (*DF* III: 284).

Gibbon's literary technique, which deliberately used language in the classical style (Ayres 1997: 60–1), required a build-up of extravagance and grandeur, the Golden Age, before he could contrast this with decline and fall. The end of the attributes of elite civilisation valued by Gibbon could only be portrayed by him as decline. Indeed, even the prospect of reading texts in vulgar Latin as research for his work, as opposed to those written by his 'assiduous companions' (Gibbon 1966: 132) of classical Rome, repelled him, as did Byzantine culture. This intensified the image he portrayed of decline and the 'darkness of the middle ages' (ibid.: 147; also see Dawson 1934: 171; McKitterick 1997: 166). Gibbon speaks of 'the declining age of learning and of mankind' and the 'decline of arts and of empire', showing his attitude to this later period. As Matthews (1997: 32) has suggested, this method of studying the late Roman period, and judging it by the standards of an earlier age, has certainly survived to this day (e.g., B. Ward-Perkins 2005).

This contrasts greatly with the language used by Gibbon to describe cities and public buildings before the decline. Of the public buildings and other monuments, Gibbon declares that their 'greatness alone, or their beauty, might deserve our attention' but they were also important because they connected 'the agreeable history of the arts with the more useful of human manners' because many were built at 'private expense' for 'public benefit' (*DF* I: 70). Bathhouses had been constructed 'with Imperial magnificence' and 'elegance of design' (*DF* III: 184); the *Forum* of Rome was described by Gibbon as being 'proud' because it was 'decorated with the statues of so many gods and heroes' (*DF* III: 204). For Gibbon, these 'exquisite statues . . . displayed the triumph of the arts' (*DF* III: 81). Buildings had 'beauty', examples being the circus at Constantinople (*DF* II: 597) and the 'majestic dome of the Pantheon in Rome' (*DF* III: 80). With the emphasis Gibbon placed upon magnitude, grandeur, and convenience, the aqueducts were seen as the 'noblest monuments' (*DF* I: 74) and 'stupendous' (*DF* III: 184).

That Gibbon considered the public buildings to be the most important features of a Roman city is also shown by the language he used to describe their later histories: The 'fairest forms of architecture were rudely defaced' (*DF* III: 374), the 'most exquisite works of art were roughly handled', and the palaces were 'rudely stripped of their splendid and costly furniture' (*DF* III: 204). Cities and their public buildings were central to the Roman Empire; through the violation of the city, Roman civilisation was threatened.

2.4.3 *Gates and civilisation*

Gibbon's distaste for the 'swarms of barbarians' (*DF* I: 276), and what they did to the towns and public buildings in the late Roman period, is reflected in the violence that is expressed as they approached city gates and entered 'civilisation'. The gates of Carthage, for example, were described as being 'thrown open' in A.D. 535, and the invaders 'burst open the gates' of Naples in A.D. 537 (*DF* IV: 631, 656). Similarly, the gates of Constantinople were 'thrown open' and at a later date 'three gates were burst open' (*DF* VI: 683, 690). In other instances Gibbon describes the danger of barbarians pressing up against the gates of the cities: The barbarians spread 'terror as far as the gates of Rome' (*DF* I: 296) and in the time of Aurelian 'the barbarians were hourly expected at the gates of Rome' (*DF* I: 309). At a later time, the barbarian Rhodogast 'marched from the northern extremities of Germany almost to the gates of Rome' (*DF* III: 143). In Rome the untrustworthy masses, 'an innumerable people', 'pressed, with impetuous zeal, against the gates of the palace' (*DF* III: 42). Gates could admit beneficial or bar harmful events: 'the citizens refused to open their gates' (*DF* I: 369); 'the gates of the city were shut against [Maxentius]' (*DF* I: 423); '[Severus] found on his arrival the gates of the city shut against him' (*DF* I: 409); but 'Tarsus opened its gates, and the soldiers of Florianus . . . delivered the empire from civil war' (*DF* I: 335).

Gates were also used as geographical markers of civilisation: Theodosius had his head-quarters at Thessalonica, for instance, so that 'the irregular motions of the Barbarians' could be watched 'from the gates of Constantinople to the shores of the Hadriatic' (*DF* II: 1075). Other references include 'as far as the gates of Ctesiphon' (*DF* I: 313), the 'long march from Thessalonica to the gates of Constantinople' (*DF* III: 136), and reference to Alaric, who resolved to 'conquer or die before the gates of Rome' (*DF* III: 136). The city gates for Gibbon were important for controlling movement, and by seeing them in this way he largely divorces towns from the rest of the landscape.

2.4.4 *Gibbon and pre-Roman settlement*

The pre-Roman significance of landscapes played little role in Gibbon's understanding of the Roman town, except for the way in which they were transformed: '[T]he spirit of improvement had passed the Alps, and been felt even in the woods of Britain, which were gradually cleared away to open a free space for convenient and elegant habitations. York was the seat of government; London was already enriched by commerce; and Bath was celebrated for the salutary effects of the medicinal waters' (*DF* I: 74–5). Here Gibbon is clearly applying his modern views of the towns to the past.

Of course, at the time in which Gibbon was writing, there was very limited knowledge in Britain of pre-Roman settlement sites such as *oppida*. Work by William Camden (1551–1623) and John Speed (1542–1629) linked names mentioned within the classical texts with those found on pre-Roman coinage, such as Ver for Verulamium and Camv for Camulodunon (Hingley 2006a: 333); Horsley's *Britannia Romana* (1974; originally published in 1732) also demonstrates awareness of sites of pre-Roman Britain. This suggests that, at this early date, pre-Roman peoples were being linked with known places and monuments in the landscape (ibid.), which Gibbon would have been able to draw upon for his understanding of Roman and pre-Roman Britain. These places were being identified at a period in time when the ways of understanding and interpreting landscape and urbanism were changing rapidly (see Chapters 3 and 4). It is not possible to criticise Gibbon's approach to pre-Roman settlement because 'archaeology' and 'prehistory' in their modern sense had no meaning in work at this time (cf. Hingley 2008).

It is useful, however, to examine the way in which Gibbon described the settlement of the period. His attitude to the role of woodland, wetlands, and other natural places in the lives of the indigenous peoples drew upon the classical texts but also the political context in which Gibbon was writing. This context had little or nothing to do with attitudes in prehistory or the Roman period. Gibbon writes, for example, that the 'only temples in Germany were dark and ancient groves, consecrated by the reverence of succeeding generations' (*DF* I: 245) and '[T]he sacred wood, described with such sublime horror by Lucan, was in the neighbourhood of Marseilles; but there were many of the same kind in Germany' (*DF* I: 245, n. 63).[16] With regard to the Suebi, Gibbon draws on the writings of Tacitus in the *Germania*. 'In that part of Upper Saxony beyond the Elbe, which is at present called the Marquisate of Lusace, there existed, in ancient times, a sacred wood, the awful seat of the superstition of the Suebi' (*DF* I: 271).[17] He also refers to the Alamanni with their 'native deities of the woods and rivers' (*DF* IV: 759–60).

For indigenous, that is barbarian, settlements, Gibbon drew on descriptions in Caesar's *Bellum Gallicum*, which describes strongholds of woods and marshes: '[W]e can only suppose them to have been rude fortifications, constructed in the centre of the woods, and designed to secure the women, children and cattle, whilst the warriors of the tribe marched out to repel a sudden invasion' (*DF* I: 235).[18] Woods were used by Gibbon as a method of emphasising the savagery and danger of the barbarians. Attacks from barbarians came from woods, in contrast to the civilisation of walled towns: 'The crafty barbarians, who had lined the woods, suddenly attacked the legions' (*DF* I: 308–9). Other phrases include 'the savage warriors of Scythia issued from their forests' (*DF* III: 121), 'a crowd of naked savages rushed from the woods' (*DF* III: 281), 'the secret paths of the woods' (*DF* II: 1066), 'dark recesses of the woods' (*DF* II: 1077), and the 'thick and gloomy woods' (*DF* II: 124).

The term 'woods and morasses' (bogs or marshes) occurs a number of times throughout the work, emphasising the barbarity of the indigenous peoples compared with the civilisation of the Romans. Woodland clearance and the drainage of marshland by the Romans were considered to represent improvement, civilisation, and rationalisation, as

---

[16] Marcus Annaeus Lucanus (A.D. 39–69) was a poet whose works included (his only surviving work) the ten-volume *Pharsalia* (The Civil War), describing the contest between Caesar and the Senate. In Book III he describes a sacred grove in the vicinity of Marseilles (Luc. III, 399–432).

[17] On this subject Tacitus, to whom Gibbon refers in footnote 81 of Chapter X, wrote that 'at fixed seasons all tribes of the same name and blood gather through their delegations at a certain forest and after publicly offering up a human life, they celebrated the grim initiation of their barbarous worship' (*Germ.* XXXIX).

[18] Caesar refers to the significance of woodland for the indigenous peoples: The Suebi sent 'their children and all their stuff to the woods' (*B Gall.* IV.19) and the 'Menapii had all hidden in their densest forests' (IV.38). On Caesar's second invasion of Britain he mentions how Cassivellaunus 'concealed himself in entangled positions among the woods' (V.19) and that the stronghold of Cassivellaunus was 'fenced by woods and marshes' (V.21). Caesar goes on to write that 'the Britons call it a stronghold when they have fortified a thick-set woodland with rampart and trench' (V.21).

was the drainage of the Fenland in Gibbon's time (Darby 1973; Rogers 2007). Economic exploitation of woods and land was to be favoured, as it was within the British colonies of Gibbon's day, where Western concepts of 'landscape' were implanted on other regions.[19] Commenting on more recent times, Gibbon wrote that, in Germany, the 'immense woods have been gradually cleared' and the 'morasses have been drained' (*DF* I: 232). It 'is the happy consequence of the progress of arts and agriculture' that instead of 'some rude villages, thinly scattered among its woods and morasses, Germany produced a list of two thousand three hundred walled towns' (*DF* III: 512). He then uses the imagery of woodland and marsh to illustrate the 'decline' of the West after Rome: 'Gaul was again overspread with woods' (*DF* III: 481), and in Britain 'an ample space of wood and morass was resigned to the vague dominion of nature' with areas returned to their primitive state of a 'savage and solitary forest' (*DF* III: 502–3).

It is clear from these passages that Gibbon did think about the impact of Roman conquest on the pre-Roman indigenous settlements and natural places, but he also considered these pre-Roman places to be inferior to the towns and civilisation that the Romans were introducing. Our knowledge of pre-Roman Britain now indicates that there was much woodland clearance before the conquest (Haselgrove 1999), but areas of trees and other natural places, such as watery contexts, are likely to have been special places (Chapter 3). More significant, however, was Gibbon's metaphorical use of these landscape features as images of barbarity to demonstrate the benefits of civilisation. The changes to towns in the late Roman period were envisaged by Gibbon as equivalent to the decline of civilisation as he understood it, and the commencement of the fall. Gibbon's attitudes to pre-Roman and late Roman settlement have remained influential in the interpretations of the archaeology of these periods. New approaches have been taken in Iron Age studies, but late Roman studies also have to be transformed.

[19] In the footnotes of Gibbon's text he records that America 'must preserve the manners of Europe' (*DF* III: 514), such as the organisation of landscape, and on the colonisation of Australia and New Zealand he wrote that 'five great voyages were undertaken for 'the pure and generous love of science and of mankind'. They also 'introduced into the islands of the South Sea the vegetables and animals most useful to human life' (*DF* III: 516).

CHAPTER 3

Approaches to Roman urbanism and studying the late Roman town

The concept of decline and fall, then, has been a dominant theoretical framework used to explain the archaeology of towns in the late Roman period in Britain and elsewhere. The Golden Age of classical urbanism is followed by decline; as Haverfield (1924: 265) stated, 'no Golden Age lasts long'. Tied in with this view is a preoccupation with economic interpretations of the evidence. Until relatively recently, studies of Roman Britain did not cover the late Roman period in as much detail as the Golden Age (e.g., Frere 1967; Haverfield 1912; Wacher 1975). A few studies have proved important exceptions (e.g., P. J. Casey 1979; Esmonde Cleary 1989), but the specialism inherent in Roman urban archaeology has meant that work has remained largely uninfluenced by the advances in theory and practice in other areas of archaeology. In Iron Age archaeology, for example, methodologies are increasingly challenging culture-specific assumptions and new approaches are being attempted (cf. Haselgrove and Moore 2007a; see Chapter 4).

Researchers often ask the question 'what is a town?' when they are discussing urbanism in the late Roman period (e.g., Halsall 1996: 276–7; R. White 2000: 107), but they usually answer it without giving a sufficient discussion of the complex issue of urbanism in the earlier Roman period and any pre-existing contexts in which towns were set. Towns in Roman Britain are generally considered to be one of the more straightforward and easily understood features of the Roman period, with urbanisation representing unproblematic progress from pre-existing settlement patterns. Researchers of the late Roman period have often taken the nature of the town for granted before they begin their analyses of decline and change. Some more challenging approaches include those by Christie (2006), Esmonde Cleary (1989, 2001), Fulford et al. (2006), Lavan and Bowden (2003), Leone (2007), and Wickham (2005). There is still, however, a need to address the way in which urbanism in later Roman times and the Roman period more generally has been approached for Roman Britain. A key aim in this chapter is to raise awareness of the way in which towns have been studied so that we can move towards a new understanding of urbanism and towns in the later Roman period.

3.1 Thinking about civilisation and decline in towns

Towns and their public buildings have been central to many works on the later Roman period. They have often been used to measure the extent of the impact of Roman values on the provinces. Changes to towns have been taken to represent the end of these values and to indicate the decline of the Empire as a whole. As a result, urbanism is a major issue in the archaeology of the later Roman period (cf. Cameron 1993a: 152; 2003: 10). Change and adaptation are now important themes, especially in the Mediterranean and North Africa (Christie 2006; Leone 2007; B. Ward-Perkins 1984, 2005), but there is still a need to consider the subject through the use of more overtly theoretical approaches, a situation that is partly the result of the context in which Roman archaeology and urban studies developed.

The nineteenth and early twentieth centuries in Britain, when Gibbon's work was especially influential, saw a number of excavations of Roman towns in Britain, including Caerwent (Ashby, Hudd, and King 1910), Silchester (Fox and St. John Hope 1890; Joyce 1866), Wroxeter (Wright 1872), and Verulamium (Page 1914). For these excavators, alternative visions from the Golden Age image of Roman urbanism were rarely sought: Fox and St. John Hope, for example, wrote of the 'desirability of the complete and systematic excavation of the site of Silchester' (1890: 733), which meant identifying the plans of stone buildings and *insulae* without addressing phasing and other types of structures.[1] As a result, information concerning the late Roman period will have been lost; more recent excavations of the Silchester *basilica* have uncovered the Victorian trenches and demonstrated the extent of the damage to archaeological deposits that these caused (Fulford and Timby 2000: 80).

Classical texts and images of Roman elite living were highly influential within Roman studies at this time (cf. Hingley 2000), which had an impact on archaeological work. Earlier, during the Renaissance, interest in both classical texts and Roman remains was growing throughout Europe.[2] The early and mid-sixteenth century saw a number of discoveries of Roman buildings and statues, and architectural components were reused; monuments were of great interest to humanists and early antiquaries (cf. Moatti 1989). This interest in the Roman period also had the effect of associating Renaissance understanding of urbanism with the Roman period (Carter 1972: 17); attitudes to and understanding of the city were projected back from Renaissance present to Roman past. Visible remains also attracted interest in Britain: the 'Jewry Wall' in Leicester, the Newport Arch in Lincoln, and the 'Old Work' at Wroxeter were all studied, drawn, and engraved, often being romanticised.[3] This projected contemporary views and attitudes onto the Roman remains, in much the same way as artists had done in Rome.

Studies of Roman urbanism in Britain have mainly taken the elite Roman perspective, seeing urbanisation in terms of the introduction of progressive and desirable forms of settlement, institutions that were judged to be hugely beneficial to the indigenous barbarian peoples. Haverfield (1913: 123), for instance, wrote that 'the regularity of the (town) plan is plainly the work of civilized man. When the Celts were brought to live in a Roman city, care was taken that it should be really Roman'; whereas for Frere (1967: 203) Roman

---

[1] Of course, excavation and recording techniques have greatly changed since then, partly as a result of these early excavations, and now it is possible to identify far greater detail in the data.

[2] Classical works, such as *De architectura* by Vitruvius, were being increasingly relied upon to create the Renaissance 'ideal city'. Contemporary publications were written on the subject drawing upon Vitruvius. *De re aedificatoria* (1452), for example, by Leon Battista Alberti (1404–72), published in ten books, stated that the art of building consisted of locality, area, compartition, wall, roof, and openings, and the style of the advocated architecture mirrored the classical tradition closely (trans. Rykwert, Leach, and Tavernor 1999).

[3] An example is the 1798 watercolour of the 'Old Work' by Thomas Girtin (1775–1802), a painter who specialised in landscapes. It has a pond and shrubs added to the foreground to make it more 'idyllic' (White and Barker 1998: colour plate 1). The 'Old Work' was also the subject of an engraving by D. Parkes in 1812 (ibid.: 14).

'civilised life was inconceivable . . . without a city as its stage'. Hingley (2000) has shown
that these attitudes are partly related to the development of Roman archaeology within
the context of British imperialism in which the elite of the day identified itself with Rome.
Archaeology has often concentrated on the 'civilising' aspects of Roman culture such as
villas and towns (Hingley 2000: 149–52). Thus Richmond (1963: 55) wrote that 'the instru-
ment of civilisation used by Rome in achieving results was the town' and for Collingwood
and Richmond (1969: 95) towns were 'bulwarks of loyalty'. They were centres of civilised
life with administration, education, trade, amusement, amenity, and protection (Wacher
1975: 26). This emphasis on civilisation can be seen in the classical sources that were used,
where the absence of the city is synonymous with savagery and towns are expressed as
tools to civilise the natives (cf. Perkins and Nevett 2000: 213–14). Examples include Strabo
referring to mainland Europe in his *Geographia* (IV.1.5),[4] probably written around the
time of Tiberius (A.D. 14–37), and Tacitus (*Agr.* XXI) referring to Britain in the late first
century B.C. and early first century A.D.[5] These attitudes can also be seen in earlier Greek
writing (Laurence 2000: 346), such as Aristotle's *Politica*,[6] and have clearly influenced
studies of late Roman urbanism.

In the early excavations of towns some discoveries considered to represent later phases
of towns were occasionally made, but these were usually placed within the context of
dramatic events inflicted on the towns. Excavations at Silchester in 1833, for example,
located a skeleton in the baths of the *mansio* (Anon 1833); this was considered to be the
result of 'violence and fire' (Kempe 1838: 418) and to represent the end of civilised standards
and of law and order (Boon 1974: 81–2).[7] Similarly, Thomas Wright's nineteenth-century
excavations at Wroxeter located twelve skeletons within the hypocaust of the baths, which
were interpreted as people who had 'fled from the massacrers [*sic*]', when 'the town was
attacked and destroyed' by Anglo-Saxon invaders (Wright 1872: 68, 143).

As Esmonde Cleary has shown (2004: 418), the Wheeler excavations at Verulamium
between 1930 and 1933 (Wheeler and Wheeler 1936) were perhaps the first major excavations of a Romano-British town that recognised chronological changes. Wheeler's interpretations, however, were based on his background as a classicist and as a military man
(Cunliffe 1999: 371).[8] Wheeler described the late town as being in a 'ruinous condition':
'nothing constructive belongs of this age'; it resembled a 'bombarded city' (Wheeler and

---

[4] Strabo wrote that 'instead of carrying on war' they (the Massiliotes) 'turned to civic life and farming'. He goes
on that 'all the men of culture turn to the art of speaking and the study of philosophy', activities that are
centred on 'the city' (IV.1.5).

[5] Tacitus, writing at the end of the first century A.D., wrote that 'In order that a population scattered and
uncivilised, and proportionately ready for war, might be habituated by comfort to peace and quiet, he
[Agricola] would exhort individuals, assist communities, to erect temples, market-places, houses' (*Agr.* XXI).

[6] For Aristotle, the city 'exists for the good life' and those without cities are 'either low in the scale of humanity
or above it' (*Pol.* I.1.8–9).

[7] This find was reported in the *Reading Mercury* on 18th February 1833 (Anon 1833) and in *The Gentleman's
Magazine* in the same month (Kempe 1838). These excavations were carried out by the Rev. Mr. Coles,
rector of the parish, and 'aided by the exertions of another neighbouring clergyman' (Anon 1833). They do not
seem to have been part of any of the programmes of excavations at the site and appear to have been a one-off
(Boon 1974: 24). The first major interventions at Silchester were undertaken by John Stair (1708–82) and then
by the Rev. J. G. Joyce (1819–78) before those of the Silchester Excavation Fund between 1890 and 1909
(ibid.: 22–7).

[8] Wheeler's degree was in Classics and his father was also a Classicist (cunliffe 1999: 371). After Verulamium,
Wheeler went on to excavate the Iron Age hillfort at Maiden Castle and vividly described what he saw as
evidence for the invading Romans and attacks on the local people (1943).

Wheeler 1936: 28). For Wheeler, the 'social and economic standards of the Verulamium citizens had fallen too far for more than a momentary redemption'; the 'spacious residential quarter in the south part of the town decayed rapidly to slum conditions or even to desolation' (Wheeler and Wheeler 1936: 30). With no salvation from civilising external forces, there could only be decline. For Wheeler, the end of the perceived Golden Age was inevitably followed by decline. Collingwood, drawing upon Wheeler's analysis, described mid-fourth-century Verulamium in a similar fashion: 'the greater part of Verulam was uninhabited, a waste of empty houses. Here and there squatters lived among the ruins' (Collingwood and Myres 1936: 206); this was considered to be typical of the period. Collingwood also refers to evidence of the 'squatters' occupation at Silchester and of the deserted and ruined *forum* at Wroxeter' (ibid.). Frere's (1983) study of Verulamium proposed a long chronology but there was a notable decline in living standards in the later Roman period.

The views of Wheeler and Frere were still influential in the 1980s and into the 1990s. Reece (1980), in more dramatic terms, proposed that the Roman town in Britain was effectively dead by the mid-third century, as a result of the third-century crisis,[9] and had completely gone by A.D. 350: 'the third century intervened and the town, a tender Mediterranean plant in foreign soil, failed' (Reece 1980: 78); what remained was an 'administrative village' (ibid.: 89–90). By asserting that towns never fully developed in Roman Britain, such an emphasis on decline is avoided but it also suggests that any settlement that was not in the image of the classical city was inferior. This 'administrative village' model has been influential; see, for example, Esmonde Cleary's (1989) important synthesis of the late Roman archaeology of Britain. He does, however, argue for a greater level of continuity of town life up to the later fourth century, rather than the early date for change advocated by Reece.

In *The Decline and Fall of Roman Britain*, a title that draws on Gibbon, Faulkner (2000a) argues for the 'decline of classical urbanism', with towns becoming fortified strong points of the military government: 'the booming civil towns of the golden age had been superseded by the gloomy police towns of an age of blood and iron' (ibid.: 130). The civic centres were replaced by areas devoted to large military piazzas and store buildings (ibid.: 128–9), whilst for most of the population there was a 'shanty town of huts and shelters' (1996: 94). His views were coloured by an emphasis on classical elite culture, large townhouses, and monumental public buildings, and neglected other meanings and forms that the settlements could take. For Faulkner, the end of classical urbanism is marked by the cessation of the construction of monumental public buildings and 'civilised' living (2000b: 47); for him it was irrelevant that occupation continued within towns: 'there are no sites where a level of activity has been recorded for the late fourth century *sufficient to justify the case of the term "town" to describe them*' (2004: 7; Faulkner's italics).

Faulkner (2004) formed his arguments by using a number of characteristics to define the Roman period: broadly uniform cultural assemblage across the Empire, including buildings; numerous high-status settlements; evidence of a centralised authority manifest in street-grids and roads; many elaborate public buildings; much use of mortared masonry; mass production and distribution of artefacts; and architecture that is rooted in

[9] The 'third-century crisis' is a term often used for a series of events in the Roman Empire during the third century that included military collapses on frontiers, internal civil war, and economic problems (Faulkner 2000a: 80–7). Diocletian's reforms at the end of the third century were an attempt to save the Empire from destruction (Mitchell 2007: 55–62).

Greco-Roman culture. These criteria, however, equate largely with the concept of 'romanisation' outlined by Haverfield (1912), which provides a simplistic way of understanding Roman Britain; features such as monumental townhouses and rural villas were in the minority compared with the number of small rural sites in the settlement record (Hingley 1989; Mattingly 2006a). It is necessary to recognise and value the vast quantity of evidence of activity in towns during the late Roman period.

International work on the later Roman period has discussed the issue of decline in a more balanced manner, including the dialogue on the subject in Lavan's (2001a) *Recent Research in Late Antique Urbanism*. In this book the main argument for decline is set out by Liebeschuetz (2001), for whom it is a value-free concept with which to record changes in the archaeology as manifest in the decay of town centres, the replacement of stone with timber, the fall in populations, and the reduction in trade. Others, however, are more critical of a simplistic vision of decline (e.g., Cameron 2001; Lavan 2001b). Cameron (1993a, 1993b, 2001), for example, considers 'decline' to be a subjective term that should be avoided, and she questions the assertion that such factors as timber replacing stone can be taken as obvious examples of decline. She also makes the important point that 'it is not the historian's place either to sit in moral judgement on his subject or to impose inappropriate classical norms' onto the data (1993a: 198). Other works such as *Towns in Transition: Urban Evolution in Late Antiquity and the Early Middle Ages* (Christie and Loseby 1996) attempted to avoid the term 'decline.'

The debate concerning decline shows the complexity of the concept as a socially constructed idea. It is also tied into the predominance of economic interpretations of towns and their settings, which is considered further in a later section of this chapter.

3.2 The historical context of late Roman urbanism

When studying late Roman urbanism, we cannot, of course, ignore the history of the Empire at this time, and there are historical documents such as the *Codex Theodosianus*, the *Notitia Dignitatum*, and the *Notitia Galliarum* that can help us. These are important sources that give insights into the role of Christianity, bishops, and the military, and into activities within towns, such as the closure of temples and the presence of government-run *fabricae*. Nonetheless, there are also problems with their use, including corruption of the texts, the motives behind their production, and the extent to which they are relevant to late Roman Britain on the periphery of the Empire. Roman archaeology, however, can have a distinct role within broader classical conceptions, one that helps to justify the subject. The archaeological evidence can be considered as a material 'text' that contains patterns and significance and can enable a different story to be told (cf. Mattingly 1997b: 15).

3.2.1 *Historical events*

Historically dated frameworks and events into which the archaeology of late Roman Britain is often set include the revolt of Carausius and Allectus,[10] the barbarian conspiracy of

[10] Carausius, and his successor Allectus, were usurper emperors in Britain in the late third century, making Britain and parts of northwest Gaul independent from the Empire. Allectus was suppressed in A.D. 296 and Britain was restored to the Empire. Current knowledge of this episode in the history of Roman Britain is still only slight (P. J. Casey 1994).

A.D. 367,[11] and other barbarian invasions; and they do indicate that late Roman Britain was a vibrant place. There are a number of studies that deal with these events in detail (e.g., P. J. Casey 1994; Faulkner 2000a; S. Johnson 1980), and Faulkner's study of Verulamium (1996) identifies a number of phases in the development of the town according to this historical framework. Esmonde Cleary (2004: 409), however, has made the point that texts referring directly to Britain are rare and contain limited information, as Britain was probably only of occasional interest to writers and also because some texts will have been lost. The significance for Britain of Empire-wide events may sometimes be given too much emphasis, because it is uncertain how much they would have affected individual towns.

The late Roman history by Ammianus Marcellinus (ca. A.D. 325/330–after 391), for example, describes the 'barbarian conspiracy' of A.D. 367 in Britain (XXVII.8). However, Marcellinus was writing within the court of Theodosius I, whose father, Count Theodosius, had defeated the revolt, and this will have influenced his account of events (P. J. Casey 2002: 85). Elton (2006: 193) has also made the important argument that dates recorded in documented laws are unlikely to reflect the actual dates on which they were implemented in Rome. In peripheral parts of the Empire, such as Britain, the implementation of laws may well have been much later than in Rome or, indeed, not at all (ibid.). Another problem with some of the historical texts is that they were not written to provide direct factual accounts of the past: this is especially the case for later works such as Gildas' (ca. A.D. 494/516–570) *De excidio et conquestu Britanniae* and Bede's (ca. A.D. 672–735) *Historia ecclesiastica gentis Anglorum*. They do include some information about the state of Britain at this time and, as texts, they indicate that there must have been intellectual training available for authors to write such works (Wood 2004: 431). What is problematic is that they are written from a Christian moral standpoint and they mix fact, fiction, and legend, and are thus unlikely to be historically accurate.

Britain would, at least to some degree, however, have been affected by changes and events on an Empire-wide level. Diocletian's reforms of the Empire, including its division into two halves, the creation of the tetrarchy, and the splitting of provinces into smaller areas (Mitchell 2007: 55–62), had an impact upon Britain. These changes saw the division of Britain into the four provinces *Britannia Prima*, *Britannia Secunda*, *Maxima Caesariensis*, and *Flavia Caesariensis*, with Cirencester, York, London, and Lincoln as their capitals (P. J. Casey 2002: 79). From the political and administrative function performed by these towns, it can be inferred that they continued to be important places and focal points within the landscape. This political significance outweighs claims for the early decline of towns based on economic factors. The economic state of the Empire would also have influenced Britain. In the later Roman period, there was inflation and a reduction of interregional trade as a result of the ever-burgeoning cost of the army and the bureaucracy (Mattingly 2006b: 283). As a result, there was an increase in the collection of taxes in kind, the *annona*, (P. J. Casey 2002: 79), which has caused Faulkner (2000a) to view British towns in the later

[11] The barbarian conspiracy in A.D. 367 was an event in which a number of groups combined in an attack against Britain. They included the Anglo-Saxons and Franks from the North Sea, the Picts and Attacotti from Scotland, and the Scotti from Ireland (Esmonde Cleary 1989: 44). Valentinian I employed Theodosius to restore the situation in Britain. The event is recorded in the history of Ammianus Marcellinus (XXVI.4–5, XXVII.8, and XXVIII.3).

Roman period as military and supply bases. Although towns were probably involved in the collection of the *annona* (Esmonde Cleary 1989: 8), it also indicates their continued role as important places, demanding study of other activities within them at this time, assessing what new insights archaeological data and theory can provide.

3.2.2 *Bishops and the Church*

The rise of the Church and the role of bishops are often considered central to our understanding of towns in the later Roman period, especially after Christianity became the official religion in A.D. 312 (B. Ward-Perkins 1998: 392). As noted in connection with the writings of Gildas and Bede, however, the history of the Church is often problematic because of the Christian messages that the writers presented to their audiences. The continuation of towns and the construction of new public buildings are often attributed to the work of bishops (e.g., Liebeschutz 2000). Most writing on the subject focuses on the central parts of the Empire and the East, but it is generally assumed that Britain followed a comparable path. Liebeschutz (ibid.) charts what he sees to be the rise of the bishop in the later Roman period: With the conversion of Constantine, the Church was arranged into a structure with provinces and dioceses that was comparable to the organisation of the Empire (ibid.: 137–9). As the secular government declined, the administrative tasks gradually fell to the bishops. Described as the new elite (Bowden 2001), bishops were powerful figures who could be involved in lawmaking whilst being exempt from laws themselves (Hunt 1998: 274), although some have argued that their influence should not be overemphasised (e.g., Wickham 2005). Textual evidence does give some indication of the bureaucratic impact of bishops in the Empire, suggesting that they would have had some influence on the towns (Hunt 1998: 238).[12] Documents also indicate that martyrs were important in continuing religious activity and spreading Christianity within towns (e.g., Bede I.7; Gildas X.1–2).

Much more documentary evidence concerning bishops survives for Gaul than for Britain. The *Notitia Galliarum*, composed in the late fourth to early fifth century, lists the *civitas*-capitals of Gaul with bishops and there are also the *acta* of church councils that name the bishops that attended. In Britain the evidence is far scarcer. One of the main sources of information is the proceedings of the council of Arles, the *Acta Concilii Arelatensis*, held in A.D. 314 (Petts 2003: 38). This appears to mention four delegations from Britain that are usually ascribed to the four provincial capitals of the later Roman period (e.g., Esmonde Cleary 1989: 47); however, the information is very limited. The *acta* lists the following (Munier 1963: 15, lines 54–8):

> Eborius episcopus de ciuitate Eboricensi prouincia Britania.
> Restitutus episcopus de ciuitate Londenensi prouincia qua supra.
> Adelfius episcopus de ciuitate Colonia Londenensium,
> exinde Sacerdus presbyter, Arminius diaconus.

This is taken to record a bishop Eborius from York, Restitutus from London, Adelfius from Lincoln (if *Londenensium* was perhaps a corruption of *Lindensium*), and a priest and deacon from another place (possibly Cirencester if the place was another provincial

---

[12] Documents record, for example, how bishops created a strain on the *cursus publicus* as they moved to church councils under the instruction of the Emperor (Hunt 1998: 238 from Amm. Marc. XXI.16.18).

capital). Although this seems to indicate bishops in Britain, there is clearly insufficient information and considerable doubt regarding the organisation of British bishops at this time. There is also a small amount of information regarding the Pelagian heresy in the A.D. 420s and 430s (see Mattingly 2006a: 534–5); these are events that, though still not completely clear, demonstrate that the Church in Britain must have be strong by the 420s but its exact involvement in towns at an earlier date are still unclear.

There are some important archaeological finds with possible references to bishops in Britain, such as the Risley Park Lanx, the Shavinton salt-pan, and the pewter *tazza* from the Isle of Ely (Petts 2003: 38–9).[13] Nevertheless, this evidence is scarce and perhaps does not really have much value in assessing the religion of the people in Britain at this time. In fact, surviving pagan attitudes may be indicated by the ways in which these artefacts were deposited and destroyed. The Shavinton salt-pan was found cut into eight pieces, perhaps a deliberate act for religious deposition; the Ely *tazza* came from a river, again suggesting religious deposition, but possibly within a Christian context. After use, it may have been necessary to deposit the vessels in sacred places; these locations will also have been associated with pre-Christian ritual and belief (cf. Rogers 2007). Many of the religious watery places were probably assimilated rather than suppressed in Christian times. The presence within Britain of bishops and clergy need not have greatly affected general religious practice and belief at this time. There will also have been a gulf between laws banning pagan ritual and what actually happened in the local setting: 'laws do not a Christian make' (Hunt 1993: 143–4).

Early scholarship tended to emphasise the evidence of Christianity, as in the identification of the 'church' building at Silchester (Fox and St. John Hope 1893: 563–8). This desire to identify the earliest Christianity may have been linked to the wish to limit the involvement of paganism in the history of Roman Britain. The large number of clergymen taking part in antiquarianism and early archaeology, as in the early excavation of Silchester (Boon 1974: 22–7), was also perhaps a factor in this search for early Christianity.

3.2.3 *The Theodosian Code*

For discussing Christianity within towns in the later Roman period there is the Theodosian Code, a compilation of over 2,500 edited constitutions completed in A.D. 437 under Theodosius II (Harris 1993: 1; Matthews 1993: 19). Although it was compiled at this late date, it contained laws from as early as A.D. 313 (Matthews 2000: 11) and so has been used to understand the Empire in the early fourth century or even earlier. The laws cover aspects of political, social, economic, cultural, and religious life in the late Empire, and they include many rules and regulations concerning the use, reuse, and protection of public buildings (e.g., regulations 15.1.10 and 15.1.25).[14] These include demands for the

---

[13] On the base of the silver Risley Park Lanx was written 'Bishop Exuperius gave this to…' together with a *chi-rho* symbol (Petts 2003: 38–9), whilst the pewter *tazza* from the Isle of Ely was inscribed with 'this belongs to/for the furnishings of the bishop and the clergy' (*ibid*.: 39). Another piece, the lead salt-pan from Shavinton (Cheshire), has 'Of Viventius, the bishop' written on it (*ibid*.).

[14] Regulation 15.1.10 of the year A.D. 362 reads as follows: 'If any person of any order or high rank should obtain any public building in any manner by an obscure interpretation, he shall, without any question, be deprived of the fruits of such benefit' (Sirmond and Pharr 1969: 424). Regulation 15.1.25 of A.D. 389 states that 'It is disgraceful that the ornaments of public splendour should be ruined by the attachment thereto of private buildings' (*ibid*.).

closure of temples and the end of pagan rituals and ceremonies (e.g., regulations 16.10.4 and 16.10.7),[15] but there are also demands for the protection and preservation of temples as monuments (e.g., regulation 16.10.15).[16] These laws have been used by archaeologists to interpret, and to date, the end of use of temples and other public buildings in the archaeological record across the Empire, including Britain, and the spread of Christianity (e.g., Liebeschuetz 2000; Watts 1991, 1998). Although the code can give valuable insights into life and conditions in later Roman times, there is a need for caution. These texts may not necessarily reflect activity across the whole Empire, where there will have been differing reactions to the laws at different times.

3.2.4 *The military*

The military is also seen as playing an important role in influencing the nature of towns and town life in the later Roman period. Faulkner (2000a: 130), for example, describes the development of military towns in late Roman Britain where production and organisation of space was geared towards war. One of the main texts used to support this view is the *Notitia Dignitatum*, which lists the offices, military units, and government installations under the control of the Masters of the Offices of the Eastern and Western Empires in the early fifth century (S. James 1988: 257). It includes lists of state *fabricae* and workshops used to supply the army with its weapons and equipment, and it has been used as one interpretation of the industrial activity within public buildings in the later Roman period in Britain (e.g., Fulford and Timby 2000: 579; see Chapter 7). In this case, public life had been given up for the sake of military security.

In fact, no *fabrica* mentioned in the *Notitia* has yet been identified with certainty in the archaeological record, and so caution is required when one is interpreting the data. Britain is even more problematic because none of the provinces here are mentioned in the *Notitia* at all. James has suggested that this may have been because Britain no longer had a large army and so did not need its own arsenals (1988: 323). James does point out that the order of the list might suggest that Britain would come at the end, the part most vulnerable to damage (ibid.: 259), but this cannot be used to suggest that Britain certainly did have *fabricae*. The circumstances surrounding the text and Britain's omission are uncertain, but it is clearly not possible to rely on the *Notitia* to explain the evidence of metalworking within the public buildings of towns in late Roman Britain.

3.2.5 *The appeal to Honorius*

The historian Zosimus in the *Historia nova*, probably written around A.D. 500 but also drawing upon a fifth-century history by Olympiodorus (Mitchell 2007: 24), wrote that 'the

---

[15] Regulation 16.10.4 from A.D. 346 states that 'It is Our pleasure that the temples shall be immediately closed in all places and in all cities, and access to them forbidden, so as to deny to all abandoned men the opportunity to commit sin' (Sirmond and Pharr 1969: 472). Regulation 16.10.7 of the year A.D. 381 declares that 'If any madman or sacrilegious person, so to speak, should immerse himself in forbidden sacrifices, by the day or by the night, as a consulter of uncertain events, and if he should suppose that he should employ, or should think that he should approach, a shrine or a temple for the commission of such a crime, he shall know that he will be subjected to proscription' (ibid.: 473).

[16] Regulation 16.10.5 from A.D. 399 reads, 'Just as We forbid sacrifices, so it is Our will that the ornaments of public works shall be preserved' (Sirmond and Pharr 1969: 474).

barbarians from beyond the Rhine overran everything at will and reduced the inhabitants of the British Island and some of the peoples in Gaul to the necessity of rebelling from the Roman Empire and of living by themselves, no longer obeying the Romans' laws' (VI.6). This is often taken in conjunction with the reference that Zosimus made to a letter the Emperor Honorius supposedly wrote to Britain in about A.D. 410, telling the towns to look to their own defence (VI.10.2). That the validity of the reference to Britain has been questioned is well known. Some prefer the place name to be read as Bruttium in Italy, arguing that the letter had been copied wrongly and that a reference to Britain at that point in Zosimus' narrative would have been out of place (Bartholomew 1982: 262). Others continue to refute this and argue for its authenticity in referring to Britain (e.g., Birley 2005: 461–2; E. Thompson 1982).

3.3 Beyond the economic: town and landscape

The influence on Roman archaeological tradition of the link between post-medieval social changes and the popularity of Roman culture should not be underestimated (Ayres 1997: 84–90). This might also explain why prehistorians have been more willing to challenge modern social attitudes in their interpretations of the past. They have criticised perceptions of life in the past that have assumed too much familiarity with our present economically dominated world (e.g., J. D. Hill 1995a; Thomas 1991).

3.3.1 Economics in Roman urban studies

In the nineteenth and early twentieth centuries, influential writings on cities by political economists and sociologists such as Max Weber (1864–1920)[17] were also encouraged by their contemporary economic situation. Although Weber's work was important, its application to the Roman period might be more problematic. *The City* (1921; translated into English, 1958) argued that the elite in Roman times used the rents from their agricultural estates to pay for their conspicuous consumption within towns; this 'consumer city' model was different from the 'producer city', where urban growth was a result of economic production and enterprise (Weber 1958; Grahame 1997: 151). The emphasis on economic aspects within studies of Roman urbanism, and of Roman archaeology more generally, has meant that other areas of Roman life and the way in which the town and its location were experienced have not been given sufficient attention. Influential supporters of Weber's model in studies of the classical world were Finley in *The Ancient Economy* (1973), and A. H. M. Jones in *The Roman Economy* (1974); both had primitivist views of the economy. Wacher's analysis of towns in Britain (1975), too, envisaged the town as the organiser and exploiter of the countryside and stressed the connection between the urban elite and the countryside and the use of the city to fulfil the elite's desire for commodities. Although Roman society may have worked in this way to some extent, this approach provides a narrow view of the town. Mattingly (2006b: 286) has also indicated that there would have been many regional differences in economic activity, with no single integrated economy.

---

[17] Weber was one of a number of sociologists in the late nineteenth and early twentieth century who were concerned principally with the rise of capitalism and the evolution of tribal societies to civilisation (Grahame 1997: 152).

Studies of urbanism have also compared 'industrial' and 'pre-industrial' cities and in many cases have considered the pre-industrial examples of the past as inferior, being similar to the settlements of modern-day pre-industrial peoples (e.g., Sjöberg 1965).[18] Related to the economic emphasis in studies of Roman urbanism is the reliance on modern conceptions of commerce that is often encountered; it is necessary to think beyond the market economy in relation to commerce in the Roman world. The idea of the 'embedded economy', as opposed to the 'market economy', for past societies was first argued forcefully by Polanyi (1957). He argued that in such societies exchange was 'embedded' in social relations and the modern concepts of 'economy' and 'economic life' had no meaning. The modern notion of the economy and the science of its study was more an invention of individuals such as Adam Smith (1723–90) and Thomas Malthus (1766–1834; see Morley 2004: 34). Polanyi's substantivist viewpoint was opposed to the formalist opinion that economic theory could be applied to all periods and all places (ibid.: 43). This was adopted by Hodder (1979) in his study of the use of pottery and coinage within Iron Age and Roman Britain. The idea of a market economy is also simplistic in the context of Rome, because gift giving and obligations of patronage often played a part in methods of exchange (Salway 1993: 427–9). Economic theory developed as a way for us to comprehend the modern capitalist economy, and it is questionable whether this can be fruitfully applied to non-capitalist and non-Western economies (Morley 2004: 34). Highlighting how twentieth-century attitudes often influence such studies, Greene (2005: 11–13) reminds us that the ways in which production and exchange were conceptualised and undertaken in the Roman period differed from present ideas. Influences will have survived from the pre-Roman period, where production and the movement and acquisition of goods will have been considered and conducted in terms beyond those of modern economics.

Industrial activity and its relationship to towns also require re-evaluation. Until recently such activity has not been the subject of as much consideration as other areas of Roman urban studies and has mainly been perceived through modern perspectives. There are some negative attitudes towards industrial activity in the classical sources, which may have influenced this early neglect of the topic in scholarship.[19] Finley's (1973) *The Ancient Economy* and A. H. M. Jones' *The Roman Economy* (1974) concentrate on agriculture, with only limited attention given to metal production. There have, however, been some useful attempts to look at other areas of production in a detailed way (e.g., Mattingly and Salmon 2000). Attitudes against industrial activity have now been shown to be largely idealist rather than representing reality in the Roman period, because the elite of the city seem to have made substantial use of production (Wallace-Hadrill 1991: 245).

In modern Western society, technology exists in a category distinct from religion and ritual, ideology and magic. However, this is a product of centuries of social change from the Middle Ages onwards, including the Enlightenment, the Industrial Revolution, and

[18] In *The Preindustrial City: Past and Present* (1965), Sjöberg makes the implicit link between so-called pre-industrial cities of today with the ancient past and suggests that they share a number of 'structured characteristics', namely in areas of class, family, the economy, politics, religion, and education.

[19] Well-known passages from Cicero include views such as these: 'of all revenue-producing activities none is finer, more productive, more agreeable, more worthy of a free man than agriculture' (*Off.* I.150–1), whereas 'vulgar are the means of livelihood of all . . . workmen . . . [and] merchants' (ibid.). The writers Juvenal (*Sat.* XIV.201–7) and Martial (*Epig.* III.59) express similar negative views towards tradesmen and craftsmen; according to Martial (ibid.) a craftsman is 'no person at all'.

modernism (Bergstøl 2002: 78). Technology is now geared towards maximum production and economic success; indeed, the words 'industry' and 'industrial' themselves have highly modern connotations and are not useful terms for the past. Modernist thinking tends to deny the human component of technology and industry and its symbolic and social role within society (Barndon 2004: 21; Reid and MacLean 1995: 145), which is important in pre-industrial and contemporary non-Western societies. This aspect of industrial activity requires further analysis. Like open spaces, metalworking and other crafts were often a significant part of late pre-Roman Iron Age precursors to many of the town sites in Roman Britain (see Chapter 5). Metalworking was also a significant activity in the public buildings of towns in the late Roman period; this is addressed in detail later (Chapter 7).

Though economic interpretations are important, they have come to dominate our understanding of many aspects of urban life and the interaction between towns and landscape. The emphasis on economic aspects in reconstructing the past has been influential in many areas of Roman archaeology; by recognising this, we can make new suggestions about the way in which urbanisation and urbanism, especially in the late Roman period, can be approached. Concentrating on the city's economic function neglects social aspects and reduces everything to economic activity. Recognising this emphasis on economic viewpoints is useful for examining towns in the late Roman period from new angles, because arguments for decline are often based on economic perspectives.

3.3.2 Landscape and town location

Economics and rationality have been influential in the consideration of Roman town planning. Some information, ideas, and attitudes concerning these issues are represented in ancient texts. Vitruvius outlines the most suitable locations to build a city (De arch. I.4.1–12),[20] whereas Cicero describes reasons of economy, security, and hygiene for the location of the town (Rep. II.2.3). Greek authors such as Plato and Aristotle express similar views in their writings (e.g., Arist. Pol. VII.10.1–8).[21] The orthogonal street-grid is often seen to be a symbol of order, advancement, and civilisation. Haverfield (1913: 11) was a strong instigator of the importance of Roman town planning,[22] and he emphasised the fact that only certain periods in time had been capable of town planning, including the Roman and the modern day.

Aspects of Roman town planning, however, went beyond technical and practical considerations. Rykwert (1976: 44–60) has documented the myths and rituals mentioned in the classical texts concerning the foundation of towns, which included taking the auspices and ritually outlining the boundaries of the town with a plough. A few important studies have attempted to analyse these in the archaeological evidence, including that in Britain (e.g., Creighton 2000: 209–13; Woodward and Woodward 2004). The preoccupation with

[20] The passage begins with 'For fortified towns the following general principles are to be observed. First comes the choice of a very healthy site. Such a site will be high, neither misty nor frosty, and in a climate neither hot nor cold, but temperate' (I.4.1).

[21] Aristotle writes that 'the city should so far as circumstances permit be in communication alike with the mainland, the sea and the whole of its territory. The site of the city itself we must pray that fortune may place on sloping ground' because of health, political, and military considerations (Pol. VII.10.1).

[22] Haverfield (1913: 11) emphasised 'the art of laying out towns with due care for the health and comfort of inhabitants, for industrial and commercial efficiency and for reasonable beauty of buildings'.

the practicalities of town foundation, however, has meant that there has been less consideration of how pre-Roman ideas and attitudes towards place and landscape influenced the establishment of towns. The town was not simply a physical entity, but also a space that was shaped, invented, and conceptualised by social actors over time (cf. Lefebvre 1991: 73; Rykwert 1976: 24). It was an interactive stage on which inhabitants and visitors orientated themselves through personal experience of their environment (Favro 1996: 227). The significance attached to the locations in which towns were placed in the pre-Roman period, across the Empire, will have influenced in some way the nature, understanding, and use of the towns and their setting.

Like town planning, location has traditionally been studied in terms of rational and economic factors emphasising military strategy, communication, and trade (though there are some important publications moving beyond this; see, e.g., Creighton 2006). In the 1960s and 1970s, central place theory was a popular analytical technique that was used to examine Roman town distribution (e.g., Hodder 1972).[23] This approach is now regarded as having a more limited value for studying landscape and settlement patterns in prehistory, but there continues to be an emphasis on rational reconstructions of the landscape in the Roman period, seeing towns as located at sites for optimal commercial value and military considerations (e.g., Qualmann et al. 2004: 90–1; Wacher 1995). These factors were important – Fulford (2002: 55), for example, suggests that the development around Verulamium was related to its location along Watling Street, which created considerable economic power with goods flowing north – but it is unlikely that the landscape would have been understood and experienced solely in these terms. To approach towns, their foundation, and their settings in more complex ways, which is a prerequisite for studying late Roman urbanism (the continuation of these places), we must address the dominance of both economic and modernist concepts of 'landscape' within studies. Figure 3.1 depicts the Brayford Pool in Lincoln, which has now been greatly reduced and confined to an economic and rational setting. In prehistory and the Roman period, however, it was larger and formed part of a highly meaning-laden and ritualised landscape (see Chapter 4; Jones and Stocker 2003).

Roman-period 'landscape' is generally assumed to have been understood, experienced, and to have functioned in a similar way to its modern counterpart, including an emphasis on its economic exploitation. This will have influenced the way in which towns and their locations in the Roman period in Britain have been studied, including their development from pre-Roman places. The term 'landscape' itself is a specific way of viewing the world originating within Western society amidst the economic and social changes of the post-medieval period (Cosgrove 1984). There has been much written on this subject and it is useful to summarise some of the arguments here. 'Landscape' is the product of an arrangement and structuring of the environment in a very specific period of change within society (Lemaire 1997: 5). Its emergence as a concept was heavily intertwined with the growing preoccupations with the economy and consumerism within Western society from the Renaissance onwards. The word 'landscape' entered English usage in the late sixteenth century as a painting term from the Dutch *landschap* (Cosgrove 1984: 120; Hirsch 1995: 2),

---

[23] The central place theory was taken from the concept of new geography, putting an emphasis on economic and rational motives in site location; in archaeology it was used to look at Iron Age hillfort distribution (e.g., Clarke 1968; Cunliffe 1984; also see Haselgrove 1992).

an artistic tradition influenced by Cartesian perspectivalism and a product of the Renaissance viewing of space as geometric, rectilinear, and abstract (Chapman 1997a: 4). Painting the land, and terms such as 'picturesque', objectified and distanced it, separating people from it (Bevan 1997: 181; Hirsch 1995: 11). Common themes of landscape paintings were aristocratic estates, and these were often conceptualised in comparable terms to Roman villas.

There was also an increasing perception of land as a commodity to be exploited to the full, culminating in the enclosure system, drainage operations on wetlands, and new farming techniques and machinery (Darby 1973). The result was that people were distanced further from the land and there was a greater emphasis on the visual landscape (Bender 2001: 3). M. Johnson (2007: 129) notes that even words such as 'farm' and 'farming' only really took on their modern meanings in the context of this eighteenth-century ideology of improvement. The rationalisation of the landscape led to its secularisation and the neglect of landscape as cosmology and mythical geography (the mingling of landscape, cosmology, and mythology) with ancestors, spirits, and gods, and invoked through memories, myths, rituals, and ceremonies (cf. Derks 1998: 135).

Merrifield (1987: 3–4) has argued that archaeology was too often considered in scientific terms, with an emphasis on measuring and quantification at the expense of other areas of human activity. Studies of landscape have been influenced greatly by the British empirical school, which has been principally concerned with surveying and mapping land (Thomas 1993: 19). Much of this work is of great value, but there has been a tendency to isolate interpretations of the landscape and separate these from the people of the past (C. Evans 1985: 80); scientific techniques have rationalised the way in which landscape was used and understood. Mapping techniques and aerial photography are 'reflectionist', because they impose modern expectations of searching for patterns onto the past as well as emphasising the aesthetic (Chapman 1997a: 10; M. Johnson 2007: 85–95), and they artificially expose everything to academic researchers or 'spectators' (Thomas 1993: 25). Space is conceived in terms of its 'formal essence' through mathematical spatial analysis (E. Casey 1996: 19–20).

The methodologies of processual archaeology created an artificial surface in which human action occurred (Tilley 1994: 9). Publications on landscape archaeology have tended to neglect the people themselves and the way in which they constructed and perceived the landscape in which they lived (Thomas 1993: 25–6). Survey projects of Roman landscapes and the production of maps of Roman provinces have generally neglected the cultural and social significance of the landscape (cf. Hingley 2006a). For Ingold (2000: 151), the notion of land as a surface to be occupied is a colonial viewpoint and is combined with the belief that the present takes over from the past. In actuality the 'landscape' will have been experienced in much more complex terms and with considerable references to the past.

General discussions of the Roman countryside have considered it predominantly in rational terms, with an emphasis on economic exploitation. This is especially noticeable in studies of villa landscapes (e.g., Branigan 1977) and discussions of the relationship between Roman towns and their hinterland (e.g., Wacher 1975). In early excavations, the villa and town mosaics that were found were sometimes placed within the house of the local estate (e.g., Upex 2001: 62–3), projecting modern elite understandings and experiences of landscape as well as perceptions of the classical past into Roman

FIGURE 3.1. Photograph of the Brayford Pool, Lincoln, in its modern setting (photograph by A. C. Rogers).

times.[24] British aristocrats were associating themselves with the Roman past, perhaps to justify their position and power in the present (Ayers 1997: 165; Hingley 2001: 149).

Studies of 'landscape' within prehistory have begun to move beyond preoccupations with the economic by placing an emphasis on humanised and meaning-laden space and attempting to explore how individuals perceived and engaged with the landscape, and constructed their identity within it (Knapp and Ashmore 1999: 9; Tilley 1994: 7–8). Bradley's (2000) study of 'natural places' has suggested that these too played an important part in social and ritual life. He has shown, for instance, that ritual deposition often had a role in negotiating the significance of the landscape in which people lived (ibid.: 5).[25] Man-made monuments were important (e.g., Thomas 1993; Tilley 1994), but so were natural features (cf. Insoll 2007; Rogers 2007).

Rather than using the value-laden and economically dominated term 'landscape' for understanding towns and their interaction with pre-existing settlements, it might be preferable to use 'place' – an entity for seeing, knowing, and understanding the world (Cresswell 2004). Places can be considered as foci of human feeling and thought, central to experiences of the environment; they are constructed in human movement, memory, and encounter (Taylor 1997: 193) and they gather and have a hold on what occurs there (E. Casey 1996: 24–5). For Ingold, similarly (2000: 149), a place is created when people

[24] During excavations of the villa at Cotterstock in the eighteenth century, for example, the Fourth Earl of Cardigan placed an uncovered mosaic on the floor of a summerhouse in the garden of the house in his nearby estate (Upex 2001: 62–3), associating his concept of the estate with that of the Roman period.

[25] In Chapman's study of prehistoric Hungary (1997b), he emphasised the importance of so-called flat sites, that is, non-monumentalised settlement sites within the landscape, which accumulated place-value over time.

inhabiting the land are drawn to a particular focus, with the act of movement to and from the sites also forming an important part of their meaning. Meaning can also differ depending on the people who are experiencing it, and their world-view and beliefs (Tilley 1994: 11). Much of understanding the 'landscape', including hills, rivers, and wetlands, was entwined with religious belief (Muir 2000: 147). The issue of ritual landscapes in Roman Britain, however, has only been briefly, although usefully, discussed (e.g., Hingley and Miles 2002; Rogers 2007; Taylor 1997).

The concept of the ritual landscape can be considered in relation to Roman urbanism by examining the significance and role of water and watery contexts within the landscape and how towns utilised and modified these resources – a topic often preoccupied with 'hard practical considerations', which are, in many cases, in actual fact 'modern, Western-derived assumptions' (M. Johnson 2007: 129).

3.3.3 Roman and indigenous attitudes to water

Within prehistory it is now generally recognised that water and watery places, including rivers, springs, lakes, bogs, and islands, amongst other natural places, played an important part in the social lives and religious beliefs of the indigenous peoples of Western Europe; they had a numinous quality (e.g., Derks 1998; M. Green 1986: 166; Kamash 2008; J. Webster 1995: 449–51).[26] These places will have influenced, and been consciously modified by, Roman urban development. It could be argued that anthropological, ethnographic, and archaeological studies of religion has often attempted to explain and comprehend it through a mindset based on the so-called world religions, with written scripture and an identifiable god, as in Christianity and Islam (Bowie 2000: 8, 25). Religion is also often considered a separate entity from everyday life and in terms of beliefs that need to be explained (Asad 1993: 40–4; Dowden 1992: 8; Graddel 2002: 6).

For Iron Age northwest Europe, it has been acknowledged that religion recognised the supernatural in all areas of life, including the natural surroundings. Consequently ritual activity was often associated with 'natural' features and especially those connected with water (P. J. Casey 1989: 37; M. Green 1986: 167). The source and confluences of rivers were important, with sanctuaries and ritual deposits known, for example, at the sources of the Seine, Marne and Yonne, and at the confluence of the Roer and the Meuse (Derks 1998: 138–9). It is unlikely that the role played by water in religious belief and activity in the Iron Age will ever be completely understood. Water is necessary for life and seems to have taken on a special significance, being considered the focus of the life-force and having regenerative powers (Derks 1998: 141; M. Green 1986: 166). Liminality may also have been a factor, with water being seen as the interface between the earthly and supernatural worlds where communication with the supernatural or entry to the 'other world' could be made (Cunliffe 1988: 359; Derks 1998: 141). Excavated sites such as Flag Fen near Peterborough, Fiskerton in Lincolnshire, and Llyn Cerrig Bach in Anglesey (Field and Parker Pearson 2003; C. Fox 1946; Pryor 2001) have demonstrated that they were foci for ritual deposition with large collections of metalwork. There are also well-known individual items from

---

[26] Records of the Second Council of Arles in A.D. 452 document the Church's discussion of how to prevent the worship of 'arbores fontes' and 'saxa' (trees, springs, and rocks; see Munier 1963: 126, I.20).

rivers such as the Battersea Shield from the Thames in London and the Witham Shield from Lincoln. Across Europe, wetlands are recognised as having been significant places throughout prehistory through the discovery of unusual finds (e.g., Coles 2001). Deposition into these contexts, as well as pits, will also have tied in with chthonic beliefs in which, as well as the visible landscape, there was a religiously imbued belowground where gods resided (cf. Cunliffe 1992, 2004).

Ritual deposition, of course, need not have been a prerequisite for the appreciation of the significance of natural places in prehistory, but it does seem that watery areas were important contexts for religious expression. Islands were also foci of attention perhaps because of their boundedness and close relationship with water (J. Webster 1995: 451); it is worth thinking about the potential ritual association of such contexts. Islands are mentioned in the classical sources as religious places (Pompon. III.48; Strabo IV.4.6; Tac. *Ann.* XIV.30; *Germ.* XL).[27] Archaeological research has demonstrated the importance of islands in British prehistory, and continuing into the Roman period, with sites such as the Hayling Island temple (King and Soffe 2001) and Llyn Cerrig Bach on Anglesey (C. Fox 1946). Some Roman towns in Britain closely associated with islands were Lincoln, Winchester and London.

Many accounts of Roman religion have tended to concentrate on the documented gods and the religious activity that took place within structurally defined temples (e.g., Henig 1984; A. Woodward 1992). Watery locations, however, were important in ancient Greece and Rome: 'all water in antiquity was sacred' (Camp 1988: 172). Gods were associated with many forms of water in Roman times, including oceans, rivers, and marshland, and in some aspects they will have invoked veneration for different reasons. The plaque dedicated to Ocean and Tethys, his divine sister-wife, found at York dating to the A.D. 80s, for example, related to the exploration of Britain's offshore islands at this time and the desire that it be conducted safely (Braund 1996: 12). Britain's location across the ocean will have meant that the land was always considered in special terms by the Romans. Rivers were considered special as local gods, and wetlands, whilst being rich in resources, were also transitional zones between land and water. Here they were being neither one nor the other but a part of both, and constantly transforming – at times water, inhabited by spirits, would dominate the land (Giblett 1996: 3).

The divine presence in springs, pools, and other watery locations is also represented in classical texts such as *De aquae ductu urbis Romae* by Frontinus, written at the end of the first century A.D., which states that 'esteem for springs still continues, and is observed with veneration' (I.4); for Servius, who wrote a fourth-century commentary on Virgil, 'there is no spring that is not holy' (Servius VII.84). Such locations were consequently often incorporated into cult sites (Scheid 2003: 72), as Pliny the Younger records (*Ep.* VIII.8.5–6) when he describes the shrines connected with the tributaries of the Clitumnus (Ferguson

---

[27] Pomponius (III.48) states that 'in the Britannic Sea, opposite the coast of the Ossimi, the isle of Sena belongs to a Gallic divinity and is famous for its oracle, whose priestesses, sanctified by their perpetual virginity, are reportedly nine in number'. Strabo (IV.4.6) records that in 'the ocean, he (Posidonius) says, there is a small island, not very far out to sea, situated off the outlet of the Liger River; and the island is inhabited by the women of the Samnitae, and they are possessed by Dionysus and make this god propitious by appeasing him with mystic initiations as well as other sacred performances'. Tacitus (*Ann.* XIV.30) records the 'circle of Druids, lifting their hands to heaven' on Anglesey and also that a number of Germanic tribes worshipped the goddess Nerthus on an island in the sea that had a holy grove (*Germ.* XL).

1970: 66–7). Rome itself was located next to the River Tiber, which was venerated (Braund 1996: 19; Creighton 2006: 95; Dion. Hal. *Ant. Rom.* II.73; Varro *Ling.* V.83).[28] Its flood plain and surrounding meadows required drainage and considerable reclamation, which would not only have been considered in practical terms but also as a demonstration of power and control over nature (Purcell 1996c). This is reflected in the meanings attached to, and uses of, this area as documented in detail by Purcell (ibid.), one use being the construction of monuments. Pliny the Elder states that the flooding in the City of Rome was thought of as 'relating to religion rather than a threat of disaster' (*HN* III.55). Flooding was also exacerbated by the natural springs in the surrounding hills (Aldrete 2007; Ammerman 1990: 636–9).

Ammerman's (1990) study of the *Forum Romanum* has indicated that the *forum* basin was likely to flood because it was low lying; it required much reclamation and this may indicate that its location was a deliberate attempt to command nature or to draw upon an association with a religious place. The *Circus Maximus* was constructed over tributaries of the Tiber and also flooded on a number of occasions (Holland 1961: 34). Flood control and drainage would not have been a straightforward practical issue; it has been argued that the *Cloaca Maxima* (main sewer) in Rome may even have taken such a winding course through the city because the engineers feared forcing the natural river here from taking its original path (Aldrete 2007: 219; Holland 1961: 32).[29] Water and the controlling of water were important features of life in ancient Rome, and this is likely to have had an impact on the way in which watery locations in conquered parts of the Empire were considered.

Studies have demonstrated that the importance attached to water and natural places within prehistory continued into the Roman period in Britain and Western Europe (e.g., Merrifield 1987). Discussions on water in connection with Roman towns in Britain have tended to concentrate on important issues such as the technical and practical aspects of supply and drainage, including pipes and aqueducts (e.g., Burgers 2001; T. Williams 2003). Though not specifically discussing Roman Britain, Ellis (1997) has briefly looked at the religious implications of aqueducts drawing water from sacred places. The objects of Roman date from Fiskerton (Field and Parker Pearson 2003) and Piercebridge, County Durham (P. J. Casey 1989), illustrate the continuing interest in watery locations from the Iron Age into the Roman period.[30] The large number of metalwork objects from the Walbrook stream, which ran through Roman London, can also be interpreted as ritual deposition (Merrifield 1995). Although it cannot be certain who deposited the artefacts, it can be inferred from the finds at sites such as Piercebridge and London that incomers to Britain also acknowledged the significance of these locations.

---

[28] Varro writes that the *pontifices* are the high-priests and that 'the name comes from *pons* "bridge"; for by them the Bridge-on-Piles was made in the first place, and it was likewise repeatedly repaired by them, since in that connexion rites are performed on both sides of the Tiber with no small ceremony' (*Ling.* V.83). Likewise Dionysius Halicarnassensis writes about the priests: 'one of the duties they perform, namely, the repairing of the wooden bridge, are in their own language called *pontifices*' (*Ant. Rom.* II.73).

[29] Holland's (1961) study of religious belief connected with water in ancient Rome suggested that the construction of bridges and the diverting of rivers would not only have been considered in practical terms.

[30] At Piercebridge, numerous Roman artefacts have been dredged from the River Tees at the point where the Roman bridge crossed the river (P. J. Casey 1989).

A number of studies have demonstrated the continuation of use or reuse of earlier monuments, indicating the survival of religious places (Dark 1993; Gosden and Lock 1998; Hingley 1999; Miles et al. 2003: 245; H. Williams 1998; A. Woodward 1992: 26; Woodward and Leach 1993). This can also be applied to 'natural' features such as rivers and marshlands, in relation to Roman towns in Britain, which were venerated. The use of the past helped to reproduce social relations and identities in the present; it was rituals that had the role of 'remembering' the past from the mythological associations invested in monuments (H. Williams 1998: 71).

Landscapes are not dead or static, but continue to be used in significant ways, with their power surviving and incorporated in different forms, the present being orientated through recognition of the past (Bradley 2002; Gosden and Lock 1998). Places have biographies that shape communal experience and create memories (Alcock 2002: 31). Chapman (1997b: 158) has identified such sites as 'timemarks': places where significant social action occurs over time, creating history and mythology; it becomes difficult to break away from these places. One of the strongest expressions of place-value is a people's choice to live in a particular area, with continued use of the same location over time leading to increasing ancestral power. Roman towns can also be studied in terms of their continuing place-value. Through their ongoing importance, they continued to invoke experiences, interactions, and the creation of memories.

3.4 A final point: the Golden Age of towns

It is often assumed that we are familiar with Roman towns. Many accounts of towns in Roman Britain take descriptive and romanocentric approaches, but this is not the case for all studies. Merrifield (1995), for example, has highlighted the pervasiveness of pre-Roman religious activity within London through a study of ritual deposition, and Fulford (2001) has argued a comparable perspective for Silchester and other towns. Studies have also explored the role of religious ceremony within towns (e.g., Esmonde Cleary 2005); these activities will have drawn on the past as well as introduced new rites.

Millett's (2001: 64) research agenda for examining Romano-British towns called for an examination of the distribution of ritual space within towns, but it only referred to temples and not to other ways in which belief was expressed. This includes the meaning attached to the 'landscapes' in which towns were placed. The agenda Millett outlined is still largely from a romanocentric viewpoint and does not seek to explore urbanism from the types of perspectives discussed here. Iron Age specialists, by contrast, have redefined their approaches (Burnham et al. 2001; Haselgrove et al. 2001), indicating the way in which the methodologies of the two periods often conflict. Ideally the perspectives of both period specialisms should be combined to gain a more comprehensive view of urbanism. The 'Golden Age' period of towns is a term that has been rightly refuted by Mattingly (2004: 22) for its simplicity and romanocentric stance. With timber buildings remaining important in towns throughout the Roman period and public buildings often being poorly constructed (e.g., the *basilica* at London; Milne 1992) or even unfinished, as some have argued for the *basilica* at Silchester (see Fulford and Timby 2000), it is clear that classical notions of Golden Age towns should not form the only comparison for towns in later Roman Britain.

Moving beyond the notion of a Golden Age leading to decline can be aided further by taking more account of the peculiarities or specificities of town foundation and early development, especially relating to the pre-Roman use and conception of the sites. There was a variety in the outcomes of towns and in the response and needs of the local population. There was no clearly defined Roman blueprint for urban development following a cycle of growth, Golden Age, and decline, but towns were places that can be studied in terms of their use, experience, and meaning.

CHAPTER 4

Establishing the urban context: pre-Roman place and Roman urbanism

It is necessary to depart from the more conventional linear route to an analysis of towns in the later Roman period by turning to an earlier period in the use of these sites. The processes that created urbanisation in Roman Britain occurred in the context of pre-existing places and became part of them, as well as bringing new aspects of land use and organisation; the sequence of activity at these places continued into the late Roman period and sometimes beyond. It has been emphasised that ways of understanding land would have been different in the past and factors such as religious belief would have played a much more significant role in this experience than they do today. This chapter examines some of the evidence reflecting the meanings of the places prior to Roman urban development.

Many of the locations in which the Roman towns were placed were already socially important. Even if there was no direct link between them and the Roman towns through to the later Roman period, they form an important analogy of ways of conceptualising late urbanism differently. According to Lemaire (1997: 7), 'in non-Western and pre-modern cultures there is a mythical space in which places are qualitatively different and meaningful referring to a sacred cosmos in which the human world is participating' (cf. Moore 2007: 90). Antiquarianism, and then archaeology with its interest in the context of finds through excavation, also played its part in the rationalisation and modernisation of land (Lemaire 1997: 16; Schnapp 1996: 179–219). Brück (2007: 244) has pointed out that antiquarianism was one of a range of pursuits dominated by the aristocracy during the eighteenth century (travelling, gardening, painting, and drawing were others), which influenced and created perceptions of landscape. An example of this has been explored in Gibbon's work with his use of antiquarian studies of Roman remains and his attitudes towards pre-conquest Britain, which were reflected in his reading of classical texts. Space and place should ideally be studied by exploring how they were structured from the perspective and way of life of the people that dwelt within them.

Drawing on discussions in Chapter 3, this chapter devises a number of criteria for assessing the nature, significance, and conceptualisation of sites in the pre-Roman period that were later used for Roman towns. Although the more practicable elements of Roman town foundation and development, such as strategic and economic considerations, would also have been issues, they would not have been in isolation of many other factors. The criteria of analysis are as follows. First, there is site location, with an emphasis on interpreting landscape and the religious and mythical significance that may have derived from 'natural' features. Watery contexts (including rivers and their flood plains, confluences, marshland, crossing points, springs, and freshwater–seawater interfaces) are the main example, although other features such as hills, wooded areas, and rocks may also have been important. Second, there is the presence of structural remains, which might indicate the special use of the sites. Third, there is the presence of industrial activity, especially metalworking and coin production, which may have had religious and social significance (cf. Creighton 2000; Giles 2007). Fourth, there is the nature of the finds assemblages.

It must be acknowledged that these criteria are devised as part of a modern agenda to study the sites, because we cannot place ourselves in the minds of pre-Roman and Roman Britons, but they do provide us with an important tool to help us understand the sites from new angles. A further difficulty that we must bear in mind could be projecting the known importance of these sites during the Roman period back into the Iron Age, but the purpose here is to attempt to examine them through pre-existing meaning.

4.1 A brief background to Iron Age settlement

The main period of hillfort building occurred in the sixth and fifth centuries B.C. in southern Britain, as at Danebury and Maiden Castle (Haselgrove 1999: 120–1). The traditional understanding of these sites as defensive settlements at the top of the settlement hierarchy is now being questioned with greater frequency (e.g., Haselgrove 1992; J. D. Hill 1995a). They seem to have been part of a much larger and complex range of sites.

In the second and first centuries B.C., another form of earthwork site appears, mainly in southern England, which is called the *oppidum*. There has been much discussion about the function and nature of *oppida* and their role within the wider settlement pattern (e.g., G. Woolf 1993). The term *oppidum*, from the Latin for 'town', was used by Julius Caesar in the *Bellum Gallicum* to describe the late Iron Age sites that he saw in Gaul. By labelling these sites as *oppida* he was interpreting them through his own elite Roman mindset.[1] The use of the term to identify these sites within archaeology has contributed towards the traditional notion of late Iron Age *oppida* as meaning primitive forms of urban settlement. These were then replaced, in the classical and modern mind, through an act of progression, by Roman forms of urbanism. However, our understanding of these sites is still very basic and this in turn has led to a simplistic understanding of the process of urbanisation. The earthworks and dykes have traditionally been interpreted as defences (e.g., Boon 1974: 42; Fulford 1984: 288; Hawkes and Hull 1947: 45). The fact that they do not easily enclose areas, however, and are often extensive in length indicates their impracticability for defence and argues for more symbolic functions (Haselgrove and Moore 2007b: 6). There were motives other than those of practicality behind the decisions made to locate activity at these places.

Oppida have been grouped into two types, 'enclosed' and 'territorial', with the 'enclosed *oppida*', including Oram's Arbour in Winchester, Salmonsbury in Gloucestershire, and Bigbury in Kent, appearing first (Haselgrove 1999: 121). They seem to have a definite earthwork enclosure as opposed to the 'territorial *oppida*', which consist of discontinuous

---

[1] Caesar writes about the Helvetii, for example, 'Ubi iam se ad eam rem paratos esse arbitarti sunt, oppida sua omnia, numero ad duodecimo, vicos ad quadringentos, reliqua private aedificia incendunt'. The word *oppida* here is always translated as town: 'As soon as they considered that they were ready for the enterprise, they set fire to all their own towns (about twelve in number) and to about 400 villages, as well as all their private buildings' (*B Gall*. I.4). Caesar's categorisation of sites here also influenced the way in which they have been considered in archaeology.

earthworks covering large areas of land and often apparently containing more than one focus, such as Verulamium (St Albans) and Camulodunum (Colchester); it is often not clear what the earthworks were attempting to demarcate or define (Haselgrove and Moore 2007b: 6). It might be that this was symbolic of places that were focal points where people came together (Sharples 2010: 173). The names 'Verlamion' and 'Camulodunon' are often used to distinguish the Iron Age period settlements from the Roman towns. These have been reconstructed from lettering on Iron Age coinage, although the exact names and spellings are still uncertain (Potter 2002: 21). These two names will be used for the Iron Age settlements here so as to avoid confusion with the Roman towns that followed.

Oppida and hillforts comprised only a small proportion of the large variety of settlement types across Iron Age Britain, and they themselves were probably parts of larger complexes of different enclosed and open sites (cf. Moore 2006). Many Roman towns have traces of pre-Roman activity that do not fall within the traditional *oppidum* category. Lincoln, for example, has some evidence of earthworks, and sites without any traces of earthworks could also have represented important places in the landscape. Other late Iron Age settlement types include a wide range of farmsteads and open settlements and a number of shrines. Other types of religious sites, including natural places (cf. Bradley 2000; Derks 1998), have been neglected, affecting our understanding of many of the places preceding Roman towns in Britain. It may be that the Romans chose to locate forts and develop towns at places that were already socially significant within indigenous society, perhaps being religious and meeting places (Creighton 2001). Even though practical considerations were important, the nature of the Roman settlements may been influenced by the meanings attached to these places. Establishing the significance of these sites will provide some information as to how the creation of Roman urbanism was conceptualised. This will aid in our understanding of the long-term biography of towns.

4.2 The sites

It appears that only York, Caerwent, Carmarthen, Aldborough, and Wroxeter have produced no definite pre-Roman evidence as yet. Aldborough, Caerwent, and Wroxeter have produced Iron Age coins, but these may have been post-conquest arrivals. Some of the sites lay outside the area of habitual coin use in the late pre-Roman Iron Age (Haselgrove 1987), so it may be that the locations were visited, used, or important in some way in prehistory, but this is more difficult to prove with certainty; excavations at these sites have tended to not go below the first- and second-century layers.

All of the towns except Caerwent were located next to rivers, flood plains or marshland areas, crossing points, and sometimes islands, indicating that water, movement, communication, and experience were important factors in the significance of the places. Springs were also features at a number of the sites. At Caerwent, the small Nedern Brook flowed around 250–300 m to the south of the Roman town (Brewer 1993: 56). The various watery contexts will have had different practical values: marshland for food and material resources and grazing, springs for sources of clean water, and rivers for resources and transport (cf. Rippon 2006). These uses will have remained important throughout the Roman period, demonstrating an aspect of the continued functioning of the sites. However, they will also have been associated with other meanings, adding considerable significance to the experience of these landscapes. A number of sites consisted of more than one focus of activity with different areas of apparent importance, including earthworks, enclosures, and industrial activity. The ways in which people moved in and negotiated these places constituted a major part of the meaning with which they were imbued. The topographies in which the towns and public buildings were constructed were already highly ritualised. Towns appropriated these landscapes and were, in some respect, shaped by them.

There is evidence of metalworking at several of the sites including moulds that were probably used in coin production, whereas in the case of Cirencester there is evidence of coin production relatively nearby at Bagendon in a marshy context.[2] In some cases there is less evidence of late Iron Age material than in others. J. D. Hill (2007: 30) has highlighted the massive increase in material culture in the late Iron Age, especially at *oppida*, compared with earlier settlements but this need not necessarily mean that sites that lack similar quantities of material culture were regarded as inferior; instead this lack of surviving material may have related to cultural preference and values.

4.3 Dating

Dating is important when we consider these sites. Several scholars have emphasised that most of the *oppida* were late constructions – the late first century B.C. and continuing into the early first century A.D. – and are on sites that do not exhibit much evidence of earlier occupation (e.g., Creighton 2006; Moore 2006). This need not necessarily mean, however, that the sites were not being used prior to the construction of earthworks. At some *oppida* in northern France, for instance, it has been suggested that the earthworks represent the monumentalisation of places with earlier significance where activities such as meetings and ceremonies took place (Metzler, Méniel, and Gaeng 2006). This would be difficult to identify with certainty in the archaeological record, but features such as rivers and marshland that attracted religious veneration indicate that at least some of these sites were meaningful before the construction of earthworks.

The passage by Strabo (IV.5.2), written at the end of the first century B.C., and describing pre-Roman settlement in Britain as spaces in forests made for huts and animals but not 'with the purpose of staying a long time', might be useful here (though he was probably drawing on what Caesar recorded). It is likely that there will have been some seasonal movements with cattle and sheep, according to the agricultural year, which were important activities in the landscape, and people will have met other communities for feasts and ceremonies at settlements or 'empty areas'. Moore (2006), for instance, has demonstrated that Bagendon was later in date than the surrounding settlement system. It was not part of earlier settlement but it may already have been important as a luminal watery place used for meetings, exchange, and religious activity. Over time, some places of these periodic meetings, markets, and rituals perhaps became more permanent and monumentalised. Meanings attached to these places will have gradually accumulated and continued into the Roman period.

The Bagendon earthworks near Cirencester were not established until the early first century A.D. (Trow 1990: 111). At Verlamion (Verulamium), construction of the dykes did not begin until about the mid-first century B.C., with the earliest possibly at Wheathampstead,

[2] There has been debate (as there has with the role of the coinage itself) about whether these moulds or trays represent coin production or simply the working of precious metals (e.g., Haselgrove 1987: 28–9; Niblett 2001: 42–3; Tournaire et al. 1982: 429–32). Either would indicate activity of considerable importance.

and the building of these earthworks continued into the early first century A.D., together with the enclosures at St. Michael's and Gorhambury (Haselgrove and Millett 1997: 284; Neal, Wardle, and Hunn 1990; I. Thompson 2005: 27–32). The majority of the dykes at pre-Roman Camulodunum (Camulodunon) were of the first century B.C. or immediately pre-conquest, although there do appear to have been two that were constructed post-conquest (Hawkes and Hull 1947: 45).[3] At Silchester, the dates of the two main earthworks remain problematic but the 'Inner Earthwork' is thought possibly to be of late-first-century B.C. or very early-first-century A.D. date and the 'Outer Earthwork' is thought to have come later (Fulford and Timby 2000: 545). The 'Entrenchments' at Chichester were also of the first century B.C. or first century A.D., although there is some evidence of the infilling and redigging of ditches after the Roman conquest (Bradley 1971; Magilton 2003: 156–9).

Oram's Arbour may have been the earliest of the *oppida* on or near the sites of Roman towns. Its construction date is still uncertain, but Middle Iron Age saucepan pottery[4] from the primary fills of the earthworks could indicate a date between the end of the fourth and mid-first centuries B.C. (Qualmann et al. 2004: 4, 90). The pottery may fall nearer to the end of this period or relate to disturbed earlier activity on the site (early Iron Age pottery may also indicate preceding activity here). A later construction date would fit with the evidence from other earthwork sites and currently a late-second- or first-century-B.C. date seems most likely. Traces of an earlier earthwork constructed at Canterbury around 300 B.C. (P. Blockley 1987) have been found, but its extent, and the way in which it related to enclosures of the first century B.C. and early first century A.D. here (as at the Marlowe car park site; K. Blockley et al. 1995: 27–51), are unclear.[5] The dykes and enclosures at Canterbury do, however, indicate that this area remained a focus of activity over a long period in prehistory.

At many sites where there is pre-Roman activity, but apparently no *oppidum*, the excavated evidence is equally late, as at Leicester, Exeter, Lincoln, and Gloucester, where it is of the first century B.C. and early first century A.D., but the landscapes do indicate longer histories. Within the River Witham at Lincoln, and further downstream at sites such as Fiskerton, there have been a number of late Bronze Age metal finds, including swords, axes, and spearheads (Jones and Stocker 2003: 24–6). These indicate that this was a place of religious veneration of greater antiquity. At London, too, it can be inferred from the finds from the Thames, such as human skulls of Bronze Age date (Bradley and Gordon 1988), that there was religious activity over a long period of time. The significance of these places pre-dates the construction of earthworks and other activities. The absence of an obviously continuous archaeological sequence need not indicate discontinuous importance during this time.

[3] Hawkes and Crummy (1995: 67) have suggested that the post-conquest dykes were part of a Roman refortification of the *oppidum*. Witcher (1998: 67), however, argues that this construction activity and reuse of earlier dykes may have had a more symbolic function, disrupting the pre-existing understanding and experiences of the landscape, perhaps as a sign of domination. This suggests a Roman recognition of the significance and threat of these places and a consequent desire to alter and control them. Infilling and redigging of some ditches after the Roman conquest may also have been identified at Chichester (Magilton 2003: 156).

[4] Saucepan pots were traditionally pots with upright or slightly bulging sides and simple or beaded rims dating from the late fourth or third to the first centuries B.C. Decoration on the pots can be rectilinear or curvilinear. They have a southern distribution from Somerset to Sussex and Surrey (Gibson and Woods 1997: 243).

[5] An important consideration is the extent to which these smaller enclosures at sites such as Canterbury were comparable with the monumental earthworks on other sites, and whether they should also be given the term 'earthwork'.

4.4 The *oppida*

4.4.1 *Verlamion (Verulamium)*

The apparent main pre-Roman focus of Verulamium (Verlamion), including the St. Michael's enclosure, lay in the Ver valley next to the river and within its flood plain; monumental earthworks lay in the environs, perhaps defining a much larger area (Figure 4.1). The land by the river was drained in later periods but would have been much more waterlogged and marshy during the late Iron Age (Niblett 2005b: 8). The St. Michael's enclosure was a 2-ha earthwork enclosure with a large boundary ditch, part of which was identified in the grounds of St. Michael's church. It underlies the central area of the town with the *forum–basilica* next to the theatre, bathhouse, and temple. This complex in the early stages of the Roman period resembled certain rural religious sanctuaries (Niblett 2005a: 105) such as Sanxay in France (Horne and King 1980) and Frilford in Britain (Hingley 1985; Lock et al. 2003), suggesting a 'role of combined *civitas*-capital and what in France would be described as a sanctuary site or cult centre' (Niblett 2005a: 105), thus apparently building on, and continuing, the religious significance of the area.

Unfortunately, the St. Michael's enclosure at Verlamion has only been very partially excavated. A short length of ditch was uncovered by Frere in 1956 (Frere 1983: 193–4) and by John Lunn in 1955 (I. Thompson 2005: 32–3). A number of pits associated with the enclosure were found in Lunn's excavations, containing material that included pottery and animal bones. Examining the nature of the finds and drawing on the work of authors such as J. D. Hill (1995b), Woodward and Woodward (2004) suggested that the material represented feasting activities and religious activity followed by votive deposition. Interpretations of the site have included a farmstead or a *templum* used in the process of taking the auspices during town foundation (Creighton 2000: 210; Woodward and Woodward 2004: 81–2). The setting of the site, in what would have been a watery location, has led others to argue against the idea that it was a farmstead, instead favouring a sacred space and meeting area (Haselgrove and Millett 1997: 284; I. Thompson 2005: 32–4).

A timber causeway, initially interpreted as a military installation, was constructed across the river around the A.D. 40s (Anthony 1970; Niblett 2005a: 64–5). Objects found during its excavation were probably deposited into the marshy area from the causeway; these included a gilt bronze *patera*, a late pre-Roman black ceramic bowl, coins, brooches, cavalry helmet fragments, and metalworking moulds (ibid.). Though the river and marshland would have had some practical uses, this area was also venerated and part of the symbolic landscape. During the Roman period, the causeway remained in use, with a road leading from it to the Folly Lane temple complex outside the town and then to Colchester (Anthony 1970; Creighton 2006: 124–5; Niblett 1999).

Other areas of late Iron Age activity have been identified by coins, brooches, and pottery found during excavations of the triangular and *insula* XVI temples (Lowther 1937; Wheeler and Wheeler 1936: 114). Although all the Iron Age coin finds from Verlamion fall within the first century A.D., it is not impossible that there was an earlier focus here that did not produce coins (Haselgrove 1987: 177). Bryant (2007: 71–2) has interpreted the monumental Beech Bottom Dyke, across the Ver and past Folly Lane, as a route to the ritual centre at St. Michael's. Additionally, and perhaps interrelated with ceremonial and ritual activities,

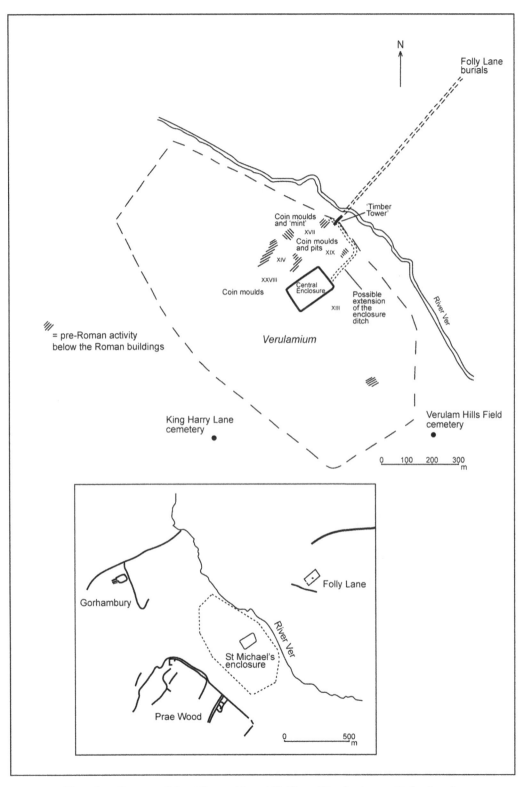

FIGURE 4.1. Plan of pre-Roman activity at the *oppidum* at St Albans (Verulamium or Verlamion; drawn by A. C. Rogers; adapted from Niblett 2001, Figure 19 and I. Thompson 2005, Figure 3.1).

TABLE 4.1. *Table showing evidence for metalworking connected with pre-Roman activities at or near the sites of Roman towns*

Town	Location	Date	Type of metalworking	Evidence	References
Canterbury	Under the public baths on the Marlowe Car Park site	Late 1st c. B.C. to ca. A.D. 70/80	Bronze-working, gold-working and coin casting	4 hearths, bronze slag, and coin moulds; associated with a group of buildings consisting of 2 roundhouses, a sunken-featured building, and a stake-built structure	K. Blockley et al. (1995: 27–51)
	44 Watling Street	Late pre-Roman Iron Age	Bronze-working	Hearths in the floor of a structure, bronze fragments, drops of metal, and crucible fragments	Frere and Bennett (1987: 117)
Cirencester	Bagendon Ditches	Late pre-Roman Iron Age 2nd c. or 1st c. B.C. to mid-1st c. A.D.	Coin casting	Coin moulds	Clifford (1961) Trow (1988)
Colchester	Sheepen	Late pre-Roman Iron Age	Object production; coin casting	Coin moulds and metalworking debris	Hawkes and Crummy (1995: 70); Hawkes and Hull (1947)

(continued)

TABLE 4.1 (*continued*)

Town	Location	Date	Type of metalworking	Evidence	References
Leicester	Bath Lane	Late pre-Roman Iron Age	Coin casting; precious metal-working	1 near-complete coin tray and 3 mould fragments; crucible fragments; molten lump of silver and copper	Clay and Mellor (1985); Kipling et al. (2007)
Silchester	Beneath the site of the *forum–basilica*	ca. 15 B.C. to A.D. 50–60	Bronze-, iron- and silver-working (incl. the production of horse-harness fittings and coin casting)	Iron-working slag, crucibles, horse-harness, and coin moulds; these were associated with rectangular timber buildings with a possible planned layout and surrounded by a palisade	Fulford and Timby (2000); Richards (2000: 421)
Verulamium	Beneath *insula* XVII	Late pre-Roman Iron Age	Coin casting	Coin moulds possibly associated with a timber structure, the 'metal workshop'	Frere (1983: 30)
	Site of *insula* XXVII building 3	Late pre-Roman Iron Age	Coin casting	Single fragment of a coin mould	Frere (1983: 30)
	Bluehouse Hill	Late pre-Roman Iron Age	Coin casting	Shallow pit containing coin moulds	Frere (1983: 31)
	Timber Tower causeway	Late pre-Roman Iron Age	Coin casting	Large deposit of coin moulds	Anthony (1970); Niblett (1999: 411)
Winchester	Cathedral Green beneath the *forum*	Late pre-Roman Iron Age	Coin casting	Coin mould	Biddle (1966: 320)

the dykes may have directed cattle and other livestock to the centre.[6] Like grain surpluses, livestock, especially cattle, are likely to have been indicators of status and sources of power at this time (Albarella 2007: 395). In all interpretations of function, the dykes reflect the way in which movement through the ritualised landscape was conducted and experienced.

Most of the evidence for metalworking is in the form of crucible fragments and coin moulds found in large quantities to the immediate north and west of the ditched enclosure (I. Thompson 2005: 32–4). Other sites include Bluehouse Hill (Frere 1983: 31–2), *insula* XXVII (ibid.: 30), and a large pit of moulds in *insula* XIX near the later bathhouse (I. Thompson 2005: 35). This concentration of coin moulds in and around the St. Michael's enclosure in its watery setting supports the notion that the enclosure was not a farmstead as we would understand the term today, although agricultural activity could have been part of its function. A number of moulds were also found at the 'Marsh Bank' near the 'Timber Tower' and lay beneath the later town wall. Frere interpreted this as a mint (1983: 30, 102–4) but definite evidence for this is lacking. The presence of moulds, however, indicates that they were probably deposited into the water after use, reflecting the connection between the ritual significance of metalworking and water.

Metalworking (Table 4.1) and the manufacture of items such as weapons and tools were highly ritualised acts, as was their deposition into pits, rivers, lakes, marshland, and wells (see Chapter 3; Giles 2007). Indeed, such deposition continued well into the post-Roman period. Metalworking influenced perceptions of the locations where it took place. Little is known about the social context of production in pre-Roman Britain; metalworking does seem to have been an important part of activity at *oppida* in the late Iron Age (Creighton 2000) but it also took place on other types of sites and so its significance at *oppida* is uncertain. Minting on these sites is likely to be indicative of wider social changes and may relate to an administrative and political function (Haselgrove 1987; Trow 1990: 109), though the discovery of coin moulds on a range of site types has led to the suggestion that coin production was not necessarily under central control (Tournaire et al. 1982).

The religious significance attached to metalworking in prehistory makes a ritual aspect to the minting of coinage unsurprising (Haselgrove and Wigg-Wolf 2005: 12). Because the activity was often located in significant 'natural' locations, such as within flood plains, it can be inferred that minting was placed under the control of local gods (ibid.). In many cases, production may have been associated with an elite group, perhaps because of the value of the metal or the significance of production as a religious activity and symbol of power. Other *oppida*, which did not become Roman towns, have also indicated evidence for industrial activity. At Stanwick, especially in the Tofts area, metal billets, crucibles, ceramic moulds, tuyères, and copper waste have been found (Haselgrove, Turnbull, and Fitts 1990: 4). A hoard of Late Iron Age horse-harness fittings and weaponry was discovered in 1843, 3 km away at Melsonby (Fitts et al. 1999). Excavations at Hobditch and Gussage Cow Down were very small in scale, so the potential still exists for similar discoveries.

4.4.2 *Camulodunon (Camulodunum/Colchester)*

Settlement in the area of Roman Camulodunum (Camulodunon), Colchester, was also heavily intertwined with rivers that surrounded it, with much of this complex being

---

[6] Strabo's (IV.5.2) reference to the export of cattle and hides (along with grain, gold, silver, iron, slaves, and dogs) from late Iron Age Britain suggests that cattle played an important part in the creation of wealth and power.

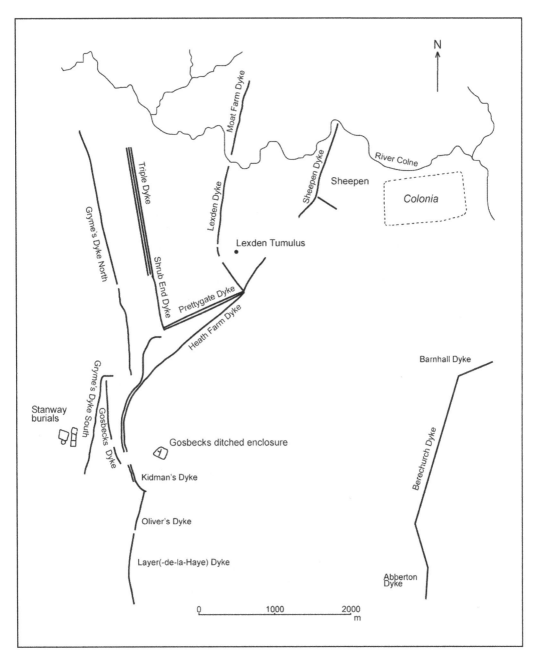

FIGURE 4.2. Plan of dykes, earthworks, and burial areas at Colchester around the Roman town of Camu-lodunum dating from the first century B.C. to the first century A.D. (drawn by A. C. Rogers; adapted from Hawkes and Crummy 1995, Figure 6.1).

bounded by the River Colne and a smaller watercourse known as the Roman River (Figure 4.2). Accounts of the Roman town have predominantly placed an emphasis on practical and strategic considerations of its development: to be in command of waterborne transport, to control river crossings into the *oppidum*, to be close to a good water supply, and to be located on a promontory to overlook the rest of the *oppidum* (P. Crummy 1997).

Although these are important considerations, they have meant that an understanding of the pre-Roman *oppidum* and its setting has been influenced predominantly by Roman (and modern) conceptions.

Camulodunon was a large *oppidum* with numerous foci of activity. The site at Sheepen 0.75 km northwest of the Roman town centre, for example, was located within the flood plain of the River Colne at the point at which it is joined by several tributaries (Willis 2007b: 121). The flood plain is wide here and has changed since the Iron Age, when there would have been areas of standing water. The location was also the lowest downstream point of the river which is non-tidal, suggesting that a deliberate acknowledgement was being made of the distinction between freshwater and seawater. Although this junction will have been useful for waterborne transport, Willis' study suggests that it was also a culturally meaningful boundary, perhaps because freshwater and seawater were associated with different deities or because seawater was regarded as unclean (ibid.: 121–2).[7]

Excavations at Sheepen have produced a large amount of debris from industrial activity including metalworking waste, moulds for coin production, and remains from pottery production and glass-working, indicating a major industrial and trading area (Hawkes and Crummy 1995: 70; Hawkes and Hull 1947). Willis' (2007b: 121) study of the finds from this site highlighted the rich material culture found here, including coins, brooches, and pottery (including amphorae, samian, and Gallo-Belgic wares), from which may be inferred feasting, festivals, and offerings relating to religious activity contemporary with the industrial activity. He argues that the industrial activity was deliberately located in this area because religious intervention was considered crucial to the productive cycle, production and religion being closely linked at this time. The relatively large number of Iron Age coins here also indicates an important focus of activity (Haselgrove 1987: 163). The continued significance of this area can be inferred by the presence of a large number of temples in the post-Boudican period (ibid.; Hawkes and Hull 1947; Hull 1958). These temples could have had a role in trade, manufacture, and storage activities (see Section 5.5) as well as the dedications prior to waterborne travel, but they could also have been tied into the longer-term religious meaning attached to this watery area.

It has also been argued that the fortress at Camulodunum was placed in an area of pre-Roman activity (Brooks 2006: 7): Iron Age coins, although small in number and from Roman contexts, and Iron Age pottery, have come from excavations within the fortress. It is likely that the construction of the fortress would have removed and destroyed evidence for earlier activity (ibid.), and this could also explain the presence of the finds in early Roman layers. There need only be slight, if any, traces of pre-Roman activity, if the kind of sacred enclosure on the site did not involve the construction of buildings; so the Roman fortress here could have been acting as a symbol of domination over a religious site. Iron Age coins have also come from the Abbey Field and the Union cemeteries (Hull 1958: 254–6), but their relationship to the Roman burials is uncertain. They may instead be disturbed evidence of earlier activity or alternatively dumped material from the construction of the fortress and *colonia*.

An apparently similar enclosure to St. Michael's in Verulamium has been identified at Gosbecks, Camulodunon, but this has not been excavated. What seem to be roundhouses within it were identified by aerial photography, and the site appears central to a group

[7] Morris (2007), for example, has highlighted the possible significance in the locations where seawater and freshwater come together and has suggested that salt production from seawater may have involved ritual and magic, and should not be considered in modern economic terms.

of droveways (P. Crummy 1997: 16–18; Hawkes and Crummy 1995: 95). This enclosure has often been interpreted as a farmstead (e.g., Hawkes and Crummy 1995: 174). The droveways suggest that there may have been some kind of agricultural function here, where sheep and cattle were brought in from the surrounding areas, but this may also have tied in with other sources of meaning and power. The construction of temples and a theatre here in the Roman period may indicate a continuation of religious functions (see subsequent text), which in the Iron Age had been combined with administrative and social activities at the site. A geophysical survey and limited excavation on the site of the Roman temple at Gosbecks has revealed traces of earlier activity that may provide further information on the function of the enclosure. Traces of what was considered to be an earlier temple were identified (P. Crummy et al. 2007: 447–50). Alternatively, it was thought that the rectangular-shaped pit on the central east–west axis of the enclosure near the Roman temple may have been a burial chamber similar to that at Folly Lane at Verlamion (Verulamium; ibid.), but further excavation is required to provide a conclusive answer. Either an early temple or an elite burial site would indicate that this site was more significant than a farmstead. Like Verlamion, the earthworks here may have been connected with movement and ritual across this landscape.

4.4.3 *Canterbury*

The Roman town at Canterbury was set within the flood plain of the River Stour, which is still wide and likely to flood today. Low river terraces to the northeast and southwest of the site provided an early crossing point (Lyle 2002: 15–16). Strategic and commercial advantages provide some reasons for the location of settlement here, but the river and its flood plain could also have been viewed and experienced in more religious and symbolic terms. Actions of movement across the river and its flood plain by crossing points would have been imbued with meaning and would have focused attention onto this area.

An analysis of pre-Roman coin distribution, including potins[8] and bronze coinage, has indicated some kind of nucleated settlement next to the River Stour beginning around the third quarter of the first century B.C. (Haselgrove 1987: 139–45). There are traces of pre-Roman activity beneath the Roman temple precinct in the centre of the town and within the flood plain of the river. At 77–79 Castle Street (Frere 1977: 423; Wacher 1995: 194), excavations uncovered traces of buildings and Iron Age coins, which might represent evidence for a pre-Roman religious sanctuary or enclosure (ibid.). The location of a shrine in this flood plain area would strengthen the link between watery sites and places of religious meaning. On the site of the Marlowe Car Park there is also excavated evidence of part of a triple-ditched enclosure containing roundhouses that were located close to the later temple precinct (K. Blockley et al. 1995: 34–6). There was also evidence for gold- and bronze-working associated with the structures, including metalworking hearths, debris, and coin moulds; other interesting finds including horse-harness fittings. As at Verulamium, the *forum–basilica*, St. Margaret's Street bathhouse and theatre were located in the area of this pre-Roman enclosure and roundhouses, an area that produced a large number of Iron Age coins. The public buildings here continued to emphasise this area of the landscape. Coin distributions indicate that there may have been a shift in occupation

---

[8] Potins were coins of bronze alloy with a relatively high tin content, which first began to be produced in the second century B.C. in southeast England. They were cast in moulds joined by runners, which left a section of the joining portion on the coins (de Jersey 1996: 14, 20).

from the enclosure to a location nearer to the river in the early first century A.D. (Haselgrove 1987: 141), although far too little is known to identify the full extent and pattern of activity in this area.

4.4.5 Winchester

The Oram's Arbour earthworks at Winchester (Figure 4.3) were sited on the western side of the Itchen valley and the flood plain of the River Itchen (Qualmann et al. 2004: 86–7; Zant 1993: 3–4). Within the river and its flood plain there was an island of tufa, an area of slightly higher, firmer ground formed by the accumulation of large amounts of alluvial chalk tufa (Zant 1993: 3). Tufa is formed as a precipitate of calcium carbonate from groundwater in a humid and marshy environment (ibid.). This was later used for the centre of the Roman town and was a crossing point and ford in the Iron Age. The Oram's Arbour earthworks, and the later town overlapping them, used the river and its flood plain as one boundary of the settlement. During the later Iron Age, increasing evidence for activity occurred closer to the river and nearer to where the town was placed (Biddle 1966: 320; Qualmann et al. 2004: 91–3).

Excavations within and outside Oram's Arbour have revealed traces of roundhouses and other structural evidence, including ditches and gullies of middle to late Iron Age date (Qualmann et al. 2004). Only around one-third of the area surrounded by the Oram's Arbour earthworks appears to have been occupied, indicating an integral relationship with a 'natural' or 'empty' space that was an important part of the complex. Many of the *oppida* included more than one focus of activity, so movement between these would have been an important aspect of the experience of place. One fragment of an Iron Age coin mould and pottery sherds came from the Cathedral Green, the site of the *forum–basilica*, in the 1960s (Biddle 1966: 320), but this evidence is as yet too slight for any conclusions to be made about the nature of activity in this area, although another focus within the flood plain of the river is possible.

4.4.6 Chichester

Roman Chichester lay close to the River Lavant around 6 km to the northeast of Chichester Harbour, which also contained Thorney and Hayling Islands, the latter with its later Iron Age and Roman temple (Downey, King, and Soffe 1979; Wacher 1995: 259). The available evidence indicates that the site embraced a large area incorporating numerous rivers. Several Iron Age coins have been found in the area between Fishbourne and the Roman town (Haselgrove 1983: 138). The 'Entrenchments' consist of at least fifteen linear earthworks. Their date is still uncertain, but small-scale excavations indicate that they were not all built at once, but between the first century B.C. and early first century A.D. (Bradley 1971; Magilton 2003: 156). Suggested functions have included land divisions and stock control (Magilton 2003: 156–9), but they may also have had a symbolic significance. It is possible that livestock were brought here for grazing in the saltwater marshes (cf. Rippon 2006); a water source would also have been useful for the slaughter process.

Excavations beneath the town have been limited but there is increasing evidence to demonstrate late pre-Roman Iron Age activity, although its precise nature and extent are uncertain. Most excavations have produced Iron Age pottery, including imported late Augustan to early Tiberian finewares; some of the pottery was of an early Iron Age

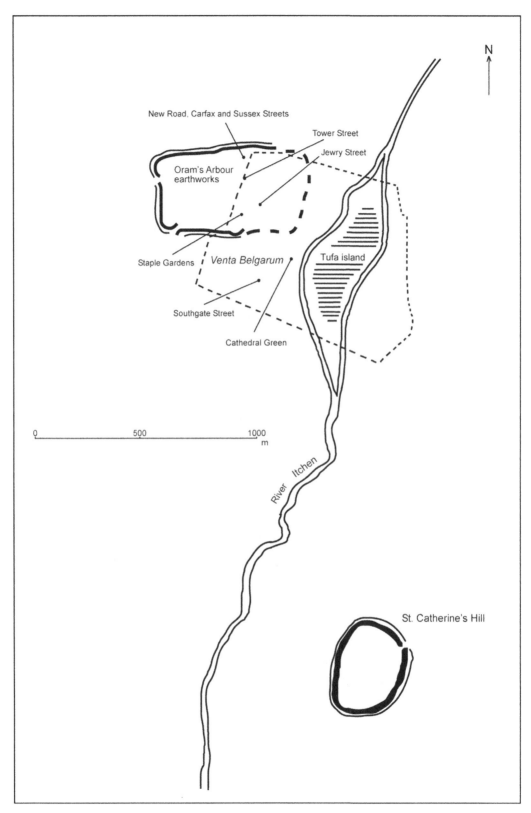

FIGURE 4.3. Plan of the pre-Roman activity at Winchester, including the Iron Age *oppidum* of Oram's Arbour and key excavations producing Iron Age material (drawn by A. C. Rogers; adapted from Qualmann et al. 2004, Figure 1).

date indicating earlier activity (Down and Magilton 1993: 19). An analysis of the Iron Age coin distributions also suggests a pre-Roman focus here, although another possibility may be a mid-first-century-A.D. military site here bringing non-local coins to the area (Haselgrove 1987: 149, 458–61). Some traces of roundhouses have been found, although their dates are unknown (Chichester District Sites and Monuments Record CD3797; CD2183). Excavations east of Fishbourne Palace in 1999 and 2002 uncovered a section of ditch containing large quantities of pre-conquest pottery and animal bones. This might indicate feasting activities (Manley and Rudkin 2005), although more work is needed before definite conclusions can be drawn. There is as yet little evidence for metalworking, although this may reflect the limited extent of excavation that has taken place. Two sherds of late Iron Age crucibles have come from St. Peter's North Street (Down and Magilton 1993: 43–8).

4.4.7 Silchester

The *oppidum* at Silchester lay close to the Foundry Brook and there were also a number of springs in the area, including near the amphitheatre and bathhouse (Boon 1974: 85). There is a clearer indication of Iron Age occupation beneath the centre of the Roman town, although its extent is uncertain (Figure 4.4). Excavations revealed a sequence beginning with at least three roundhouses, dating to around 15 B.C.–A.D. 25, which were then replaced by rectangular structures with metalled streets and surrounded by a timber palisade (Fulford and Timby 2000: 8, 20–4). What might be considered to have been fairly high-status material came from this area, including Iron Age coins, copper-alloy brooches, and toilet instruments. Pottery included *terra nigra* and *terra rubra* wares[9] and some early samian ware from ca. A.D. 30 onwards, and there were also large numbers of pig bones and oyster shells (ibid.). Other activity includes early-first-century-A.D. pits near the later South Gate (Fulford 1984: 27–30; Fulford and Timby 2000: 547) and pits and a silver coin of the Durotriges from the temple precinct in *insula* XXX (Anon 1854: 57; Boon 1974: 156). The Inner Earthwork 'enclosed' around 32 ha and underlies the Roman town. The Outer Earthwork is more discontinuous and later in date, perhaps of the early first century A.D. It may have been part of further dyke systems to the northwest of the town (Fulford 1984: 79–83), implying that the site incorporated a much larger area than that indicated by the Inner Earthwork.

There is important evidence for metalworking, including waste from the production of bronze horse-harness gear and silver coins associated with the palisaded enclosure (Fulford and Timby 2000: 419–20; Richards 2000: 421). There was also over 9 kg of iron slag representing hearth bottom material and hammerscale, much of which had been disposed of within a pit that lay inside the enclosure (Fulford and Timby 2000: 30–1).

4.5 Non-*oppida*

Studies of Roman towns where there was apparently no *oppidum* have often concentrated on military origins, leading to important pre-Roman activity being given less prominence.

[9] These fine polished Gallo-Belgic wares were imported into Britain in the late pre-Roman Iron Age and were also being manufactured before A.D. 43 around Colchester and Verulamium. The *terra nigra* vessels were grey-black in colour whereas *terra rubra* were orange-coated cream to buff vessels (Swan 1980: 11).

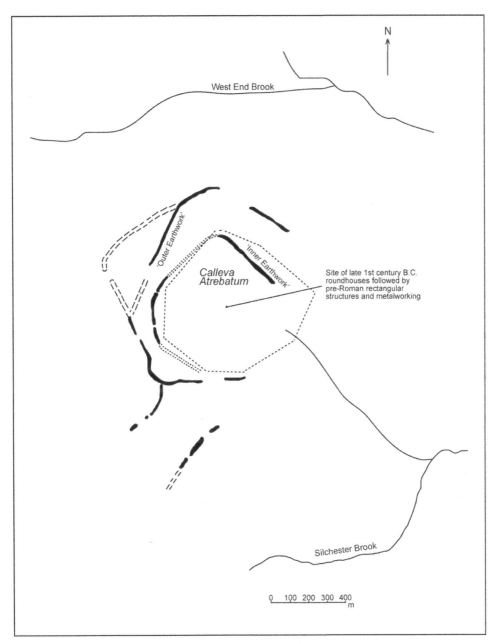

FIGURE 4.4. Plan of the late pre-Roman *oppidum* at Silchester (drawn by A. C. Rogers; adapted from Creighton 2006, Figure 7.4 and Fulford 1984, Figure 85).

The term *oppidum* may not always be entirely helpful because it puts emphasis on the earthworks and their role in the enclosure of the settlement. It omits sites that do not have obvious traces of earthworks but that do have some of the other features that have been taken to define *oppida* and constitute important places. The absence of monumental earthworks does not mean that the sites were not also important places with long sequences of use, incorporating both 'natural' and constructed features.

4.5.1 *Lincoln*

The Roman town at Lincoln lay next to the River Witham and the large natural body of water known as the Brayford Pool, formed where the Rivers Till and Witham meet (Figure 4.5). This pool was much larger in the late pre-Roman Iron Age than today's canalised form (Darling and Jones 1988: 1), and it contained a number of islands that are now lost (M. Jones 2002: 21–4). The rivers, Brayford Pool, and surrounding marshland indicate that, on occasion, there would have been flooding and drainage problems for any settlement in the vicinity (ibid.). Strategic and transport benefits, as well as food resources, are often considered to have been important for the siting of the Roman town here (ibid.). From the finds of Bronze and Iron Age metalwork from the Witham, however, it can be inferred that the river and surrounding wetlands also had religious connotations. Downstream is the timber causeway at Fiskerton, where items were deposited into the marshland from the Bronze Age onwards (Field and Parker Pearson 2003).

Traces of pre-Roman activity in the area of the *forum–basilica* include late Iron Age pottery spreads, coins, and a pit containing burnt bone; the bone was radiocarbon dated to the late first century B.C. (Jones and Stocker 2003: 28–30). It has also been argued that the fortress, in a prominent position on the crest of the hill, may have been placed on the site of a pre-existing, perhaps religious, Iron Age enclosure (Gilmour 2007: 231), but as yet there is little evidence to support this, although, of course, only a very small proportion of the area has been uncovered. The well on the site of the Roman *forum* may have originated in the pre-Roman period as part of this ritual site, but there is no dating evidence for verification, as it was cleared out in the medieval period (ibid.). It has also been recognised that part of the fortress was constructed over the 'Jurassic Way', an ancient routeway that follows the line of the Jurassic limestone ridge through Northamptonshire to Lincolnshire (ibid.), so it does seem unlikely that the fortress and town would have developed without some knowledge of the pre-existing significance attached to this place.

Excavations have located activity on what, before land reclamation from the medieval period onwards, would have been an island within the Brayford Pool (Darling and Jones 1988; M. Jones 2002: 21–4). The structural evidence here consisted of the curving gullies of a possible roundhouse and a series of post-holes indicative of a rectangular building or perhaps drying racks. Unfortunately, there were no contemporary floor levels or finds to suggest a function, although the location on the island may imply something more than a domestic farmstead. The date of the structure is equally problematic, but the few sherds of late Iron Age pottery found make a late Iron Age date likely (Darling and Jones 1988: 5). There were only a few finds from the site and these do not help with interpretation. The objects consisted of a Langton Down brooch, a clay toggle, and late Iron Age shell-tempered indigenous pottery (ibid.). Probably also from pre-Roman layers, although less certain, was an iron spearhead and a fragment of copper-alloy tweezers – the dating of the activity was problematic but an analysis of the stratigraphic layers does indicate that the earliest structural remains were late Iron Age.

There is also an extensive triple linear ditch and bank system to the north of the later town that contained pottery of the second and first centuries B.C. The function of this system is uncertain, although one suggestion has been for stock movement controls (e.g., Cunliffe 2004; 2005: 421–4). Other possibilities, which are not necessarily mutually exclusive, are control over local agricultural production (Champion 1994: 140), an expression of

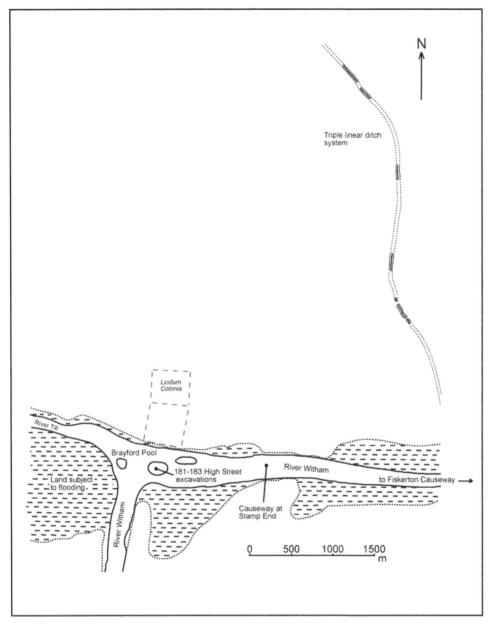

FIGURE 4.5. Plan of late pre-Roman activity at Lincoln (drawn by A. C. Rogers; adapted from Jones and Stocker 2003, Figure 5.10).

territorialism (Palmer-Brown 1993), or an attempt to focus on a religious place or ceremonial site (Jones and Stocker 2003: 30–1), which perhaps centred on the Brayford Pool area. Activity associated with the wetlands near Lincoln, such as the Fiskerton causeway constructed across the wide flood plain of the River Witham (Field and Parker Pearson 2003), indicates that movement between these places across the watery area was a meaningful act. The Roman town would have become part of this landscape.

Similar ditch systems do occur elsewhere in the Midlands and they might sometimes indicate possible *oppidum*-type settlements; one such example is Hobditch in Warwickshire (Cracknell and Hingley 1996). Further afield there is the group of triple ditches at Gussage Hill in Wessex (Barrett, Bradley, and Green 1991), which also represents a focus of activity in this area. In some cases there are earthworks that do not seem to enclose much, if any, evidence of occupation, such as the North Oxfordshire Grim's Ditch earthworks (Cunliffe 2005: 192) and the Dorsey in Northern Ireland (Aitchison 1993).[10] Places defined in the landscape through the construction of substantial earthworks need not include much evidence of occupation. This has implications for understanding the importance of the landscape of places that contained Roman towns, such as Lincoln. Another comparison for analysing the function of earthworks is at Friar's Wash near the source of the River Ver, 15 km to the northwest of Verulamium (Niblett 2006: 22). Here the earthworks focus on the watery location and an early enclosure, 'suggesting the presence of a religious place' (ibid.), which is also supported by the later siting of two Romano-Celtic temples here. The activity at this location is likely to have been linked through movement to the earthworks and activity at Verulamium itself further along the river; the whole Ver valley is likely to have been imbued with meaning.

4.5.2 *Cirencester*

The Roman town and preceding activity at Cirencester were also intertwined with their watery setting (Figure 4.6). The Roman settlement was located in a low-lying area between the River Churn and the Daglingworth Brook, and even today it is subject to flooding (Darvill and Gerrard 1994). The town is in the direct path of floodwaters as they come down the valleys and meet (Reece 2003: 276). The original fort was located on a small gravel spine between the two rivers, but this proved small for the town that, as it expanded, spread out into the flood plains of the rivers. It was necessary to redirect the courses of both rivers and, as Reece points out (ibid.: 277), the maintenance required to prevent leakage and flooding will have been a constant part of life within the town.

Some traces of pre-Roman occupation have been excavated in Cirencester itself but they are not well understood. This includes pits and ditches at Queen Elizabeth Road that were probably Iron Age, but there is little good dating evidence (Barber and Collard 2000). A stake circle was found at 17 The Avenue (Wacher and McWhirr 1982: 28), although the extent, nature, and date of the activity this represents are uncertain. As at Lincoln, however, there need not be extensive evidence of occupation for the importance of the place to be inferred. Indeed, this low-lying wetland area may have been an integral part of the 'complex' of interrelated sites in the vicinity, including Bagendon and the Ditches (North Cerney) enclosure (cf. Moore 2006).

Reece (2003: 276) has drawn attention to the fact that both Ermine Street approaching the area from the southeast and Fosse Way from the southwest deviate from their projected courses to come to this low-lying watery area. They then return to their original courses

---

[10] Initially the North Oxfordshire Grim's Ditch earthworks enclosed around 13 km² and then as much as 80 km² and dated to the late first century B.C. (Cunliffe 2005: 192). The Dorsey is a large earthwork enclosure in Dorsy, County Armagh, Northern Ireland, near the Dorsy River; it is associated with a large area of marshland. There is very little evidence for occupation or activity within the enclosure. Traditionally seen as a military installation, it may instead have functioned as some kind of sacred enclosure (Aitchison 1993).

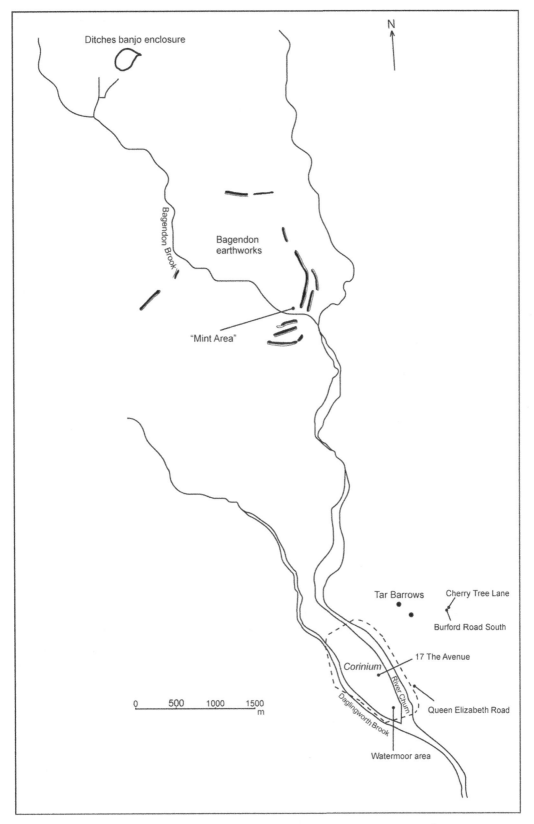

FIGURE 4.6. Plan of late pre-Roman activity around the Roman town of Cirencester. Sites where coins, ditches, and other Iron Age material have been found are marked (drawn by A. C. Rogers; adapted from Creighton 2006, Figure 7.1, Trow 1988, Figure 1, and Wacher and McWhirr 1982, Figure 1).

once they have left the area of the town. There is a late Iron Age burial mound complex on a hill in Tar Barrow Field to the northeast of the later town (Creighton 2006: 148; O'Neil and Grinsell 1960: 108). A geophysical survey of the area indicates that the complex was more extensive than once thought and it was also used for burial in the Roman period (Holbrook 2008: 308–10).[11] Reece (2003: 276) argues that the Roman roads deviated from their courses to avoid the burials, but it may also be that the Romans wanted to reach an important low-lying area whilst keeping the drier higher ground on the approach.

4.5.3 Gloucester

Gloucester was located in a curve of the River Severn at the lowest point at which the river could be bridged before the twentieth century. There is growing evidence of pre-conquest activity at and near Gloucester, but the significance of the area at this time is still poorly understood and requires further work. There may, however, have been more activity here than has previously been suspected. Structural remains and domestic debris were found at the sites of Saintbridge (Atkin 1987; Darvill and Timby 1986), Abbeymead (Atkin 1987), and Cherry Tree Lane (Mudd, Williams, and Lupton 1999: 70). An analysis of the pottery from the Coppice Corner site near the Kingsholm fort, 700 m north of the Roman town site, has led to suggestions of an Iron Age settlement here, even an *oppidum* (Hurst 1999a: 119; Timby 1999). However, without a further detailed analysis of this important site, recovered in difficult conditions with little contextual information, it is difficult to appreciate its significance fully. A number of coins of the Dobunni and Durotriges have come from the area (Haselgrove 1989: 51–7), but these may also relate to early Roman activity. Whether pre-conquest activity was a reason for the establishment of the fort here (Hurst 2005: 299–300) remains uncertain without further work. It seems possible that there were a number of foci of activity across this area combining settlement, movement, and ritual in a watery setting, as around Cirencester.

4.5.4 Leicester

At Leicester excavations are also increasing our knowledge of late pre-Roman activity, which here seems to have focused near the River Soar in the area of the Roman town after known earlier settlements in surrounding higher areas appear to have gone out of use in the first century B.C., such as Elms Farm, Humberstone (Cooper and Buckley 2004: 51–2). This may have led to an increased focus on the river valley, which was possibly already imbued with religious meaning and power. Breeze (2002) has suggested that Corietavi, the name recorded for the local people, might mean 'army of many rivers' or 'host of (the region of) many rivers'. If this is the case, it would draw attention to the significance of the watery nature of the area and the importance of the rivers. It has also been suggested that *Ratae* from the Roman name for Leicester meant earthen rampart (Rivet and Smith 1979: 443) and, if so, there may have been some kind of earthwork construction here, although there is still no evidence of this.

Various pits, gullies, ditches, and coins dating to the late first century B.C. and early first century A.D. have been found on a number of sites in the modern town, including St. Nicholas Street, St. Nicholas Circle (Clay and Pollard 1994: 1), and beneath the 'Jewry Wall' bathhouse (Jarvis 1986; Kenyon 1948). Traces of a possible roundhouse were found

---

[11] The geophysical survey was undertaken by a team led by Peter Guest from the University of Cardiff.

at Thornton Lane (Clay and Pollard 1994: 37, 44). One near-complete coin tray and a number of coin mould and crucible fragments were found in 2007 from an Iron Age ditch and surroundings at Bath Lane, and three coin mould fragments came from earlier excavations here (Clay and Mellor 1985: 18, 20, 30, 69; Kipling, Parker, and Cooper 2007), hinting at the importance of this area. One large ditch was found across the Merlin Works site at Bath Lane, but the dating and extent of this feature is uncertain and more work is needed before an *oppidum* or other earthwork site can be suggested (Kipling et al. 2007). The presence of coin moulds at many of the *oppida* indicates that coin production was an important function of these sites, but their discovery at other sites such as Leicester is a reminder that coin casting also took place on other types of site.

4.5.5 Exeter

The Roman town at Exeter, built on the site of the fortress, was located on a spot overlooking a crossing, the lowest fordable point, of the River Exe, which was also a large marshy area (Bidwell 1979: 3). The Roman town extended beyond the confines of the fortress, taking the settlement even closer to the river. The flood plain of the valley was, until the construction of the Exeter Flood Defence System between 1965 and 1977, prone to extensive flooding, as demonstrated by a major flood in the city in 1960 (Johns 1969: 283).

Like Leicester, the Exeter area has now produced evidence of pre-Roman activity, including traces of roundhouses of probable Iron Age date at Holloway Street, Trichay Street, and the Southernhay East car park, and also two Iron Age coins, although these are of non-local origins (records accessed from the Exeter Urban Archaeology Database: 10000, 10001, 10002, 10003, and 11553; Stead 2004). The two coins were an Armorican silver issue of ca. 50 B.C. found in 1871 and a Durotrigian bronze type found in 1978, both of which, and especially the latter, may have reached the site after the Roman conquest. One ditch on the Southernhay East car park site contained over 100 sherds of late Iron Age pottery. Whether this represents a concentration of activity focused on the river is uncertain, but with the islands and flood plain here this area is likely to have been associated with special meaning, which may even have attracted the development of the Roman town here.

4.5.6 Dorchester

Roman Dorchester, close to the Iron Age hillfort of Maiden Castle, was located next to the River Frome in an area that seems to have been hugely important from an early date (P. Woodward, Davies, and Graham 1993: 1). The Dorchester area has a concentration of prehistoric monuments including the hillforts of Maiden Castle and Poundbury, and the Neolithic henge monuments of Maumbury Rings (Bradley 1975; Gale 2003) and Mount Pleasant (Wainwright 1979). Excavations at the Greyhound Yard site within the modern and Roman town uncovered a series of large post-pits that seemed to be of later Neolithic date and, if continuous, formed a large timber circle (P. Woodward et al. 1993: 351). This was located within a small coombe running down to the flood plain of the River Frome and that may have been imbued with religious meaning. P. Woodward et al. (ibid.: 361) have argued that this is a likely place to find an Iron Age shrine, providing a link between previous activity and the Roman period, but so far there is no supporting evidence. A small number of coins of the Durotriges have come from Dorchester, although these are mostly of an uncertain provenance (Haselgrove 1983: 136, 150), and Sparey Green (1986) has catalogued evidence of a number of ditches found across the town, which he argues may relate to late Iron Age activity. The dating evidence from all of these features is sparse, however, and more work is needed before any continuity for activity in the area from the Neolithic to the Roman period can be established.

It would seem unlikely, however, that this area was not also important in the Iron Age, perhaps focused on the watery area of the Frome. The Roman amphitheatre was constructed on top of Maumbury Rings, making the arena unusually large for the amphitheatres in Britain (Bradley 1975). There may well have been continuity in the use of this site through the Iron Age, the evidence of which would have been lost in the building of the amphitheatre.

4.5.7 *London*

The site of Roman London was divided by the Walbrook stream and other tributaries (Perring 1991a: 1). There were also islands and marshy areas around the Thames at South-wark facing the Roman town (Heard, Sheldon, and Thompson 1990), and semi-marshland existed in a broad strip along the river (Marsden 1980: 12). Pre-Roman metalwork finds have come from along the Thames, albeit over a fairly long stretch, including the Battersea Shield and the Waterloo Helmet (Merrifield 1995). Fitzpatrick (1984) documents over 100 finds of La Tène metalwork from the Thames, with much being found during dredging operations. There is also the collection of human skulls from the Walbrook that seem to date from the Bronze Age and the late Iron Age to Roman period. The majority of the skulls were of young males, suggesting that they were deliberately selected; the lack of mandibles points to some kind of special treatment (Bradley and Gordon 1988). These factors, together with their context, suggest that they were ritual deposits (Bradley and Gordon 1988; Marsh and West 1981). Radiocarbon dating gave Bronze Age to Roman dates for the skulls,[12] indicating veneration of this area over a long period from prehistory into Roman times.[13]

It is often stated that Roman London was founded for economic reasons on an unoc-cupied site (e.g., Rowsome 1998: 35), but there is evidence for arguing that the location was already important in the pre-Roman period. Holder and Jamieson's (2003) study of the prehistoric area around London has highlighted the level of truncation caused by Roman and later activity in the city and also the extreme difficulty of excavating to the great depth necessary to identify the earliest deposits. What is known so far, however, does not seem to indicate extensive pre-Roman occupation in the area, although some Iron Age coins have been found (Kent 1978). The prehistoric and Roman metalwork from the Thames and Walbrook indicates that the area was frequented and of importance for religious activity, which continued in the Roman period (Mattingly 2006a: 315–16; Merrifield 1995; Wardle 1998). The islands within the Thames at Southwark have more evidence of Iron Age occupation, including traces of roundhouses, pottery, and inhumation burials (Beard and

---

[12] Radiocarbon dating of three skulls from the Walbrook yielded dates of 100 cal. B.C. to cal. A.D. 390 for one skull, between 110 cal. B.C. and cal. A.D. 130 for another, and between cal. A.D. 140 and cal. A.D. 460 for the final one (Bradley and Gordon 1988: 507). This would definitely suggest deposition in the late Iron Age, continuing into the Roman period. Radiocarbon dating taken from skulls from the Thames yielded Middle and Late Bronze Age dates, suggesting that some skulls were deposited at the same time as the Bronze Age metalwork (ibid.: 508).

[13] Anglo-Saxon objects, including weapons such as spearheads from the Thames (Bradley and Gordon 1988: 508), suggest veneration in the early medieval period as well.

Cowan 1988; Cowan *et al.* 2009), perhaps indicating that they were a more important focus at this time than the area of the later town (cf. Drummond-Murray and Thompson, with Cowan 2002: 5–6).

4.5.8 *Caistor-by-Norwich*

Caistor-by-Norwich lay in the valley of the River Tas near the confluence of this river and the Yare (Wacher 1995: 243). Current excavations within the town have encountered traces of Iron Age activity, including coins and pottery, but so far little contextual information is known (W. Bowden, personal communication). A geophysical survey, however, has identified a number of circular and subcircular anomalies including gullies and ring ditches beneath the Roman town (Bowden and Bescoby 2008: 332). These appear to indicate a settlement here, but further work is needed to identify its nature and date. It was at one time thought that a series of ditches identified by aerial photography and some excavation apparently surrounding the area of the later town were Iron Age features, perhaps even indicating an *oppidum* (Davies 1996: 80). However, the large-scale survey of the area now suggests that these ditches were in fact of Roman date and may indicate an early form of enclosure around the town (Bowden and Bescoby 2008: 328–9). This does not mean, however, that this area was not important for Iron Age activity. The Roman temple to the northeast of the Roman town has produced Iron Age coinage and pottery (Gregory 1991) that might indicate that there was also pre-Roman activity here, and perhaps a religious place, although the coins could also have reached the site after the conquest. Creighton (2006: 144) has suggested that the site of this shrine may have been the location of a Late Iron Age princely tomb, but there is as yet no evidence to support this. A number of enigmatic enclosures have been identified in the surrounding area, such as at Harford Park (Ashwin 2000), which point to a considerable amount of activity here that seems to revolve around the two rivers. Neolithic monuments and Bronze Age barrows (records accessed from the Norfolk Historic Environment Database: 6100, 9582, 9743, and 9789) indicate a ritualised landscape of far greater antiquity.

4.6 People and place

Consideration must also be given to the people involved in the activity at these sites; people are evidently fundamental to the construction of the significance of place (cf. E. Casey 1996). People and their activities also formed an important part of towns in the later Roman period. Simplistic assumptions concerning the constituents of society in the late Iron Age have often influenced interpretations of sites such as *oppida*, their practical roles as settlements, and their position in the wider settlement hierarchy. Traditional views of the late Iron Age have argued that most of the towns were located within tribal centres that had been established with greater stability prior to the conquest (e.g., Cunliffe 2005). Lives of individuals, such as Commius, Dubnovellaunus, Verica, and Cunobelin, were reconstructed through coin distributions and references within classical texts, such as Caesar's *Bellum Gallicum* and the history by Cassius Dio.[14] This is despite uncertainties

---

[14] Cassius Dio (ca. A.D. 164–after A.D. 229), a Greek senator, wrote an eighty-volume *Roman History* between the late second and early third centuries A.D., which only partly survives today. It covered a period of over 980 years and ended around the time of his death (Rich 2003: 299–300).

about their accuracy and the nature, and even existence, of tribes (as the term is understood today) that the individuals represent.

A number of authors have argued that tribal groups will have been more complex and variable than static models of tribal divisions in pre-Roman Britain suggest (e.g., Laurence 2001; Mattingly 2004). It is also likely that ethnicity, and identity more generally, was highly fluid in nature (cf. S. Jones 1997). Mattingly (2004: 13) argues that rather than being affiliated with particular and relatively static tribal groups, people may have considered themselves followers of a specific leader in a situation in which circumstances and allegiances would have been constantly changing. Creighton (2006) argues that at Camulodunum and Verulamium, the Roman townscapes developed to enshrine and reinforce the memory of the 'kings' or other leading individuals who ruled these areas before and immediately after the Roman conquest. If so, these were probably new political positions, evolving as a result of changing relationships with Rome. J. D. Hill (2006: 177–8) emphasises the likely instability of these leaders; being dependent on Roman support, they may have made up the rules as they went along. There are still a lot of unknowns about the use of these places, but what is especially important is that these sites, which were often places of greater antiquity, appear to have been locations at which power, identity, and being were negotiated. They were highly ritualised and meaning-laden places. The complexity of social structure at this time highlights the problems in identifying the importance of some sites, such as *oppida*, over others that did not possess monumental earthworks. Examining the people is difficult: Ingold (2000: 151) even argues that to describe indigenous people in terms of those that were 'there first' 'situates them within a history conceived as a narrative of colonial conquest and state formation'. Late Iron Age people are likely to have had a different concept of being and time.

The population of these places in the late pre-Roman Iron Age, in terms of ethnicity, status, and gender, will always be a difficult area to pursue, as demonstrated by the many studies of identity and ethnicity in the past (e.g., Díaz-Andreu 2002; S. James 1999; S. Jones 1997; Mattingly 2004) and of romanisation (e.g., Mattingly 1997b). Sharples (2010: 173) has argued that though the earthworks of *oppida* reflect special places and the presence of elites, they do not include the coalescence as groups of single indivisible communities that we would understand today. Instead they were focal points of networks where people were bound together by personal allegiances. The issue of agency (cf. Gardner 2004) is also important, because different people will have experienced and understood the sites in different ways. The Roman viewpoint, traditionally dominant in most studies of Roman Britain and its people, is important but must be considered as only one of many viewpoints. In the Roman period, towns will have been inhabited by many diverse types of people from across the Empire (Mattingly 2006a: 292–5), but local people, and their concept and experiences of place, time, and movement, would have been a major part of this. To the local people in the late Iron Age, the significance of these places, many of which had longer histories of activity, will have influenced activity and remained strong into the Roman period. These sites were important in late pre-Roman times without classical-style monumentality and their continued use during the Roman period will have added to their importance and meaning.

CHAPTER 5

Structures of the public buildings in the later Roman period: framing place and space

To examine the use of public buildings in the later Roman period, we must first review current knowledge and interpretations of public buildings in Romano-British towns and the evidence of their structural state in the later Roman period. The emphasis here, however, is on how this can be used to indicate experience and use of space. Public buildings were hugely symbolic features of the townscape (Revell 2009) and also formed part of wider ritualised landscapes encompassing longer histories. Although the buildings had complex biographies with structural changes, and some were partially demolished, the spaces within them remained important and were adapted for new uses, as needs and desires developed, whilst also retaining older functions. The demolition of some structures also represents the vibrancy of place and the creative reuse of building materials and spaces.

With difficult urban excavations, the identification and interpretation of public buildings is not always easy. Their function is also a complex subject: buildings were not usually restricted to single roles and this adds a greater complication to the analysis of their late use. Mackreth (1987) defined the Roman public building as 'a structure which was put up to fulfil a public function and was open to the public itself'. This is useful because it is wide-ranging definition and can include buildings such as palaces because they had an administrative as well as residential function. Although to date no such buildings have been identified in Britain, Lavan (2001c) has argued that the *praetoria* of the later Roman period – residences of the civil or military governor – also had a number of similar functions to public buildings, including their role as places for ceremonies and administrative activities. Black's (1995) study of *mansiones* indicates that they could have served a large number of functions beyond their role in the *cursus publicus* (see Section 5.7). The *cursus publicus* was the system by which messages and officials moved around the empire by using the road network. *Mansiones* are included in this study as are monuments such as town gates, which were important points of passage and interaction. Monumental arches were also used in the organisation of space and the manipulation of movement (MacDonald 1986: 74); although often built for a specific commemoration, they were involved in 'invoking things sacred and temporal' (ibid.: 99).

Buildings and their architecture defined space, but the ways that people experienced and interacted with the buildings contributed to the creation of their significance over time. In this respect, the monumental architecture itself would have been only one element in the importance of the places (see the subsequent text; cf. Häussler 1999). Large open areas were also used as public spaces but they have rarely been considered in the same category as the public buildings, despite the possibility of having some comparable roles (see Chapter 6). The significance attached to space is important to consider when one is examining changes to public buildings in the late Roman period. Evidence of architectural changes to public buildings has often been described in terms of decline leading to the fall of towns (e.g., Liebeschuetz 2000; B. Ward-Perkins 2005). However, concentrating on the structural elements alone will give only a partial, and mainly negative, understanding of towns during the later Roman period. What requires further consideration is evidence of the way in which the structures continued to frame activities and maintain their importance as places. Feld (1996: 91) remarks, 'as place is sensed, senses are placed; as places make sense, senses make place' – in other words, it is necessary to consider the ways in which the buildings were used and experienced.

Architecture is a stage for movement and interaction, where performances are enacted in physically and symbolically bounded space (Edensor 2000: 123). Walking within and around public buildings and using them will have contributed towards creating the meaning attached to them (Simonsen 2003: 167–8). Acknowledging the difficulties in dating late phases of structures including demolition or collapse, an analysis of their structural state in the later Roman period indicates that at least parts of many of them survived into the late Roman and post-Roman periods; the buildings continued to have an impact on the landscape, as they had done in the earlier Roman period. An analysis of their use in the following chapters will indicate that they were not merely empty shells but continued to build upon the meanings attached to these places.

5.1 Studying public buildings

The post-colonial reaction to elitist and military themes within Roman archaeology (e.g., Mattingly 1997a; Webster and Cooper 1996) has led to an increase in studies of indigenous settlement and landscape patterns. These works are hugely welcome and have added significant information to our knowledge of Roman Britain (e.g. Fincham 2002; Hingley 1997a; Mudd et al. 1999; Taylor 2001). Nevertheless, this reaction does not mean that our understanding of public buildings is complete.

Tilley, addressing prehistoric remains, defined architectural space as the 'deliberate attempt to create and bound space, create an inside, an outside, a way round, a channel for movement' (Tilley 1994: 17). The phenomenological approach to space, emphasising its creation through relations between people and place, has become influential within studies of monumental landscapes in prehistory as a reaction against the scientific conceptions of space of New Geography and New Archaeology (Tilley 1994: 7–8, 11). Studies now attempt to understand how landscapes were experienced and understood, and how movement was conducted within and around them (Thomas 1993; Tilley 1994; Witcher 1998). Both Favro (1996) and Boman (2003) have argued that the space that was enclosed by walls and roofs of Roman and Greek buildings was as important as the architecture itself. Boman (2003) has explored Greek architecture and public space through the ways in which it permitted and denied movement; this influenced the conceptualisation and use of the space that was enclosed. Laurence's (1994) analysis of Pompeii also examined the way in which public buildings controlled movement and created identities and experiences, especially as areas of propaganda.

Roman architectural structures can be studied as highly visible and enduring enclosures around space. They often reflect power and wealth (Trigger 1990: 128), with significant buildings designed for maximum visual effect to communicate messages; buildings were 'stamped' with Roman ideology (Zanker 1989) and used to dominate and persuade (Häussler 1999). The way in which Augustus rebuilt large parts of Rome to draw on the past and create a new mythology conveyed through visual imagery and architecture has been an important theme of study (e.g., Sear 1982: 49; Wallace-Hadrill 1993: 50; Zanker 1989: 4).[1] The public buildings within the towns of Roman Britain created new spaces at pre-existing sites, and this will have influenced the experiences of the people who visited and moved through these buildings. Indigenous people will also have had their own concepts of space that will have influenced the ways that they experienced these buildings.

5.2 The *forum–basilica* complex

The *forum* and *basilica* were, according to Zanker (2000: 34), who draws heavily upon the writings of Vitruvius in *De architectura*, the symbol of the town, occupying a central location. They were key features in the urban landscape providing, from an elite Roman viewpoint, the 'stage and the facilities for an urban way of life' (Häussler 1999: 5).

The *forum* was principally an open space that allowed public congregation, commercial, political, judicial, and religious events, and entertainments (Perring 1991b: 280–1; Thorpe 1995: 32). Some of the earliest were delimited in simple ways such as at Cosa, western Italy, where a small number of trees seem to have marked out its location (Gros 1996: 208), but over time, the *forum* became increasingly monumentalised, allowing movement to be controlled and creating a source of power and indoctrination (Perring 1991b: 280). Entering the *forum*, perhaps through monumental arches and colonnades, would have been a meaningful act for many people: 'to the visitor of any Roman *forum*, there unfolds the picture of power relationships' (Häussler 1999: 6). *Fora* were not 'neutral entities' but charged with power and symbolism (Revell 1999: 57). Favro's study of the Augustan *Forum Romanum* has demonstrated how visitors would have 'experienced a carefully choreographed environment' (1996: 198). She examined the way in which the walls of the Augustan-period *Forum Romanum* were angled, the locations at which the statues and memorials were placed, and the locations of the entry points. Those using the structures in provinces such as Britain, where they were new phenomena, would have been encouraged to behave in a new way that was suitable for them (Revell 1999: 54).

The *basilica* was usually an aisled hall, often laid out to standardised measurements, but its origins have been the subject of much debate (e.g., Anderson 1997: 252–3; Welch 2003). Vitruvius writes that the '*basilica* should be situated adjoining the *forum*, on the warmest side, so that the merchants may assemble there in winter, without being inconvenienced by the cold' (*De arch.* V.1.4). In Britain, the *basilica* was attached to one side of the *forum*, with which it had an integrated role. Its likely uses were for commerce, politics (including the location of the *curia* for town council meetings), and religious activity: shrines and temples were important parts of the *forum–basilica* complexes. In Britain it is generally assumed that the *curia* was part of the *basilica* building and that it was not a separate structure within the town. Not enough is known about the *basilica* or town plans to be definite about this, and it is possible that there were *curia* in other areas of towns in the later Roman period.

---

[1] Suetonius (*Aug.* XXIX.1; XXVIII.3) records how Augustus 'built many public works' and had found Rome built of 'brick and left it in marble'.

TABLE 5.1. *Details of the known date of the latest structural alterations and demolition of the* forum–basilica *complex in each town*

Town	Alterations	Date of demolition	References
Aldborough	Little known about the *forum–basilica*	Uncertain	
Brough-on-Humber	Little known about the *forum–basilica*	Uncertain	
Caerwent	Evidence of reconstructions and alterations in the late 3rd to early 4th c.	Very late 4th or early 5th c.	Brewer (1993: 63–4)
Caistor-by-Norwich	Rebuilt in the mid-3rd c. after a fire, but little is known about later activity because of damage to the remains; 4th c. pottery might suggest that the building continued standing to this date	Uncertain; there is evidence of 4th c. pottery on site	Frere (1971)
Canterbury	Possible evidence of some rebuilding in the mid- to late 4th c.	Uncertain but presence of later 4th c. pottery	Frere and Bennett (1987: 93–8)
Carmarthen	Nothing is known about a *forum–basilica*	Uncertain	
Chelmsford	Nothing is known about a *forum–basilica*	Uncertain	
Chichester	Little is known about the *forum–basilica*	Uncertain	Down (1988: 31)
Cirencester	Alterations were evidenced in excavated areas with new walls constructed and new floors laid	Continuing use into the 5th c.; uncertain about demolition	Holbrook (1998: 117–19)
Colchester	Nothing is known about the *forum–basilica*	Uncertain	
Dorchester	Little is known about the *forum–basilica*	Uncertain	
Exeter	Alterations and extensions made in the mid-4th c.	Late 4th or early 5th c.	Bidwell (1979: 110)
Gloucester	Removal of the paving stones of the *forum* in the 4th c. but there was a continuation of activity	Uncertain; mid-4th c. pottery suggests a date of the late 4th c. or later	Hurst (1972: 58)

(continued)

TABLE 5.1 *(continued)*

Town	Alterations	Date of demolition	References
Leicester	Evidence of fire in the second half of the 4th c. but some evidence of the continuation of activity	Uncertain; there is evidence of wall-robbing in the post-Roman period	Buckley (2000); Hebditch and Mellor (1973)
Lincoln	Refloorings in the late 3rd to 4th c. and building work including the construction of a church in the *forum* in the 4th c.	Part at least may have remained standing, as shown by the Mint Wall	Gilmour and Jones (1980)
London	Repairs were made to the building in the second half of the 3rd c.	Demolition in the late 3rd or early 4th c.; part of the structure may have remained standing	Bateman (1998: 51); Brigham (1990)
Silchester	Few apparent changes made to the *basilica* after its construction in masonry in the mid-2nd c.; in the 5th c. there is evidence of the insertion of a hypocaust into the southern ambulatory of the west range and access to the west ambulatory was blocked off	Possible partial demolition in the 5th c. with the main shell of the building still standing into the 6th and 7th c.	Fulford and Timby (2000: 78, 581)
Verulamium	Little evidence of alterations because the area of excavations was too small but there is possible evidence of the continuation of use	Uncertain: the area of excavation was too small; there does not appear to be any evidence of deliberate demolition in the Roman period and the building may have remained standing to a later date	Frere (1983: 57–8); Montagu-Puckle and Niblett (1983–1986: 180); Niblett (2005a: 83)
Winchester	Alterations in the north wing of the *forum* in the 4th c.	Uncertain because of the small area of the building uncovered by excavation; parts may have remained standing into the post-Roman period	Teague (1988: 6–8)
Wroxeter	The building was destroyed by fire in the late 3rd c. but it may have continued in use afterwards	Uncertain; parts may have remained standing into the post-Roman period	Atkinson (1942: 106); White and Barker (1998: 112)
York	Nothing is known about the *forum–basilica*	Uncertain	Ottaway (1993: 87)

Knowledge of the *forum–basilica* complexes within each town in Roman Britain varies widely, with only the *basilica* hall at Silchester having been completely uncovered by use of modern excavation techniques, although even here the surrounding rooms and *forum* are poorly known (Fulford and Timby 2000). The complexes at Wroxeter (Atkinson 1942), Caerwent (Ashby 1906; Ashby, Hudd, and King 1909), and Caistor-by-Norwich (Frere 1971) were excavated on a large scale, although not to modern standards. Caerwent's *basilica* has since been re-excavated, although on a smaller scale. A possible *curia* was identified in the discovery of the positions of timber benches and a table in one of the excavated rooms of the *basilica* (P. Guest n.d.); this is the only such example discovered in Britain. At Wroxeter, it has been suggested that the large collection of metalwork, comprising locks, hinges, and a fragment of military diploma from within West Room 1 of the *basilica*, indicated that this room was an office or archive (Atkinson 1942: 103; Revell 2009: 40). However, other interpretations of the finds are possible, including a collection of metalwork for recycling (see Chapter 7), because no other similar collections of finds have come from other buildings. Structural changes to *forum* and *basilica* complexes are often considered to represent the decline of governance within the town and of urban function (Liebeschuetz 2000: 34, 41; Perring 1991b), but the analysis here will emphasise where possible their continued importance.

Out of the seventeen towns where something is known about the *forum–basilica* complex, thirteen have evidence of at least part of the buildings standing into the late fourth or early fifth centuries and later (Table 5.1). There is insufficient evidence from the other four to make analysis possible. In some cases there is evidence of the deliberate demolition of some parts of the complex, perhaps as a result of structural decay and the expense of repairs, whilst other parts remained standing and in use. The structures continued to be central to the urban space and a focus in the road system. Although most eventually collapsed or were demolished by the early medieval period, the dating of this event for some of the buildings is not easy to establish.

5.2.1 *London*

There have been a number of small-scale excavations on the site of the *basilica* and *forum* in London, the largest area being the Leadenhall Market site across the east end of the *basilica* (Figure 5.1; Milne 1992). The results from this excavation suggested that this area of the *basilica*, at least, was demolished in the early fourth century and the stone cleared away. This was indicated by the fact that the surviving bases of the walls were at the same level as the early-fourth-century occupation layer in the area. The final floors were then covered in silt, indicating a period of inactivity before the site was put to further use in the medieval period. Greater clarity regarding the sequence of demolition or destruction of the building is difficult because of truncation caused by later activity on the site (Brigham 1990: 77). Excavations between 1995 and 2000 in the southwestern corner of the *forum*, at 168 Fenchurch Street, seem to support the evidence for demolition around the early fourth century (Dunwoodie 2004: 34). The results from excavations on the site of the eastern portico at Whittington Avenue (Museum of London Archive and Research Centre record: WIV88) and 20–21 Lime Street (Museum of London Archive and Research Centre record: LIE90) indicate that the portico was probably demolished before the main building, perhaps in the late third century.

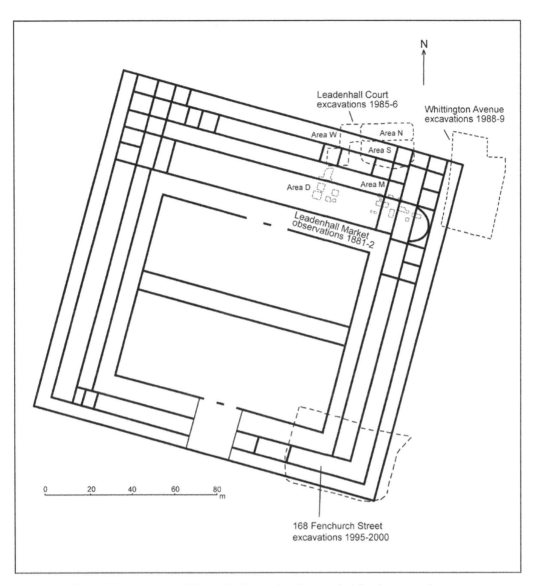

FIGURE 5.1. Plan of the reconstructed *forum–basilica* at London, marked for the areas of excavation mentioned in the text (drawn by A. C. Rogers; adapted from G. Milne 1992, Figures 2 and 4).

There are indications, however, that not all parts of the *forum–basilica* were demolished at this time (Bateman 1998: 51), demonstrating a complexity in the late and post-Roman use of the structure and its survival. At the extreme eastern end of the *basilica*, the survival of walls and tiled and tessellated floors of the eastern antechamber, the apse, indicate that this part remained standing to a later date, possibly even remaining above ground into the fifteenth century when the Leadenhall was built (Brigham 1990: 77; Milne 1992: 29–33). Observations of the area in the early 1880s, during the construction work of the Leadenhall Market, identified surviving Roman architecture 'showing the great extent of Roman building, and the thickness of walling' (Brock 1881: 90; see also Lambert 1916: 225–6), which contrasts with the evidence from the later excavations. Other areas where walls survived include parts of the south wall of the nave and some rooms off the nave (Brigham 1990: 77). These indicate survival to a post-Roman date, but too little is known to comment on the extent of this survival.

It is inferred from this analysis that parts of the complex survived, including the area of the apse, and remained in use beyond the fourth century, whereas other parts were demolished. Only further excavation will reveal more details and the extent of activity here. This demonstrates the difficulties of determining destruction dates of buildings: it should not be assumed that evidence of demolition from one excavation can necessarily be applied to the whole building.

5.2.2 Cirencester

Excavations on the site of the *forum–basilica* at Cirencester have also revealed a complex sequence of activity. The published excavations suggested that the *basilica* was demolished in the late fourth or early fifth century (Holbrook 1998: 111). Pits that cut into the *basilica* floor contained Oxfordshire colour-coated ware of A.D. 325–400. One pit contained a coin of Honorius (A.D. 395–402). These pits were sealed by the demolition debris of the building – consisting of masonry, mortar, and roofing slates – which itself was not dated. This means that the building could well have remained standing later than the dating evidence gained from the pits. This is supported by the evidence from the *forum* (Figure 5.2), where there were some major alterations to the structure in the mid- to later fourth century, including the enclosure of the colonnade of the portico, the rendering of walls with pink plaster, and the laying down of new mosaics (ibid.: 116).[2] Mosaics were also laid in the northwest range of the *forum*, although the dating is more problematic because the excavation did not continue to earlier layers beneath the mosaic.

It is possible that the *basilica* remained standing alongside the *forum*, but if it had been demolished at an earlier date then the *forum* would have become an independent structure. Wacher (1995: 314) has suggested that these alterations to the *forum–basilica* may have been for the creation of an administrative palace for the new province of *Britannia Prima*. This administrative change is not known to have occurred until around A.D. 314 (Holbrook 1998: 116), which is too early for these changes. The unusual nature of the building also has no parallels with known palaces (Lavan 1999). More work is required on the building, but what is clear is that a large part, if not all, remained standing and in use to a late date.

5.2.3 Silchester

Excavations at Silchester concentrated on the site of the *basilica* and there is only very limited modern information for the *forum*. The main *basilica* hall was uncovered in excavations between 1980 and 1986 but was also investigated in the Victorian period (Fox and St John Hope 1893), which destroyed much of the stratigraphy within the building (Fulford and Timby 2000: 80). From the excavated data it seems that there was an early phase of demolition in the later fourth century, when some of the interior walls and the colonnade of the building were removed to ground level. A coin of A.D. 360–8 was found

---

[2] The new mosaics were placed over a make-up of stone, loam, and plaster where a coin of Constantine II provides a terminus post quem of A.D. 335.

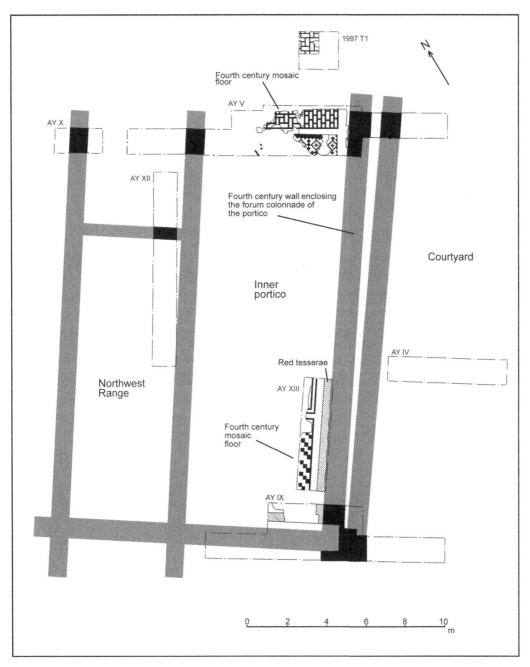

FIGURE 5.2. Plan of the excavations demonstrating fourth-century structural changes to the *forum* at Cirencester, including the enclosure of the *forum* courtyard and the laying down of new mosaics (drawn by A. C. Rogers; adapted from Holbrook 1998, Figure 73).

within a pit cut into the foundations of the colonnade at the north end where a stylobate block had been removed, but the foundation left. It provided a terminus post quem for the robbing of this wall (ibid.: 79–80). The main walls of the *basilica*, however, were robbed to their foundations at a later date, in the sixth or seventh century or possibly even later (ibid.), indicating that the main frame of the building remained standing and in use.

Apparently contemporary with the first phase of robbing was the insertion of a hypocaust under the floor in the west range of the *basilica*. It was only partially excavated and there is little dating evidence, although it appears to have cut a layer containing fourth-century pottery (ibid.: 75). Not only were these rooms still maintained and used in the west wing, but at least one was now heated. In this area was also a sherd of engraved glass dating to the late fourth or fifth century, though unstratified, and a piece of window glass of the seventh to ninth century (ibid.: 76–8), which might give a date to which activity continued. Late use is also indicated by a sherd of engraved glass vessel dating to the late Roman or early post-Roman periods (Price 2000: 320–1).[3] Late layers, one containing a coin of Eugenius (A.D. 392–5), completely covering a statue base within the *forum* (Fulford and Timby 2000: 75) suggest that the area remained in use alongside the *basilica*. This evidence also suggests that statue(s) had been removed from the *forum* at an earlier date.

5.2.4 Wroxeter

Like Silchester, Wroxeter's *forum* produced layers indicating use into the late fourth century and beyond (Atkinson 1942). Unfortunately, the complex was not excavated to what would be considered modern standards, so some caution is required when one is examining evidence from these later layers.[4] The *basilica* hall survived poorly and was only partially excavated but the western and southern range survived better. Within these ranges, Atkinson identified some traces of late use, including new walls, the alteration of rooms, and the laying of new floors (ibid.: 108–9). There was little dating evidence, although unstratified coins above one new floor included one of Victorinus (A.D. 268–70/71) and two of Tetricus I (A.D. 270/71–73/74), emperors of the Gallic Empire. Despite the limited evidence, it is possible that at least the east wing of the building remained in use.

5.2.5 Other towns

Further towns are examined in brief because there is less material available. At Exeter, only a small corner of the complex was excavated but it is evident that structural changes were being made up to around the mid-fourth century, which included the extension of the *basilica* (Bidwell 1979: 104–5). The excavated area suggests demolition in the early fifth century, with the only dating evidence, provided by burials across the southwest of the nave wall (ibid.: 108–10), giving a terminus ante quem of around A.D. 450. These burials need not indicate the demolition of the whole building, other parts of which may have remained standing. Only further excavation will determine this. The burials may even indicate a continued focus of activity here (see Section 8.5 on burials).

At Verulamium the *forum–basilica* has only received limited excavation (Corder 1940; Montagu-Puckle and Niblett 1983–1986), but there were traces of rebuilding and alteration

[3] Whilst there were ninety fragments of cast matt-glossy window glass that was in use to around A.D. 300, there were also ten fragments of pale green, cylinder-blown double-glossy window glass that was in use from the beginning of the fourth century. There were also nine fragments of dark greyish blue-green, cylinder-blown window glass likely to belong to post-Roman use of the building, which is especially well known at Anglo-Saxon ecclesiastical sites. These later fragments may represent replacements to the windows of the *basilica*, indicating the hall remained in use and in a state of good repair possibly into the seventh or eighth century (Fulford and Timby 2000).

[4] There is also no archive surviving for these excavations and so the evidence and interpretations in the report cannot now be checked easily. Knowledge of the site would benefit greatly from re-excavation.

in the third and fourth centuries, and later-fourth-century pottery suggested use at least to the end of the fourth and into the fifth century (Montagu-Puckle and Niblett 1983–1986). The level of accumulated material within the structure might indicate that demolition did not occur until the post-Roman period (Frere 1983: 57–8; Niblett 2005a: 83). At Caerwent, the small area of the nave and rear range of the *basilica* that was re-excavated in the late 1980s provided some more information on the sequence of the structure (Brewer 1990: 81; P. Guest n.d.). It would seem that demolition, dated by coins, took place in the late fourth or early fifth century. Other parts, however, would certainly appear to have been standing until a later date, with some walls even being incorporated into nineteenth-century farm buildings (Brewer 1993: 61). As in London this evidence indicates a complexity of use into the post-Roman period, with some parts remaining standing whilst others were demolished.

Very little is known about the *forum–basilica* at Canterbury, with only a small area being uncovered through excavation, but a section of exposed wall did appear to show evidence of rebuilding in the mid- to late fourth century (Frere and Bennett 1987: 93–8). At Lincoln, the survival of the 'Mint Wall', a section of the *basilica* wall 22.5 m long and 7.25 m high (Gilmour and Jones 1980), indicates that at least part of the *basilica* remained standing into the post-Roman period and beyond, and the excavations of the east range of the *forum* (Steane 2006) have demonstrated that this part also remained standing. The small area of the *forum–basilica* excavated at Winchester (Teague 1988) points to alterations in the fourth century. At Leicester, although the site suffers from much disturbance and truncation, there is evidence of structural alterations and new floors within the building after a fire in the second half of the fourth century (Hebditch and Mellor 1973).

Where there is evidence available, then, there does seem to have been structural contin-uation of at least part of each building to a late date, often into the post-Roman period. This may well also be representative of more that has not survived in the archaeological record, perhaps including timber structural components (see Chapter 8). Structural alterations to the buildings could be seen as demonstrating the decline of the building as originally constructed, but equally they indicate that the buildings continued to be foci of attention and centres of activities within the towns.

5.3 Public bath buildings

Public baths could be monumental buildings covering large parts of the town. The largest buildings, especially the Imperial baths, had many functions in addition to bathing.[5] It has been argued that it was the Imperial baths (*thermae*) that played an important part in making baths more popular and respected within towns, because during the Republic baths were smaller, less organised, and not always considered socially respectable (DeLaine 1999a: 70); they also generally concentrated more on the bathing function at this time (Thorpe 1995).[6] The Imperial baths, with their facilities, marble plaques, statues, and paintings (Gros 1996: 397), promoted the role of public baths as important social places and foci for display and propaganda. In the larger towns, public baths were often outnumbered

[5] The Baths of Trajan, built during the first decade of the second century, for example, contained exercise halls and also accommodated meetings, lectures, and performances (Anderson 1997: 275), whereas the Baths of Caracalla built in Rome in the A.D. 210s had gardens, fountains, and a running track (Thorpe 1995: 59–60).

[6] In the *Epistulae* (LXXXVI), Seneca, writing in the first century A.D. contrasts the small and dark bathhouse that Scipio Africanus had in his house at Liternum in the second century B.C. with the extravagant baths of his day (Thorpe 1995: 57).

by commercial baths, and it is these that are likely to have fulfilled the basic bathing needs of the population (DeLaine 1999a: 72), leaving the public baths more as centres of social activity.

They were important places of social interaction (DeLaine 1999b: 7–9; Yegül 1992: 1–4). Vitruvius states, for instance, that the baths should be placed directly under light so that 'the bystanders do not obscure the light with their shadows' (*De arch.* V.10.4), clearly indicating the presence of many people who were not bathing. Bathhouses were often associated with religious sanctuaries, indicating that they were also part of religious ceremony. In Britain examples include that at Verulamium, where in the centre of the town there was an early complex of monumental buildings including a temple, bathhouse, and theatre (Niblett 2005a: 105). Other sites include Bath (Cunliffe 2000) and sanctuaries such as Lydney (A. Woodward 1992: 49, 77).

In some parts of the Empire there is good evidence of the continued importance of bath buildings in the late Roman period, and they even influenced the architecture of other types of building. The *Basilica Nova*, built in Rome in the early fourth century, for example, took the form of the *frigidarium* (the hall for the cold baths) of a bathhouse rather than drawing on the architectural tradition of the *basilica* (Thorpe 1995: 47). Documentary evidence demonstrates that baths took on some important roles in late Roman times: in A.D. 245 in Antioch, for example, the governor Julius Priscus held his judicial meetings within the baths of Hadrian rather than the *basilica*. Surviving written sources state that the Emperor Valerian (A.D. 253–60) used the public baths as his headquarters (SHA *Aurel.* X.3, XIII.1; Thébert 2003: 445).[7] Later there are records that the A.D. 411 Council of Catholic bishops took place within the baths of Gargilius in Carthage (ibid.: 445), the *Secretarium Thermarum Gargiliarum*.[8] The changing official use of baths is occasionally reflected in archaeological evidence, as when marble statues of the imperial family were transferred to the bathhouse at Thubursicum Bure in Tunisia (DeLaine 1999a: 72; Thébert 2003: 413).[9] Bath buildings often remained important places in the late Roman period, which has implications for examining the surviving evidence from bathhouses in Britain.

Within the towns of Roman Britain (Table 5.2), bathhouses have been identified in all the towns except Cirencester, Colchester, and Gloucester; however, often the excavated area of the building was small, as at Canterbury (K. Blockley et al. 1995) and Verulamium (Niblett 2001: 65, 77), making interpretations difficult. Remains of a bathhouse were uncovered in York in 1839 but details are scant (Ottaway 1993: 87). Some towns, such

[7] Passages in the Scriptores Historiae Augustae include 'At this time ... Ulpius Crinitus gave thanks formally to Valerian as he sat in the public baths at Byzantium saying that he had done him great honour in giving him Aurelian as deputy. And for this reason he determined to adopt Aurelian' (*Aurel.* X.3). Another is that 'when Valerian Augustus had taken his seat in the public baths at Byzantium, in the presence of the army and in the presence of the officials of the Palace ... (he) spoke as follows: The commonwealth thanks you, Aurelian, for having set it free from the power of the Goths' (*Aurel.* XIII.1).

[8] The function or nature of the *secretarium* is not known, but it may have been where laws were drawn up (Leone 2007: 86) and apparently it had moved into the baths.

[9] At Thubursicum Bure, between A.D. 260 and 268, the baths were given the name of the Emperor and saw considerable aggrandisement. The statues suggest that the building was now an important location for propaganda and may have been where meetings and even administration took place. In Liternum, Campania, in 383 an inscription records how the governor moved statues 'from a hidden place in the town to the thronged Severan baths' (CIL, X no. 3714), whereas at Beneventum a curator *rei publicae* of the late third or early fourth century (CIL, IX no. 1588) brought a statue 'from a hidden place to the use and splendour of the baths' (Yegül 1992: 322).

as Canterbury and London, have multiple bathhouses and it is unlikely that all were public buildings (K. Blockley et al. 1995; Frere and Stow 1983; Rowsome 1999). The more clearly defined function of bathhouses than other types of building is useful because it makes change of use more readily identifiable, and this provides a pattern of comparison for changes of use in other public buildings. Of the towns studied, twelve bathhouses are likely to have been at least partly standing into the later fourth or early fifth centuries. The end date of the use of the bathhouses as functioning baths is often difficult to identify because they may have operated in a reduced fashion. The bathhouses at Canterbury, Dorchester, and Chichester show definite evidence of changes or additions to the structures in the fourth century, demonstrating that these buildings were still functioning in some capacity. For other bathhouses, only a terminus post quem for their destruction or change of use can be identified. In many cases the function as a bathhouse probably ceased earlier than the use of the buildings themselves, which were then utilised for other activities.

5.3.1 Leicester

The bathhouse at Leicester was excavated in the 1940s but no later levels within the baths themselves survived, or were recognised. There was, however, a series of late layers within the courtyard containing fourth-century pottery and coins (Kenyon 1948: 34), which might relate to the continued use of the building even if its function had changed. That at least a section of the baths remained standing into the late Roman period and beyond is indicated by the survival of the 'Jewry Wall', which was part of the unheated rooms of the baths. This was incorporated into a later church on the site (ibid.: 7) and still stands next to a church today. Although there is no direct evidence, this part of the baths may have functioned as a church or an administrative or judicial building in the late Roman period, especially because it later became the site of a medieval church. It is uncertain for how long other parts of the bathhouse remained standing with this wall and whether there were selective stages of demolition.

5.3.2 London

Excavations of the Huggin Hill baths in London have shown that at least the excavated areas had gone out of use by the mid-second century. This has sometimes been taken to indicate an early decline of the town despite the fact that there are likely to have been many other bathhouses (Marsden 1976: 20; Rowsome 1999: 269–70).[10] Despite the early demolition of some areas of the Huggin Hill baths, there is evidence that at least some of the walls remained standing throughout the Roman period and into the early medieval period. A document of the ninth century records large, standing masonry referred to as the Hwaetmundes stan in the area of the baths (T. Dyson 1978: 209). If this is connected with the baths, it would indicate that parts of the building survived to the end of the Roman period and beyond, although their function in the late Roman and post-Roman periods is unclear.[11] The excavations carried out by Marsden (1976) in the 1960s, and the

---

[10] One example recently found was at 172–6 The Highway, the site of the 'Babe Ruth' diner. It would have lain outside the walls of the Roman town and was in use from the second to the early fifth century (Museum of London Archive and Research Centre record: HGA02).

[11] A land grant from Queenhithe of A.D. 889 refers to a market courtyard as an ancient stone building called Hwaetmundes stan. T. Dyson (1978: 209) has placed the area mentioned in this grant to the location of

TABLE 5.2. *Details of the known date of the latest structural alterations and demolition of the public bath buildings in each town*

Town	Alterations	Date of demolition	References
Aldborough	Nothing known of the bathhouses	Uncertain	
Brough-on-Humber	Nothing known of the bathhouses	Uncertain	
Caerwent	The later 3rd c. saw the addition of a new wing to the baths and in the 4th c. a timber building was inserted into the ruins of the colonnade of the building	Uncertain: part of the building at least may have remained standing into the 5th c.	Nash-Williams (1930)
Caistor-by-Norwich	Rebuilt in the late 2nd c. after a fire but little is known about its later phases because of damage on site	Uncertain	Frere (1971)
Canterbury	St. Margaret's Street: alteration in the early 4th c. with rebuilding and the construction of a *laconicum*	Uncertain; the structure seems to have remained standing into the 5th c.	K. Blockley et al. (1995: 188–91)
Carmarthen	Little known about the bathhouse but finds suggest a continuation of use into the 3rd c.	Uncertain; in use into the 3rd c.	H. James (2003)
Chelmsford	Nothing known of the bathhouses	Uncertain	
Chichester	Evidence of the repair of pumping equipment into the late 4th c.	No evidence of demolition available	Down (1988: 42)
Cirencester	Nothing is known about the bathhouses	Uncertain	
Colchester	Nothing is known about the bathhouses	Uncertain	
Dorchester	Finds suggest that the building continued in use to the end of the 4th c. or later but little else is known about it	Uncertain of demolition date but coins and pottery into the 5th c.	Keen (1977); Putnam (2007: 70–1)
Exeter	The *natatio* and drain were filled in during the late 3rd c. but the main building may have continued in use	Uncertain	Bidwell (1979: 122)

(continued)

TABLE 5.2 *(continued)*

Town	Alterations	Date of demolition	References
Gloucester	Nothing is known about the bathhouses	Uncertain	
Leicester	No later levels within the baths survived but in the courtyard a succession of floors suggests the continued use of the building into the 4th c.	The survival of the Jewry Wall suggests that at least part of the building remained standing	Kenyon (1948: 7)
Lincoln	Repairs or rebuildings probably took place in the Antonine period but little is known beyond that date	Uncertain; activity does not seem to have continued beyond ca. A.D. 350	M. Jones (2003: 127)
London	Huggin Hill baths: after the early demolition new buildings were constructed on site	Careful demolition took place in the mid-2nd c. but part of the building may have remained standing into the medieval period	Marsden (1976: 23)
Silchester	Use continued into the 4th c.	Part of the south *caldarium* had probably been pulled down by the 4th c.; uncertain about the rest of the building	Boon (1974)
Verulamium	The *insula* III bathhouse may have been derelict by the late 3rd c.	Demolition in the late 3rd c.; still a possibility that it was rebuilt in the 4th c.	Niblett (2005a: 85–6)
	The Branch Road bathhouse had fallen into decay by the mid-3rd c. and silt accumulated in the hypocausts	The building may have naturally decayed after abandonment	Niblett (2005a: 83–5); Wilson (1975: 258)
Winchester	Little is known about the bath building but there was possible use into the early 4th c.	Demolition sometime in the 4th c.	Winchester Museums Service archive record: SQ 88
Wroxeter	A number of structural alterations in the 3rd and into the 4th c. The *frigidarium* may have remained standing and in use with a different function	The Old Work suggests the survival of at least the *frigidarium* beyond the 4th c.; other parts of the baths may also have stood to a late date	Ellis (2000: 55)
York	Little is known about the baths	Uncertain	Ottaway (1993: 87)

later excavations in the 1980s (Museum of London Archive and Research Centre record: DMT88), were not extensive enough to preclude the possibility of the continued existence of some walls to a late date.

5.3.3 *Wroxeter*

Like the Jewry Wall in Leicester and the Hwaetmundes stan in London, the 'Old Work' at Wroxeter indicates that at least part of the public bath building remained standing and probably in use, although not necessarily for its original purpose, into the late and post-Roman period. Excavations have shown that the Old Work formed part of the *frigidarium*, which appears to have survived well beyond the collapse or demolition of other parts of the building (Barker et al. 1997: 138). Its survival, combined with its east–west orientation and evidence of a vaulted roof and late burials in the surrounding hypocausts, has led to the suggestion that it functioned as a church in the late Roman or early post-Roman periods (White and Barker 1998: 125). There are many other functions that the building could have performed, including a meeting place of some other kind or a granary (ibid.). The structure definitely appears to have been valued and in use in the fifth century and later, a theory supported by the fact that it was surrounded by numerous newly built timber structures at this time (Barker et al. 1997: 138–68).

5.3.4 *Other towns*

At the Canterbury St. Margaret's Street bathhouse, the excavation of part of the building showed clear alterations to its structure in the early part of the fourth century. The infilling of the *piscina* with rubble was identified, along with the construction of a *laconicum* over the site, but by circa A.D. 350 this too was being put to another function (K. Blockley et al. 1995: 171, 188). The building was not demolished, so it is likely that much of it continued to have some kind of function. At Chichester, dendrochronology of surviving oak timbers lining the cistern (main well) of the bathhouse indicates that it was still being used and repaired in the late fourth century (Down 1988: 42).[12] There also appeared to be no evidence of abandonment, suggesting that the building remained standing to at least the end of the Roman period (Down 1978: 152), although there had been much post-Roman robbing of the latest layers.

Late activity at the baths in Dorchester is indicated by the insertion of a hot tub in the late fourth century, but the overall size of the baths contracted (Keen 1977; J. Magilton, personal communication). Robbery of the plumbing and some structural features including tiles seems to have taken place in the early fifth century (ibid.), but there is nothing to indicate that the shell of the building was not standing and in use to a later date, which is likely to be the case (Putnam 2007: 70–1). Similarly, at Exeter, although the *natatio* (open pool) and an excavated section of drain seem to have been infilled in the late third century, there is no evidence that the main building had gone out of use. It can be inferred that it

---

the Huggin Hill baths, although there is no definite proof that the structure mentioned was that of the baths. Further excavation of the baths might be able to show that some parts remained standing beyond the demolition of others. It does, however, indicate that care must be taken in assuming that evidence for a demolished area represents the demolition of the whole building.

[12] From the cistern, water would have been pumped into a tank, reaching the bathhouse through lead pipes (Down 1988: 42).

continued into the fourth century and later (Bidwell 1979: 122; record accessed from the Exeter Urban Archaeology Database: 10257). The baths at Caerwent were not excavated to modern standards. However, coins of Constantius II (A.D. 337–61), Valens (A.D. 364–78), and Arcadius (A.D. 394–408) from the excavations may suggest some kind of use of the structure at this time. Other baths where nothing is known about the later layers as a result of the nature of the excavations or the disturbance of the stratigraphy include the buildings at Lincoln (Petch n.d.), Caistor-by-Norwich (Frere 1971), and Verulamium (Niblett 2005a: 85–6). Without positive evidence of the demolition of the whole of these structures, however, it is likely that parts of them remained standing and in some kind of use to the end of the Roman period or beyond.

Bathhouses are often perceived to be one of the public building types that would have been most desirable to maintain to a late date, at the expense of other buildings, because they were the most valued within the town (Liebeschuetz 2000: 39; White and Barker 1998: 88; Yegül 1992: 321). Evidence of early cases of demolition or abandonment, therefore, is taken as a clear marker of decline. In the Western Empire the end of the use of bathhouses seems to have occurred earlier than in the East, where some continued into the eighth century although on a reduced scale (Liebeschuetz 2000: 180; Yegül 1992: 315, 324–6). In Britain, the latest bathhouses seem to have lasted only until the early fifth century, and this fact is used to indicate an early decline of towns here. The rise of Christianity is sometimes given as a reason for the end of public baths because they were considered to be related to rituals of pagan religion with amoral connotations (Yegül 1992: 315). There is good evidence from parts of the Empire that baths, perhaps because of their compatible architecture and water supply, were converted into churches, as in the case of the baths of Novatianus in Rome around A.D. 400 (Hansen 2003: 146; Thorpe 1995: 81). There is also known epigraphic evidence, although now lost, dated to A.D. 384 that recorded that the bath building already had a congregation and clergy in its unmodified state (Webb 2000: 65), indicating that it was converted to a church before alterations to its structure. This might provide analogy for other bath buildings, and public buildings more generally, where textual evidence is lacking. There is also the issue of ownership in these cases where public buildings were taken over by the Church.

Viewing the disuse of the structures as baths as a symbol of decline may be simplistic, especially because in the later Roman period there appears to have been a preference across the Empire for small private bathhouses rather than public buildings (Liebeschuetz 2000: 30; Stirling 2001). Secondary uses must also be taken into account when one is looking for the 'end' date of the buildings. There are some examples where parts of bathhouses were used for different purposes whilst parts retained their original function. At Leptiminus in North Africa, for example, one area of the bathhouse had a pottery kiln installed whilst the baths remained in use (Stirling 2001). Like the *forum–basilica*, the bathhouses were often hugely monumental structures; as the Old Work at Wroxeter indicates, in many cases remains survived into the late Roman period and sometimes beyond.

5.4 Spectacle buildings

The function of spectacle buildings in Romano-British towns is not straightforward. It is unclear to what extent the theatres and amphitheatres in Britain were used for the same purposes as they were in other parts of the Empire, and their function across the Empire was hugely varied.

The archaeological record indicates that theatres were not used simply for classical theatrical performances. Across the Empire many were associated with temples, including all the known examples of theatres in Romano-British towns. In Gaul they have been identified as part of sanctuaries in rural as well as urban contexts. Examples include Sanxay (Horne and King 1980: 466–7) and Vendeuvre (Horne and King 1980: 486), both in Vienne, and Vendeuil-Caply located at the source of the River Noye (ibid.: 485; Wightman 1985: 98). Besides being spaces endowed with the divine presence, theatres were places of social interaction in which all members of society could view each other in one location (Häussler 1999: 8). Zanker (2000: 37–8) has considered theatres in terms of the way in which they reinforced the social order through their design, because different sections of society sat in different areas and physical contact between groups was minimised by the stipulation that 'many and spacious stepped passages must be arranged between the seats' to allow multiple routes of access (Vitr. *De arch.* V.3.5). Without textual evidence, it is not possible to know whether a comparable organisation of seating existed in the theatres in Britain, but it raises possibilities about their role in Romano-British towns.

Amphitheatres have been considered in a similar way: Edmondson (1996) states that by encouraging different types of people to sit in close proximity, the amphitheatres represented microcosms of society. The presentations and displays within the amphitheatre were tools for ensuring social cohesion and enforcing the Roman social structure. Like theatres, amphitheatres probably had a religious role, being convenient centres for congregation. It is unfortunate that there has not been much excavation around amphitheatres in Britain because there may be evidence for associated structures, including temples and service buildings, that would assist in understanding the use of the amphitheatres. A temple has been identified by aerial photography close to the amphitheatre at Caistor-by-Norwich (Wacher 1995: 250). Amphitheatres or semi-amphitheatres are sometimes found at religious sanctuaries in France and Britain, such as Frilford in Oxfordshire (Hingley 1985: 205–6; Lock et al. 2002: 70–3). This amphitheatre appears to have been deliberately constructed in a boggy part of the settlement, and a large number of bronze, iron, and glass objects found in this area just outside the amphitheatre may be related to ritual deposition. This evidence and the location of the building may indicate that, at least on occasion, this structure was used for religious activity.

Though there have been a number of excavations in Britain, amphitheatres have produced few finds such as large animal bones, weapons, and human bone that one might expect to be present after being used for Roman entertainments. In fact at some there have been no finds, indicating that they were used in ways distinct from theatres. Excavations at the amphitheatre at London produced samian ware with scenes of gladiatorial combat (Bateman, Cowan, and Wroe-Brown 2008), which may support the idea that some kind of spectacles took place here; the distal humerus of a brown bear from behind the arena wall may also support this (Bateman 1997: 56), and possible chambers used to keep animals have been identified at London and Cirencester (Bateman 1997: 56; Holbrook 1998: 173). Sherds of samian ware displaying gladiatorial combat have also come from the amphitheatre at Chester (Mason 2001: 142–6). It was also near the amphitheatre here that a fragment of a slate relief depicting a gladiatorial scene was found in the eighteenth century (ibid.: 146–7), and excavations of a part of the structure in 2004–5 located human bones and large stone blocks possibly where animals or humans could have been chained during spectacles (Wilmott, Garner, and Ainsworth 2006: 12). The recently discovered circus outside

Colchester also indicates Roman entertainments (P. Crummy 2008). Gladiatorial combat and fights involving wild animals are likely to have taken place within amphitheatres in Britain, especially where there would have been many people from overseas such as in London. These events could have been combined with religious activities of both Roman and indigenous character, in some cases taking on some of the roles connected with the meaning-laden places of the late pre-Roman period.

In Britain, Cirencester is the only town where both an amphitheatre and the remains of a possible theatre have been identified (Holbrook 1998: 142–5). Where only one of these occurs, an amphitheatre is usually represented, although at Canterbury, Verulamium, and extramural Colchester only theatres are known so far. Remains interpreted as a theatre-type structure were uncovered in early-twentieth-century excavations at Wroxeter, west of the temple in the southern half of the town. The remains seemed to indicate a large rectangular enclosure with double walls and rounded corners, with an alcove set in one wall and an entrance in another. It was argued that the double walls supported seating and that this structure may have been a focus for rituals and performances associated with the temple (Bushe-Fox 1916: 20–2; G. Webster 1975: 58; White and Barker 1998: 95). Details of this building are scant and further evaluation of the excavations is not now possible.

Most British amphitheatres are extramural, in common with many others across the Empire, which may relate to logistical considerations of access. Exceptions are the amphitheatre at London and the problematic example at Caerwent, where excavations in the early twentieth century uncovered a structure consisting of a single wall enclosing an elliptical-shaped area (Ashby et al. 1904: 104–5), but the definite nature of this structure is uncertain. The setting of the amphitheatre at Dorchester within the Neolithic henge monument of Maumbury Rings, an enclosure of around 2,100 m², meant that it had the largest arena in Britain. There is no evidence of the use of the henge in later prehistory, although Roman construction activity may have destroyed earlier strata. It is possible that in some way the amphitheatre at Dorchester commemorated and transformed pre-existing forms of use of the monument. The location of the amphitheatre at Chester may also be significant despite its being built on what appears to have been a new site; it was situated at the edge of the plateau overlooking the River Dee, a name that comes from Deva the goddess (Mason 2001: 106). This amphitheatre, which could have been used for religious activity as well as games and other events, may have been drawing on the religious significance of the place.

Both types of spectacle building require further detailed study in Britain, and this could determine whether both indigenous and Roman-inspired activities took place within them, and the extent to which they remained vital places in the late Roman period. In many cases in Britain, the amphitheatres and theatres remained standing into the late Roman period and beyond, continuing as monuments in the landscape, and there is often evidence of some kind of activity within them (Table 5.3). Seven of the known structures were standing into the later fourth and fifth centuries; the circumstances surrounding a further seven examples are uncertain. Only one building appears to have been demolished at an earlier date. The fact that many of these structures survived as visible earthworks into the twenty-first century indicates that they will have continued to have an impact on people within these landscapes. They remained important structures regardless of whether they continued to be used as spectacle buildings.

TABLE 5.3. *Details of the known date of the latest structural alterations and demolition of the spectacle buildings in each town*

Town	Alterations	Date of demolition	References
Aldborough	No amphitheatre or theatre known	Uncertain	
Brough-on-Humber	No amphitheatre or theatre known	Uncertain	
Caerwent	Possible evidence of an amphitheatre but the known traces are problematic	Uncertain	Ashby et al. (1904: 104–5)
Caistor-by-Norwich	Amphitheatre known through aerial photography but unexcavated	Uncertain	Bowden and Bescoby (2008)
Canterbury	The theatre was rebuilt in the early 3rd c. but it is uncertain if it was still is use in the 4th c.	The structure remained standing into the medieval period but had been demolished or robbed by A.D. 1200	Frere (1970)
Carmarthen	Amphitheatre known but little has been excavated	Uncertain	H. James (2003): 18–19; Wacher (1995: 392–3)
Chelmsford	No amphitheatre or theatre known	Uncertain	
Chichester	Very limited information known about the amphitheatre	Uncertain; has remained a visible earthwork into the 21st c.	G. White (1936: 157–8)
Cirencester	Amphitheatre: alterations to the northeast entrance and the interior during the 5th c.	Uncertain; remained standing into the 5th c. and it is a prominent earthwork into the 21st c.	Holbrook (1998: 169–71)
	Theatre: very little known about the structure and its interpretation is problematic	Uncertain	Holbrook (1998: 142–5)
Colchester	Theatre in *insula* XIII but little is known about its later history	Uncertain; no material dated to the 4th c. in the excavations	P. Crummy (1982)
	Gosbecks theatre rebuilt in stone in the mid-2nd c. but demolition in the 3rd c.	Demolition some time in the 3rd c.	Dunnett (1971: 31–43); Hull (1958: 269)
	Circus possibly built in the 2nd c. but very little known about the structure	Uncertain; it possibly remained standing, at least in part, into the post-Roman period	P. Crummy (2008)

(continued)

TABLE 5.3 *(continued)*

Town	Alterations	Date of demolition	References
Dorchester	Alterations to the entrance and interior during the late 3rd and 4th c.	Some of the superstructure may have been demolished or robbed; a large earthwork remains into the 21st c.	Bradley (1975)
Exeter	No amphitheatre or theatre known	Uncertain	
Gloucester	No amphitheatre or theatre known	Uncertain	
Leicester	No amphitheatre or theatre known	Uncertain	
Lincoln	No amphitheatre or theatre known	Uncertain	
London	A number of new floors laid in the late 3rd c.	Robbing of walls after abandonment in the late 4th c. or later; part of the structure may have remained standing into the medieval period	Bateman (1997: 68); Bateman et al. (2008)
Silchester	The structure was rebuilt in the mid-3rd c. but there is little evidence of use in the 4th c.	The walls may have been robbed in the late 4th or early 5th c.; much remains standing into the 21st c.	Fulford (1989: 58, 192)
Verulamium	The theatre was reconstructed ca. A.D. 300 but was then filled with organic earth	Uncertain about demolition	Kenyon (1935: 239–40)
Winchester	No theatre or amphitheatre known	Uncertain	
Wroxeter	No theatre or amphitheatre known, except for possible enclosure in the west of the town, which may have served as a type of amphitheatre or theatre	Uncertain	Bushe-Fox (1916: 20–2); White and Barker (1998: 95)
York	No theatre or amphitheatre known	Uncertain	

5.4.1 Dorchester

Excavations at the amphitheatre in Dorchester took place in the early twentieth century but were written up and published in the 1970s (Bradley 1975). This means that some of the evidence may be problematic, but the available data do indicate that some structural changes were made to the building in the late Roman period. Bradley (ibid.: 78) suggested that this took place after the structure had ceased to function as an amphitheatre, but this is difficult to prove with certainty because there is little direct evidence of the use of the structure in any period.

An analysis of the early excavations suggested structural alterations, including the erosion of the seating banks in the early fourth century and the end of use of the east and west recesses. The wall of the south recess was knocked through to create a new entrance to the arena, which suggests that it was still in some kind of use. The northern entrance also appears to have been rebuilt, there being evidence of what are described as 'rustic pedestals', each consisting of Purbeck marble fragments (ibid.: 56–8). There is some evidence that accompanying these two features were post-holes and a line of timber uprights, which might indicate that they continued to form some kind of gateway. The dating evidence is limited, but a sherd of New Forest ware found within one of the post-holes, and coins of Carausius (A.D. 286–93) and Constantine I (A.D. 306–12) found in the silt cut by the timber features, suggest a fourth-century date (ibid.). The surviving evidence does not allow any interpretation of function, but what can be inferred is that people continued to come to the building and perhaps to congregate here.

5.4.2 *Cirencester*

Late structural changes to the entrance of the amphitheatre have also been identified. The second half of the fourth century saw the demolition of the masonry passage walls and covering vault at the northeast entrance, and metalled surfaces being laid down over the remains (Holbrook 1998: 166). The southeast and northeast chambers were also demolished, but the arena wall was rebuilt. A coin of A.D. 270, which lay in the latest floor level of the southwest chamber, provides a terminus post quem date for the demolition of this chamber, whereas the latest coins associated with the rebuilding of the arena wall dated to the period A.D. 330–48 (ibid.). Probably in the early fifth century, stone blocks narrowed the entrance passage into the arena; a coin of A.D. 383–7 was found in a layer beneath the stones (ibid.: 169). Without more evidence it is not possible to know whether this indicates a greater need for security, but it does demonstrate that the building was still in use at this time.

5.4.3 *Other towns*

Other amphitheatres that have been excavated relatively recently are London (Bateman 1998; Bateman et al. 2008) and Silchester (Fulford 1989), but there is not the same evidence here for architectural changes made to the buildings in the late Roman period. The structures did, however, remain standing into the post-Roman period. The date of demolition of the London amphitheatre is not precisely known; however, coins in some of the robber trenches suggest a date after A.D. 367 (Bateman 1998: 52–3), indicating destruction in the late fourth century or later, as the robber trenches may only represent partial robbing in the late Roman period. Remains of the amphitheatre at Silchester survive today. Excavations indicate that in the medieval period it first contained a single-aisled hall, but by the twelfth century it was being used as a fortification (Fulford 1989: 193–5). Excavations of the amphitheatre at Chester have produced some important results for comparison. At least two of its entrances were deliberately walled up in the latest

Roman period, perhaps in the early fifth century. This might indicate some kind of defensive structure (Ainsworth and Wilmott 2005: 8). A timber structure was discovered within the arena that has been interpreted as an early post-Roman hall, possibly indicating a power base here (ibid.: 7–8), and clearly the monumental structure itself remained important.

At Canterbury the theatre has not been excavated beyond a small number of minor trenches (Frere 1970), but it is clear that it remained a significant monument, influencing the street-grid and not being robbed until after the Norman Conquest. At Colchester, the theatre at Gosbecks seems to have been demolished in the third century (Dunnett 1971: 41) but the theatre within the town may have remained standing into the post-Roman period (P. Crummy 1982), although very little is known about it. Nothing is known about the later use of the circus outside Colchester because of limited excavations and poor dating evidence (P. Crummy 2008). Similarly, the amphitheatre at Chichester was only very partially excavated in the 1930s (G. White 1936). Claims that it was demolished in the second or third century were based on the lack of later pottery, but as very few sherds were uncovered these conclusions are problematic. There is no evidence of the demolition of the theatre at Verulamium, but a structural analysis suggests that it remained a monumental feature in the town into the fifth century and later (Kenyon 1935). This building has received attention because of the late 'dark earth' material and large number of late coins from within the structure, which may indicate its continued use.

Theatres and amphitheatres in Britain may well have had a variety of uses throughout the Roman period, making specifically late use difficult to prove. Interpretations of the late use and structural change of amphitheatres in Britain include suggestions that they were made into defensible refuges because of threats of invasion and violence at this time (cf. Fulford 1989: 194; Wacher 1975: 314). There is some evidence from the Continent to support this idea, although there amphitheatres were converted to strong points incorporated into town walls, which does not appear to have happened in Britain. Examples include Amiens in *Gallia Belgica* (Bayard and Massy 1983: 222) and Tours in *Gallia Lugdunensis* (Knight 2001: 61). The amphitheatres at Dorchester (Bradley 1975: 78–9) and Cirencester (Holbrook 1998: 169–71) that are most often considered to have been refuges were not part of the walls. In Britain much less evidence survives for activity within the amphitheatres at this time compared with that on the Continent. At Nîmes, *Gallia Narbonensis*, for example, structures were built within the amphitheatre (Monteil 1999: 432–3). In Spain, too, there is evidence of buildings and other activities within some theatres and amphitheatres in the later Roman period, such as at Italica (Rodríguez Gutiérrez 2004) and Cartagena (*Carthago Nova*), where there were many market buildings (Casal and Gascó 1993: 103), though these do not seem to be related to a security issue.

It is sometimes thought that amphitheatres may have gone out of use because of the Christian condemnation of gladiatorial combat and the centres of paganism they represented (Bomgardner 2000: 201–2). Where there is evidence that the games continued to the sixth century, especially in Rome, Italy and the East (ibid: 197–220), this implies there was a benefactor able to pay for them; no evidence exists for this in Britain. Bomgardner (2000: 219) discusses evidence, for example, of chariot races in the amphitheatre at Constantinople in the sixth century and repairs and use of the Colosseum in Rome, also in the sixth century. On the Continent there is evidence that some amphitheatres retained religious and public roles after their use for games ceased. An inscription from Tarragona

(*Tarraco*), for example, indicates its repair by the Emperor Constantine (Dupré Raventós 2004: 69–72), but by the sixth century a *basilica* was built within the arena (ibid.), indicating religious activity – whether this was also a continuation from pagan ceremonies is uncertain. No inscriptions survive for Britain, but from the archaeology it can be said that in many cases the amphitheatres remained standing into the late Roman period. The evidence assessed here indicates that they continued to frame spaces and activities that took place within and around them.

5.5 Temples

Temple structures are usually recognised in the archaeological record through their distinctive building plan, either being of classical plan or, more usually in Britain, of Romano-Celtic design (Wilkes 1996: 1). This Romano-Celtic design of temple consisted of a square chamber (*cella*) surrounded by an ambulatory and this could also be set within a larger precinct (*temenos*). Despite this, there is still uncertainty about the identification of some buildings as temples in Britain. Where only small areas of the buildings have been uncovered, the interpretation of the structure as a temple is often problematic. At Gloucester, for example, the remains at Westgate Street were originally interpreted as the edge of a bathhouse (Heighway and Garrod 1980), but Hurst (1999b: 155–7) suggests that a *peribolos* (court enclosed by a wall) of a temple might be more likely. At Cirencester, excavations within *insula* VI opposite the *basilica* uncovered an area of courtyard and section of the portico of a building of monumental nature that have led to suggestions that it may have been the *temenos* of a temple, although little else is known (Holbrook 1998: 139–40). In the case of small towns, temples often seem to have been the only public building and they sometimes had a central position, as at Elms Farm, Heybridge, in Essex (Atkinson and Preston 1998), and Westhawk Farm in Kent (Booth 2001). This central location and surrounding open spaces indicate that the temples were perhaps involved in market and administration activities.

Within Roman London a number of large monumental complexes are known. Their functions remain enigmatic but perhaps included some kind of religious role without the buildings being wholly temple complexes. The complex described as an 'Allectan Palace', by the side of the Thames, excavated on small sites including Peter's Hill and Sunlight Wharf, was built in the later third century. The fact that the date of its construction in A.D. 294, dated by dendrochronology, coincides with the reign of Allectus has led to suggestions that it was a palace built by Allectus; however, there is no definite proof of this (T. Williams 1993: 28). It reused masonry apparently from an earlier complex on the site and baths here make a religious interpretation possible (T. Williams 1993: 26–32). Further masonry that apparently came from these buildings was found within the late riverside wall. This stonework displayed religious features, including depictions of gods that had come from religious monuments that had been part of the complex (C. Hill, Millett, and Blagg 1980: 125–32). It is uncertain whether the new buildings continued any of the functions of the earlier ones. Across the Thames at Southwark there was another large complex of uncertain function, which included a number of large wings of rooms and a bathhouse of comparable size to that at Huggin Hill (Yule 2005: 50–72). Some sort of religious or military role is a possibility here. Relatively few sites in urban contexts have produced many obviously religious artefacts such as statuettes and regalia. This contrasts with some rural sites such as Uley (Woodward and Leach 1993) and Hayling Island (King and Soffe 2001), and it could be the result of post-Roman reuse and disturbance of the urban sites, or perhaps of the differing rituals that occurred in the buildings.

Temples are also useful when one is considering movement around, to, and from towns because they would have played an important role in religious ceremonies and festivals (Esmonde Cleary 2005); they may well have attracted people to the towns from long distances. Some temples would also have had restrictions of access both in terms of time (of day and year) and type of person, reflecting aspects such as class (Stambaugh 1978: 574–80). This will have intensified the experience of entering the temple and worshipping within. Whereas other aspects of the landscape would have been imbued with meaning, including natural features, temples were an important way in which the religious landscape was created and negotiated. Roman temples in Britain were also apparently sometimes located on sites of pre-Roman religious importance (A. Woodward 1992: 17–30), indicating a longer-term continuity of activity (ibid.: 63).

Despite the presence of temples and shrines within towns, it must also be acknowledged that there were other forms of religious expression within the urban centres (see Chapters 3 and 4; cf. Fulford 2001). Religious activity took place at other public buildings, including theatres, amphitheatres, the *forum–basilica*, and bathhouses, and towns also formed part of the wider ritualised landscape. Temples and their precincts encouraged many diverse public activities, including meetings, business transactions, and performances (Anderson 1997: 243; Perring 1991b: 280; Stambaugh 1978). In some cases there are traces of activity beneath the temples, as at Canterbury (Frere 1977: 423) and Verulamium (Lowther 1937), and, despite the caution required in assuming a continuation of religious activity, it is possible that these were the locations of pre-Roman shrines representing continuity in the religious landscape.

A number of temples display structural alterations in the late Roman period indicating a change or continuation in use (Table 5.4). Of the thirty-eight definite temples known within the towns, fifteen buildings had at least parts of the structures standing into the later fourth and fifth centuries. A further five temples may have been standing, though there is insufficient evidence to be certain, and only three definitely appear to have been demolished by the fourth century. For a further fifteen known temples there is not enough evidence for an analysis of their structural condition in the late Roman period to be possible.

5.5.1 *Caerwent*

The temple at Caerwent, which was not built until around A.D. 330, was maintained throughout the fourth century, and into the fifth, with evidence of a number of late alterations. These included the addition of a range of rooms to the inner side of the entrance hall, suggesting that more space was needed for the activities taking place in the hall (Brewer 1993: 59). A coin of Valentinian (A.D. 364–75) was found beneath repair work to the foundations of one of the pilasters in the entrance hall (Brewer 1990: 79; 1993: 59). There have been various interpretations regarding the role of this entrance hall and rear range of rooms. Reece (personal communication) and Knight (1996: 36) have argued that the hall may have taken on the role of the *basilica*, after that had decayed, because it would have been more convenient and economical to maintain. Other interpretations have

TABLE 5.4. *Details of the known date of the latest structural alterations and demolition of the temples in each town*

Town	Alterations	Date of demolition	References
Aldborough	No temples known	Uncertain	
Brough-on-Humber	No temples known	Uncertain	
Caerwent	Addition of a range of rooms to the inner side of the entrance hall of the temple and the construction of two half-domed niches in the 4th c.	Uncertain; remained standing into the 5th c.	Brewer (1990: 79; 1993: 59)
	Possible external octagonal temple but little is known about it	Uncertain	Wacher (1995: 387)
Caistor-by-Norwich	Temple A *insula* IX: uncertain about alterations and use	Uncertain	Atkinson (1930: 99–102)
	Temple B *insula* IX: uncertain about alterations and use	Uncertain	Atkinson (1930: 99–102)
	Extramural temple: no structural changes evident in the 3rd or 4th c. but the temple may have continued in use	Uncertain	Gurney (1986)
Canterbury	Central temple precinct: a new courtyard surface was laid in the 4th c. made out of reused stone	Uncertain about demolition; courtyard use continued into the 5th c.	Bennett and Nebiker (1989); Frere (1977: 424)
	Temple at St. Gabriel's chapel: construction of a timber building within a pre-temple 'townhouse'	Demolition in the 4th c.	Driver et al. (1990: 89–91)
	Temple at Gas Lane: uncertain because of disturbance	Uncertain because of disturbance	Bennett et al. (1982: 44)
	Temple at Burgate Street: Built in the mid-3rd c.	Destroyed by the late 4th c.	Frere and Stow (1983: 41–9)
Carmarthen	Temple built in the 1st c. but out of use by the 2nd c.	Demolition in the mid-2nd c.	H. James (1984: 51; 2003: 150)
Chelmsford	Octagonal temple built in the 4th c.	Demolition in the late 4th c. or early 5th c.	Wickenden (1992: 39–41, 141)

(continued)

TABLE 5.4 *(continued)*

Town	Alterations	Date of demolition	References
Chichester	Very little known about the temples of Chichester	Uncertain	
Cirencester	*Insula* VI building temple? New floor surface in the courtyard laid in the 4th c.; the corridor was paved with a tessellated floor of chequerboard pattern ca. A.D. 330	Use into the 5th c. but uncertain about the demolition	Holbrook (1998: 134–5)
Colchester	Temple of Claudius: structural alterations in the 4th c. now doubted but probable continuation of use into the 5th c.	The building was probably still standing into the Norman period	Drury (1984); P. Crummy (1997: 120)
	Balkerne Lane temple: demolition of the ambulatory in the late 4th c. leaving the *cella* standing	The *cella* may have remained standing into the post-Roman period: the foundations survived to the height of the latest surviving Roman layer	P. Crummy (1984: 125)
	Balkerne Lane shrine: uncertain about later alterations	The building was demolished in the 5th c.	P. Crummy (1980: 267–8; 1984: 124)
	Grammar school temple: uncertain because of poor survival	Uncertain	Hull (1958: 236–8)
	Gosbecks temple: uncertain because of poor survival but possible use into the 4th c.	Uncertain	P. Crummy (1980: 260); Hull (1958: 264)
	Sheepen large temple; St. Helena's School: use into the 4th c.	Careful demolition in the 4th or 5th c.	P. Crummy (1980: 252); Hull (1958: 230)
	Sheepen small temple; St. Helena's School: uncertain or late changes	Uncertain	P. Crummy (1980: 252)
	Sheepen temple: uncertain	Uncertain	P. Crummy (1980: 252)
	Sheepen temple: uncertain of later alterations; possibly out of use by the 4th c.	Uncertain	P. Crummy (1980: 252)
Dorchester	No temples known	Uncertain	
Exeter	No temples known	Uncertain	

(continued)

TABLE 5.4 *(continued)*

Town	Alterations	Date of demolition	References
Gloucester	Temple precinct: demolition in the 4th c. but then further construction on site followed by a covering of metalling over the whole site	Demolition after ca. A.D. 370	Heighway and Garrod (1980: 78); Heighway et al. (1979: 163)
	Northgate Street temple: refloorings and structural alterations with some internal walls being converted to colonnades	Date of demolition uncertain; use may have continued into the 5th c.	Hurst (1972: 65)
Leicester	St. Nicholas Circle temple: little evidence of structural changes but use continued into the 4th c.	Uncertain	Wacher (1995: 359); Wilson (1970: 286)
Lincoln	Lower town temple complex: little is known	Uncertain	Stocker (2003)
London	Temple of Mithras: structural alterations in the 4th c. included the removal of the columns that had divided the nave from the aisles	It is uncertain whether the building was demolished or left to decay	Henig (1998); Shepherd (1998: 84)
	Riverside temple complex: possibly out of use by the 3rd c. or it may have continued in use when the remains from the first complex were used to build a new complex	Demolition of components of the structure in the 3rd c.; some evidence of the robbing of rebuilt parts in the late 4th c.	T. Williams (1993)
	Tabard Square temples, Southwark: they may have remained standing into the 4th c.; the deposition of a dedicatory plaque in the 4th c. might suggest that the temples had changed use or were demolished; deposition here might also indicate that the religious nature of the area was still recognised	Not completely certain but possibly in the 4th c.	Durrani (2004)
Silchester	*Insula* VII temple: uncertain about late phases	Uncertain	Fox and St. John Hope (1894: 206–9)
	Insula XXX temple precinct: uncertain about later structural changes but probably continued in use into the 4th c.	Uncertain	Boon (1974: 155–6); Fox and St. John Hope (1890: 744–9)

(continued)

TABLE 5.4 *(continued)*

Town	Alterations	Date of demolition	References
	Insula XXXV temple: uncertain	Uncertain	Boon (1974: 153); St. John Hope (1908: 206–8)
	Insula XXXVI temple: uncertain but probable continuation of use into the 4th c.	Uncertain	Boon (1974: 153)
Verulamium	*Insula* XVI temple: 2 wings were added in the 3rd c. and in the later 4th c. the east gate was demolished and a new gateway constructed on the west	It is uncertain whether the building was demolished or decayed naturally	Kenyon (1935: 241); Lowther (1937: 33–4)
	Triangular temple: repairs to floors in the 3rd c. and continuation of use into the 4th c.	It is uncertain whether the building was demolished or decayed naturally	Wheeler and Wheeler (1936: 117)
	Folly Lane temple: largely fallen into decay by the 3rd c. but may have continued in use	The absence of building material may suggest that it was deliberately demolished; uncertain of date	Niblett (1999: 71, 417)
Winchester	The use of the temple ceased in the 3rd c.	Demolition in the 3rd c.	Biddle (1975: 299)
Wroxeter	Uncertain of structural changes but use may have continued into the 4th c.	Uncertain	Bushe-Fox (1914: 9)
York	Wellington Row ?temple: extension in the 3rd c. and then use into the 4th c.	Uncertain	Ottaway (1993: 112–14; 1999: 147); Whyman (2001)

included priests' quarters and shops selling religious votive gifts and souvenirs (Wacher 1995: 386). The hall appears to have remained in use into the fifth century, although there is no definite evidence of its use and, as discussed, there are reasons to suggest that at least parts of the *forum–basilica* remained standing to a contemporary date.

5.5.2 *Colchester*

At the Balkerne Lane temple in Colchester there is evidence of differential robbing activities. The ambulatory of the temple was completely robbed, including its foundations, in the late Roman period (P. Crummy 1984: 125), but the foundations of the *cella* survived to the height of the latest Roman layers, indicating that it was only after abandonment of the building that these walls were demolished or had collapsed. It would appear that the *cella* stood in isolation in the fourth century, which might indicate a different function; the excavator suggested a church (ibid.) but its continuation as a temple or for another use is also quite possible.

Little is known of the Temple of Claudius in Colchester but some of its walls are visible within the cellars of the medieval castle. Studying the known evidence and plan, mainly from excavations in the 1930s, Drury (1984) suggested that there was evidence of a 2-m-thick wall built across the front of the temple in the fourth century and also for the demolition of the temple façade. He suggested that this created a long and narrow space with an apse, a church being formed by the conversion of the building. The latest coins on the site were of Valentinian II (A.D. 382–93) and Theodosius I (A.D. 379–95), and pottery found dated up to A.D. 360–70. Excavations in 1996 beneath the castle in the supposed location of the wall, however, failed to support these earlier findings, arguing that this had merely been a hypothetical projection (P. Crummy 1997: 120), but the building appears to have remained standing. This need not necessarily mean that the function of the building did not change in the later Roman period and, though clearly not enough evidence exists, a piece of pottery with a *chi-rho* symbol was found there in the 1996 excavations.

5.5.3 *Verulamium*

Another example of a temple where conversion to a church has been suggested is the *insula* XVI temple in the centre of Verulamium near the theatre, although the excavations of this structure took place in the 1930s. Lowther (1937: 33–4) suggested that at around A.D. 400, indicated by coins of the House of Theodosius, a new gateway to the building was constructed in the centre of the colonnade on the west side of the temple. This western gateway appeared to replace the earlier eastern entrance (ibid.) and therefore might indicate a change in orientation of the building. Although this need not equate with its conversion to a church, it would indicate that the building remained in some kind of use into the fifth century and possibly beyond.

5.5.4 *Canterbury*

At Canterbury, the small excavated areas of the central temple precinct indicate that demolition and robbing of the precinct portico and levelling of at least some internal buildings took place in the fourth century; the area was covered by a new courtyard surface on which were many fourth-century coins (see Section 6.2.1; unpublished excavations, P. Bennett personal communication; Frere 1977: 424). The new surface indicates that the area continued to be important within the town centre. The other temples known at Canterbury are only partially excavated and many have been badly disturbed. The temple at Gas Lane has coins dating to A.D. 330–40 in disturbed layers (Bennett, Frere, and Stow 1982: 44), but there is nothing to indicate that it was demolished and it may have remained standing to a later date. The Burgate Street temple has late-fourth-century pottery in its demolition layer (Frere and Stow 1983: 47), but this need not necessarily indicate the date at which the building was destroyed because the act of demolition can disturb earlier layers.

5.5.5 London

At London, masonry of the riverside temple complex was incorporated into later buildings on the site and elsewhere, indicating that it had been destroyed by the end of the third century (T. Williams 1993: 11, 27). The monumental nature of the structures that were then built on the site may, however, suggest a continuation rather than change in use (ibid.: 28–9). At the temple of Mithras there are alterations to the structure in the fourth century with the removal of the columns that had separated the nave from the aisles, apparently creating a larger open space (Shepherd 1998: 84). This appears to have coincided with the burial of many religious sculptures within the building. The definite function of the structure is uncertain[13] but it remained standing into at least the sixth century (ibid.: 97). Internal alterations to the building in the late fourth century, creating a more open space, suggest that many people were still using it.

5.5.6 Other towns

Late phases of temples from the other towns in the study have not survived well. These include the temples at Caistor-by-Norwich (Atkinson 1930; Gurney 1986), Wroxeter (Bushe-Fox 1914), and Leicester (Wilson 1970: 286), although there were some late-fourth-century coins from this latter site. At Winchester, the temple was demolished in the third century (Biddle 1975: 299). No temples have been identified with certainty at Cirencester, although the enigmatic monumental building in *insula* VI, of which only a small area has been excavated (Holbrook 1998: 135–8), may have been one. Results from this site, including well-worn coins of ca. A.D. 400, indicate that it remained standing into at least the fifth century (ibid.: 135–8). At Gloucester, there is an equally problematic building excavated at 63–71 Northgate Street that, it has been argued, functioned as a temple. The excavations indicated floor resurfacings that sealed coins of the fourth century and changes to the internal walls, these seemingly being converted into arcades or colonnades in a later period (Hurst 1972: 65). This would demonstrate use well into the fourth century and perhaps beyond.[14]

That the use of temple buildings in the Roman period was variable, with many activities taking place within and around them (Stambaugh 1978), makes studying their function in the late Roman period more complex. It is perhaps overly simplistic to rely on historical documents such as the Theodosian Code, which banned the use of temples for pagan religion and ordered their preservation for alternative use, to date the end of use of the buildings (see Section 3.2.3 for these code entries). There are well-known examples in Rome where temples were converted into churches (Webb 2000), but there is very limited evidence in Britain for such use of these structures. Examples include the temple of

---

[13] The presence of a sculpture of Bacchus led Henig (1998) to suggest that the building had now become a *bacchium*. Croxford's (2003) analysis of the material from this building, however, suggested that the large number of sculptures found in the excavations indicated that they had been collected together from other places and brought to the building. He doubts whether any of the sculptures can be used to describe a definite use of the building, although clearly something was going on here.

[14] Rural temples demonstrate similar complex evidence for late use, often beyond apparent evidence for their structural decay, including such important sites as Hayling Island (Downey et al. 1979) and Uley (Woodward and Leach 1993).

Fortuna Virilis, which became the church of Santa Maria ad Gradellis between A.D. 872 and 880, and the church of San Nicola, which was constructed in the *Forum Boarium* out of the parts of three adjoining temples (Hansen 2003: 182). It is not easy to determine similar processes in Britain, and the location of temples within the townscape and wider ritualised landscapes may also be an important reason why some of the sites remained in use. It is important not to see evidence of structural decay as always indicating the end of the value of a site.

5.6 The *macellum*

The *macellum*, a market building (Sear 1982: 31) generally consisting of rows of rooms around a courtyard, would also have been a location for social interaction. Only a few examples of *macella* have been identified in Britain (Table 5.5), although open spaces such as gravelled areas were probably also used for market activities. Buildings identified as *macella* through their structural plan of a central space with small 'shops' around the outside have been found at Verulamium (Niblett 2001: 77),[15] Wroxeter (Ellis 2000), Cirencester (Holbrook 1998), and Gloucester (Rhodes 1974: 31). Positive evidence of the function of these known buildings is lacking and their identification is not always secure. At Wroxeter, the plan of the building does suggest a *macellum*, with small rooms around three sides of a courtyard and the fourth side fronting Watling Street (Ellis 2000). Surviving traces also point to an upper storey, but it is not possible to discern the functions of individual rooms. What is revealing is that the building was an integral part of the bathhouse complex, which indicates some of the wide range of activities that would have taken place in this *insula*. At some towns, the evidence is much more limited, as at Cirencester, where the site of a *macellum* has been suggested only through an exposed colonnaded external portico with possible rooms to the rear (Holbrook 1998: 180).

Where *macella* have been identified they do appear to have continued to a late date, which might indicate continued market functions within the town. Pits containing food and craft waste have come from late phases of the *macellum* at Wroxeter (Barker et al. 1997: 55–7), and glass-working waste has come from the *macellum* at Leicester (Cooper n.d.; Wacher 1995: 362). There is also evidence of timber structures built within and around public buildings in the late Roman period that have produced evidence of market activity, indicating that this took place in locations other than *macella*.[16] At Verulamium, alterations to the *macellum* in the late third to fourth century included the addition of two central walls with piers that divided the building into three aisles. There is no definite evidence of the demolition of this building in the Roman period, and there remains the possibility that it continued to stand into post-Roman times (Niblett 2005a: 105).

At Cirencester, use of the *insula* II structure continued into the fifth century with new floors and structural changes (Holbrook 1998: 183–5). Another possible *macellum* at Gloucester appears to have received new floors and a reconstructed verandah during the

---

[15] For Verulamium, Niblett (2005a: 105) has recently suggested that a structure identified as a *macellum* may instead have functioned as a *nymphaeum* because water management seems to have been a major preoccupation throughout the life of the building. This is still uncertain but it does emphasise further the problem of assuming the function of archaeological structures with little supportive evidence.

[16] Market activities, of course, will have taken place in many locations, including open areas (e.g., Heybridge, Essex), late pre-Roman period open places, and Roman *fora*.

TABLE 5.5. *Details of the known date of the latest structural alterations and demolition of the* macella *in each town*

Town	Alterations	Date of demolition	References
Aldborough	No *macellum* known	Uncertain	
Brough-on-Humber	No *macellum* known	Uncertain	
Caerwent	No *macellum* known	Uncertain	
Caistor-by-Norwich	No *macellum* known	Uncertain	
Canterbury	No *macellum* known	Uncertain	
Carmarthen	No *macellum* known	Uncertain	
Chelmsford	No *macellum* known	Uncertain	
Chichester	No *macellum* known	Uncertain	
Cirencester	Structural alterations in the 3rd and 4th c. and continuation of use into the 5th c.	It is uncertain whether or when the structure was demolished	Holbrook (1998: 186)
Colchester	No *macellum* known	Uncertain	
Dorchester	No *macellum* known	Uncertain	
Exeter	No *macellum* known	Uncertain	
Gloucester	New floors and reconstruction of the verandah in the 3rd or 4th c.	It is uncertain whether the structure was demolished	Rhodes (1974: 33)
Leicester	Fire destroyed some of the building in the late 4th c. but there is evidence of the continuation of activity in some parts	Fire damaged occurred in the late 4th c. but it was not demolished	Cooper (n.d.); Wacher (1995: 362)
Lincoln	No *macellum* known	Uncertain	
London	*Macellum* remains problematic	Uncertain	
Silchester	No *macellum* known	Uncertain	
Verulamium	Structural alterations occurred in the late 3rd to 4th c., including the addition of two central walls with piers that divided the building into 3 aisles	Demolition is uncertain; it may have remained standing into the post-Roman period	Niblett (2005a: 105)
Winchester	No *macellum* known	Uncertain	
Wroxeter	Repairs and new floors were laid in the 3rd c.	Destruction and robbing possibly took place in the 4th c.	Ellis (2000: 57–8)
York	No *macellum* known	Uncertain	

late third and fourth century (Rhodes 1974: 33). The *macellum* at Leicester suffered from fire in the fourth century but there are some indications of repair work, including new floors laid over the debris (Cooper n.d.; Wacher 1995: 362). At Wroxeter, the *macellum* has evidence of new herringbone floors laid in the late third to early fourth century (Ellis 2000: 55–6), and the structure remained standing in the fourth and fifth centuries and possibly beyond.

5.7 *Mansio* buildings

Mansiones were the official stations in the *cursus publicus* system across the Empire, although it was not always the case that a specifically built structure was used for this purpose (E. Black 1995: 9). There is no detailed description of a *mansio* in literary sources, making identification difficult (ibid.: 17).[17] In Romano-British towns, recognised *mansiones* take the form of large courtyard structures, usually near the edge of the town on the road network, although it is not always possible to distinguish them from courtyard houses with complete certainty. *Mansiones* may have had a wider variety of functions than the specific role that they played in the *cursus publicus*, over time acquiring other functions such as providing the setting for transactions of local government (ibid.: 94). Black draws particular attention to the tripartite entrance hall identified in the plan of some *mansiones*, including those at Silchester and Verulamium, and discusses the likelihood that the main hall would have been used for formal functions of government. Their prominent positions within some towns where few or no other public buildings are yet known, such as Chelmsford (Drury 1988) and Godmanchester (H. Green 1975), indicates that they probably performed some similar functions to the *forum–basilica* complexes here. In some cases 'small towns', such as Brandon Camp and Leintwardine, developed around *mansiones* (E. Black 1995: 29–30).

Possible *mansiones* have also been identified at Aldborough, Canterbury, and Carmarthen, although very little is known about the structures because of the small scale of the excavations. At Wroxeter, a possible *mansio* has been recognised through aerial photography and geophysical survey (White and Barker 1998: 75), whereas excavated examples come from Silchester (Boon 1974: 81), Verulamium (E. Black 1995: 81–2; Wheeler and Wheeler 1936: 95), and two at London (Bateman 1998: 56; Cowan 1992). A courtyard structure has recently been excavated at Leicester on the Vine Street site, in the northeast section of the town. The plan and location of the building suggests that it may have been a *mansio* or alternatively it could simply have been a townhouse (T. Higgins personal communication).

Of the identified buildings (Table 5.6), there would appear to be a number in which at least part of the building remained standing into the fifth century and beyond, including the Leicester Vine Street building and the Chelmsford, Southwark (London), Silchester, and Verulamium buildings. There is insufficient data on the *mansiones* in Aldborough,

[17] Black (1995: 17–18) uses the *mansio* at Inchtuthil as a type-site for examining evidence for *mansiones* in Britain, although there is no documentary or epigraphic evidence stating that this was definitely a *mansio* itself. Features included barrack-like buildings for accommodation, an entrance hall, a bath building, possible stabling, and yards. Some rooms with under-floor heating were interpreted as higher-class accommodation. It lay near the fortress gate and next to the main road.

TABLE 5.6. *Details showing the known date of the latest structural alterations and demolition of the known* mansiones *within each town*

Town	Alterations	Date of demolition	References
Aldborough	Very little is known of the structure because of the small scale of the excavation in the 19th c.	Uncertain	North Yorkshire Sites and Monuments Database record: MNY 11278
Brough-on-Humber	No *mansio* known	Uncertain	
Caerwent	No *mansio* known	Uncertain	
Caistor-by-Norwich	No *mansio* known	Uncertain	
Canterbury	There is a possible *mansio* on the Tannery site but very little is known about it	Uncertain: very small area excavated	P. Blockley (1987: 314)
Carmarthen	Changes evident in the 3rd c.	Evidence of wall-robbing in the early 4th c. and reuse of the site in the A.D. 350s; other parts of the site may have remained standing	H. James (2003: 201–3)
Chelmsford	There is evidence of rebuilding and repairs in the late 3rd and early 4th c.	Evidence of destruction and robbing, possibly not until the early 5th c.	Drury (1988: 34)
Chichester	No *mansio* known	Uncertain	
Cirencester	No *mansio* known	Uncertain	
Colchester	No *mansio* known	Uncertain	
Dorchester	No *mansio* known	Uncertain	
Exeter	No *mansio* known	Uncertain	
Gloucester	No *mansio* known	Uncertain	
Leicester	Possible *mansio* building at Vine Street; it appears to have structural changes well into the 4th c. and possibly later	Uncertain of date of demolition or destruction; appears to be in the post-Roman period	T. Higgins (personal communication)
Lincoln	No *mansio* known	Uncertain	
London	Old Bailey site: possible *mansio* built on site of an earlier building in the 3rd c.	Possibly demolished in the mid-4th c. with the latest coin on site being A.D. 335–41	Bateman (1998: 56)

(*continued*)

TABLE 5.6 *(continued)*

Town	Alterations	Date of demolition	References
	Southwark Street: evidence of rebuilding and structural alterations in the 3rd and into the 4th c.	Part of the building was demolished and robbed in the earlier 4th c.; other parts appear to have remained standing much later and possibly into the post-Roman period	Cowan (1992: 53–61)
Silchester	*Mansio* within *insula* VIII but little is known about the phases of activity as a result of the early date of the excavations	Uncertain; appears to have remained standing at least into the 4th c.	Boon (1974: 81)
Verulamium	The structure appears to have been altered in the early 4th c. with the extension of rooms and a tripartite entrance hall	The date of destruction or demolition is uncertain; it probably remained standing into the post-Roman period	E. Black (1995: 81–2); Wheeler and Wheeler (1936: 95)
Winchester	No *mansio* known	Uncertain	
Wroxeter	Possible *mansio* identified through aerial photography and geophysical survey	Uncertain: the building has not been excavated	White and Barker (1998: 75)
York	No *mansio* known	Uncertain	

Canterbury, and Carmarthen to be certain about their late use. Parts of the *mansio* at Southwark appear to have been demolished in the early fourth century, but other parts of the structure (mostly beyond the limits of the excavation) seem to have remained standing and in use to a much later date (Cowan 1992: 60–1). That *mansiones* probably had a number of roles adds complexity to understanding their use in the later Roman period. If *mansiones* did take on some formal functions of local government, as argued by Black (1995: 94), then this role may have become more significant in the late Roman period in some towns if the *basilica* was no longer used for such functions.

5.8 Porticoes

Porticoes and colonnades were public structures in their own right, but they were also used to define the spaces of other buildings. Porticoes were used to surround many public buildings, including *fora* and temples, but they also provided monumental walkways around *insulae* and became places to congregate, shelter, and sell wares (Anderson 1997: 247–9); they were an influential part of daily life and invited people to meet and interact (Zanker 2000: 39; Perring 1991b: 280). They connected one public building with another, and they played a part in the movement of people around the town (MacDonald 1986:

117–18). Porticoes were classical forms of town organisation but it seems there were fewer in Romano-British towns than in the towns of other provinces.[18]

Known porticoes in Britain include those outside the St. Margaret's Street bathhouse and around the temple precinct in Canterbury (Bennett 1981; K. Blockley et al. 1995: 98–100), in front of buildings in *insulae* XIV and XXVII at Verulamium (Frere 1983: 84, 203), around the baths complex at Wroxeter (Ellis 2000: 19–25), and in front of the *forum* at Lincoln (M. Jones 1999: 66).[19] Their association with the classical world has meant that evidence of their demolition or change of use in the towns of Roman Britain in the late Roman period is often considered to represent decline. There is some evidence that porticoes along streets and attached to public buildings were transformed in the late Roman period. Rather than decline, however, the evidence could indicate vitality with a more intensified use of space. Many of the porticoes that were originally free from material, suggesting that they were kept clear in the Roman period, now have evidence of timber stalls and activity continuing into the fifth century; such is the case at Wroxeter, Canterbury, and Leicester (K. Blockley et al. 1995; Ellis 2000: 58–68; Cooper n.d.). This activity within the porticoes will have had an impact on movement around the towns, but it also represents vibrancy and the continued importance of the town centres.

5.9 Monumental arches

Monumental arches also played a role in the organisation of space and the regulation of movement of people within the town (MacDonald 1986: 74–6). Arches were mechanisms of transition and also connected areas of the town (ibid.: 32, 74). Evidence from Rome shows that monumental arches were often decorated with scenes and images celebrating the emperors and important military victories (J. Ward-Perkins 1981: 429–30). There were sometimes four-square arches (*quadrifrons*) positioned at armature junctions; these structures were also sometimes placed at spots where significant actions had taken place in the past (ibid.: 87–91). Very few monumental arches are known in Britain, but it appears that the Balkerne Gate in the town walls at Colchester was originally a monumental arch prior to the construction of the defences (P. Crummy 1984: 15, 122), whereas at Verulamium, it seems that three monumental arches marked boundaries of earlier forms of the settlement (Frere 1983: 75–9; Wheeler and Wheeler 1936: 76–8, 129). Another arch is known from London, represented by monumental stone reused in a fourth-century section of the town wall (Blagg 1980).

It appears that the identified examples did undergo changes in the late Roman period. The remains of the arches at Verulamium are very scanty because of heavy robbing, which probably took place within the late Roman period (Frere 1983: 75–9). This would indicate changes in the organisation of the town but there is also evidence of much activity taking place in the town at a contemporary date. A monumental arch in London is known only through the stonework used in later structures (T. Williams 1993), but its demolition certainly did not indicate the decline of the town.

---

[18] They were probably also found only rarely in 'small towns'. An example in timber was possibly found surrounding a gravelled area in Godmanchester (H. Green 1975).

[19] At Lincoln known remains of the portico in front of the *forum* have been termed the 'Bailgate colonnade' and the column positions are marked out in the modern road and pavement (M. Jones 1999: 66).

5.10 Town gates and town walls

Town gates will also have functioned as zones of passage and transition. They were on the town boundaries, which will have been defined through ceremony and ritual at the time of town foundation. Rykwert (1976: 136) describes the *pomoerium* at Rome, a strip of land used to define the town and build the town walls. This boundary had religious significance: the 'gates were bridges over a forbidden tract of earth charged with menacing power' (ibid.: 137). Crossing the town boundary will have been an act imbued with meaning (Perring 1991b: 282). As Rykwert states (1976: 139), 'to cross over such a bridge [the passage through the *pomoerium*] is in itself a religious act'. The gates marked the only sanctioned crossing points and the town walls would have had a symbolic as well as functional importance.

For Rome we have sources referring to gods associated with the gates and boundaries of the city – Janus was the god of the gates (ibid.: 137–9). Although this probably applied to towns across the Empire, we have no definite evidence relating to Britain. Creighton's (2006) work has argued for the ritual foundation of towns in Roman Britain (see Chapter 4), and evidence of religious deposits also indicates that boundaries around settlements were meaningful in prehistory (e.g., J. D. Hill 1995b; Hingley 2006b). Gibbon's impression of city gates (Chapter 2) reflects the view that they represented markers and the boundaries of civilisation, with barbarity lying outside. Knowledge of town gates in Roman Britain varies greatly. Remains of gates have survived at Silchester (Fulford 1984), Lincoln (M. Jones 2002: 59–60), and Caerwent (Ashby et al. 1904; Manning 2003), whereas those at towns such as Leicester (Cooper and Buckley 2004) have survived poorly as a result of intense later occupation.

Many of the defensive circuits around Romano-British towns were constructed earlier than in other provinces and began as earthworks, for example at Caerwent (Manning 2003: 168–73), Verulamium (Niblett 2001: 71–2), and Wroxeter (White and Barker 1998: 98). They were then replaced with stone walls that usually followed the same circuits rather than reducing the size of the enclosed area, as often occurred in late Roman Gaul. Mattingly (2006a: 332) has suggested that the continued importance of these large enclosed areas might indicate links with memories of a proto-urban past in Britain. Other authors have also raised the possibility that Roman town walls might invoke the past of *oppida*, with the size of the enclosed area having more to do with Iron Age notions of power and display than with the desire to be seen as Roman (e.g., White and Gaffney 2003: 231). This may also relate to the need for large open gatherings and sales of produce and livestock as part of the function of these sites.

In a few cases there is evidence from the late Roman period that town gates were blocked (Table 5.7); this has been explained in terms of increased insecurity and economic decline (e.g., Ashby et al. 1904: 92). The example of the Ridingate (or Riding Gate) at Canterbury, however, indicates that despite the blocking of part of the gateway in the late third century (P. Blockley 1989: 130), the structure continued in use, now being used for metalworking (see Chapter 7). At Caerwent and Silchester there is some structural evidence of blocked gates (e.g., Ashby 1906: 111–12; Fox and St. John Hope 1894: 237), as there also is at Colchester with the Balkerne Gate (P. Crummy 1984: 122–3). Rather than being signs of the decline of order and civilisation, the alterations to gates represent changes in the organisation of space, and as such are similar to changes to monumental arches, porticoes, and

TABLE 5.7. *Details of the town gates known to have been blocked or demolished in the late Roman period*

Town	Gate	Evidence of blocking	Date	References
Caerwent	South Gate	Blocking with a well-built and mortared stone face	Late 3rd c.	Ashby (1906: 111–12)
	North Gate	Blocked when the gate was already ruinous and included reused material	4th to 5th c.	Ashby et al. (1904: 92)
Canterbury	Ridingate	South carriageway blocked and the space used for metalworking	Late 4th c.	P. Blockley (1989: 130)
Colchester	Balkerne Gate	Demolition of the monumental arch along with part of the northern footway and then the construction of a thick wall filling the gap	Uncertain; probably late Roman	P. Crummy (1984: 122–3)
Silchester	South Gate	Rubble found between the in-turns of the gate	Uncertain	Fulford (1984: 75)
	South East Gate	The rear face of the blocking within the gate has survived; indicates courses of flints and *tegulae*	Uncertain; probably late Roman	Fulford (1984: 76)
	West Gate	Fragments of stonework were found by the West Gate especially associated with the south carriageway	4th to 5th c.	Fox and St. John Hope (1890: 756–7); Fulford (1984: 75)
Verulamium	Chester Gate	A thick layer of burnt material containing roof-tile, suggesting a partial destruction of the gate	Late 4th c.	Wheeler and Wheeler (1936: 70)
	London Gate	Extensively robbed	4th c.	Wheeler and Wheeler (1936: 66–7)

colonnades; certainly at all of these towns there is still considerable evidence of activity at the time of the changes in the late third and fourth centuries.

5.11 Statues

Another way in which space was organised was by the placement of statues around and within public buildings and towns. Very few are known in Britain, although there may originally have been many more (Table 5.8). Remains of statue bases have been found within the *fora* at Silchester, Wroxeter, Verulamium, Chichester, and Gloucester (Atkinson 1942: 104–6; Down 1988: 31; Frere 1983; Fulford and Timby 2000: 55–6; Hurst 1999b: 158). Pieces of bronze statuary have come from public buildings in Cirencester, Gloucester, and Silchester, probably indicating that they were recycled in metalworking activities. Their removal may represent a change to the classical order of towns (cf. MacDonald 1986) but also implies new priorities and uses of the buildings at this time.

5.12 Discussion

Evidence of the changing structural nature of public buildings in the later Roman period, including the partial demolition of some sections of them, can be seen across the Empire. Of the public buildings excavated at Amiens (*Samarobriva*) in *Gallia Belgica*, for example, part of the public baths (les thermes de la rue de Beauvais) was demolished around A.D. 275 but the rest remained standing and in use (Frezouls 1982: 90). The amphitheatre was incorporated into the town walls and its external entrances blocked, although it remained usable (Bayard and Massy 1983: 222). In Paris (*Lutetia Parisiorum*), *Gallia Lugdenensis*, there is evidence of new walling and a reshaping of the entrance of the *forum–basilica* in the late third or fourth century (Busson 1998), indicating its continued importance within the town.

Although late Roman phases of buildings are increasingly being documented, as at Amiens (Bayard and Massy 1983), Paris (Guyard 2003), and Arles (Heijmans 2004), there is seldom much debate regarding the length or importance of use of the buildings in the late Roman period (e.g., Beaujard 2006). A rare example concerns the bathhouse of the rue du Languedoc in Toulouse, where an examination of pottery from the site led Baccrebère (2001) to argue that use of the building continued into the fifth and possibly sixth century, whereas Bouet (2003: 307) argued for the more conventional complete abandonment in the fourth century.

In Spain, the varied and complex ways in which public buildings continued to be used in the fourth and fifth centuries and later can be seen in the case of the *forum–basilica* of the upper town at Tarragona (*Tarraco*). Here, inscribed statues erected by provincial governors and other high-ranking officials in the first half of the fourth century (Arce 2002: 54; Keay 1996: 28–9) indicate a continuation in the original use of the *forum–basilica* and maintenance of the organisation of space.[20] In the fifth century some *forum* paving stones were removed and refuse pits dug, but in other parts the paving remained, indicating the main area continued in use. There is also evidence of market activities and light industry

[20] An inscription dating to A.D. 472 to Anthemius and Leo, found at an early date in the town, may also have come from the *forum*, although this cannot be proven with certainty (Aquilué Abadías 2004: 53).

TABLE 5.8. *Details of the known evidence of statues placed within the* forum–basilica *complexes of the towns of Roman Britain with some additional information from other buildings*

Town	Public building	Evidence	Date	References
Chichester	*Forum–Basilica*	The base of a possible statue or column of Jupiter was found within the location of the *forum*	Possibly 3rd c.	Down (1988: 31)
Cirencester	*Forum–Basilica*	A bronze eye from a statue was found in the 19th c. and may represent a statue that was cut up in the 4th c.	Uncertain	Holbrook (1998: 108–9)
Gloucester	*Forum–Basilica*	On the east side of the courtyard was a substantial base (approx. 4 × 3 m) of finely cut oolitic limestone blocks joined by anathyrosis; the base had been rebuilt with reused material in the late Roman period, suggesting that the statue may have remained in place to a late date; cut up fragments of a bronze statue were also found in the locality	Early 2nd c. onwards	Hurst (1999b: 158)
Lincoln	Pre-*Forum–Basilica* temple?	Evidence of statue bases on a paved floor	1st c.	M. Jones (1999: 169–70)
Silchester	*Forum–Basilica*	Remains of a brick foundation set on the gravelled surface in the *forum*; this may have been an altar base instead	1st c.	Fulford and Timby (2000: 55–6)
	Forum–Basilica	Bronze statue fragments were found within the *basilica*	3rd to 4th c.	Fulford and Timby (2000: 72)
Verulamium	*Forum–Basilica*	Statue base or podium	1st c.	Frere (1983); Niblett (2005a: 82)
Wroxeter	*Forum–Basilica*	Statue bases within the *forum*	2nd c.	Atkinson (1942: 104–6)
	Temple	Collection of bronze fragments, including pieces of statue	Late 4th to 5th c.	Bushe-Fox (1914: 2–9)
York	*Principia*	Evidence of pedestals for statues	Late 4th c.	Phillips and Heywood (1995)

in this area (Arce 2002: 54), whereas material from the pits indicates the town's vitality at this time, with pottery and other finds from the Mediterranean (Aquilué Abadías 2004: 53). Together, the evidence from this site suggests an intensification of use of the building. A similarly well-excavated *forum* is at Zaragoza (*Caesaraugusta*). Excavations elsewhere in the city have indicated changes and a reduction in civic maintenance in the fourth and fifth centuries, including evidence of the silting up of drains and loss of the sewage system, even in the *forum* itself (Cepas Palanca 1997: 162; Kulikowski 2004: 125). The discovery of a statue with a fourth-century inscription (Kulikowski 2004: 125), however, suggests a continuation of political activity, including meetings of the *curiales*. The *forum* apparently lost its paved floor at this time, indicating less emphasis on upkeep, but there was also evidence of continuing activities here, including waste in rubbish pits.

Bath buildings did not go out of use even if they lost their bathing function. At Écija (*Astigi*), for example, excavations showed that the *natatio* and *palaestra* of the baths were filled with rubble in the early fourth century, but there is evidence that the building remained standing and that these rooms and others continued in use for some other function (Keay 2003: 202). The bathhouse at Zaragoza also appears to have been no longer functioning as such by the fourth century (Kulikowski 2004: 227), but more work is needed to identify whether the building was still in use at this time for other activities. At *Tarraco* there is a fourth-century inscription (RIT 155[21]) recording restoration of the *thermarum montanarum* bathhouse by the provincial governor, M. Aurelius Vincentius (Arce 1982: 101; 2002). The actual building has not yet been identified, preventing further study, and indicating how much information about the late use of bathhouses and other public buildings is missing. From evidence available it would seem that many bathhouses ceased to retain their original function at an earlier date than the *forum–basilica* complexes. With little textual evidence, however, information has to be gained from detailed studies of the archaeological deposits.

Work across Italy and North Africa has also documented complex changes to public buildings in the later Roman period but has also demonstrated their continued use, although, especially in the areas where there has been considerable use of the sites into modern times (Christie 2006: 215), too often the late Roman phases of the sites are poorly understood. In some cases complex continuities of use can be identified such as at Terracina in central Italy, where a large church was constructed over the temple in the *forum* but the surrounding space continued to be used as a market as it was previously defined (ibid.). In North Africa the *forum* at Iol Caesarea (Cherchell) exhibited structural changes but it clearly remained an important focus of activity (Potter 1995). Leone (2007: 82–96) has demonstrated that despite the appearance of public buildings changing, the structural restoration of many of the buildings continued in North African towns until at least the end of the fourth century; it remained important that they could still be used. There appeared to be a special emphasis on the restoration of the *basilica* complexes, *fora* and *curiae*, suggesting that there was still a need for judicial and senatorial buildings. Examples include the reflooring of the *basilica* at Bulla Regia in Zeugitana and alterations to the *basilica* in Lepcis Magna, Tripolitana (ibid.: 90–2). The repairing of public baths also occurred in a number of towns, including at Belalis Maior in Zeugitana and Thysdrus in Byzacena. It does seem, then, from these examples from across the Empire, that when

---

[21] RIT = Die römischen Inschriften von Tarraco (Alföldy 1975).

economically viable, the buildings were maintained where possible. In Britain, where there was perhaps less financial means, buildings were retained as best they could but without the more monumental repair work.

Architectural changes emphasise the long and diverse biographies of buildings and their use. Movement through the buildings was an important way in which they were experienced, and it was often regulated through particular routes and rights of access. Different activities within the buildings in the late Roman period will have altered such organisation, creating new experiences and opportunities, and adding to the vitality of the places. Towns continued to contain monumental buildings that would have formed foci of attention and activity.

In Britain it appears that part of the function of the *basilica* was to house the *curia*, but it need not necessarily have met within public buildings in the late Roman period: instead smaller structures or sometimes even open spaces are possible venues. Wickham (2005: 597) has argued that it was not until the fifth and sixth centuries that the role of the *curia* in running towns and raising taxes across what had been the Roman Empire declined and ended. Civic officers became less prominent and local senators and bishops took a more central role. During the fourth and early fifth centuries, however, *curiae* are still considered to have been prominent entities within the town. With little documentary or epigraphic evidence from Britain, it is difficult to judge whether the *curiae* were still in operation. Simply looking at the architectural evidence has led to negative conclusions (e.g., Faulkner 2000a), but the absence of a fully functioning *curia* need not indicate the decline of a town. At Wroxeter (White and Barker 1998), for example, it has been suggested that the community was led by individual leaders in the late to post-Roman periods.

The insertion of a new hypocaust into the southern ambulatory of the west wing of the *basilica* at Silchester might indicate at least one area that continued to be used as offices (Fulford and Timby 2000: 75), as might the alterations to the *forum–basilica* at Cirencester. The survival of the apse of the *basilica* in London also might indicate the continuity of official use (Brigham 1992: 94–5), as might the survival of the Mint Wall at Lincoln. There were also opportunities for other types of public building, including bathhouses, to be used as *curiae* in the late Roman period, and Reece's (personal communication) analysis of the temple entrance hall next to the *basilica* at Caerwent suggests that it may have taken over the role of *curia*. If there were continuing *curiae* into the late fourth and possibly fifth centuries, then evidence of structural changes to public buildings need not be an accurate reflection of declining towns.

The continued visual impact of these structures in the surrounding landscape will have been an important element of the surviving significance of these places. This would be true regardless of whether the buildings continued to be maintained or whether some parts had been demolished. Demolition may well even have been aimed at the preservation of other sections: the process of demolition takes considerable effort, time, organisation, and resources and so was a very deliberate and considered act. Selected demolition can be viewed in terms of continued vitality and even as an act of regeneration in town centres. Similarly, Revell (1999) argues that fires within public buildings could be important stages in the life of the buildings – they allowed renewal and should not be viewed in terms of crisis or decay. It could be argued that some monumental buildings continued to exist because they were too much trouble to demolish but whilst they remained standing they could continue to be important structures within the town and put to use.

It is difficult to determine the appearance of the structures by the late Roman period –
in some cases it may have been quite different from the original designs. Nonetheless,
changes were important stages in the biographies of the buildings: viewing buildings in
static terms, in their newly constructed forms, misses the long sequences of alterations and
additions that constituted the life of the buildings (cf. Revell 1999). Many of the buildings
did eventually disappear through structural decay, demolition, and stone robbing in the
post-Roman period, although some survived longer, influencing locations of churches and
forms of settlement in the medieval period (Bell 2005). The spaces remained important
beyond the economic viability of funding structural maintenance. In E. Casey's words
(1996: 121), 'there are no places without the bodies that sustain them . . . (and) there are
no lived bodies without the places they inhabit and traverse'. The analysis of evidence of
activities within the buildings, conducted by the bodies, will argue that it cannot be taken
simply to represent declining standards but was symbolic of the continued significance of
the sites and even of generation and vitality.

CHAPTER 6

New public structures within towns in the later Roman period

Another important area to consider comprises new structures dating to the later Roman period that have the appearance of being public buildings. The most common type is a rectangular aisled building, although there are other forms, including large gravelled or paved areas. The size and location of many of these suggest some kind of public function. The rectangular aisled structures have usually been interpreted either as churches or agricultural storage buildings (e.g., Esmonde Cleary 1989; Faulkner 2000a; Wheeler and Wheeler 1936), although there is often much uncertainty about their use.

Some of the 'church' buildings were excavated in the late nineteenth or early twentieth century, and the interpretation of their function has been questioned in later times (e.g., at Silchester: Fox and St. John Hope 1893: 563–8; King 1983). The identification of churches in Britain has often been encouraged because of known events in the Empire, such as the conversion of Constantine (Mitchell 2007: 259–65) and the order to close temples in the Theodosian Code (Sirmond and Pharr 1969). Gibbon's narrative of the Christianisation of the Empire will also have encouraged people to search for churches. The identification of agricultural storage buildings within late Roman towns in Britain is also based partly upon Empire-wide events, with Diocletian reforms resulting in late Roman taxes being collected in kind, the state *annona* system (e.g., Faulkner 2000a: 112–14). As with the so-called churches, this interpretation of the function of the buildings is not always straightforward. What these structures do indicate, however, is continuing construction activity within towns, alongside alterations to and use of existing public buildings.

The interpretation of these structures has implications for our understanding of the function of towns at this time and their role as religious centres. Some archaeological studies of late Roman towns in other parts of the Empire have demonstrated that the first churches were often located away from the centre of towns, where the public buildings remained in use (Krautheimer 1983). The first church in Rome, for example, built by Constantine, was away from the centre, perhaps to avoid causing unrest amongst the pagan population (ibid.). In many cases in the latest Roman and post-Roman periods, churches gradually moved from the periphery to the town centres, making a statement of power and achievement (B. Ward-Perkins 1998: 257, 400). There is insufficient evidence from Britain to assess this pattern for the late Roman period.

6.1 Masonry aisled buildings

6.1.1 Possible churches

Much has been written about the rise and function of the Church in the late Roman town, especially on the Continent and in Italy, Africa, and the East (e.g., Leone 2007; Liebeschuetz 2000). The possible examples in Britain, however, are all problematic and no example of a church building has yet been identified with certainty in a town of Roman Britain.

Colchester (Butt Road)

A strong case for a church has been made for the extramural building excavated at Butt Road in Colchester (N. Crummy, Crummy, and Crossan 1993). This building was around 7 m by 24 m with an apse at the east end and two internal rows of post-pits indicating an aisle. There was no flooring; this may have originally been simply of sand and earth (ibid.: 163–6). Alternatively, it may have been robbed at a later date, or the removal of the floor could even represent a later change in use of the structure.

A cemetery around this building is one of the main sources of evidence used to suggest that this was a church. There were two periods of burials here, the first being pagan with grave goods and only the second, with few grave goods and the burials facing east–west, possibly being Christian (Millett 1995). The building itself faced east–west and had an apse and basilical plan, common features of early churches, contributing to its interpretation as a church (N. Crummy et al. 1993: 163–6). The dating, however, is problematic because the early-fourth-century coins, taken to indicate the construction date, had an insecure stratigraphic context (Millett 1995). Millett has argued that the building was earlier in date and possibly functioned as a pagan funerary banqueting hall rather than a church (ibid.). On balance, the earlier date would argue against the building functioning as a church when it was first built, though it may have been used as a church at a later date when the Christian burials took place.

Also problematic is the feature known as 'Hull's Pit', excavated by Hull (1958), which lay in the south aisle at the east end of the building. The pit probably dated to the fifth century, based on its stratigraphic relationship with the building (N. Crummy et al. 1993: 176),[1] and it contained a varied selection of artefacts.[2] These may simply have come from a disturbed grave (ibid.), but it is also possible that they were a ritual deposit showing continuing pagan activity on the site. Apart from the finds from this pit, there were few artefacts from the site and nothing that might help to identify its use, although a religious function cannot be ruled out. Coins indicate use into at least the fifth century, with five coins of A.D. 388–402, but the possible robbed floor indicates that use may have gone on to a later date.

---

[1] There is some uncertainty about the date of the pit. Hull (1958: 245) suggested that it was of a late-second-century date on the basis of the discovery of five coins, despite the fact that there were far more coins of the fourth century within the pit.

[2] The artefacts included a silver amulet, silver ring, iron stylus, iron knife, a possible frying pan, parts of a large bowl, many iron nails, a number of coins, pottery, some painted wall-plaster, bird bones, a piece of marble, part of a human skull, and a human thigh bone (N. Crummy et al. 1993: 175–6).

Silchester

The 'church' building near the *forum–basilica* at Silchester has also been reanalysed, with doubts raised concerning its date and function after being first discovered in the nineteenth century (Fox and St. John Hope 1893: 563–8). The building has both an apse and aisles, but with its probable third-century construction date (Frere 1975: 291) it is likely to be too early for a church in Britain. Cosh's (2004) study of the style of the mosaic within the building, comparing it with dated mosaics of similar designs, may even indicate a late-second-century date for its construction. The nave of the building has a red tessellated pavement with a square panel of mosaic of a black and white chequered scheme (Fox and St. John Hope 1893: 563–8). King (1983) suggests that an alternative, non-Christian, religious function is possible, although as yet there is insufficient evidence to identify which religion this might have been, or whether the building had an altogether different function.

Verulamium

At Verulamium, there are two equally problematic buildings. Eighty metres from the London Gate at the Verulam Hills Field site there is a structure excavated in the 1960s, around 8 m wide and at least 11 m long, with a semi-circular apse at its northwest end (Niblett 2005a: 98–9). As a result of serious erosion it was not possible to ascertain a construction date, although the surrounding area produced around twenty late-second- and third-century inhumations. These burials seem to have pre-dated the building and there was no late Roman cemetery here. The building was constructed within a mid-first-century-A.D. ditched enclosure containing both early cremations and inhumations, and objects had also been deposited within the ditches (Niblett 2005a: 98). Finds included a large piece of a *lorica segmentata* of the first century A.D. and a fragment of a life-sized statue. This may have been some kind of ritual enclosure, but whether the rectangular building also had a religious function is uncertain and there is no evidence to suggest that it was a church.

The other building was identified during a watching-brief in *insula* IX, which Wheeler interpreted as a church (Wheeler and Wheeler 1936: 122–3). There was no dating evidence for this structure but it had a basilican plan with square projections at both ends and measured around 32 m by 12 m, leading to the interpretation that it represented a church. Wheeler also stated that the 'character of the masonry . . . pointed to a late Roman date' (ibid.: 123), presumably because he felt that a building of the Golden Age would have been constructed from monumental stone blocks. The surviving material indicated walls of mortared flint with tiled courses, which need not necessarily have been late in date. Niblett (2001: 136–7; 2005a: 99) has argued that the thickened foundations at the northeast apse indicate a tall structure or tower here, and the building may have been an aisled barn with a granary. This seems the most likely interpretation but the lack of dates and artefactual evidence makes interpretation difficult.

Accounts of the martyrdom of Alban, a citizen of Verulamium, in Bede and Gildas describe the construction of a shrine on his grave. This might indicate that there was at least one church at late Roman Verulamium, but no archaeological evidence of this has yet been found; activity instead may have focused nearer the later abbey.

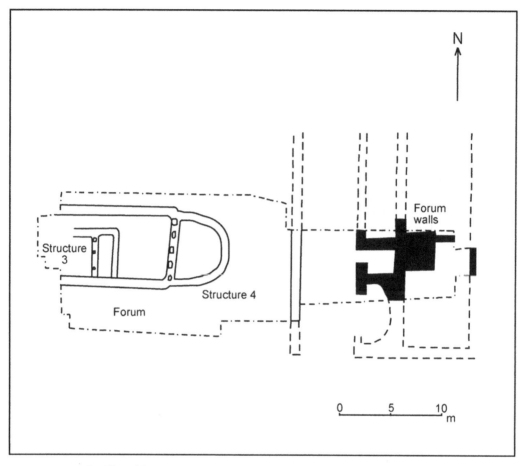

FIGURE 6.1. Plan of the excavation and timber structures at the St. Paul-in-the-Bail site within the *forum* at Lincoln. These timber structures may have been early churches, but this interpretation is uncertain (drawn by A. C. Rogers; adapted from figures in Steane 2006).

Lincoln

A problematic structure has also been found in Lincoln at the Flaxengate site in the southeast part of the lower walled town. This was a large, stone, rectangular building, apparently without aisles. Suggestions as to function have included a church, an audience or assembly hall, or a storage building, but there is no surviving evidence to allow a more definite interpretation, which only further excavation might provide (Colyer and Jones 1979: 51–4; M. Jones 2003: 129).

   The sequence of timber structures within the *forum* at the St. Paul-in-the-Bail site at Lincoln has been thought to provide more definite evidence of a church (Figure 6.1; also see Steane 2006: 154–5). Their location on the *forum* site, and proximity to a medieval church, might support this view, but the plan of the first structure in the sequence is problematic and the finds do not assist with identifying the function (Gilmour 2007: 233). The dating evidence for this building is poor: a coin of the House of Theodosius (A.D. 388–402) may either have come from the floor of the first timber building or from a late floor of the *forum*, which, in this case, would only provide a terminus post quem date

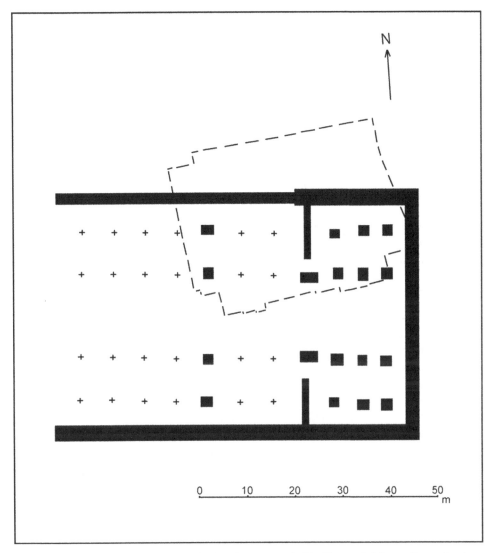

FIGURE 6.2. Plan of the excavated area of the fourth-century aisled building at Colchester House, London. The function of this building is uncertain, although a church, temple, *basilica*, or meeting chamber are possibilities (drawn by A. C. Rogers; adapted from Sankey 1998, Figure 17).

of A.D. 388 for its construction. As yet, then, no late Roman church has been positively identified in Lincoln, despite the indications of a bishop here as early as A.D. 314, recorded in the *acta* of the Council of Arles.

London

Excavations at the Colchester House site in London uncovered one section of a large rectangular stone structure with aisles that seems to have been built on a previously open site after around A.D. 350 (Figure 6.2). The dating was indicated by Portchester D ware (early to late fourth century) that was found beneath it (Sankey 1998: 78). The excavated remains consisted of a 2- to 3-m-wide exterior wall with two lines of pier or column bases in the interior, the whole being constructed on timber piles (Museum of London Archive and Research Centre record: PEP88). Because only a small area has been uncovered, neither the width nor length of the building are known but the remains indicate a large structure, which has led to parallels being drawn with churches such as the Cathedral of St. Tecla in Milan (Sankey 1998: 80). Alternative suggestions have included a civil *basilica*, audience chamber, other administrative building, or a state *horreum* (granary) used for the collection of taxes (Museum of London Archive and Research Centre record: PEP88; Sankey 1998: 80–1). There were also very few finds from the site that might help to interpret the building's function.

6.1.2 *Possible agricultural buildings*

Some of these rectangular structures have also been interpreted as agricultural buildings. This includes the *insula* IX building at Verulamium and the Colchester House building in London discussed in earlier text.

Colchester (Culver Street)

A structure excavated within *insula* XXXV at Culver Street in Colchester, which measured at least 45 m in length and 17 m wide, was probably built in the late third century (P. Crummy 1992: 112). Like the Butt Road building, it possessed two rows of columns and there is no evidence of a laid floor – it may simply have been sand or one of raised timber. The building was located near a corn-drying oven with remains of free-threshing wheat, barley, rye, and oats, which might support the interpretation of some kind of barn, although there were two adult burials placed under the north aisle (ibid.: 114). These were without coffins and were orientated north–south, which might indicate a pagan rather than Christian context (ibid.: 116). Whether the burials indicate a function other than that of an agricultural barn is uncertain. Their association with an agricultural context may be deliberate (cf. Scott 1991 on animal and infant burials in such contexts).

Verulamium

A possible agricultural building has been identified within *insula* XXVII at Verulamium. This was around 43 m long and 17 m wide; it was constructed over a courtyard structure probably in the late fourth or fifth century (Frere 1983: 226). Frere argues that it was a barn structure (ibid.: 224–5), although there is no evidence to support this with certainty.

Dorchester

Two late Roman aisled structures, built in the late fourth century, have been identified in Dorchester, one at the Greyhounds Yard site and one at Colliton Park (RCHME 1970: 560). The Greyhounds Yard structure, Building 2700, was approximately 13 m wide and 24 m long (P. Woodward et al. 1993: 80). There were few finds from the site and there is nothing to support a definite function for either building, although without good preservation it is unlikely there would be finds to indicate that they had been agricultural buildings. Unfortunately no phosphate analysis of the soils has taken place, which might have been able to provide some information on the use of the buildings. The plan of the Greyhounds Yard structure and its association with a courtyard building may suggest that a use for crop storage and processing is most likely (ibid.: 366–7).

6.1.3 *Discussion*

All these buildings represent activity within towns in the late Roman period, but the function and date of many of them remain uncertain. Perhaps they are most likely to have been put to a variety of different uses, and their function may have changed over time. These buildings, at first identified as churches, are all now regarded as problematic.

The problematic situation regarding current knowledge of the Church and bishops in late Roman Britain makes an assessment of their role in towns more difficult. Limited documentary evidence, including the *Acta Concilii Arelatensis* and the events surrounding Pelagius, suggests that towns would have been involved in late Roman Christianity, and they provide some hint as to the prominence of the Church in Britain at least by the 420s–30s. Without more evidence, however, it is difficult to say how they influenced towns in the late fourth and early fifth centuries other than that they are likely to mean that public spaces remained vibrant with meetings, markets, and other activities. In many cases this is likely to have become part of the activities that were already taking place within towns, thus intensifying the use of space. Churches will have attracted people and activities that were not only related to Christian practice, and religious leaders would have been important figures with power within the towns.

There is more evidence of Christianity within towns in other parts of the Empire that may be of use to compare with Britain. Documentary evidence for a Christian presence and for bishops in France is more abundant than that for Britain, and certainly by the later fifth and sixth century there is archaeological evidence for bishoprics in towns (e.g., Guyon 2006). There are also a number of examples of possible late Roman churches including new structures, such as within the medieval amphitheatre at Metz (Frezouls 1982: 327), and the conversion of public buildings. Excavations within the cathedral on the site of the Roman baths at Reims, for example, revealed what may have been a church and baptistery dating to the early fifth century (Bromwich 2003: 315). At Tongeren (by this time in *Germania Inferior*), a large apsidal building beneath the later cathedral may have been a church (Wightman 1985: 231) and at Trier there was a cathedral connected with the baths of Constantine (Loseby 1996: 58). At Limoges there is evidence of what may have been a church constructed on the site of a bathhouse (Knight 2001: 122).

It is often assumed that many of the temples in France were converted into churches in the late Roman period, but Heijmans (2006: 27–9) has demonstrated that this was probably not especially common. There are few definite comparable examples with the Temple of Augustus and Livia in Vienne, *Gallia Narbonensis*, which became the church of Notre-Dame-de-la-Vie (ibid.). At Toulouse, excavations of the *forum* temple suggested that much of it was deliberately demolished in the late fourth or early fifth century, but the main shell of the building remained standing and in use (Arramond and Boudartchouk 2001: 443). This may well have become a church but equally could have remained a pagan religious site. There appear to have been more cases where the *forum–basilica* became the site of church complexes in the early medieval period, such as at Aix-en-Provence, Apt, Carpentras, Cavaillon, Fréjus, and Toulouse (Heijmans 2006), but it is still uncertain in these cases whether there was also a Christian presence in the later Roman period. The extent of Christianisation within the towns of late Roman France is still uncertain, but, as in Britain, it would be useful to consider the evidence for Christianity as part of the continuation of the religious importance of these places drawing on longer-term histories of action.

There is also documentary evidence relating to Christianity within towns and to the role of bishops in Spain. There are records, for example, that church councils were held in Tarragona in A.D. 310 and 419 (Kulikowski 2004: 223). At Tarragona a fifth-century Christian cemetery to the east of the town contained a basilican building that was probably a church, whilst in the upper town a large building with parallel halls was constructed in the late fifth century, also interpreted as a church (ibid.: 221–3). A possible church dating to the fifth century was discovered in excavations beneath the cathedral of Santa Eulalia in Barcelona (Arce 1982: 94; Cepas Palanca 1997: 10). The building was on the edge of the Roman town when the major focus of the settlement was still in the area of the Roman public buildings. Only in the medieval period did the focus move to where the cathedral was later built (Granados 1995). This is similar to *Complutum*, where the fourth-century Christian complex became the settlement focus during the medieval period (Kulikowski 2004: 229), whereas in the late Roman period the public buildings of the town remained central. It appears, then, that both Christianity and pre-existing foci of power were important in late Roman towns, which may well also have been the case in Roman Britain.

Leone's valuable work on North Africa (2003, 2007) has played an important role in documenting the increasing influence of bishops and the Church in the towns there by looking at both documentary evidence and archaeological traces of church complexes and the wider activities of the Church across the towns. Churches suggest intense building activity here by the end of the fourth century, with both new structures away from the town centres and the reuse of some public buildings. The development of the Church and the growth of Christian space within Italian towns have also been very well documented because of the rich data surviving for this area (e.g., Cantino Wataghin 1999, 2003; Christie 2006). Although the strength of the Church's involvement in the continuity, revitalisation, and organisation of towns is perhaps more specific to areas such as Italy, North Africa, and Spain, the evidence does raise important possibilities for Britain, where so little evidence now survives. Another possibility for some of the buildings identified in Britain is that they were used as meeting or congregation places, not necessarily as part of Christian activity, but also indicating the continued need for such public spaces.

Agricultural storage buildings and granaries represent other functions (Esmonde Cleary 1989; Faulkner 2000a; Reece 1980). There do appear to have been some more farm-like buildings within towns in the fourth century, with land perhaps being farmed inside and outside the boundaries of the town, but these occurred mainly in areas of the settlements that were not used much in earlier periods (e.g., the Beeches Road site in Cirencester; see McWhirr 1986: 77–8). At Lincoln, excavations by the waterfront found huge quantities of cattle bones from butchery processes dating to the late fourth century (Dobney, Jacques, and Irving 1996). There is also evidence that there may have been heated buildings there, such as granaries, because the earliest example of a cockroach in Britain was found in waterlogged deposits, although the traces of the buildings themselves have not yet been located (M. Jones 2003: 103). The large-scale nature of the activities at Lincoln at this late date implies the involvement of civic authorities. An 'administrative village' model is an important economic interpretation of towns, but it tends to imply that there was little else going on within towns at this time, and this is not reflected in the evidence. An agricultural presence was probably also usual within towns throughout the Roman period in Britain (cf. Willis 2007a) and was part of the vitality of these places, including the movement of animals and harvests of grain. A related issue is the state *annona* system, a priority across the late Roman Empire (Mitchell 2007: 345–6), but without good textual or archaeological evidence it is uncertain whether it operated effectively in Britain. If it did (cf. Faulkner 2000a: 113), collection points for produce could have been in towns but more evidence is needed before the *annona* system can be linked to these buildings.

Agriculture was also associated with procreation, growth, and vitality in indigenous society (cf. Giles 2007; E. Scott 1991); this might explain such finds as the infant burials within the aisled building on the Greyhounds Yard site at Dorchester (P. Woodward et al. 1993: 57–9). The heightened importance of agriculture in late Roman towns could have been a sign of regeneration and prosperity. Whatever the function of these late buildings, they indicate that town space continued to evolve and renew itself.

6.2 Late Roman paved areas

This renewal of space is also reflected in another form of monumental structure: in the centre of some towns there is evidence of an expansive paved or gravelled area, laid down in the late Roman period. The extent of these areas points to some kind of public building function and space connected with issues of assembly and movement.

6.2.1 Canterbury

In Canterbury there is evidence that a new courtyard surface was laid over the temple precinct in the town centre during the fourth century. This consisted of building debris including sixteen different types of marble, ornamental stone, limestone, and brick (Figure 6.3; P. Bennett personal communication; Bennett and Nebiker 1989). The temple structures may have been demolished at this time (ibid.), although as only a small area of the precinct has actually been excavated, some parts of the complex could have remained standing. The new surface continued beyond the area of the precinct, over the demolished porticoes that separated the temple from the *forum*, and seems to have joined onto the *forum* courtyard itself, creating a large expanse of paving in the centre of the town (Bennett and Nebiker 1989).

The large quantity of late Roman pottery and fourth-century coins from the site indicates that the area was heavily used. Some kind of market activity is a possibility (Lyle 2002: 33), but the location of the courtyard surface on the site of a temple complex could indicate the continuation of religious ceremonies and large gatherings. The coins could either have been offerings or the result of market activity. A late-fourth- or early-fifth-century group burial on the edge of the temple precinct (Bennett 1981) may even have been the result of religious activity (see Section 8.5). There is a long sequence of activity on this site, including the late pre-Roman shrine, suggesting that this was a hugely important part of the town.

6.2.2 Gloucester

At Gloucester there is comparable evidence that the large central temple precinct, excavated at numbers 1 and 30 Westgate Street, was covered by a thick layer of metalling in the late Roman period (Heighway and Garrod 1980: 82–5). Some other discoveries in the area indicate that the surface extended beyond this site and up to the *forum*. In 1900, a builder uncovered a Roman road near the site that was covered in the same late gravelling (ibid.), so it would seem that a large central area was included in this metalling, which

TABLE 6.1. *Evidence of early gravelled areas within towns (including examples from 'small towns')*

Settlement	Location	Date	Description	References
Chichester	Underneath the *forum–basilica*	Early post-conquest date	Large area of thick gravel; may represent the levelling-up of the area prior to the construction of the central public buildings, or may have been used as an open space	Wacher (1995: 262)
Cirencester	Eastern corner of *insula* II adjacent to the *forum* and under the possible *macellum*	ca. A.D. 70 to mid-2nd c.	Metalled area formed by extension of a gravelled area of the street	Holbrook (1994: 62; 1998: 178–80)
Dorchester-on-Thames	Laid on east side of the main north–south road	Constructed in the 1st c.	Wide area of thick metalling at least 37.5 × 33.8 m	Frere (1984: 98–100)
Exeter	South Street next to the Roman *forum*	Uncertain; probably contemporary with the *forum–basilica* built ca. A.D. 80	Extensive layer of cobbling extending to at least 67 × 32 m	Bidwell (1979: 80)
Godmanchester	Laid between two roads running parallel in the centre of the settlement	Laid in the early 3rd c. A.D.	Gravelled open space of approx. 67 × 30 m; there is also possible evidence of timber arcade along 3 sides	H. Green (1975: 204)
Harlow	Associated with the temple	Constructed ca. A.D. 80	Area of graded flint pebbles creating an area extending 27.4 × 15.2 m	France and Gobel (1985: 32, 35)
Heybridge	Associated with the temple	Originated in the early 1st c. A.D.	Extensive gravelled area in centre of the settlement	Atkinson and Preston (1998: 94–8)

(continued)

TABLE 6.1 (*continued*)

Settlement	Location	Date	Description	References
Irchester	South of the temple	Uncertain of date; probably associated with the temple	The extent of this gravelled area is uncertain; possibly approx. 30.5 m²	Knight (1967: 102)
Leicester	Underneath the *forum* and *macellum*	Roman but pre-dating the *forum*; pottery over the gravelling dating to A.D. 70–120	Layer of small cobbles laid on a surface of weathered sand; size of the expanse is uncertain: there may have been a number of gravelled areas	Hebditch and Mellor (1973: 7)
London	Underneath the *forum–basilica*	Pre-Boudican ca. A.D. 50–60	Layer of metalling of gravel between 0.075 and 0.125 m thick laid on a de-turfed area; exact extent is uncertain but it was possibly approx. 33 m wide east–west and at least 40 m long north–south with an overall area of >1,320 m²	Marsden (1987); Philp (1977: 8)
Silchester	Surrounding the *forum–basilica*	Uncertain; probably same date as the *forum–basilica* built ca. A.D. 85	Layer of cobbles extending to location of the later 'church' building	Boon (1974: 110–11)
Verulamium	Outside the northeast entrance of the *basilica*	Constructed in the late 1st c. with evidence of resurfacing into the 4th c.	Wide area of gravelling stretching back to the River Ver	Niblett (2001: 135)
	Beneath the theatre and *insula* XVI temple	Laid after the Roman conquest; pre-dated the theatre, built ca. A.D. 150–60 and the temple built ca. A.D. 90	Well-maintained gravelled area continuing in use after the temple had been built and before construction of the theatre	Frere (1983: 73–4)
Wroxeter	Beyond the *forum*	Uncertain; probably same date as the *forum*	Large gravelled area	G. Webster (1975: 58–9)
Wycomb	West of the temple	Uncertain	Gravelled area with drains	Timby (1998: 297–8)

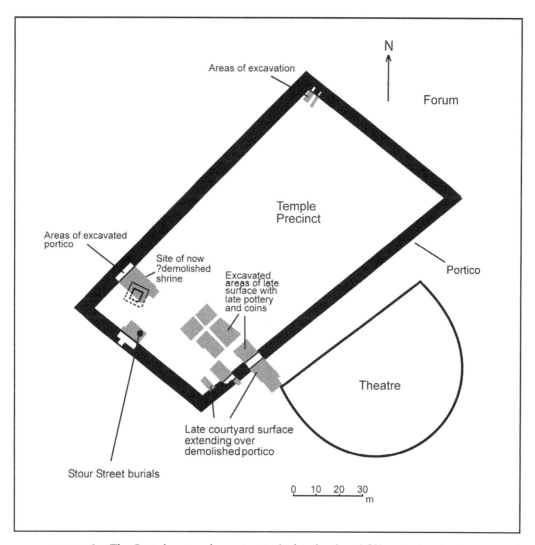

FIGURE 6.3. The Canterbury temple precinct in the late fourth and fifth centuries, showing excavated areas and the evidence for the new surface laid over the precinct (drawn by A. C. Rogers; adapted from Bennett and Nebiker 1989, Figure 2 and Bennett 1980, Figure 3).

would have demanded considerable resources and organisation. The large number of cattle bones from the site, consisting mostly of the scapula, pelvis, and femur, all showing evidence of butchery marks, suggests that animal slaughter and market activity took place here (ibid.). From the latter it can be inferred that large numbers of people came here and that other activities probably took place at the same time, including meetings and displays. It is also possible that there was continued religious activity here.

6.2.3 Discussion

Faulkner (2000a: 126–8) has interpreted these large open areas as components of towns that became late Roman military establishments used for the congregation of soldiers and supplies. There are no finds to support this interpretation but, if correct, the periodic assembly of the military need not have excluded other functions for these sites. The real extent of the security crisis at this time is also unclear and may well have been exaggerated. Open spaces also raise relevant similarities with some of the sites in the late pre-Roman period that were also foci for agricultural production, livestock, and ceremonial activities, reached by moving through the landscape.

It is significant that large surfaces areas (Table 6.1) have also been found within the centres of towns in the earliest Roman period beneath the public buildings, and in 'small towns', often associated with temples, including Elms Farm, Heybridge (Atkinson and Preston 1998), Godmanchester (H. Green 1975), Harlow (France and Gobel 1985), and Irchester (Knight 1967). They were in their own way public monuments where people met to engage in a variety of activities. In the earliest phases of large towns there is evidence of gravelled areas, perhaps fulfilling the role of the public building prior to construction. The main examples are Leicester (Buckley 2000; Hebditch and Mellor 1973: 7; Wacher 1959: 113–14) and Verulamium (Frere 1983: 73–4). These areas were probably used for markets, meetings, displays, and religious activities. They may also have been drawing on the importance of the open space in sites in the late pre-Roman period, reflecting social traditions. It is clear that monumental public buildings were not the only significant areas of towns.

Rather than being part of the decline of towns, then, these open areas symbolise a reshaping but continuation of the central spaces to meet circumstances and needs. They reflect functioning entities without necessarily having a classical form of organisation. They also drew on longer traditions of the significance of the open space.

CHAPTER 7

Industrial activity within public buildings

One of the major types of evidence of new uses of public buildings in the later Roman period is industrial activity. The nature of this activity leaves obvious traces in the archaeological record, and there were probably other contemporary uses of the space that are not represented in what has survived. The industrial evidence has generally been considered to represent the decline of the buildings, with living standards across the towns much reduced. In some other parts of the Empire, especially Italy and North Africa, however, interpretations of industrial activity are now placing more emphasis on the themes of change, adaptation, and continuing dynamism (Christie 2006; Leone 2007). For Britain, by scrutinising the evidence and possible interpretations, a different and more dynamic understanding of public buildings, and towns in general, can be proposed.

Evidence of industrial activity includes iron-working, bronze-working, lead-working, pewter manufacture, and coin production, along with glass-working and bone-working (Figure 7.1). One case of lime production, for use in mortar and plaster, was identified within the baths-*basilica* at Wroxeter (Barker et al. 1997: 96), suggesting continual structural regeneration. The vast majority of buildings with evidence of industrial activity had at least some parts of their structures still standing at this time. Metalworking constitutes the majority of the evidence so it will provide much of the focus here. Within Roman archaeology, studies have often concentrated on the practical, economic, and technological aspects of metalworking without considering the social and religious elements, which can be important for analysing its significance with regards to late Roman urban space.

7.1 Metalworking evidence

Iron- and bronze-working dominate the metalworking evidence, but there are also traces of lead-working and pewter manufacture. There is virtually no evidence of the items produced, but there are strong indications that recycled metal played a part in production.

7.1.1 The forum–basilica complex

In Figure 7.2 the metalworking evidence is shown in relation to building type. Nine *forum–basilica* complexes and the fortress *principia* at York have produced evidence of metalworking. In none of the other towns, except possibly Verulamium, has the complex been excavated extensively enough to produce similar detailed evidence. The

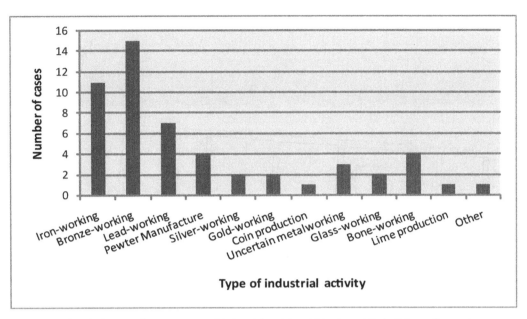

FIGURE 7.1. Graph showing the occurrence of industrial activity within the public buildings of towns in Roman Britain (drawn by A. C. Rogers).

concentration within the *forum–basilica* complex compared with other public buildings, however, does suggest a deliberate desire to focus the activity here.

At Caerwent (Figure 7.3), iron-working activity was found in Room 9 in the east end of the north aisle of the *basilica* where there was a furnace and pits containing iron-working waste; associated with this were several circular hearths, surrounded by stake-holes, within

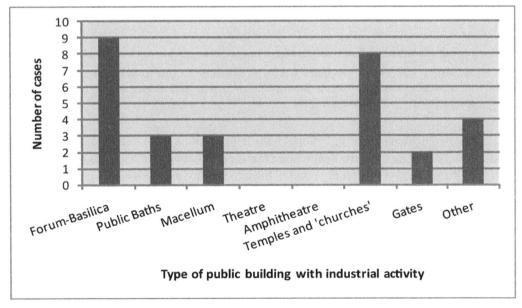

FIGURE 7.2. Graph showing the type and number of cases of industrial activity occurring within each category of public building in the towns of Roman Britain (drawn by A. C. Rogers).

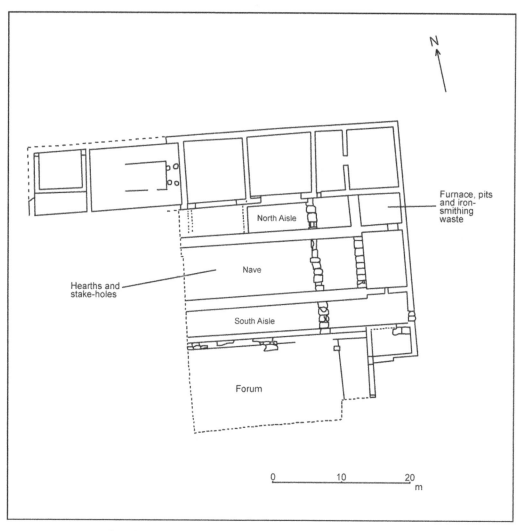

N

Furnace, pits
and iron-
smithing
waste

North Aisle

Nave

Hearths and
stake-holes

South Aisle

Forum

0   10   20
                         m

FIGURE 7.3. Plan of the excavated section of the *forum–basilica* complex at Caerwent showing the location of the metalworking activity in the fourth century (drawn by A. C. Rogers; adapted from unpublished excavation reports, P. Guest n.d.).

the nave (Brewer 1990: 82; P. Guest n.d.). The activity appears to have dated to between A.D. 330 and 360 and was then followed by the demolition of at least part of the building at the very end of the fourth or start of the fifth century, as indicated by coins of A.D. 389–402. At London, excavations at Whittington Avenue revealed a section of the east portico of the *basilica* that seems to have been demolished in the mid-third century. Hearths were then constructed here that left slag from iron-working (Brigham 1992: 91; Museum of London Archive and Research Centre record: WIV88). Contemporary with this were iron-working hearths in the east range of the *basilica* (Brigham 1992: 91). Excavations of the *forum–basilica* at Wroxeter (Figure 7.4) uncovered a furnace associated with iron slag in the east of the portico, in front of East Room A of the *basilica* against the back wall of the colonnade. Coins suggested a date of the third quarter of the fourth century and later for this activity (Atkinson 1942: 108–9). The large collection of metalwork from Room 1 of

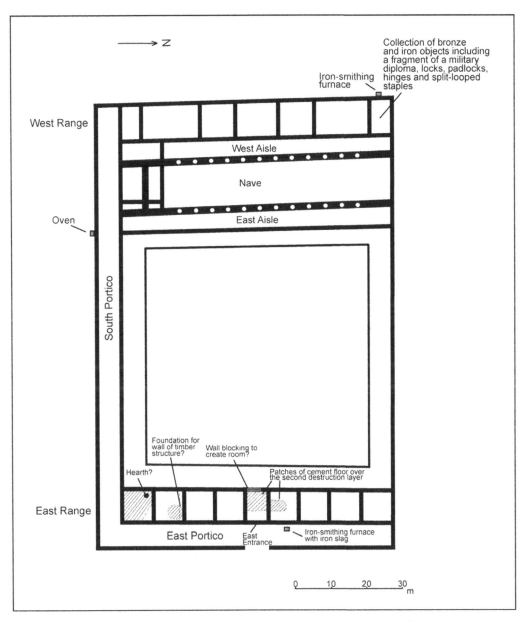

FIGURE 7.4. Plan of the late features associated with the *forum–basilica* at Wroxeter, including an iron-smithing furnace (drawn by A. C. Rogers; adapted from Atkinson 1942, plate 73 and R. White and Barker 1998, Figure 44).

the west side of the *basilica* was probably for recycling, and there was also a furnace on the outer wall of this room. At Lincoln, a clay and tile hearth, scrap metal, and slag were found in the excavations of the east range of the *forum* dating to the late third and into the fourth century (Steane 2006: 186).

Better known is the evidence for iron-working from the *basilica* at Silchester (Figure 7.5; Fulford and Timby 2000). Victorian and Edwardian excavations had removed much of the stratigraphy within the building; the extent of lost evidence will never be known. What survives consists mainly of features cut into the *basilica* make-up that contained iron slag. Altogether, 42 kg of forging slag, suggesting smithing rather than the smelting of iron, was recovered from features. These seemed to demonstrate a concentration towards both ends of the hall, with less activity in the centre (Fulford and Timby 2000: 74). Twelve of the features containing iron slag have produced coins dating to the fourth century, between the A.D. 320s and 370s, with one small pit or post-hole (F58) containing a coin of Theodosius (A.D. 383–8). Pits containing scrap from bronze-working appeared to be earlier in date, perhaps from the late third century (ibid.: 72).

Room 12 in the south wing of the *forum–basilica* at Leicester also contained bronze-working evidence in the form of a hearth and bronze fragments. This was located above the robbing of an earlier floor and can be dated by coins to the late third century (Hebditch and Mellor 1973: 18). The excavation of a small area of the *basilica* at Exeter produced evidence of a large pit, Pit 22, containing bronze-working waste dug down into the demolition debris of this part of the building (Bidwell 1979: 110–11). Broken tiles covered by a layer of burnt clay to the side of the pit appear to be the remains of a hearth, and it seems likely that the pit was dug to extract clay for crucibles and furnace linings. There is no good dating evidence for the metalworking, although stratigraphically, from the dating of earlier phases, a late date is likely – perhaps in the late fourth or earlier fifth century. Later burials dating to around A.D. 450 cut into the building near to these metalworking features, although this need not necessarily indicate that the activity had ceased.

Excavations of the southwest corner of the *basilica* building at Cirencester, Rooms 2 and 3/4, produced traces of hearths and finds of scrap bronze (Holbrook 1998: 108–9). Finds including a fragment of bronze statue in the form of an eye, found in the late nineteenth century by Cripps (1898), are suggestive of metalworking. Both excavated rooms contained coins of the House of Theodosius. This, together with the fact that the hearth within Room 3/4 seems to have been replaced by an oven, would suggest that the activity went on to a late date. Evidence for lead-working has been found at Dorchester that was probably associated with the *forum*. Its exact context is uncertain because little is known of this building, but a hearth was dug down into a gravelled surface and was associated with lead waste and late pottery (RCHME 1970). Other types of metalworking within the *forum–basilica* complexes include pewter manufacture, with moulds found in the Silchester *basilica* and the York *principia* building (Fulford and Timby 2000: 73; Phillips and Heywood 1995: 66–7). At York, the fortress *principia* has produced evidence for iron-working in the rear range with hearths, charcoal, and iron-working waste. This probably dated to the late fourth and fifth centuries, although there is little definite dating evidence (Phillips and Heywood 1995: 66–7); in the east range there was waste from bronze-working (ibid.).

7.1.2 *Bathhouses*

There is less evidence for metalworking in the bath buildings, with only three examples known (Figure 7.2), but fewer bathhouses have seen extensive excavations. In the St. Margaret's Street bath building in Canterbury both the robbed *laconicum* and the *piscina* contained evidence for iron-working that dated to the second half of the fourth century, with iron-working waste and hearths (Figure 7.6; K. Blockley et al. 1995: 185). Within the *laconicum* were three phases of timber structures associated with hearths and iron slag. The dating of these structures is problematic, although a coin of A.D. 345–8 was found in

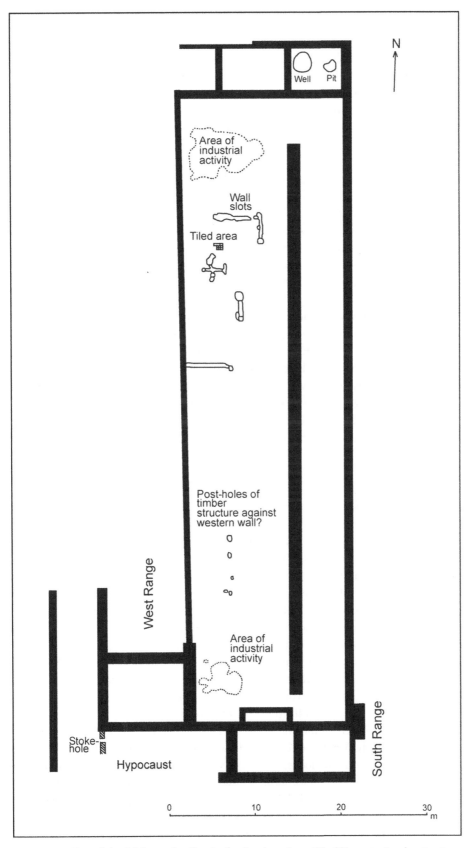

N

Well Pit

Area of
industrial
activity

Wall
slots

Tiled area

Post-holes of
timber
structure against
western wall?

West Range

Area of
industrial
activity

Stoke-
hole

South Range

Hypocaust

0   10   20   30
                                    m

FIGURE 7.5. Plan of the Silchester *basilica* in the fourth and possibly fifth centuries showing traces of timber structures, metalworking, and a possible tiled shrine (drawn by A. C. Rogers; adapted from Fulford and Timby 2000, Figure 71).

silt beneath the second phase structure and two coins of the House of Theodosius were found over the third phase structure (ibid.). It is uncertain, however, whether this layer sealed the structures or represents its use.

Iron-working was also part of the industrial activity that took place on the site of the Huggin Hill public baths in London in the late second to third centuries. This evidence was uncovered in the 1989 excavations on the site of Dominant House near Upper Thames Street (Museum of London Archive and Research Centre record: DMT88) in an area close to that excavated in 1964, as detailed by Marsden (1976). Marsden recognised no industrial activity, although it is uncertain if it was missed or if there were no traces on this site. There was also a limestone mould for pewter manufacture (Museum of London Archive and Research centre record: DMT88). It is uncertain how long metalworking took place here, but it may well have continued throughout the third century until some masonry buildings were constructed on the site in the fourth century (Rowsome 1999).

At Wroxeter, the *basilica* associated with the public baths has produced evidence for metalworking (Figure 7.7). Within the two rooms of the annexe of the *basilica* there were at least two phases of bronze-working belonging to the late fourth century (Barker et al. 1997: 72–9). There is little direct dating evidence from the annexe itself for this activity, but a coin of Gratian (A.D. 367) came from the layer within the nave believed to be contemporary in date (ibid.). The evidence within the annexe consisted of two phases of timber structures associated with hearths, casting pits, and bronze waste. From the early fifth century there is evidence of activity within the baths-*basilica* itself, consisting of timber structures, hearths, bronze and lead waste, casting moulds, and a lime pit that had later been adapted for lead-working (ibid.: 91–5).

7.1.3 *Temples*

Examples of metalworking have also come from what were probably religious buildings. Excavations at 1 Westgate Street in Gloucester were undertaken in the vicinity of what has been argued was the *peribolos* of a temple precinct (Hurst 1999b: 155–7). Beneath the demolition material of the structure were three oolitic limestone moulds for the casting of pewter and a group of iron objects suggestive of scrap metal (Heighway and Garrod 1980: 79). This demolition has been dated to the late fourth century because of the presence of late Roman pottery, including shell-tempered ware. The nature of the destruction means that there is little other evidence for the latest phases before demolition, although one hearth was uncovered, and so the extent of the industrial activity is unclear. The *insula* VI courtyard structure at Cirencester (probably a temple) had a timber structure VI.7 built within the courtyard in the fourth century associated with slag and fragments of iron as well as copper alloy (Corinium Museum Archives record: CIR 1974 K). Burnt soil and lumps of charcoal may represent the presence of hearths here.

More inferred evidence for metalworking comes from the temple at Wroxeter that was excavated in the early twentieth century. Here, a large collection of bronze and iron objects, including iron hooks, loops, clamps, rivets, around 1,300 nails, and fragments of bronze statuary, was found in a location that was described as being 'between the north wall and the pedestal in front of the podium' (Bushe-Fox 1914: 2–9). Without evidence of metalworking waste, it is uncertain whether the activity took place here or the material was collected to be taken elsewhere, perhaps to the *forum–basilica*. At the Butt Road

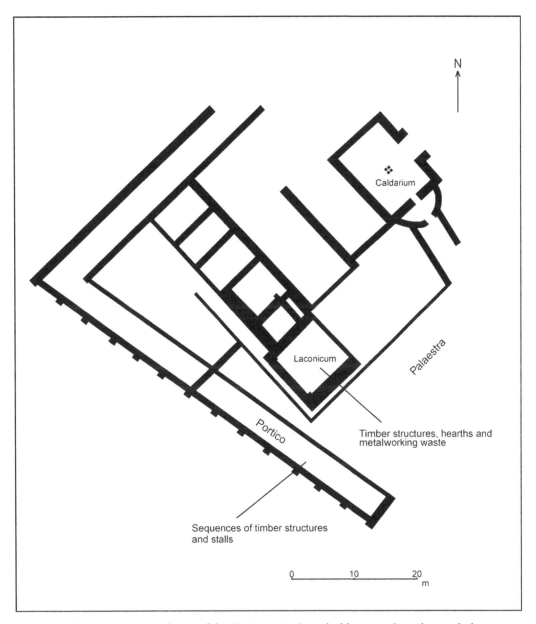

FIGURE 7.6. Plan of the excavated parts of the St. Margaret's Street bathhouse in Canterbury with the evidence for activity within the *laconicum* and portico in the later fourth and fifth centuries (drawn by A. C. Rogers; adapted from K. Blockley et al. 1995, Figure 92).

structure in Colchester a piece of lead sheet, perhaps from the roof, was found, folded and placed, probably in the fifth century, within a hole made by a removed post (N. Crummy et al. 1993: 184; P. Crummy 1997: 124). The deposition of this material within a pit, a type of context known to have received deposits (cf. Fulford 2001), may indicate that it had religious connotations, but this need not mean that it was not also intended for later metalworking.

7.1.4 Other buildings

A lead ingot was found deliberately buried in a carefully sealed pit within the late phase of a room of the Vine Street courtyard structure in Leicester (T. Higgins personal communication); this may have been ritual activity but it also suggests that there had been lead-working in the area. Further traces of metalworking have been found in the latest Roman phases of the southeast corner of this building, associated with timber structures and partitions constructed within it. Iron- and bronze-working took place here, represented by waste metal, hammerscale, and a possible hearth (T. Higgins personal communication). Also in Leicester, at the *macellum* there was a furnace in the external portico of the west range associated with a bloom of cupellation waste (15 percent copper, 55 percent lead, and with a trace of silver) apparently dating to the late fourth or early fifth century, which Wacher has argued came from the extraction of silver from coinage (Wacher 1995: 353). Although this is unproven, the bloom does show that some form of metalworking, perhaps recycling, was taking place here. Glass waste also indicates that the furnace was used for glass-working at some point. This may indicate the continuation of craft activities in the *macella* to a late date.

Excavations of the Ridingate in Canterbury, in the southeast of the town, revealed that in the late third or early fourth century the southern carriageway was blocked off, creating a room that was then used for bronze-working. Evidence consisted of ash and charcoal, a hearth base, and bronze waste (P. Blockley 1989). At the South Gate at Silchester, where there are indications that the gateway may have been blocked in the fourth or fifth century, excavations beside the gate produced waste from the working of copper alloys and lead, including lumps of metal in fourth-century deposits (Fulford 1984: 75). There were also three fragments of non-ferrous hearth bottom from lead or copper alloy working. Because no hearths were found in situ, it is uncertain whether the metalworking actually took place at the gate or whether the waste was perhaps dumped there from elsewhere (ibid.: 120).

7.2 Other industries

Unlike some other regions of the Roman Empire in the later Roman period, such as North Africa (Leone 2003), there seems to be only limited evidence for pottery and lime production within the public buildings of Britain. One lime pit has been identified within the baths-*basilica* at Wroxeter dating to the early fifth century, and this most likely relates to the layers of slaked lime discovered within the nearby annexe (Barker et al. 1997: 96). The duration of use was short, however, as the pit was subsequently used for casting lead. The small quantities of lime represented here are perhaps more likely to relate to timber building construction, such as whitewashing, rather than building in stone. Glass-working in the Leicester *macellum* has been mentioned and glass-working was also identified, together with metalworking, at the site of the Huggin Hill public baths in London (Museum of London Archive and Research Centre record: DMT88).

During what was possibly the latest phase of occupation within the monumental complex at the Winchester Palace site in London, bone-working is attested (Figure 7.8; also see Yule 2005: 76, 78–9). The stratigraphy is not entirely clear but the evidence consists of rough-cut and unfinished bone pins as well as a number of complete pins. These appear to be associated with the demolition layers of the complex, indicating that production had

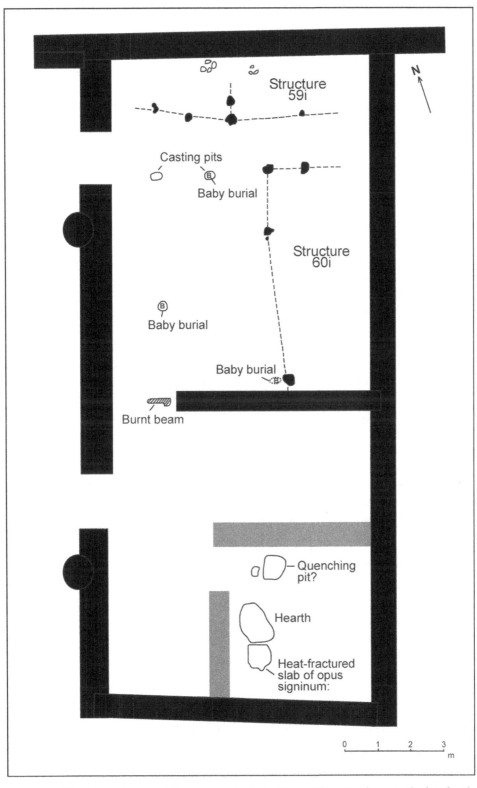

FIGURE 7.7. Plan of the Annexe of the Wroxeter baths-*basilica* in Phase W1 dating to the late fourth century, showing timber structures, hearths, and casting pits for bronze-working, and the location of baby burials that seem to have been associated with the industrial activity (drawn by A. C. Rogers; adapted from P. Barker et al. 1997, plan A61).

taken place immediately prior to demolition or perhaps within the ruins of the building (ibid.). Bone-working is also attested in the latest phases of the portico of the St. Margaret's Street baths in Canterbury, associated with the timber stalls and again from the area of the *palaestra* (K. Blockley et al. 1995: 199–201). The evidence consisted of large quantities of cattle metapodials, fragments of bones, and numerous unfinished pins. The fact that the material was fairly spread out, and that some became incorporated into later layers, suggests a degree of disturbance on the site and the possibility that the material represents rubbish derived from elsewhere. Alternatively, bone-working may indeed have taken place within the baths portico, with the waste then spread out into the nearby areas. Large-scale butchery was identified within the latest Roman layers of the fourth-century Flaxengate basilican building at Lincoln (data from the Lincoln Archaeology Services archives).

A few needles from the late phases of the baths-*basilica* at Wroxeter may indicate some kind of cloth-working. They came from floor surfaces, making it more possible that they related to activity within the building. There were three needles from the nave, one from the north aisle and one from the north portico belonging to Phase W (late fourth century), and one needle from the north aisle and two from the north portico belonging to Phase Y (early to mid-fifth century). Three further needles came from the Phase Z (fifth or sixth century) rebuild. Needles are amongst the finds assemblages from other sites,[1] although it is uncertain whether they represent anything more than small-scale needlework, were unrelated to this activity, or simply dumped on the site from elsewhere. Spindle whorls have been found amongst finds assemblages in some public buildings, but mainly in earlier periods, and some were in make-up debris and other deposits. The *Notitia Dignitatum* mentions a *gynaeceum* (cloth factory) at Venta, *procurator gynaecii (in Britannis) Ventensis* (Seeck 1876: 151), which has been interpreted as Winchester (Biddle 1975: 299), but it may well have been referring to another town. No definite structural traces have been found, although speculation has led to the suggestion that a late Roman oblong structure containing hearths and ovens, apparently built on the site of a demolished temple, may have functioned as the *gynaeceum* (ibid.).

7.3 Interpreting the metalworking

Metalworking and other industrial activities within public buildings in Britain are usually assumed to form part of the general decline of the towns and civilisation, with the buildings being taken over by degenerate activity. Rarely has it been given detailed attention and analysis that could lead to alternative possibilities.

7.3.1 Production

Very little is known about the actual items produced by the metalworking activities. At Silchester, a large number of nails were associated with the iron-working evidence, although it is uncertain whether these were a product of the activity or if they were intended for recycling (Fulford and Timby 2000: 74). A large quantity of nails was also

[1] Buildings include the Leicester *forum–basilica* in a third-century context (Hebditch and Mellor 1973), the Winchester Palace site in the 'dark earth' (Yule 2005), and the Southwark *mansio* in a second- to third-century context (Cowan 1992).

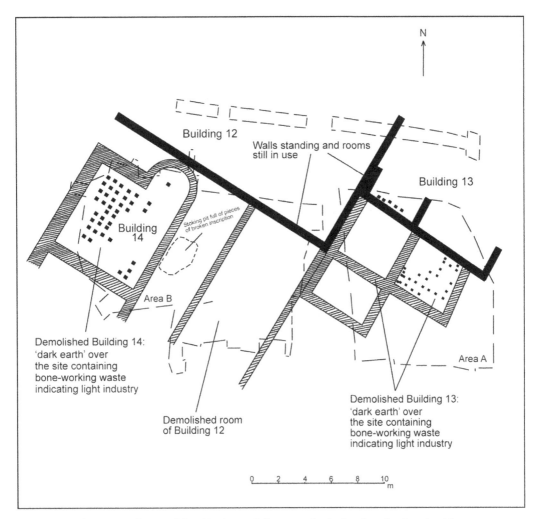

FIGURE 7.8. The excavated areas of the Winchester Palace complex in London, Southwark, with traces of possible fourth-century activity within the building (drawn by A. C. Rogers; adapted from Yule 2005, Figure 45).

found contemporary with the metalworking debris at Lincoln (Steane 2006), although again their relationship to the process is uncertain. It has been suggested that iron nails were amongst the products of the iron-working in the *basilica* at Caerwent, because there were nails in the debris here (P. Guest personal communication). The production of nails would clearly have been of considerable importance in the maintenance and construction of town buildings including new timber structures. The ritual connotations of nails (see Section 7.3.3) may also suggest that the character of production had symbolic elements.

In a few rare instances mould fragments have been found. Brown (1976) has highlighted the lack of surviving mould debris from known bronze-casting workshops of the Roman period. The small number of finds need not reflect the level of activity. Within the *basilica* at Silchester, though unstratified, half a mould for casting copies of the coins of

Tetricus II (A.D. 273–4) was recovered (Fulford and Timby 2000: 72).[2] The oolitic limestone moulds from the temple building at Gloucester were for casting pewter vessels (Heighway and Garrod 1980). Limestone moulds also came from the site of the Huggin Hill baths (Museum of London Archive and Research Centre record: DMT88) and from within the *basilica* at Silchester (Fulford and Timby 2000: 73), which in both cases seem to have been for the production of bronze or pewter vessels. A fragment of a pewter vessel mould was found amongst the metalworking waste in the *principia* at York (Phillips and Heywood 1995: 66–7). It was not possible to determine the type of object made within the casting pits of the baths-*basilica* annexe at Wroxeter (Barker et al. 1997: 81–6). The limited data available do not provide much evidence for the objects that were manufactured. However, it seems that the metalworking involved the production of items for use – iron tools, bronze objects, pewter vessels, and even coins – and structural parts for repairing or constructing buildings.

Most of the evidence for iron-working within public buildings is for smithing rather than smelting, which can be identified through the waste material (Richards 2000: 421). This suggests that iron objects and structural parts were being recycled. The collection of scrap metal has implications for the role of towns, and recycling iron requires resmithing at very high temperatures, which demands significant organisation and skill, whereas bronze can be remelted and reshaped at lower temperatures, making this technologically easier (Tylecote 1976: 22, 162–3). Iron smelting has been identified in some late contexts such as at Silchester in *insula* IX (Fulford et al. 2006), although not on the site of the *basilica*. Only one piece of bloomery slag was found on the *basilica* site, indicating that smelting is unlikely to have taken place within the building (Richards 2000: 421); this suggests that old iron objects were resmelted or new material was brought in and used.

The recycling of metal is also indicated by collections of scrap metal found in towns. The objects from Room 1 of the west range of the *basilica* at Wroxeter most probably represent a collection of scrap metal for recycling. The same is also likely for the large collection of metal objects found in the temple near the *forum–basilica* at Wroxeter in the early twentieth century (Bushe-Fox 1914: 9). Metalwork was also ritually charged (see Section 7.3.3), perhaps especially if it was intended for reworking, and may well have been treated with caution. Hoards of metal items and currency bars that could be reworked were ritually deposited in prehistory, the transformative processes of the metalworking adding to the symbolism attached to the objects (Hingley 2006b). Some of the bronze fragments from the collection seem to have originated from statuary, because there were patterns representing hair and drapery (ibid.: 2–9). Certain public buildings may have been chosen as safe depositories for scrap metal and the material may then have been taken to the central *forum–basilica* for reworking. Other bronze statue fragments associated with metalworking evidence have been found in the *basilica* buildings at Cirencester (Holbrook 1998: 108–9) and Silchester (Fulford and Timby 2000: 72). It seems most likely that towns were able to make use of a range of sources of metal and were able to adapt when new circumstances arose, taking advantage of material when it became available.

---

[2] An unstruck coin blank was also found within Roman layers, dating to the second half of the fourth century, of an enigmatic rectangular structure at Frilford (Lock et al. 2002: 76); this might suggest that coins were also copied here.

7.3.2 *Commerce*, fabricae, *and the Church*

One interpretation of the industrial evidence within the public buildings is that of com-mercial activity. Perring (1991a: 103) argues that the sites of public buildings may have remained in the ownership of the town after their disuse and that they were rented out to craft-workers to generate revenue. Without documentary evidence, however, it is not possible to know for certain whether this occurred. It is equally possible that the public buildings remained in use for public activities whilst some areas were used for metalwork-ing. A number of cases where commercial activities might be suggested include the activity within the portico and *laconicum* of the St. Margaret's Street baths at Canterbury and the porticoes of the baths at Wroxeter. The hearths and metalworking identified within the portico of the *forum* at London also faced onto the street. The metalworking within rooms in the east range of the *forum* at Lincoln could have exploited its close proximity to the street, as might the metalworking in the Vine Street building in Leicester.[3]

Some writers have argued that government control may have been an important factor in industrial activities. Mattingly (2006a: 336–7), for example, emphasises that the metal-working evidence within the *basilicae* at Silchester, Caerwent, and Exeter was relatively well ordered and indicates a regulated reuse of public space, whereas Fulford and Timby (2000: 579), discussing the Silchester *basilica*, also suggest that centralised control was important; they point to the possibility that the *basilica* was an imperial *fabrica* producing weaponry and recycling metal. This is the argument adopted by Faulkner (2000a: 128) in his discussion of urbanism in the later Roman period, which sees towns becoming centres of the state's 'total war mentality', with the establishment of military workshops making them 'gloomy police towns of an age of blood and iron' (*ibid.*: 130). Much of our understanding of state *fabricae* comes from late documentary sources, especially the *Notitia Dignitatum* (Seeck 1876). The *Notitia* indicates that the *fabricae* were highly organised establishments, many being devoted to one specific area of production, but there is nothing from any of the buildings in Roman Britain to indicate that production was geared towards any specific item of military equipment. *Arcuaria*, for example, referred to workshops making bows whereas *ballistaria* made artillery, *hastaria* made spears, and *sagittaria* produced arrows (S. James 1988). The *Notitia* does record some more general workshops, *fabricae armorum*, which produced a mixture of weapons and armour (ibid.), but the available evidence does not prove the existence of these in Britain.

The state-controlled *fabricae* are also a popular explanation for the industrial activity identified within public buildings in other parts of the Empire. At Amiens (*Gallia Belgica*), for example, part of the *forum* was levelled, probably in the second half of the fourth century, and then used for metalworking (Bayard and Massy 1983: 239, 252; Bayard and Piton 1979: 162). Parts of the building lying outside the excavation could also have been in use at this time, although further excavation would be required to provide this information. This evidence has been interpreted as a possible *fabricae* (Bayard and Massy 1983: 239, 252), but despite the *Notitia Dignitatum* mentioning the presence of a shield and sword factory in Amiens there is no positive evidence in the form of inscriptions, documents, or products from the site that can support this. The apparent continued use of the *forum* also

---

[3] Courtyard houses could also exploit their position along the streets, with outer rooms serving as workshops and shops (cf. Jones and Robinson 2004).

suggests that the metalworking, as at Silchester, was only one part of the function of the complex at this time.

The 'small town' of Argentomagus (*Gallia Aquitania*) has evidence of late metalworking in the theatre, consisting of hearths and debris, with most of the evidence concentrated within two corridors (Dumasy 2000: 218–23). It has also been interpreted as representing the presence of a military workshop for the production of armour and weaponry (ibid.) but, again, there is no positive evidence for this. It is possible that the hearths were placed within the corridors rather than the arena because they produced a lot of smoke (ibid.). This would suggest that the arena was still being used for other purposes at this time and that there was an intensification of use of the building rather than decline. Some kind of officially run factory is often favoured, because this fits in with the Empire's greater concern for defence in the later Roman period, especially in the centre of the Empire such as Italy (Christie 2006: 216, 312–13). Though *fabricae* undoubtedly existed, there is a danger in assuming the British evidence can be interpreted in this way.

The Church is another organisation that could well have taken over buildings to carry out industrial activities. Often based on the close proximity of a church, evidence suggests that they took advantage of the spaces to make goods for their own use and as an income (cf. Christie 2006: 214–17). Leone (2003) has demonstrated that, in North Africa, areas of production including olive presses and pottery kilns, often in public buildings and other public spaces, were located near churches. This suggests that the activities were regulated and organised. Moreover, these structures need not have been removed from public use entirely and may indeed have encouraged people to use these spaces more. Excavations within the theatre at Italica in Spain indicated partial robbing of the structure in the fourth century, but at the same time it continued to be used for many activities. Evidence included an oven, a series of hearths, an olive mill, and a bone workshop (Rodríguez Gutiérrez 2004). The arena was also used as a cemetery, which indicates a religious focus here and possibly a church.

It is more difficult to consider Church involvement in Roman Britain because of the problematic identification of churches, as we have seen. A lead sealing from one of the rooms in the west range of the Silchester *basilica* had a *chi-rho* symbol and the letters 'PMC' (for *Provincia Maxima Caesariensis*) inscribed on it. This might suggest a Christian presence within the building at the same time as the metalworking, although the object may not necessarily have been connected with the Church (Fulford and Timby 2000: 580). The *frigidarium* at Wroxeter, which leads directly into the baths-*basilica*, may have been converted into a church (Ellis 2000: 55; White and Barker 1998: 125), but this is uncertain and there are also the problematic timber buildings within the Lincoln forum where there was metalworking in the east range (Steane 2006: 54–7).

7.3.3 *Metalworking, space, and ritual*

Stirling (2001: 69) has argued that public buildings provided convenient locations for metalworking because of their stone walls, high roofs, and large spaces, and their proximity to roads and water. These are important considerations, but in Britain it appears that many instances of the metalworking took place within rooms or areas on the edges of the buildings or concentrated at the ends of main rooms within them, such as in the *basilicae* at Caerwent, Cirencester, London, and Silchester. This implies that central parts of the buildings were still being kept for other purposes. The *laconicum* of the St. Margaret's

Street baths in Canterbury lay in the furthest southeast corner of the baths and the *piscina* lay on the western side, so other parts of the baths may well have remained in use or have been put to different functions. People will have continued to congregate and interact in these buildings at the same time as the metalworking was being undertaken. They were not simply derelict spaces for reuse. Local governments may have continued to use the buildings and perhaps the metalworking was an aspect of their continued power. Its concentration within the public buildings, especially the *forum–basilica*, may also indicate a social role for the metalworking, perhaps drawing on pre-Roman practices, where people gathered, interacted, carried out ceremonies, and feasted, with the metalworking forming a focus to the activities.

Linked with this is the potential religious significance of the metalworking, which could have had an impact on the way in which the activities and their spatial context were perceived. Studies of Iron Age metalworking have emphasised its religious symbolism, moving beyond purely technological considerations (e.g., Aldhouse-Green 2002; Giles 2007; Hingley 1997b). This aspect has not received so much attention in Roman studies, especially of the late Roman period. Recent work on iron deposition and the significance of iron in the Roman and late pre-Roman periods is an important exception (Haselgrove and Hingley 2006; Hingley 2006b). The evidence from Roman public buildings can be analysed in the light of reappraisals of industrial processes in the past as meaningful beyond the basic parameters of economic production.

Ethnographic studies, especially on iron production in Africa, demonstrate there are alternative ways of thinking about metalworking that contrasts with Western technological and economic understanding. Though, of course, not directly applicable to the Roman West, studies have shown that iron production often involved complex rituals, with smiths sometimes holding the status of religious leaders. Haaland's (1985) work on iron production in the Sudan and Reid and MacLean's (1995) in East Africa demonstrated links between iron production and human fertility and procreation, with smelting considered a procreative act in which furnace and bellows took the roles of the sexual partners (ibid.: 149). The cognitive link between iron production, transformation, and human procreation was also the major theme of Herbert's work *Iron, Gender and Power* (1993) on the smelting rituals of a number of groups in Africa.

Other ethnographic studies connected with metalworking include Barndon (2004) and Gansum (2004), but there are far fewer studies of these aspects of technology within archaeology. Though it is not wise to use ethnography to provide 'answers' about the past, it can give examples of how actions and processes can be conceptualised in different ways, which is vital for archaeology. Moving beyond modern Western assumptions can help to demonstrate that people in the past will have experienced their worlds differently. Hingley's (1997b) study of British Iron Age iron production drew on Herbert's (1993) work to examine possible ritual activity associated with smelting and smithing sites. He examined especially the possible symbolism of passage and rebirth in the location of the metalworking on sites. Aldhouse-Green (2002) has considered links between collecting iron ore, producing iron and agricultural activity, cooking, and nourishment;[4] whilst also working on the Iron Age, Giles (2007) has examined the symbolic links between metalworking, agricultural production, and procreation. The significance of iron in pre-Roman Western Europe is

---

[4] There are also hoards of deposited metalwork, including iron sickles and cauldrons, which might indicate this link to agricultural activity and cooking, such as that from the Llyn Fawr lake in South Wales (Aldhouse-Green 2002: 13).

also implied in classical texts. Tacitus records in the *Germania* (XL.2–5), for example, that a number of the tribes worship Nerthus, a goddess of agriculture, and they could only carry out their annual festival once all iron objects had been hidden away (Aldhouse-Green 2002: 9). Blacksmiths may have had special status in pre-industrial periods, as suggested in texts from early historic Ireland.[5]

The inclusion of iron-smiths' tools within ritual hoards indicates the special significance of iron-working in the Iron Age and the continuation of these attitudes and beliefs in the Roman period. Relevant hoards include those at Llyn Cerrig Bach on Anglesey (C. Fox 1946), Waltham Abbey in Essex (Manning 1972: 231), and Fiskerton in Lincolnshire (Field and Parker Pearson 2003). The tools are usually in good condition, suggesting that they were not thrown away because they were broken; nor was the act likely to relate to changes in technology. The finds do not consist of complete sets of smith's tools, but they are often accompanied by other types of objects, which argues against their being deposited for safekeeping by craftsmen (Manning 1972: 238–9). The significance of iron-working and its products is also inferred by the large number of Iron Age and Roman date iron-work hoards catalogued and studied by Manning (1972) and more recently by Hingley (2006b). Given the symbolism attached to iron objects through their manufacture, the number of accidental losses would have been small; even iron nails had religious meaning and they were used in religious activities such as *defixio* (Dungworth 1998: 153).[6]

Iron artefacts are not the only metal items known in hoards: Poulton and Scott (1993) have documented a large number of late Roman pewter hoards across Britain often found in wells, rivers, and pits, suggesting a conscious association of religiously imbued metalwork with watery places. These hoards are often regarded simply as dinner services deposited for safekeeping (e.g., Brown 1973: 201–4; Lethbridge and O'Reilly 1933: 166),[7] but the collections rarely make sense as dinner services and they often appear unused even though this material can be easily marked or damaged. The pieces may even have been deliberately produced for deposition, which has implications for the significance of metalworking within public buildings. Likewise, Budd and Taylor's (1995) examination of bronze-working has emphasised the need to put the 'magic' back into studies of ancient metalworking and attempt to conceptualise the activities as ritual and symbolic rather than economic. The procedures of bronze-working would have been passed on through rituals and spells, and metalworking would have had a special place within prehistoric society. Like other ritual activity and ideas about space and place, this undoubtedly continued in

---

[5] The *Triads of Ireland* record that the blacksmith was associated with supernatural items such as the anvil of the mythical god Dagda. Smiths and their powers are also mentioned in recorded legends; in the *Scéla Eogain*, for example, the druid-smith is recorded putting five iron protective rings around the newly born baby of the smith's daughter (B. Scott 1984: 154).

[6] Dungworth (1998: 153–4) draws attention to records that nails were driven into temple walls to ward off evil and that curse tablets were activated by nailing. Nails are also used ritually amongst the Bakongo of Congo, where wooden statues are heavily decorated with nails (ibid.: 149). He argues that the hoard of nearly 1 million nails found at the Roman fortress of Inchtuthil in Scotland, claimed to have been preventing 'later recovery . . . by the natives' upon abandonment of the site (Pitts and St. Joseph 1985: 109–12), was more probably a ritual deposit relating to the power attached to nails.

[7] The Appleford hoard was found during gravel extraction and consisted of twenty-four pewter vessels apparently deposited in two piles, one of small bowls and one of plates. With the hoard was a group of iron objects, including a cauldron chain and steelyard, quern stone fragments, pottery mostly of the fourth century, animal bones, and parts of human skull (D. Brown 1973). Another example is a hoard of five pewter plates from a gravel pit at Shepperton, Surrey, which is likely to be an extinct watery context (Poulton and Scott 1993: 116).

the Roman period (cf. Merrifield 1987). Metalworking activities were bound up with ritual and belief, their presence within public buildings bringing notions of regeneration and renewal and forming a focus for associated activities.

Within the annexe of the baths-*basilica* at Wroxeter, contemporary with or directly succeeding the bronze-working, the bodies of four foetuses or newly born babies were deposited, one of which was directly within a casting pit and another next to a post-hole of a timber structure that was associated with the metalworking (see Figure 7.7; Barker et al. 1997: 81–6). Metalworking continued here after the baby burials, with new hearths constructed that were associated with metalworking debris (ibid.: 83–4). A further burial was in the floor near the exit from the northern half of the annexe to the southern half, whilst the fourth was that found by Kenyon in her 1930s excavations in the northwest corner of the north room (Kenyon 1938: 188). There are some classical sources (e.g., Plin. *HN* VII.15; Plut. *Mor.* 612a) referring to infant burials being placed within settlements rather than in cemeteries with graves and burial rites, because it was believed that as children the infants did not possess souls and they were not yet part of the earthly community; nothing survived them after death.

In Britain, however, there were few infant burials known in either settlement or external contexts (Philpott 1991: 97), and it is likely that local practices also continued and infant bodies were treated in a variety of ways.[8] At Silchester, for example, the bones from a minimum of four infants were discovered, apparently having been deliberately placed within pits not as complete skeletons and combined with animal bones (Snelling 2006: 200–5). The clear concentration of burials within the baths-*basilica* at Wroxeter associated with the metalworking does, then, appear to be significant, demanding explanation, perhaps relating to ideas of regeneration attached to the metalworking. At Leicester two baby burials were found in the same location as metalworking within the Vine Street building (T. Higgins personal communication), which may also support the connection between ritual and metalworking. This association may have had symbolic and ritual meanings linked with regeneration on a wider scale, the practice drawing on pre-Roman beliefs, which Scott (1991: 119–20) saw as integral to the infant burials that she studied on Roman rural sites.

In the *basilica* at Silchester (see Figure 7.5) there is also evidence that indicates religious activity associated with the metalworking. Contemporary with the phase of iron-working that concentrated at both ends of the hall, was a tiled area, laid down within the hall, now represented only by a few remaining tiles (Fulford and Timby 2000: 74–5). There were also traces of slots indicating a timber structure that may have enclosed it (ibid.). There was markedly less iron slag and other iron-working debris in this vicinity, which would suggest that it was deliberately kept clear. There was also a large number of late-third- and early-fourth-century coins in this area and two oak leaves cut from sheet lead (although one was unstratified; ibid.: 72–5, 578). These finds indicate that a domestic interpretation for the structure is unlikely and that the evidence may represent a shrine, in use at the same time as (and perhaps associated with) the industrial activity.

---

[8] The poor survival of infants in the archaeological record should also be taken into account as an important factor in the lack of known examples. There is also the possibility that there were separate areas for infant burials, as identified at Cirencester (Cool 2004: 289–90), as well as other ways of deposition such as into rivers (Barber and Bowsher 2000: 313).

Well F127 and adjacent pit F107 in the nearby north range of the *basilica* contained a large number of bird and fish bones as well as sheep bones, the remains of two neonatal pigs, and iron slag (ibid.: 69–71). Pit F18 within the northern area of the metalworking, near the tiled area, and the general occupation layer within the building (Phase 7.13) also produced a high incidence of bird bones.[9] Fulford and Timby (2000: 577–8) argue that this may relate to feasting and sacrifices taking place within the *basilica* and is unlikely to represent solely domestic occupation. Its association with the metalworking evidence points to these religious and ritualised activities being intertwined with the industrial processes. Such an interpretation may also be supported by the evidence from the rear range of the *principia* at York, where there was a late-fourth- or fifth-century horizon of young pig bones contemporary with the metalworking debris (Phillips and Heywood 1995: 64). The large assemblage of young pigs may suggest elite activities, perhaps feasting, rather than simply butchery on the site (ibid.). The deposition of waste material into pits at the end of the metalworking process, as found in the Exeter *basilica* (Bidwell 1979: 110–11), may also relate to the religious significance of the material (Giles 2007; Hingley 1997b) and tie into the broader practice of ritual pit deposits (e.g., Fulford 2001; J. D. Hill 1995a). Within the *basilica* at Cirencester, Room 1 was blocked off around the same period as the metalworking activity within an adjacent area of the building. Nineteenth-century excavations within the room by Wilfred Cripps uncovered a large number of oyster shells together with a dog skeleton (Holbrook 1998: 108). Dog burials have been associated with ritual deposits both in prehistory and the Roman period (e.g., Smith 2006), and it is possible that there was some kind of religious activity taking place that was connected with the life of the building and involving the metalworking.

The industrial activity indicates that the public buildings in the heart of the towns were real and symbolic centres of people, production, and regeneration, and that metalworking, and the rituals associated with it, represented renewal and continuity. It is even possible that the industrial activity, and its symbolic significance, was a response to perceived changes to the towns. It would also have altered movement and enriched experiences within the buildings, contrasting with earlier organisations of space, but other parts of the buildings may have been used for their original functions, indicating the intensification of use of the structures, including meetings and the *curia*. A controlling authority is likely, suggesting continued leadership within the towns as a whole. Metalworking within public buildings in the later Roman period could be a symbolic representation of the vitality of towns at this time. In the late pre-Roman Iron Age, metalworking and other activities were integrated with the elite presence and religious nature of sites (cf. Haselgrove and Millett 1997). Combining practical, political, and religious considerations, the *forum–basilica* and other Roman public buildings could have now been adapted to fit local traditions where the forge or hearth was central to meetings, networking, social activity, power, and ritual. These were places of events and actions and not the decaying vestiges of one-time greatness.

[9] Serjeantson's (2000: 500) study of the bird bones from Period 7 highlights the high proportion of these bones in the assemblages compared with other animals and suggests this is unlikely to reflect overall food consumption patterns across the town, thus indicating special activity.

CHAPTER 8

Timber buildings and 'squatter occupation' within public buildings

Timber structures, sometimes associated with industrial activity, also altered the organisation of space within public buildings whilst indicating their continued use. Other traces of activity within the public buildings are also examined here, including spreads of pottery sherds, coins, and animal bones. These remains, however, are usually considered to relate to a period after the buildings had ceased to be maintained or had been abandoned. Along with the timber structures, they have been regarded as representing the 'slum conditions' of town centres (Wheeler and Wheeler 1936: 30), squatters amongst the ruins (Collingwood and Myres 1936: 206), and a 'degenerate' situation of 'shanty towns of huts and shelters' (Faulkner 1996: 94; 2000a: 124) at a period when Roman civilisation and order had decayed and vanished. This interpretation is used to support notions of decline because it contradicts perceptions of economic vitality and Golden Age images of urbanism.

Ward-Perkins (2005: 94–5) considered timber structures to represent 'the disappearance of comfort' and the end of civilisation. His excavations on a small area of the *forum* at Luni in northern Italy, which uncovered traces of two timber buildings cutting into the robbed *forum* floor, became a well-known type-site to support his argument for the decline of towns (1978, 1981); however, Cameron (1993a: 198) sees this as applying 'inappropriate classical norms' to the evidence. An approach that avoids more negative interpretations is more helpful. Mattingly (2006a: 534) has drawn attention to the fact that the latest activity evidenced within villas is often labelled 'squatter occupation' by the excavators because of the poor survival of the remains and because it does not correlate with expected images of Roman civilisation. Instead of reoccupation within a ruined or derelict structure, however, he argues that the evidence is more likely to relate to final adaptations to the buildings. This positive approach to the material can also be taken for public buildings in towns, emphasising the continued use of the buildings. There is generally less evidence of material culture in late Roman layers, which has been a contributing factor in interpretations of the decline of towns. Fulford et al. (2006: 280), however, have questioned the assumption that a developed material culture is a necessary indicator of urbanism in the archaeological record, suggesting that such an approach hinders studies of late Roman towns where there was continuing vitality. Any surviving evidence is also likely to reflect more information that has not been preserved; thus analysis of this evidence can indicate more about activities taking place within buildings before they were eventually abandoned or demolished.

Timber structures and stalls were always a common accompaniment to *fora* and temples – the evidence of their presence in the late Roman period would therefore suggest continuing activity rather than decline (cf. Potter 1995). Potter's (1995) excavations of the

forum at Cherchel (*Iol Caesarea*) in Algeria identified what appear to have been timber stalls constructed in the fourth century, clearly indicating activity still taking place
here and use of this public area. In some cases the structures indicate additional uses to
which the buildings were being put (Wickham 2005). It must, of course, be borne in mind
here that excavation conditions can affect analysis. The five *forum–basilica* complexes with
traces of timber structures in Britain, for example, were all excavated after 1960 (Cirencester, Lincoln, London, Silchester, and Winchester). Of the complexes where no timber
structures have been found, including at Wroxeter, Verulamium, and Caistor-by-Norwich,
excavations were not undertaken to what would be considered modern standards. Traces of
timber structures may have been lost or not recognised. Positive evidence that late public
buildings did not have traces of timber structures is also important, however, because it
implies that the building spaces continued to be kept clear for other uses. Examining the
nature of the timber constructions also provides useful information regarding the state of
the public building structures themselves at this time.

8.1 Early timber phases of public buildings

Before the late Roman timber structures are examined, it is worth noting that in some cases
timber phases of public buildings have been recognised in the early stages of towns. This
includes the site of the *basilica* at Silchester (Fulford and Timby 2000: 44–58) and some
amphitheatres, theatres, *macella*, and *mansiones* (Table 8.1). Traces of timber structures of
more uncertain nature have been found beneath the *forum–basilica* complexes at London
(Philp 1977: 7–16), Winchester (Biddle 1966: 320), and Lincoln (Steane 2006). These
structures demonstrate that much remains unknown about the development of Roman
towns and the biographies of public buildings. They also raise issues of how to interpret
the public buildings of the late Roman period where there are traces of timber structures.
Timber structures were also often parts of these sites in the late pre-Roman Iron Age (see
Chapter 4). This long-term use of timber indicates that such structures need not have been
considered less significant than stone buildings.

8.2 The timber structures

8.2.1 *Buildings represented by post-holes and stake-holes*

The majority of the timber structures identified within public buildings are represented
solely by post-holes and stake-holes dug or pushed down into existing floors. This type of
evidence can often be problematic because of the dating of the post-holes and the difficulty
in understanding their distribution in the ground. An example comes from the excavations
of the *forum–basilica* at 11–17 Southgate Street in Gloucester, where there were three square
post-holes, dated by pottery to the fourth century, dug down into the *forum* courtyard after
paving slabs had been removed (Hurst 1972: 53). There is insufficient evidence to interpret
this structure, but its existence does not mean that the rest of the building complex did not
remain standing and in use at this time. Equally problematic are the four post-holes dug
into the south corner of the internal colonnade of the Verulamium *mansio* (Wheeler and
Wheeler 1936: 96). These were interpreted as representing a structure of approximately
3.75 m by 4.5 m but there was no evidence to indicate its date, nature, or function.

TABLE 8.1. *Details of the known timber phases of public buildings before they were built in stone*

Town	Public building	Date	Reference
Caerwent	Beneath the temple were traces of a timber building around 16 × 10 m; its function is uncertain	Date is difficult to establish; possibly built late 1st c. to early 2nd c. A.D.	Brewer (1993: 58)
Canterbury	The portico excavated on the Marlowe Car Park site was built over a timber structure that seems to have been of the same alignment	Dates to the 1st c. A.D.	K. Blockley et al. (1995: 98)
	A timber structure was identified under the stone 'temple' at Burgate Street; the timber structure seems to have been built on a previously unoccupied site	Built ca. A.D. 200	Frere and Stow (1983: 43)
Chelmsford	A timber structure, possibly also a *mansio*, preceded the stone *mansio* structure	Built ca. A.D. 125; replaced in stone soon after ca. A.D. 130–5	Drury (1988: 25)
Colchester	The earliest phase of the theatre at Gosbecks was in timber	Built ca. A.D. 100; replaced ca. A.D. 150–200	Dunnett (1971: 31–43); Hull (1958: 269)
Gloucester	Beneath the masonry '*macellum*' excavated at Northgate Street were post-holes of a timber building and verandah	Built in 1st c. A.D.	Rhodes (1974: 31)
	Timber building underlying the 'temple' excavated at Northgate Street; evidence consisted of a sill-beam and pebble floor	Built in 1st c. A.D.	Hurst (1972: 63)
Leicester	Traces of a timber building were found beneath the *macella*; little is known about the structure	Built in 1st c. A.D.	Wacher (1959: 113–14)
Lincoln	Traces of a timber building under the *forum–basilica* may represent an early timber phase of the building or possibly an early timber temple; the plan suggests that building had a corridor or verandah along its east side	1st c.: late Flavian to early Trajanic	Steane (2006)
London	Traces of timber structures on the site of the later *forum*	Built ca. A.D. 44–60	Philp (1977: 7–16)
	The amphitheatre was first built in timber; mainly survives as post-holes, robbed-slots, and waterlogged timbers	Built ca. A.D. 70; replaced by a stone structure ca. A.D. 120	Bateman et al. (2008)

(continued)

TABLE 8.1 *(continued)*

Town	Public building	Date	Reference
	A building 19 × 11 m with timber and brick-earth walls on gravel and mortar foundations was excavated at 5–12 Fenchurch Street close to the *forum*; the structure had two aisles divided into rooms by partitions, some of which contained hearths	Built 1st c. A.D.; demolished by mid-2nd c.	Perring (1991a: 35–6)
Silchester	A timber *forum–basilica* was found beneath the stone structure; the *basilica* comprised a hall divided into two by an entrance onto the *forum*; the hall also contained a nave flanked by aisles	Built ca. A.D. 85	Fulford and Timby (2000: 44–58)
	A timber structure of uncertain nature lay beneath the 'church' building	Uncertain date; possibly 3rd c.	Frere (1975: 292)
	The amphitheatre was first built in timber	Built ca. A.D. 75 and replaced by stone in the mid-3rd c. A.D.	Fulford (1989: 13–27)
Verulamium	The theatre was first built in timber	Built ca. A.D. 160	Kenyon (1935: 215)
	Traces of timber buildings were found beneath the *macellum* but of an uncertain nature	Destroyed by the Boudican fire ca. A.D. 60/1	Niblett (2005a)
Winchester	Traces of timber buildings were found beneath the *forum–basilica*	Built in the 1st c. A.D.	Biddle (1966: 320)

Post-holes of a structure were found in the 1960s excavations of the Cirencester amphitheatre but there is some doubt regarding their interpretation (Figure 8.1). Within Trench AU1, which opened a small area within the arena, there was evidence for five post-holes in the uppermost layer (Holbrook 1998: 170–1). Post-hole I, however, was of an irregular shape and may have been a soft spot in the metalling rather than a post-hole (ibid.). Post-hole V contained sherds of twelfth-century green-glazed wares, which might indicate that it was later in date than the other post-holes. The layer sealing all the post-holes, however, contained a coin of the House of Theodosius (A.D. 379–455) and in the layer beneath them were coins of A.D. 330–41. This might mean that the medieval sherds were the result of later disturbance and that there was a late Roman timber structure here, although exactly what activity it represents within the arena is uncertain. Bradley (1975: 56–8) identified post-holes and slots within the arena of the amphitheatre at Dorchester dating to around the late third or fourth century, but there is no evidence of what they represented or whether they formed structures.

Definite evidence of structures comes from the Wroxeter baths-*basilica* building (Figure 8.2). Here, meticulous excavation and recording revealed traces of a number of timber

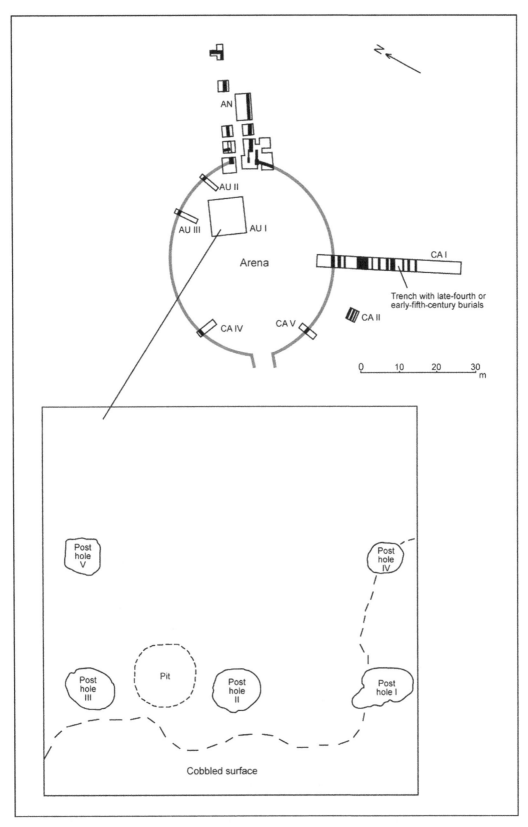

FIGURE 8.1. The excavated areas of the Cirencester amphitheatre together with possible late Roman timber structures within the arena (drawn by A. C. Rogers; adapted from Holbrook 1998, Figures 102 and 124).

structures within the annexe and the *basilica*, dating to the late fourth and fifth centuries, including those represented by post-holes and stake-holes (Barker et al. 1997: 81–2, 99). Another example is the evidence for four post-holes and a rectangular feature, accompanied by iron nails, cutting down into a stone building at the St. Gabriel's Chapel site in Canterbury dating to the late third or fourth century (Driver et al. 1990: 85). There was also a series of shallow stake-holes cutting through the northeast part of the demolished ambulatory of the octagonal temple at Chelmsford, dating to the early fifth century (Wickenden 1992: 42–3). Timber constructions, or at least partitions, have been identified within a large room in the southeast corner of the Leicester Vine Street building (T. Higgins personal communication). The recognition of such evidence in recent excavations demonstrates the level of detail that can be retrieved through careful excavation.

Generally, little can be stated about the nature of the structures represented solely by post-holes or stake-holes, but in some cases they can be of use for assessing the structural condition of public buildings. Most evidence seems to indicate insubstantial timber structures, often open-fronted lean-to structures, as in the Wroxeter baths-*basilica* (Barker et al. 1997: 81–2). This probably suggests that the public buildings were in an adequate condition to provide wall and roof support.

8.2.2 *Buildings represented by floors and bases*

Another way in which structures have been identified is by the presence of platforms and areas of surfacing around or on which they would have been constructed. Again, these surviving traces do not reveal much about the nature of the superstructures and their interpretation can be problematic. Excavations of the London *basilica* on the Leadenhall site uncovered a number of clay post-pads, rather than post-holes, over the last *opus signinum* floor within this area of the nave, which most likely supported a timber floor and dated to the early fourth century (Milne 1992: 33). This either represents a structure built within the nave or reflooring of the whole area; both options indicate continuing use of the *basilica* and the importance of timber construction in the late Roman period. At the 168 Fenchurch Street excavations, the base of another structure was found constructed over a section of the south and east wings of the London *forum* (Dunwoodie 2004: 34). Other examples include a series of floors found at the Peter's Hill site (T. Williams 1993: 26–32) within the 'Allectan Palace' complex in London, and rubble platforms across the courtyard of the *insula* VI building at Cirencester (Holbrook 1998: 135). At the Westgate Street temple in Gloucester there were surviving traces of timber planks representing the floor of a structure (Heighway and Garrod 1980: 82), and at the Leicester *macellum* there was a layer of stone, brick, and tile indicating a floor for some kind of building (Cooper n.d.).

There is no knowledge of the superstructures of these buildings, but they do suggest more substantial constructions than those represented by post-holes alone. The construction of this type of building within courtyards of public buildings may indicate that the roofed parts of the buildings remained standing and in use, demonstrating a complex use of public buildings at this time. Not only were the stone buildings themselves still in use but there was also an intensification of activity surrounding them, suggesting that they remained foci of activity within the towns.

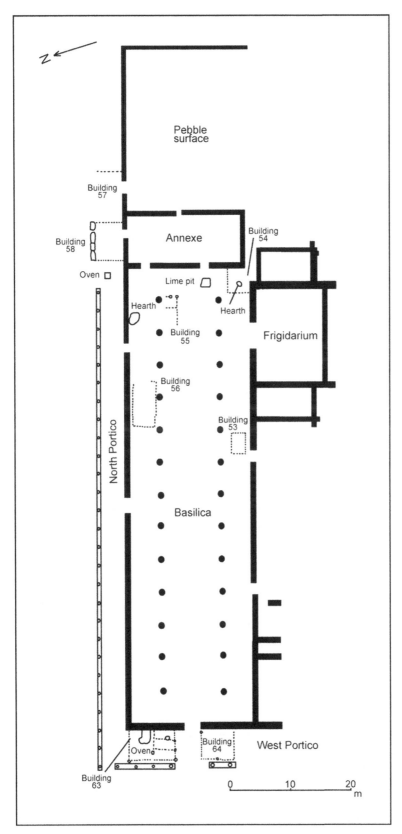

FIGURE 8.2. Plan of the Wroxeter baths-*basilica* (Phase X) dating to the end of the fourth to early fifth centuries, showing the location of timber structures and industrial activity found within the structure (drawn by A. C. Rogers; adapted from P. Barker et al. 1997, plan A9).

8.2.3 Buildings represented by floors and traces of structural evidence

In some cases, slightly more in the way of traces of timber buildings have been uncovered in the form of floor surfaces or bases for timber platforms, combined with sill beams and post-holes. Examples include the sequence of timber buildings within the *forum* at Lincoln, probably dating to the fifth century and represented by timber slots, post-holes, and small areas of paving (Steane 2006: 154–7). At Canterbury, post-holes, slots, and floors of crushed *opus signinum* dating to the late fourth to fifth centuries were found within the St. Margaret's Street bathhouse (K. Blockley et al. 1995: 190). At Wroxeter, the floors and slots found within the porticoes of the baths building indicate separate floors or stalls dating to the late third and fourth centuries (Ellis 2000: 58–9). Many of these structures appear to have been integrated into the public buildings because they relied on them for support.

8.2.4 Buildings with stone foundations

A small number of buildings were constructed with more substantial foundations, although little is known about their superstructures. The excavator of the bath building at Caerwent in the 1920s (Nash-Williams 1930) claimed to have uncovered a structure, dated by coins to the late fourth century, that appeared to lie over the demolished colonnade of the baths and used parts of the walls of the bath as its base. Watts (1998), however, argues that its identification as a new structure is questionable and the evidence is more likely to represent late alterations to the baths structure itself. Another more reliable example comes from the excavations of the Huggin Hill public baths in London, where third- and fourth-century structures reused stone from the baths in their foundations (Marsden 1976; Museum of London Archive and Research Centre record: DMT88). Although they appear to have been on a demolished area of the building, other parts probably remained standing, as suggested by references to the Hwaetmundes stan (see Section 5.3.2 in Chapter 5).

8.2.5 Other structural evidence within public buildings: new internal floors

Another type of structural evidence noted within public buildings, often after their surmised destruction by fire or demolition or a period of assumed desertion, is reflooring within rooms and corridors (Table 8.2). Within the *basilica* at Leicester, for instance, excavations indicated that a fire occurred around the A.D. 360s, which led to the assumption that the building was no longer in use. Much of the site, however, had been badly disturbed by medieval activity and so late Roman layers will not have survived well (Hebditch and Mellor 1973). Within Room 2 of the north wing of the *basilica*, and the northern portico, however, there was evidence of a new floor laid over the ash (ibid.: 17), indicating continued use and perhaps representative of much more that was not preserved. Room 5 in the west wing also had evidence of activity above the 'destruction' level.

Excavations of the east range of the Lincoln *forum* produced similarly complex details of late floor surfaces above destruction debris. In Room 2A there were traces of a sequence of floors above a layer of ash and building debris, which sealed burnt stone suggestive of a fire within this area of the building (Steane 2006: 148). The ash was sealed by a floor surface of crushed tile containing fragments of clay. This in turn was sealed by another surface

TABLE 8.2. *Details of the evidence of reflooring within areas of public buildings in the fourth to fifth centuries*

Town	Public building	Location	Evidence	Date	References
Leicester	*Forum– Basilica*	Room 2 in the north wing of the *basilica* and in the portico	Floors represented by mortar spreads, cobbles, sand and granite, tile, and sandstone rubble after a layer of ash containing a coin of Valens	4th c. with a coin of Valens within a layer of ash beneath as a *terminus post quem*	Buckley (2000); Hebditch and Mellor (1973)
	Bathhouse	Courtyard	A succession of floors within the courtyard suggests continued use	Pottery and coins show the latest refloorings in the 4th c.	Kenyon (1948: 33–4)
Lincoln	*Forum– Basilica*	East range of the *forum*	Sequences of reflooring within the rooms consisting of clay, sand, pieces of limestone, and crushed tile	The sand over the floor patchings contained late 4th c. pottery	Steane (2006: 148–50)
London	Amphitheatre	Arena	Extensive and compact gravel and sand surfaces	4th c. pottery associated with the latest floor and also late coins	Bateman (1997: 68)
Wroxeter	*Forum– Basilica*	*Forum* courtyard, east portico, and east rooms	Layers of earth, cement, and blocks of sandstone over the destruction debris	Coins suggest late 4th c.	Atkinson (1942: 108–10)
York	*Principia*	Rooms around central courtyard	Floors of crushed tile and mortar; in other areas the stone paving slabs were removed and the sand beneath used as the floor	4th to 5th c.	Phillips and Heywood (1995)

of yellowish clay followed by a floor of mortar patches and stones. Later robbing caused disturbance across the site but neighbouring rooms appear to have had the same floor sequence; unfortunately only small areas of these fell inside the area of excavation. Dating is also problematic: the latest coin from the ash beneath the floors dated to A.D. 350–64, but this may have been intrusive because there were also post-medieval glass sherds amongst the material (ibid.). The pottery from the layers, however, was more consistently late fourth to early fifth century, making it unlikely that this was residual (ibid.) and instead indicating use at least into the fifth century.

Another sequence of late activity was identified within the *forum–basilica* at Wroxeter, although the exact nature of this is not easy to discern. There does seem to be evidence of activity post-dating the second fire, which was presumed to have left the building in ruins (Atkinson 1942: 125). Layers of clay above the destruction debris in the excavated rooms probably indicate new floors, and coins associated with them were of Claudius II (A.D. 268–70), Tetricus I (A.D. 270/71–73), the Constantinian period (ca. A.D. 330–40), and Valentinian (A.D. 364–75; ibid.: 109). In other areas of the building, the laying of stone roof slates is interpreted as creating paths over the destruction layer (ibid.: 108–9).

Within the fortress *principia* at York there is evidence for the removal of flagstone floor surfaces and the accumulation of debris over this layer in the late fourth century. This was taken to indicate the stripping of the building prior to the departure of the army (Phillips and Heywood 1995: 64). The rooms remained in use, however, as indicated by the layers of crushed tile and mortar above this layer (ibid.: 65). Other long sequences of floors include those within the Leicester bathhouse courtyard, perhaps indicating continued use of the building where there was a much poorer survival of stratigraphy (Kenyon 1948: 33–4), and also the arena of the amphitheatre at London (Bateman 1998: 52–3). These floors indicate that some caution is needed before complete abandonment of a building is assumed. Careful excavation within the buildings and analysis of the evidence can identify complex histories of continuing use before eventual collapse or disuse in later times.

8.3 Studying finds: moving beyond squatter occupation and the shanty town

8.3.1 Coin assemblages

Coins are a traditional archaeological tool for dating events in the structural sequence of buildings, but they can also indicate continued activity on sites. This can often take the history of use of these structures beyond the phase of architectural alterations and structural decay of the buildings, although it is also important to remember that the absence of coins need not mean the end of use of the building. On some temple sites, it has been argued through coin evidence that there was continued veneration after the buildings had started to degrade. Excavations of the temple site on Hayling Island, for example, noted that the structural decay of the building had begun by the late third or early fourth century. Later coins on the site were suggestive of continued visits, perhaps because of the lasting sanctity of the site (Downey et al. 1979: 15).[1]

Sometimes coins have been used to date so-called squatter occupation within a building (e.g., the 'church' structure at Silchester; Frere 1975: 287), but this may be oversimplifying what the evidence represents. The difficulty is in identifying the exact circumstances leading to deposition of a coin. In the amphitheatre at Silchester (Fulford 1989: 58, 192), for example, a coin of Magnentius ca. A.D. 350–3 was found within imported material used

---

[1] At Nettleton, structural decay of the temple seems to have occurred around the early fourth century but the latest coins dated to A.D. 370–90 (Wedlake 1982: 83–6). At Pagans Hill (North Somerset), coins of Arcadius (A.D. 383–95) were found but the structural evidence was more uncertain and might otherwise have suggested disuse (Rahtz and Harris 1956–1957).

as part of the reflooring of the arena; this provides a terminus post quem for the construction of the floor. On the arena floor surface itself, however, was a coin of Constantine II ca. A.D. 324–30 that may have been dropped by someone within the structure. Its earlier date than the coin below it might indicate that the later coin was residual and highlights one of the major problems with extrapolating dates from coins. That it is common for only small areas of a building to be excavated also means that the latest coin found in the excavations need not be the latest across the site.

Once the contexts of the coins have been established, the latest coins found on the sites of public buildings might help to provide a terminus post quem for the continuing use of the buildings. This would indicate that a large number of the *fora–basilicae* known in Britain remained in some kind of use to a late date, as five out of the twelve excavated *fora–basilicae* had coins dating to the mid-fourth century or start of the fifth century, whilst five more had coins dating to the earlier and mid-fourth century. Only at Caistor-by-Norwich, where there was heavy destruction of the latest layers, did the coin list end in the third century, although there was later pottery. In the bath buildings there seem to have been fewer coins of the late fourth or early fifth century. Five baths do have coins of this time, which may represent activity to a later date, whilst another two baths have coins of the earlier and mid-fourth century.

In the case of theatres and amphitheatres, the only structures where no late Roman coins have been found are those where limited excavations have taken place, as at Chichester and Colchester. Cirencester, Dorchester, London, Silchester, and Verulamium produced coins of the late fourth century, with those at Cirencester (House of Theodosius A.D. 388–402) possibly falling into the early fifth century (Holbrook 1998: 169–71). At London, coins of A.D. 340–80 were found amongst debris that included the animal bones discussed in later text (Section 8.3.3; Bateman et al. 2008). Activity in the amphitheatre of the 'small town' settlement at Frilford, for comparison, appears to have continued to a late date with the presence of many fourth-century coins (G. Lock personal communication).

The evidence from temples within towns is quite diverse, with some examples having coins of the late fourth to early fifth centuries, probably representing activity into at least the fifth century, and others having coin lists that end in the third century. There are a number of sites where coins provided the only evidence to indicate late use of the buildings, as at the Folly Lane temple in Verulamium. Here it appears that the building had fallen into structural decay by the third century but the latest coin found within the structure was of the House of Valentinian, A.D. 364–78 (Niblett 1999: 71). The large number of fourth-century coins within the Triangular Temple in Verulamium may indicate a similar late use of this building. At Colchester, too, late activity at some of the Sheepen temples is supported by coins when little else has survived (P. Crummy 1980: 152). Coins have provided evidence for the late use of temples at a number of the so-called small towns, rural sanctuaries, and other sites such as at Heybridge, Essex (Atkinson and Preston 1998: 101–2), and Hayling Island, Hampshire (Downey et al. 1979: 15). Although the context of these coins is not always free of problems because of the disturbance of these late layers, their presence might be a strong indication of the continuation of activity.

In some public buildings, large late coin assemblages have been found and these are sometimes dated subsequent to the inception of the apparent structural decay of the buildings. Debate has centred around whether they represent coins discarded in rubbish dumped in the buildings, or whether they result from activity continuing within the buildings (Niblett 1999: 417). The value of these coins is also likely to have been low at this time (e.g., Reece 1996). Within the theatre at Verulamium there was a large number of late Roman coins, with examples dating up to Arcadius (A.D. 383–95) and Honorius (A.D. 393–5) within a thick deposit of dark earth, which has been interpreted as the product of dumping within the disused building (Kenyon 1935: 239–40). Although this might be the most likely interpretation for the information, the possibility of the coins representing activity within the building or surrounding buildings cannot be ruled out.

Within *basilicae*, there are a number of cases of large late coin assemblages. These consist of the 232 late-third- and fourth-century coins from within the *basilica* at Silchester (Fulford and Timby 2000), the 72 coins from the later fourth-century phase of the Wroxeter baths-*basilica* (Barker et al. 1997), and the 52 coins from the fourth-century phase of the Lincoln *forum–basilica* excavations (Steane 2006; as opposed to only two from Lincoln of the second century). The majority came from occupation layers, probably resulting from the commercial, market, or religious use of the buildings. Comparable large coin assemblages have come from temples, although whether these were the result of religious activities within the buildings is uncertain. In the *insula* XVI temple at Verulamium (Lowther 1937), an assemblage including 72 coins of the House of Constantine (A.D. 307–37), 22 of the House of Valentinian (A.D. 388–402), and 11 of the House of Theodosius (A.D. 379–95) was found amongst a layer of dark earth similar to that in the theatre. This may indicate that the temple was now out of use, or the material could represent disturbed stratigraphic layers of activity. The large number of fourth-century coins from the temple precinct at Canterbury might indicate the continuation of religious activity on the site, contemporary with the laying down of a new surface of reused stone over the whole complex (see Section 6.2.1 in Chapter 6). Another possible interpretation for this evidence is market activity (P. Bennett personal communication; Bennett and Nebiker 1989).

8.3.2 *Late pottery sherds*

Like coins, pottery is a very useful dating tool; late Roman pottery types found in public buildings include grog-tempered wares, Portchester D ware, Crambeck wares, Alice Holt grey wares, New Forest, Oxfordshire, and Hadham slipped wares, Nene Valley colour-coated wares, and Southeast Dorset Black Burnished ware (Tyers 1996).[2] The end date of these pottery types is not always secure; it is usually assumed to be the end of the fourth century or around A.D. 410 (Fulford 1979). Recent work on individual types, however, has started to suggest revisions to the chronology in some cases. Southeast Dorset Black Burnished ware, for example, is generally considered to have gone out

---

[2] Grog-tempered wares (late third century to the end of the Roman period) and Portchester D ware (early fourth to the end of the fourth century) were mainly distributed in the south, especially Kent, London, Hampshire, Surrey, and Sussex; Crambeck wares (early fourth century to the end of the Roman period) were mainly in the northeast of England. Alice Holt or Farnham ware was produced in the south from the mid-first century but a second major period of production took place in the late third to late fourth century. Southeast Dorset Black Burnished ware was produced in the Wareham/Poole Harbour region from the first century but distribution spread out to the midlands, southeast, and north in the third century. The slipped wares were distributed across central, southern, and eastern England and are generally considered to have been produced to the end of the fourth century (Tyers 1996).

of production by the late fourth century. More recent work on sites in Dorset, how-ever, is beginning to demonstrate that production probably continued into the early fifth century and that the pots may have continued in use later still (J. Magilton personal communication).

Late Roman grey wares have proven to be especially problematic because local types and chronologies are difficult to establish through typologies. Whyman's (2001) examination of late Roman grey ware in the north of England identified chronologies that continued later than has been supposed. Subtle differences in types are also beginning to be recognised amongst late grey ware from Lincoln, indicating that production probably continued into the fifth century (J. Mann personal communication). In some cases, the use of buildings will have continued beyond the production and use of pottery, as with the baths-*basilica* at Wroxeter. The end of large-scale pottery production and other types of manufacture in the early fifth century has implications for understanding the late Roman economy and the nature of the province at this time. The continuation of some kind of organisation within towns suggests that the economy was independent from this. Production reduced in scale considerably, indicating changes in the countryside (Faulkner 2000a: 148), but significance and meaning of place survived, indicating that decline and fall in the later Roman period should not be viewed solely in economic terms. For the majority of the population of Britain at this time, moreover, the end of large-scale production need not have been considered as catastrophic as it perhaps might today. People were able to carry out production of necessary items on a much smaller local scale and adapt to using materials that were much more readily available.

The study and publication of complete pottery assemblages from sites is rarely possible because of issues of time and expense. Traditional priorities within pottery studies have also led to a concentration on samian and other fine wares at the expense of studying or retaining the coarse wares in a systematic manner. On some sites pottery was selectively discarded by the excavators, as at the baths and *macellum* site at Wroxeter (Mould 2000: 108). An aspect of pottery use that affects its presence on the archaeological site is the curation of vessels from earlier periods; it is important to acknowledge that pottery use was not always directly functional. This can add complexity to the study of late assemblages and has implications for the identification and dating of late layers through pottery on sites.

The potential of detailed contextual studies is demonstrated by Timby (1998: 261–2), who conducted an analysis of the forms and fabrics found within each room of Building VIII of the 'small town' of Kingscote (Gloucestershire) in an attempt to identify whether the assemblages could reflect differences in use of the rooms.[3] What might also have been possible was a study of the way in which the pottery assemblages from different contexts had changed over time within each room, thus indicating changes or continuities of use. This analysis, however, whereby each individual sherd was examined in its context in a

---

[3] According to Timby's analysis, some rooms produced negligible quantities of pottery whereas others produced large amounts. Room 5 contained distinctive pots, including storage jars, cooking vessels, and serving dishes, which may indicate some kind of pantry or serving area. Rooms 8 and 15 had similar mixtures of serving, cooking, and drinking vessels, possibly suggesting these two rooms had similar functions, but of an uncertain nature. Timby also found was that within most of the rooms there was a mixture of broken sherds that did not appear to come from reconstructible vessels, suggesting that some of the pottery got there through means other than those relating to room function (Timby 1998: 261–2).

quantitative manner, would be very difficult for all but a very few public buildings in Roman Britain because of the nature of excavation and recording on many sites.

Late pottery assemblages on definite floor layers within public buildings might be able to indicate that activity continued within the buildings, often to a later date than coins would suggest. Whereas historical frameworks (such as the Theodosian Code on the closure of temples) often indicate the abandonment of buildings, the archaeological information can provide different conclusions. In some cases pottery sherds can reflect the continued use of structures; they can perhaps be especially useful in cases where the excavations have been small scale, stratigraphic levels have been difficult to identify, and there have been few other finds. Excavations of the *forum–basilica* at Verulamium, for example, have been limited, and work in 1983–6 on the site of the southeast corner of the *basilica* showed that all the later Roman evidence had been destroyed by the construction of the nineteenth-century cellar. There was, however, a small quantity of unstratified late Roman pottery, perhaps reflecting evidence of activity that has been lost (Montagu-Puckle and Niblett 1983–1986: 180). There is also no positive evidence for the demolition of the building in the Roman period (Niblett 2005a: 83) and so activity may have continued to a later date.

Analysis of the pottery found during the excavations of the *forum–basilica* buildings in Britain shows that twelve out of the thirteen, where something is known of the buildings, have pottery of the late fourth century; in some cases, as discussed in earlier text, it has been claimed that some of the pottery continued into the fifth century. More work is needed on late pottery to develop methods of distinguishing fourth- and possible fifth-century wares. In some cases, as at Verulamium, the latest pottery was unstratified and in Silchester much of the pottery came from Victorian disturbance levels. At Winchester, late pottery was used to indicate continued use of the few rooms excavated into the fifth century. The pottery here included New Forest colour coat, Oxfordshire parchment ware, grey wares, grog-tempered wares, and a sherd of fifth- to sixth-century chaff-tempered ware, although this was from an uncertain context (Teague 1988; data from the Winchester Museums Service archives).

Similar possibilities for studying continued use exist for bath buildings, where the apparent decay or demolition of the functional aspects of the baths is often taken to indicate their desertion. Examples include the bathhouse at Dorchester where excavations produced late Black Burnished ware in the Roman layers of the site, which probably continued in use into the early fifth century (J. Magilton personal communication). Oxfordshire red colour-coated pottery occurred at the St. Margaret's Street baths site in Canterbury and may indicate that it continued in use into the early fifth century (K. Blockley et al. 1995). Comparable pottery was found at the bathhouse in Chichester, where only a small area of the building has been excavated (Down 1978: 152).

There are a number of examples of temple structures with late pottery, including the extramural temple at Caistor-by-Norwich (Gurney 1986), the temple at the St. Gabriel's chapel site in Canterbury (Driver et al. 1990), the octagonal temple at Chelmsford (Wickenden 1992), and the temple at Folly Lane in Verulamium (Niblett 1999: 71, 417). Within the dark earth over the public building complex at the Winchester Palace site in Southwark, London, was Portchester D ware, Eifelkeramik, and 'calcite-gritted ware',[4]

---

[4] 'Eifelkeramik' is a collective term for coarse ware produced at a number of sites in the Eifel mountain region of Germany, including Trier, Speicher, and Mayen from around A.D. 300 to 450. In Britain most comes from

suggestive of late use (Yule 2005). The small quantities of pottery from excavations often make interpretation difficult. This is exemplified by the three sherds of grass-tempered ware from excavations of the amphitheatre at Cirencester, which could, if the number of sherds was not so small, indicate activity dating to sometime between the fifth and eighth centuries (Holbrook 1998: 169–70). There is considerable potential in the use of pottery sherds for identifying late activity, and this is important to bear in mind for future excavations.

8.3.3 *Animal bones*

In a number of cases, excavations of the latest phases of public buildings have produced large assemblages of animal bones. Where it can be discerned that they were not dumped from elsewhere, they represent some form of late activity within the buildings (Table 8.3). Animal bones from both layers and pits can be the result of dumping material, and layers can also be badly disturbed by later activity, making interpretations of assemblages problematic. The dumping of bones can, however, provide potential information on the state of civic amenities such as waste disposal facilities at this time. However, even if by the late fourth century there was no central system of waste disposal, resulting in the uncontrolled dumping of waste, the bone deposits suggest that there was still vitality within towns. The volume of meat represented by the bones, in some cases, suggests a thriving population requiring meat. Careful excavation and analysis of the contexts of the bones is, therefore, needed for interpretations to be made. The examples studied indicate the potential of such evidence.

At the temple precinct site at Westgate Street, Gloucester, demolition of at least some of the building appears to have taken place in the fourth century; however, the accumulation of debris above this demolition and traces of a timber building indicate continuing use. Associated with this use was a large quantity of animal bones, with late-fourth-century pottery. An analysis has indicated that it was probably the waste from on-site animal butchery (Maltby 1979), perhaps indicating market activity, which is supported by the other late finds from the site (see Section 7.1.3 in Chapter 7). Butchery and market activity might also be indicated by the large number of predominantly cattle bones from late levels of the Wroxeter (Ellis 2000) and Canterbury (K. Blockley et al. 1995: 200–1) bathhouse porticoes, although at Canterbury they also appear to have been associated with bone-working (Section 7.2). Public buildings, especially bathhouses, may have been a good source of water for the processes. It is also possible that there was a social function to the butchery, as there was with the metalworking, drawing on pre-Roman ideas, leading to the activities being conducted in public space. The large assemblage of young pig bones within the *principia* at York, dating to the late fourth or early fifth century, possibly relates to feasting and political activity taking place within the building, contemporary with metalworking and indicating some kind of power base here (Phillips and Heywood 1995: 64). These bones were not from pits but from occupation layers, indicating that they

mid- or late-fourth-century contexts (Tyers 1996: 151–2). 'Calcite-gritted ware' is also known as South Midlands shell-tempered ware, the production of which saw a major expansion in the early fourth century; it occurs in abundance in the late fourth century (ibid.: 192–3).

TABLE 8.3. *Details of some large late Roman animal bone assemblages associated with public buildings*

Town	Public building	Animal bone assemblage	Date	Discussion	References
Canterbury	St. Margaret's Street bathhouse	Large quantity of cattle bones, especially metapodials from the portico of the bath building	Late 4th to 5th c.	It is uncertain whether butchery took place on the site or whether the bones were dumped from elsewhere; they are also associated with possible bone-working here	K. Blockley et al. (1995: 200–1)
Cirencester	*Macellum*	Pits of animal bones displaying evidence of butchery	4th to 5th c.	These may represent the continuation of commercial activity	Holbrook (1998: 186–7)
Colchester	Butt Road 'church'	Pits of animal bones, especially sheep and pig	4th c.	The bones may represent feasting activities associated with ceremonies at the site	Luff (1993)
Gloucester	Westgate Street temple precinct	Large late Roman assemblage dominated by cattle bones; very few fragments of jaw, skull, and limb extremities	4th c.	Analysis of the cattle bones has suggested that the animals were slaughtered elsewhere and brought to this site to be cut up into joints; this might suggest market activity on the site	Heighway et al. (1979: 161); Maltby (1979)
London	Mithraeum	Groups of animal bones found within the building deposited in pits; large number of chicken bones	2nd to 4th c.	The assemblages may indicate religious activity and feasting within the building	Shepherd (1998)
	Amphitheatre	A large assemblage of cattle and horse bones; appears to represent whole carcasses	4th c.	The bones may represent the butchery of cattle within the amphitheatre, but they may simply have been dumped here from elsewhere	Bateman (1998: 52–3)
	Winchester Palace complex	Concentration of cattle horn cores and 4 articulated dog skeletons in the latest Roman layers of the site	Mid-3rd to early 5th c.	The horn cores seem to suggest bone-working in the late Roman period; the significance of the dog skeletons is uncertain but ritual activity is possible	Yule (2005)

(continued)

Table 8.3 (continued)

Town	Public building	Animal bone assemblage	Date	Discussion	References
Wroxeter	Bathhouse	Pits containing large numbers of animal bones, predominantly cattle, in the porticoes of the baths	3rd to 5th c.	The bones suggest market activity	Ellis (2000)
York	*Principia*	Large assemblage of young pig and sheep bones	Late 4th to 5th c.	The bones may represent some kind of feasting activity within the building	Phillips and Heywood (1995)

Note: Details are taken from a study of all known assemblages from the structures.

are more likely to have come from use within the building than from dumping waste.[5] A bone assemblage representing religious and elite activity from the Silchester *basilica* has also been discussed (see Section 7.3.3 in Chapter 7). Animal bone assemblages in late Roman public buildings, then, certainly need not represent squatter occupation and each case demands detailed analysis.

Another assemblage came from the London amphitheatre where the latest discernible Roman layer contained a large number of sheep and horse bones. This might be evidence of market activity within the building, although the context indicates that dumped waste is more likely. In the latest layers on the site of the possible Cirencester *macellum* there were pits cut down into the building, each containing large numbers of animal bones (Holbrook 1998: 186–7), perhaps indicating the continuation of commercial activity or other functions. Bone-working along with other craft activities on sites in the late Roman period can also be considered a sign of vitality and generation at these places.

8.3.4 *Small finds*

Small finds (generally the catalogued objects but categorised separately from the coins), especially in the late Roman period, are often more difficult to date accurately than coins and pottery, but where site phases have been dated they may help to indicate the use and changing use of the buildings. Their value should not be underestimated and, like the other types of finds evidence, they may sometimes be able to indicate continuing use of the buildings when otherwise structural decay might suggest abandonment. Here some case studies from London are explored.

The excavations of the Winchester Palace complex and *mansio* in Southwark are important because of the dark earth in their latest Roman layers and the early post-Roman

---

[5] Ritual feasting is also indicated by large animal assemblages on Roman temple sites such as Harrow Hill in Sussex (Holleymen 1937), where it would appear to have been an important part of the religious site. Hill and Semple have discussed an association between feasting debris and ancient monuments in the Late Iron Age and Roman periods (J. D. Hill 1995a; Semple 2004).

disturbance layers, which have the potential of revealing late Roman use. Current under-standing of dark earth was discussed in Chapter 1 and, although more work is still needed, it does appear that in many cases it is likely to have been the result of pre-existing strata of activity by biological and human action on the site (Yule 2005: 80). The presence of dark earth can indicate activity – people using space – and not just decay (Christie 2006: 262).

Excavations at Winchester Palace consisted of a number of sites across a large area. It was mainly on Sites A, B, and part of C that structural remains of the monumental complex, including a number of large stone buildings and a bathhouse, were uncovered; these appeared in Period 3 of the site in the second century (Yule 2005: 50–72). Periods 1 and 2 included buildings that were part of earlier phases of the complex. The end of Period 3 and then Period 4 represent activity of the fourth and fifth centuries and include the dark earth found over much of the site. There are generally very few finds across the area and 75 percent of the metalwork was not identifiable; only the identified finds have been included in this analysis.

In Period 1, Site A produced only one pin, two brooches, one copper-alloy finger-ring, and one gaming counter, and Site B produced only the remains of a copper-alloy *ligula*. The Period 2 buildings contained even fewer finds of known function, with only one brooch and one copper-alloy *ligula* from Site A and none from Site B. Site A in Period 3 produced one bone pin and one bone needle, a bone *ligula*, a copper-alloy brooch, a bone gaming counter, and bone-working waste. Site B had a bone pin and copper-alloy brooch and also an unfinished bone pin. Bone-working waste and bone artefacts also came from Period 4, which was largely the dark earth layer. Here on Site A were four bone pins, two bone needles, and waste in the form of an unfinished pin from a cattle-sized long bone. The four bone pins were all of Crummy Type 3 (N. Crummy 1983: 21–2). These were pins with roughly spherical heads, and study of the contexts of these pins from a number of sites shows that they probably began to appear around A.D. 200 and continued to the end of the Roman period (ibid.). The needles found were also of a later Roman type, Crummy Type 1 (ibid.: 65), indicating that the artefacts themselves that can be classified by types and dates support the late Roman date of the context. Site B produced no artefacts of use, but residual medieval layers over Site A produced a further three bone pins as well as a bone spindle whorl. Stratigraphic sequences show that at least part of the building remained standing into the post-Roman period (ibid.: 78), although this need not preclude use of the areas of the demolished building.

Although there are not many finds from the site, which causes problems in interpreting the use of the complex in its earlier phases, it is clear that there does seem to have been some kind of bone-working taking place here in the late Roman period, perhaps alongside many other activities. This would not have been recognised if the later layers, including the dark earth, had been removed and destroyed without detailed study. Analysis of the pottery from the dark earth indicated that there was six times as much dating evidence for the third and fourth centuries than for the first and second centuries. This indicates that the deposits were reworked late Roman horizons, perhaps after the building was eventually demolished in the post-Roman period, with relatively low levels of residual early Roman pottery (ibid.: 81).

Another complex late sequence came from the possible *mansio* structure on the 15–23 Southwark Street site. On this site, Period 3 in the A.D. 70s saw the construction of a monumental masonry structure, Buildings 4 and 5, with a courtyard 18 m across

(Cowan 1992: 24–31). The two earlier periods on the site consisted of small timber and clay structures. Period 4 in the second century saw the rebuilding of part of the structure, Building 6, and then Building 7, which followed in the third century and was the last rebuilding on the site (ibid.: 35–53). During Period 5 thirteen fourth-century burials cut through the robbed remains of part of the building; Period 6 is represented by a layer of dark earth (ibid.: 56–60). An analysis of the dark earth and its context suggested that it represented the churning up of late Roman occupation layers on the site, perhaps after later demolition, rather than material that had been dumped (ibid.). The debate concerning the origins of dark earth, however, demonstrates that there is still much uncertainty about what it represents.

The finds from Period 3 included fourteen coins, three brooches, four needles, two bone dice, one bone counter, and one iron knife blade. In Period 4 there were 206 finds, including thirty-three coins, eighteen pins, four brooches, and two copper-alloy finger-rings. There were also nine needles, a spindle whorl, writing stylus, and twelve gaming counters; where dateable the object types supported the early dates of these layers (Cowan 1992). Two clay figures, of Venus and a pigeon, probably indicate religious activity and there were nine items of personal equipment, including *ligulae*, tweezers, and spatulas. The Period 5 artefacts were mostly associated with the burials cutting into a demolished area of the building. Continued use of at least part of the building might be indicated by the finds within the dark earth of Period 6, where there were eight coins of the third and fourth centuries and three pins, and also by the burials that surrounded part of the building (see subsequent text). Disturbed levels above this produced a further forty-one coins, mostly dating to the third and fourth centuries, and more pins. It is likely that, as at the Winchester Palace site, these layers represent the disturbed latest Roman layers of the site. Use of the building continued beyond the demolition of part of the structure and the placing of burials over part of the site.

8.4 The function of the timber structures

After the analysis of finds, it is useful to return to some examples of the timber structures. A study of the finds assemblages from the buildings with timber structures might give some indication as to the use of the structures as well as the contemporary activities that took place in other parts of the buildings.

8.4.1 *The* forum–basilica *at Silchester*

Twelve *forum–basilica* complexes have been excavated to some degree within the towns of Roman Britain, but, so far, at only five of these sites have traces of timber structures been identified. The phase in which the timber structures existed within the Silchester *basilica* (Phase 7: late third and fourth centuries) saw a large increase in the number of small finds within the building. These included 259 coins (73 percent of the total finds) as opposed to 27 in Period 6 (second and third centuries), which was the main period of construction and use of the *basilica*, and 31 in Period 5, the timber *basilica*, of around the late first century. It is unclear why there is so little material relating to Period 6, but it is possible that the hall was cleared and the flooring robbed before the late use of the building (Fulford and Timby 2000: 76). If this is the case, then comparing the finds between periods is less meaningful. Alternatively, the use of the *basilica* in Period 6 need not have left much material, in contrast to the activities in Period 7, and the building is also likely to have been cleaned regularly in this period. This change in the way in which finds accumulated in the material record is valuable for considering differences in use of the building and indicates that an analysis of the finds is worthwhile.

There was a concentration of coins around the tiled area (a possible shrine), perhaps relating to religious activity (ibid.: 74). Alternatively, commercial activity within the *basilica* at the same time as the metalworking is possible. The sixteen pieces of personal ornament from Period 7 (only twelve came from Period 6) suggest that people were still using the building in spite of the industrial activity, although it is possible that some of the material was intended for recycling. The high proportion of bird, fish, and sheep bones from Well F127 and pits in the north range and nave in Period 7 have already been examined. This assemblage may relate to elite activity, perhaps involving ritual acts and feasting, and it would certainly indicate that the building remained an important place within the town.

Basilica buildings could remain centres of activity despite containing timber structures. Where there have been large-scale excavations with a detailed recording of the finds, as at the Silchester *basilica*, the distribution of the activities within the buildings can begin to be approached, although there will also have been activities that do not now survive in the archaeological record. Loseby (1996: 54) argued that timber buildings within *forum–basilica* complexes represent their redundancy and the redefinition of the boundaries between public and private space. The evidence from the Silchester case study, however, indicates that these claims are too simplistic because the finds represent evidence of their continued use. There was a variety in the late biographies of buildings that requires analysis.

8.4.2 *The Wroxeter baths-basilica*

Five bathhouses have evidence of timber structures, but eleven of those excavated so far have no evidence, although in some cases this could relate to the size and manner of excavation. Where the timber structures do occur it would indicate that the bathing function was no longer in operation, but this need not apply to the whole building, where bathing could have continued on a reduced scale. Cool's (2006) study of finds from the fortress bathhouse at Caerleon from the first to third century indicates that a working bathhouse could result in a large amount of material from activities taking place there. These included small finds, glass vessels, and animal bones, probably from eating that took place there. Such results may be useful for indicating changes to the use of baths in the late Roman period.

A detailed study was carried out of the finds from the baths-*basilica* at Wroxeter (see Figure 8.2; Barker et al. 1997), where the timber structures were associated with industrial activity but where there is also evidence of activities other than metalworking taking place within the building at this time. Although the excavations covered a large area of the building, and involved the careful recording of finds and their contexts, no layers earlier than the *basilica* in its final form were excavated (Phase S). This makes analysis of the use of the building over the longer term impossible. The finds that were examined in the excavation archive were only those that are likely to have come from primary deposits (labelled 'Category A' finds in the report; R. White 1997) and not those that were probably brought in from outside and dumped there (Category B and C finds; see Section 1.4 in Chapter 1). The reliability of these categories is not absolute, but the attempt to distinguish the different ways in which the finds reached the site improves the methodology of using finds data.

Phase S of the baths-*basilica* was the earliest excavated phase within the building and produced very few finds that came from definite primary deposits, consisting of one structural fitting and some unidentified miscellaneous artefacts. Phase T produced only one coin from the nave, two domestic objects, and an unidentified object. Phase U, of the late third to early fourth century, also produced one coin and two objects of personal ornament. Phase V had forty-two artefacts, including three coins (7 percent of the finds from the phase) and five objects of personal ornament (12 percent). Phase W, which began in the late fourth century, witnessed a substantial increase in the number of finds to 511, which included seventy-three coins (14 percent) and 225 objects of personal ornament (44 percent) including two gold finger-rings, nine copper-alloy finger-rings, and twenty-nine pins. Other objects of note included three writing styli and two seal box lids, which may relate to activity within the building. It was Phase X, dating to the early fifth century, that saw the construction of the timber buildings within the *basilica* (Barker et al. 1997: 81–4), and although there was a reduction in the number of small finds to fifty-nine, the percentage of each find type remained fairly similar to that of Phase W. In Phase Y, dating to within the fifth century, there was again a large number of finds, 271, including seventy-eight coins (29 percent) and seventy-two objects of personal ornament (27 percent).

Although it is difficult to avoid the issue of residuality in the finds assemblages, the results suggest that the *basilica* remained in use during and after the main phase of timber structures. The large number of coins and personal ornaments in Phases W and Y, of the late fourth to fifth century, compared with earlier phases may indicate that the building was no longer being cleaned in the same thorough way or it may indicate that different activities were now taking place within it. The small finds may demonstrate the presence of large gatherings of people, with the coins perhaps indicating market activities or casual losses made by people within the building. Studies of Roman clothing and jewellery (e.g., Swift 2003) indicate that many people would have worn dress accessories, including pins, brooches, and beads, which could fall off and get lost. The finds certainly indicate that the baths-*basilica* remained in general use and continued to be a valued building in the town centre.

The reuse of bathhouses for other functions is well attested across the Empire. It has been argued that they were suitable for churches because of the water supply for Christian ritual and hygiene, and the shape of the buildings meant that they could be easily converted (B. Ward-Perkins 1984: 135). This form of reuse has been identified in a number of cases such as the fourth-century *basilica* of Saint Pierre-aux-Nonnains in Metz, *Gallia Belgica*, which had originally been a bathhouse (Wightman 1985: 231). It has been suggested that the *frigidarium* of the Wroxeter bathhouse became a church (White and Barker 1998), but there is little positive evidence for this. Despite this uncertainty of function and also evidence for areas of decay and demolition of bathhouses, much activity involving large numbers of people does seem to have been taking place within this building during the late third to fifth centuries and beyond, including industrial activity (Chapter 7) and the slaughter of animals.

TABLE 8.4. *Evidence of some burials and human remains found within towns, and associated with extramural public buildings, in the late Roman period*

Town	Location	Evidence	Date	References
Caerwent	Near the public baths	2 bodies on a level with the top of a dismantled wall	Uncertain of date; may be of the 4th c. or later	Nash-Williams (1930: 230)
Caistor-by-Norwich	Small set of baths within Building IV	Presence of ~36 human skulls and other human remains; these may have come from disturbed burials in the area or may represent other activity, perhaps of a ritual nature	Uncertain; stratigraphic layering suggested that they may have been burials of the late 4th or 5th c.	Atkinson (1931: 232)
Canterbury	Temple precinct	Multiple burial of an adult male and female, 2 children, and a dog	Beads and metalwork from the burial suggest early 5th c. date	Bennett (1981)
Cirencester	Amphitheatre	2 adult burials were found at the extreme south eastern end of the trench dug into the rear of the seating bank; a child's skeleton was found just south of the crest of the bank, seemingly contained within a wooden coffin represented by 6 iron nails	First half of the 5th c.	Holbrook (1998: 169–71)
Colchester	Butt Road 'church'	2 successive cemeteries were found, the first with grave goods and the second facing east–west with few grave goods	4th c.	P. Crummy (1997: 121); N. Crummy et al. (1993: 164–99)
Dorchester	Amphitheatre	2 male and 1 female burials outside the northern entrance of the amphitheatre	Uncertain; possibly 3rd c.	Bradley (1975: 61–2)
Exeter	*Forum–Basilica*	4 burials, 3 males and 1 destroyed, were arranged in a line cutting across the southwest wall of the *basilica* nave; 1 female burial cut through levels of the *forum*; 1 further burial cut through the street levels	Carbon-14 dating of three burials suggests a date of ca. A.D. 450; one burial was dated to A.D. 1070 but this may have been contaminated	Bidwell (1979: 111–13)

(continued)

TABLE 8.4 *(continued)*

Town	Location	Evidence	Date	References
Lincoln	*Forum–Basilica*	2 north–south burials were dug over the site of the church that occupied a site in the *forum*; the skeletons were too poorly preserved for the sex or age to be identified; there was also a cist grave within the area of the church although this contained a hanging bowl of 7th c. date; an early medieval cemetery was located to the west of the *forum* church site	Uncertain; probably 5th c.	M. Jones (1999: 172); Steane (2006: 160–1)
London	*Mansio* (Southwark)	13 burials were found cutting through the robbing of an area of the *mansio*; they consisted of 1 adult female, 1 young female, 5 adult males, and 6 uncertain	4th c.	Cowan (1992: 56–9)
Silchester	*Mansio*	Excavations in 1833 found the body of a man within the cold plunge bath of the *mansio* baths; associated with a number of finds, including a greyhound skull	Uncertain; probably late 4th or 5th c.	Anon (1833); Boon (1974: 81–2)
Verulamium	'Church'	Small inhumation cemetery 50 m from the building; has been interpreted as a church but no burials show any specifically Christian characteristics	3rd c.	Niblett (2001: 137)
Wroxeter	*Forum–Basilica*	2 burials were found around the *forum*; various human skeletal parts have been found within the building	Late or post-Roman	Atkinson (1942: 112–13)
	Public bath building	12 burials were found in the hypocaust surrounding the *frigidarium* in the 19th c.	Late 4th c.	Ellis (2000: 55); White and Barker (1998: 125)
	Baths-basilica	The burial of a young man cut into the rubble platform of Building 11, which had been built over the north aisle and north *portico* of the *basilica*	The bones have been radiocarbon dated to ca. A.D. 600–790	Barker et al. (1997); White and Barker (1998: 136)

8.5 Burials around public buildings

Another indication of the continuing use of public buildings is where burials surrounded the structures or cut into sections of the buildings near other parts that were still standing (Table 8.4). During most of the Roman period, cemeteries were located outside the boundaries of the towns and were integral parts of the Roman urban landscape. The evidence within towns is often taken to indicate the presence of churches with the burials surrounding them (e.g., Bell 2005; with examples from other areas of the Empire including Christie 2006: 252–9 and B. Ward-Perkins 1984 on Italy; Leone 2007 on North Africa). Heard et al. (1990), however, have argued that the focus of burials around a building could be an indication of its continued use, and perhaps of its symbolic importance, even if it did not function as a church. Connected with this, Struck (1997: 137) has drawn attention to the fact that burials in prehistory often focused on places that had long histories of meaning.[6] The burials associated with public buildings in late Roman contexts, then, should be studied for their potential to reveal aspects of religion, ritual, change, topography, and organisation within towns (cf. Cantino Wataghin 1999; Christie 2006: 258).

Burials surrounding basilican buildings are most often interpreted as Christian. Examples include the Butt Road building in Colchester (N. Crummy et al. 1993: 164–99) and the cemetery at Verulam Hills Field at Verulamium (Niblett 2001: 137), but the nature of the cemeteries and function of the buildings are problematic (see Chapter 6 for further discussion). Six burials with radiocarbon dates of around A.D. 450 have been found on the site of the *forum* at Exeter (Bidwell 1979: 111–13). It was suggested that the row of four burials here represented some kind of planned cemetery belonging to a church, with further bodies being destroyed and lost at a later date (ibid.), although only further excavation could prove or dispute this. Although the excavated section of the *forum–basilica* appears to have been demolished in the fourth century, the burials may indicate that some part of this building, or another building nearby, remained standing and provided the focus for the burial activity. In the case of the *forum–basilica* at Lincoln (M. Jones 1999: 172), the burials found here may give some indication that at least part of the rest of the surrounding buildings remained in use. The Christian interpretation of the use of these buildings surrounded by burials might be problematic, but the burials do indicate some kind of continuing activity at these locations.

In London, burials were found associated with the *mansio* building in Southwark (Cowan 1992: 56–9). Thirteen burials cut through a robbed area of the building, but it appears that other parts remained standing: there does not seem to be evidence of robbing in the area of Rooms 9–12 of Building 4, and the remains are better preserved (ibid.). The burials appear to be divided into two groups, one aligned north–south with the heads to the north and another aligned east–west with the heads to the west (Cowan 1992: 56–9). Whether this might represent different beliefs, family groups, or even funeral societies (ibid.) is uncertain, but it does suggest that the burials do not simply represent

---

[6] There have been a number of studies on the presence of Iron Age, Roman, and Saxon period burials at prehistoric monument sites in Britain, which, it has been suggested, may indicate continued ritual activity at these sites and also the memory and commemoration of them (e.g., Dark 1993; H. Williams 1998, 2006). Some kind of meaning attached to these places often survived and was recognised. Semple (2004) has considered large early Anglo-Saxon cremation cemeteries in England in terms of 'central places' and foci for communal ritual, assemblies, and displays of power. Late Roman burials within towns could also represent foci on particular places being used for meeting and religious purposes.

decline within the town. The interpretation of this building as a *mansio* is problematic in itself and the function of the surviving part, perhaps associated with the burials, is also uncertain. If the building had originally been a temple, then the burials may indicate a continuation of religious use or perhaps a change to a Christian function, but if it was a *mansio*, then the burials may indicate a new function. Although burials can rarely indicate what activity was taking place within buildings, their presence would seem to represent some kind of deliberate focus of attention in these locations. The dating of the burials is also not always straightforward, with some cases, such as on the Exeter *forum* (Bidwell 1979: 110–11), possibly dating to the post-Roman period.

There are also a number of cases where burials are associated with amphitheatres, as at Cirencester (Holbrook 1998: 169–71) and Dorchester (Bradley 1975: 61–2). For some parts of the Empire it has been argued that burials were placed within amphitheatres and theatres when the spaces were deserted, because the walls of the structures would have kept the burials isolated from the rest of the town, which was still a socially important consideration (Cantino Wataghin 2003). This might provide an appropriate interpretation where numbers of burials are large, but in Britain there are only small numbers of burials associated with the buildings and these were on the edge or around the outside of the structures. It is possible that they represent the encroachment of suburban cemeteries, or they could relate to the use of the structures. Either way they show that spaces within the buildings could still be put to some kind of use.

In some early cases, burials associated with public buildings were interpreted in terms of the results of barbarian attacks. An example is the skeleton of a man found within the cold bath of the *mansio* at Silchester in 1833 (Anon 1833). Little can now be said about this find because 'the extraction was wholly impracticable, and but few bones were preserved' (Anon 1833), but a burial associated with nearby domestic occupation might seem more likely than the individual being a victim of violence.[7] Another case comprises the twelve burials discovered within the hypocaust system surrounding the *frigidarium* of the baths at Wroxeter (Wright 1872: 68). Reanalysis, however, suggests that these burials were probably deliberately placed here because it would have been easier to break through the raised floor of the heated rooms of the building than to dig a grave (White and Barker 1998: 125). White and Barker argued that the *frigidarium* was being used as a church at this time but there is no definite evidence of this (ibid.; also see Section 5.3.3 in Chapter 5). Wacher (1995: 412–14) highlights the textual evidence of major epidemics, including the bubonic plague, between the third and sixth centuries in the Empire that are likely to have had an impact on Britain. This may account for some cemeteries and individual bodies such as found at the Wroxeter bathhouse, but there is no positive evidence to support this.

Burials have also been explained in terms of declining standards within towns. For example, at Wroxeter, a single skeleton of a male was found on the site of the baths-*basilica* cutting through the rubble platform of Building 11 of the 'great rebuilding' phase of the site. The skeleton was orientated north–south (Barker et al. 1997: 138–68, 176) and has been radiocarbon dated to cal. A.D. 600–790, providing a terminus ante quem of A.D. 790. The burial was taken as indicating the final decay of the town (ibid.: 167–8) but, instead, it might indicate that some kind of activity was still taking place in the surrounding

---

[7] What might be significant is the discovery of the 'skull of a greyhound' apparently near the skeleton (Anon 1833), perhaps suggestive of religious activity (cf. Smith 2006) associated with the burial.

area; certainly the burial would indicate the presence of people. The Stour Street burials in Canterbury consisted of the skeletons of an adult male and female, two children, and a dog within a pit or grave at the edge of the central temple precinct of the town (Bennett 1981). Previously considered post-Roman in date, a study of the beads within the grave now suggests that the burials were very late Roman (P. Bennett personal communication). Rather than indicating declining standards, the location of this unusual burial within the temple precinct may mean the continuation of pagan religious activity and not abandonment of the site – although it should be noted that human burials are rare on Iron Age and Roman temple sites in Britain.

No interpretation of the burials associated with the public buildings is certain and there are likely to have been a number of motives involved, but the focus of the burials on these buildings might be an indication of their importance as places of congregation, ritual, and ceremony (cf. Semple 2004). Those burying the dead were perhaps drawing on the history, memories, and stories associated with the sites, or the towns on a wider scale, which in some cases could even have been from the late pre-Roman Iron Age. More work, perhaps only through further excavation, is needed to identify the types of activities taking place within buildings on which the burials focused.

What seems clear, however, is that there was considerable and varied activity taking place within the buildings and across the towns in the late Roman period and that this often occurred beyond the date at which structural decay set in. Timber structures represent the continued use or development of the buildings; often they will have changed or renewed the way in which space, and movement within the individual building, was organised. The timber structures within the Silchester *basilica* and the Wroxeter baths-*basilica*, for instance, divided up the building space in a new way. The constructions within the portico at Canterbury changed the thoroughfare to one with two rows of timber stalls and a space in between only 1 m wide for walking (K. Blockley et al. 1995: 199–201). These data can be combined with the structural evidence discussed earlier in Chapter 8 that shows that the public buildings themselves were still being altered and renewed at the same time as the construction of the timber structures. Experiences moved away from the classical norm, but this was not decline. Urban life continued, adapting to new circumstances and opportunities.

Chapter 1 discussed the problems relating to the loss of evidence of late timber structures within towns (cf. Niblett et al. 2006: 101–3). There is, however, evidence of housing and other structures around and near public buildings, such as at Canterbury (K. Blockley et al. 1995), Cirencester (McWhirr 1986), Silchester (Fulford et al. 2006), and Winchester (Biddle and Kjølbye-Biddle 2007), indicating that a substantial population still focused on the town centres. Iron-working has been located within a property in the Silchester *insula* IX excavations dating to the fourth century (Fulford et al. 2006), although only 16.43 kg of slag was found at this metalworking site compared with the 90.5 kg from the *basilica*, indicating smaller scale activities here and emphasising the larger concentration within the *basilica*. In Lincoln, iron slag was identified within a late Roman townhouse at Hungate in the lower town (M. Jones 2002: 140; 2003: 92, 134). Small-scale industrial activity may have been fairly common within townhouses and workshops in the late Roman period, as it also was in earlier periods (Fulford et al. 2006: 268; McWhirr 1986). Evidence from such locations does not, however, detract from the importance of such activity within public buildings, which until the late Roman period appear to have been kept largely clear of these processes. This remains a striking and significant aspect of the late Roman townscape. As discussed, the products of the metalworking remain largely unknown but it seems likely that there were utilitarian objects for the town inhabitants, including components for building construction and repair, linking in to the timber building evidence across the towns. Structural parts were also recycled, providing a sense of change and renewal. Town spaces were evolving and being adapted to the needs and desires of the continuing population.

CHAPTER 9

Senses of place: rethinking urbanism in late Roman Britain

This book set out to explore new ways to study late Roman urbanism in Britain. It represents an attempt to move away from unquestioning perceptions of towns in the later Roman period and urbanism in the Roman period as a whole. The approach taken also necessitated an examination of the late pre-Roman settlement pattern. Amongst prehistorians theoretical developments have greatly advanced our understanding of the late Iron Age, and their approaches can be useful for understanding aspects of the Roman period. Methodologies for studying the late pre-Roman and the late Roman periods in Britain have often differed considerably. Analysis of the late pre-Roman period is embedded in traditions within prehistoric archaeology, whilst examination of the later Roman period has drawn on perspectives from classical archaeology and ancient history. In this book, both methodologies were brought together to provide a coordinated view.

Roman towns developed within the context of pre-existing and numinous landscapes, continuing, but also transforming, aspects of the way in which certain places were experienced, a tradition that continued into the late Roman period. Rather than representing a decline in standards in late Roman towns, this perspective indicates that activity continued the use of these places in meaningful ways. They need to be considered both in terms of what occurred on these sites previously and in terms of the continued use of these places as creative and vibrant localities. Historiographical analysis within archaeology is important, as the study of Edward Gibbon's *The Decline and Fall of the Roman Empire* has demonstrated. One of the most influential texts on the Roman Empire in the English language, it was especially significant in Britain for interpreting the later Roman period.

Archaeological evidence indicates that there was still considerable activity taking place within the public buildings of towns in the late Roman period and that the structures remained architectural frames around the activity. Moreover, this surviving evidence is likely to be representative of much more that has since been lost or did not leave any trace at all. The surviving evidence includes structural changes to public buildings (sometimes with the deliberate demolition of elements of a structure in order to preserve the rest) and timber structures built within or on the sites of public buildings. One of the major types of evidence within buildings was that of industrial activity, which appeared to focus on the *forum–basilica* complexes especially.

Although historical documents such as the *Notitia Dignitatum* and the Theodosian Code can be drawn upon for understanding towns in the later Roman period, the archaeological evidence is extremely complex and requires analysis that pursues a number of methodological and theoretical perspectives. Rather than indicating 'squatter occupation' and the decline of buildings, the industrial activity was a part of the 'place-value' of towns with its ritual significance, reconfirming and reinforcing the symbolic nature of these places as parts of meaning-laden landscapes.

9.1 Place: beyond beginnings and endings

The late Roman phases of towns were part of a process of recurring and simultaneous continuity and change from earlier periods. A concentration on the scientifics of space in many studies of the past has neglected the importance of place, which can help in understanding towns and change over time (E. Casey 1996: 14). Places can be considered as entities that gather people, experiences, histories, and thoughts, and keep them to influence later action and feeling; they are bodies of collection and recollection. Ingold (2000: 149) sees places as being composed of the vitality that animates their inhabitants. Linear time may also not be so useful for understanding all aspects of places: the present in places gathers the past and future into itself and is not segregated from them (Ingold 1993: 159). Places are generative and regenerative in their own right and do not age according to any pre-established schedule of growth and decline, such as the historical events of the later Roman period (cf. E. Casey 1996: 24–6). Roman towns gathered people in deeply acculturated ways but, as we have seen, in Roman Britain and elsewhere they were also located on sites with longer histories. Roman towns were highly ritualised places and in the late Roman period would have continued to draw on the significance of the places from earlier periods. The role of memories and myths that places contained is an important area to study for reconsidering the decline of towns in the late Roman period.

Memories and myths relating to places and landscapes in Roman Britain require more attention on a general level, and it is something that is now receiving more analysis in prehistoric studies, especially in relation to concepts of time and identity (e.g., Lucas 2005; Murray 1999; Thomas 1996) and the use by people in later prehistoric times of earlier monuments (e.g., Gosden and Lock 1998; Lock, Gosden, and Daly 2005; Miles et al. 2003). Hingley (2009) has demonstrated that Bronze Age bronze objects were sometimes deliberately incorporated into activity levels of Iron Age date on sites that often had a pre-existing monumentality. He suggests that the objects may have been used as part of the commemoration of place and incorporated ideas of the mythical past into the context of the present. Gosden and Lock (1998) have argued that all societies will have been influenced by mythical and real pasts that affected the way in which continuities and change took place in the present. Most work has focused on prehistory but the arguments are equally valid for the Roman period. Ancient artefacts could be received and reinterpreted in later periods of the past, but public buildings and other structures of the Roman period can also be interpreted in terms of structural material culture (cf. Gardner 2007: 97–114) that were used, repaired, and reformed over time. The sites of Roman towns had long sequences of use before and during, and also after, the Roman period. Van Dyke and Alcock (2003: 5) write of 'places that have been inscribed with meaning, usually as a result of some past event or attachment' that continued to attract attention and activity. This might be one way of viewing towns and their importance in the later Roman period. Whilst drawing on the past, however, towns were also being used in innovative and transformative ways, continuing the dynamic nature of the places.

Memory is 'something vital to our understanding of the ancient world' (Alcock 2002: 1); it is the central medium through which identities are constituted – we are shaped by the past (Olick and Robbins 1998: 112). The issue of memory in Roman archaeology is a topic that could still benefit from more attention despite it generally being difficult to study from archaeological material. One approach is to use documentary evidence to support the material (cf. Alcock 2002: 2), but this can be biased towards particular viewpoints and has limitations in areas in which few texts exist.

An analysis of the role of memory within society over time suggests that social memory – shared remembrance – would have played an important part in the construction of identity in the Roman period, providing both an image of the past and direction for the future (Alcock 2002: 1; Fentress and Wickham 1992: 8; Le Goff 1992). Today, it could be argued that memory is often related more to the personal than the social and there has been a general devaluation of memory as a source of knowledge (Fentress and Wickham 1992: 8). Social memory is articulated through speech, performances, and ceremonies (Fentress and Wickham 1992: 47; Van Dyke and Alcock 2003: 4). Rituals also created and reinforced memories within society and passed information on. Memories are generated along the paths of movement that each person lays down in the course of his or her life (Ingold 2000: 139, 147) – this is intimately connected to the way in which the 'land' is lived and contributes to the long-term place-value of sites. Agency is also important, because individuals and groups would have had different memories and different motives in the creation of these memories.

Place, including the built environment and 'natural' places (cf. Insoll 2007), is an important arena in which memories are created and in which the society is structured and reproduced. Giddens' theory of structuration (1984) argued that routinely performed activities created the knowledge and memory of how to go on; it reproduced the society through time. The individual becomes socialised within the culture of the group whilst at the same time the group and its cultural values are reproduced (ibid.). For Tilley (2004: 12) it is also the individual who carries time into the experience of places, and his (1994) study of prehistoric monuments argued that the experience of walking along the Dorset Cursus monument was an essential ingredient of its meaning. Barrett (1988) sought to apply structuration theory to archaeological evidence, and it has been useful in studies of architecture and the organisation and layout of buildings in many periods of archaeology (e.g., Graves 2000; M. Johnson 2002).[1] For the Roman period, Favro (1996) has explored the *Forum Romanum* of Augustan Rome and the ways in which the architecture and use of space was carefully choreographed, movement controlled, and experience manipulated, creating the meaning of the site. Buildings act as 'curtains around space' (Boman 2003: 207), framing the spaces and directing the action. The involvement of people is also necessary and adds to the significance of the places; as Casey said, 'bodies build places' (E. Casey 1993: 116).

People living within towns in the later Roman period may well have possessed a genealogical understanding of the origins of these places (cf. Hingley 2009: 157) for which no written records now exist but that will have been represented in their continued actions, behaviours, and experiences of the places. That these large towns were comparatively rare in Roman Britain may also have contributed to the special nature of these places and their

---

[1] Graves (2000) sees social space as created out of social practice within physical space. Johnson's (2002) study of medieval and renaissance castles in England considered them in terms of 'active and complex pieces of landscape and material culture'.

significance in social memory. As bodies of structural material culture, towns are hugely complex sets of data, the product of the activities of many individuals over long periods of time. This will also have been recognised by the inhabitants of these places in the later Roman period, and it may well have been a positive factor adding to the importance of these places.

The architectural framing of place applies as much to 'ruins' as it does to well-maintained structures, as Edensor's (2005) study of industrial ruins indicates. Edensor argues that the importance of ruins has generally been ignored because of the predominant capitalist notion within society of the economic value of space: 'ruins and other forms of wasteland are tarnished by their association with economic decline' (ibid.: 7, 166). Ruined space is often seen as somewhere where nothing happens, but Edensor highlights the many varied uses of the buildings and the ways in which the space was comprehended. In his terms, ruins are 'haunted by a horde of absent presences, a series of signs of the past that cannot be categorised but intuitively grasped' (ibid.: 152). Activities with late Roman public buildings too were not simply taking advantage of deserted buildings but were placed and organised within them in meaningful ways, as in the case of the metalworking in the *basilica* at Silchester (Fulford and Timby 2000: 72).

Beyond the public buildings, the towns as a whole were places where movement, encounter, assembly, experience, and memory were significant factors in the creation of meaning. Towns were still places with sizeable populations in the late Roman period, which drew people from outside. Some of the public buildings retained official functions, despite also becoming centres of other activities and some parts of their structures being demolished. There were changes in the organisation of towns, in some cases moving away from the classical style of urbanism, but these need not be translated as decline. Other settlement types such as small towns, for example, became prosperous and densely populated without adopting the classical style.

9.2 Widening perspectives: small towns and villas

Small towns appear to have become more prominent in Britain in the late Roman period (Millett 1990: 143–56) and are useful for examining late Roman urbanism. Despite the term 'small town', the settlements represent success and were perhaps representing more indigenous interpretations of Roman urbanism (Hingley 1997a; Millett 2001). Some small towns were actually quite large, such as Water Newton in Cambridgeshire (Fincham 2004) and Elms Farm, Heybridge, in Essex (Atkinson and Preston 1998). Some so-called specialist religious sites such as Bath also have considerable evidence of domestic occupation (Cunliffe 2000: 118),[2] and at Frilford in Oxfordshire there are spreads of domestic occupation, as well as a large cemetery, probably indicating a fairly large number of inhabitants here (Hingley 1985: 208). The prominence of religious activity within many of the towns connected with temples, public buildings, and their settings in the landscape might also make such divisions of settlements problematic.

Many of the small towns show evidence of pre-Roman activity, but others began after the conquest, being associated with forts or Roman road networks. Though buildings within small towns were for the most part not monumental or stone built, the settlements were

[2] Excavations across the town have found traces of timber-frames and masonry buildings that indicate occupation (Cunliffe 2000).

not failures or economically poor. They suggest alternative ways of living and organising space, which included central open spaces (see Chapter 6). Temples are found at many of the small towns, indicating that these were important features of the settlements (Burnham and Wacher 1990). Some bathhouses have been identified, such as at Godmanchester (H. Green 1975: 198), but these may not necessarily have been public buildings, some instead being private ventures; others may have been attached to houses or *mansiones*, a number of which are known within small towns. What is most important about small towns for this study is that they represent the significance and value of places in Roman Britain beyond the classical form of street-grids and public buildings. They indicate a vibrancy that was based on local circumstances and interactions with their landscape, which has important implications for how we should regard the physical changes to the so-called large towns in the later Roman period. Small towns, of course, did not have the monumentality of the early large towns and would have had different genealogies of place, but they demonstrate that the vitality of places can go beyond monumental architecture.

The use of villa sites in the later Roman period could also form a comparable study to towns (also see Gardner 2007 for a detailed study of forts in the later Roman period). Like towns, villas were monumental and highly ritualised places and in a number of cases there is evidence of the definite acknowledgement of preceding activity at the sites on which they were constructed. At Barcombe in Sussex, for example, the villa was constructed around a Bronze Age burial mound that seems to have remained a prominent feature of the site throughout the use of the villa (Gammon, Rudling, and Butler 2006). This locality may have been meaningful in the Iron Age and the use of the site certainly remained important into the post-Roman period. Excavations on villa sites are now disclosing traces of late Roman activity, including industrial activity. Recent excavations at Yarford villa near Winchester, for example, revealed changes to the decoration of some rooms during the late fourth century in addition to debris from craft activities, consisting of a burnt layer with small pieces of shale and burnt antler, over the floor (King 2004); coins of the late fourth century and pottery came from this layer. There were also post-holes from timber posts cut into the floor that may have supported part of the villa roof in the late fourth or early fifth century when more substantial structural repairs were not possible as a result of a lack of materials and funds (ibid.).

Bell's (2005) work has explored the reuse of Roman villa sites in medieval Britain as locations for churches, suggesting that many of these sites remained important places that attracted attention. Work in Italy and Spain has examined the continuation and transformation of villas in the late Roman and medieval periods, with some becoming places for political and religious activity (e.g., Chavarría Arnau 2004; Sfameni 2004). Like public buildings within towns, the villa structures remained foci of activity within the landscape, often well into the medieval period.

9.3 Points for the future and final thoughts

Excavation and recording methodologies have developed in ways that are hugely beneficial to late Roman studies. Post-colonial approaches, plus advances in excavation techniques, have led to the recognition of the importance of a huge range of site types as well as the continuance of pre-existing settlements, monuments, and natural places in the geography of Roman Britain. Excavations of towns tended to concentrate on the monumental earlier

Roman periods without recognising or recording later phases in much detail. There have also been difficulties in excavating the pre-Roman phases of sites as a result of the depth of the deposits, disturbance caused by later layers, or the preference to preserve the Roman structural layers, as in the case of the Wroxeter baths-*basilica* (Barker et al. 1997: 49). It is important for the research agenda to focus on the need to record all stratigraphic layers on sites in similar detail.

When late phases of towns are encountered, it has been conventional to draw upon classical viewpoints and historical frameworks for interpretation. Although these sources are useful, the theoretical and historical constraints often led to interpretations of decline. It is important for the archaeology to be interpreted in its own terms. Finds recovery, dating, and processing constitute a crucial aspect in this. To retrieve the most information from the latest layers of the sites, a holistic approach is necessary, whereby the structural evidence is combined with the finds data in an attempt to discern what might have been taking place on the sites in the latest Roman period. The researching of these issues is sometimes made difficult because of the way in which the finds on many sites were recorded, published, and studied in the past. Problems can include the partial recovery of artefacts, especially pottery, and the lack of sufficient contextual information for each find. Only through the careful recording of each object and its context can studies exploring the continuing and changing use of buildings over time be attempted. Pottery and stratigraphic layering can sometimes indicate later dates for activity within buildings than those suggested by coins. Debate concerning the date of the latest Roman pottery on sites, such as the late grey wares from the Lincoln *forum* excavations, indicates the potential for work in the future.

Theoretical approaches within the study of Roman urbanism are also crucial. As M. Johnson (2006: 132) has put it, the role and importance of theory within archaeology is 'beyond debate'. Studies of Roman towns, however, have not traditionally embraced developments in theory from archaeology and other disciplines that can bring new angles to the subject. Roman urbanism, despite appearing familiar through references to classical texts and comparisons with modern towns, was far from straightforward and is still not adequately understood. The settlement pattern and nature of 'landscape' prior to the conquest are also only partially known. Methods for understanding settlement, landscape, place, and space in prehistory, geography, anthropology, and other disciplines can usefully be applied to the Roman period. Archaeological theory is often perceived as a distinct body of knowledge, but it should not be separated from the theories of other disciplines, nor deemed inapplicable to late Roman studies. The traditional divide between methodologies of the late Roman and early medieval periods is as problematic as the divide between the late Iron Age and Roman periods. Because no study can take place outside, and fail to be influenced by, the context of previous scholarship, historiographical analyses are also important. Ideas and approaches are inherited from earlier generations. Examining the context of study allows the discipline to take additional directions, introducing new ways of interpreting the data and moving beyond traditional themes in urban studies, such as economic development and subsequent decline and fall, which have been influenced in part by modern assumptions and prejudices.

Using the later Roman period as the core case study, this book is about, above all, re-energising Roman urban studies not only in Britain but across the Empire. Roman towns in many ways are still alien features to us with uncertainties as to how they appeared, functioned, and formed part of wider landscapes, and how they were experienced. It is not easy to make assumptions about them. Rather than viewing urbanism in terms of greatness and decline, the Roman towns, as they changed over time, were successive expressions of the enduring importance of the sites in their landscapes. A detailed study of the archaeological record from a variety of theoretical stances can begin to provide us with a new understanding of towns in both the earlier and later Roman periods.

References

Ancient sources

Ammianus Marcellinus (Translated by W. Hamilton 1986).
The Later Roman Empire (A.D. 354–378). Harmondsworth: Penguin Books.

Aristides (Translated by C. A. Behr 1981).
Orationes. Leiden: Brill.

Aristotle (Translated by H. Rackham 1932).
Politica. London: Heinemann.

Bede (Translated by J. E. King 1930).
Historia ecclesiastica gentis Anglorum. London: Heinemann.

Caesar (Translated by H. J. Edwards 1917).
Bellum Gallicum. London: Heinemann.

Cassius Dio (Translated by E. Cary 1961).
Roman History. London: Heinemann.

Cicero (Translated by W. Miller 1968).
De officiis. London: Heinemann.

Cicero (Translated by C. Walker Keyes 1928).
De republica. London: Heinemann.

Dionysius Halicarnassensis (Translated by E. Cary 1937).
Antiquitates Romanae. London: Heinemann.

Frontinus (Translated by M. B. McElwain 1925).
De aquae ductu urbis Romae. London: Heinemann.

Gildas (Translated by M. Winterbottom 1978).
De excidio et conquestu Britanniae. Chichester: Phillimore.

Hesiod (Translated by H. G. Evelyn-White 1967).
Opera et Dies. London: Heinemann.

Juvenal (Translated by G. G. Ramsey 1918).
Satires. London: Heinemann.

Lucan (Translated by J. D. Duff 1969).
Pharsalia. London: Heinemann.

Lucretius (Translated by W. H. D. Rouse 1975).
De rerum natura. London: Heinemann.

Martial (Translated by W. C. A. Ker 1920).
Epigrammata. London: Heinemann.

Pliny, the Elder (Translated by H. Rackham 1942).
Naturalis historia. London: Heinemann.

Pliny, the Younger (Translated by B. Radice 1969).
  Epistulae. London: Heinemann.

Plutarch (Translated by P. H. De Lacy 1959).
  Moralia. London: Heinemann.

Pomponius Mela (Translated by F. E. Romer 1998).
  Description of the World (De chorographia). Ann Arbor: University of Michigan Press.

Scriptores Historiae Augustae (Translated by D. Magie 1932).
  Aurelian. London: Heinemann.

Seneca (Translated by R. M. Gummere 1930).
  Epistulae. London: Heinemann.

Servius (edited by G. Thilo and H. Hagen 1884).
  In Vergilii Carmina Commentarii (DServius). Leipzig: Teubner.

Strabo (Translated by H. L. Jones 1917–1932).
  Geographia. London: Heinemann.

Suetonius (Translated by J. C. Rolfe 1913; reprinted 1970).
  Divus Augustus. London: Heinemann.

Tacitus (Translated by M. Hutton 1970).
  Agricola. London: Heinemann.

Tacitus (Translated by J. Jackson 1937).
  Annales. London: Heinemann.

Tacitus (Translated by M. Hutton 1970).
  Germania. London: Heinemann.

Tacitus (Translated by C. H. Moore 1931).
  Historiae. London: Heinemann.

Varro (Translated by R. G. Kent 1938).
  De lingua Latina. London: Heinemann.

Virgil (Translated by L. P. Wilkinson 1982).
  Georgics. Harmondsworth: Penguin Books.

Vitruvius (Translated by F. Granger 1934).
  De architectura. London: Heinemann.

Zosimus (Translated by R. T. Ridley 1982).
  Historia nova. Canberra: Australian Association for Byzantine Studies.

Modern sources

Ainsworth, S. and Wilmott, T.
  2005. *Chester Amphitheatre: From Gladiators to Gardens*. Chester: Chester City Council and English Heritage.

Aitchison, N. B.
  1993. Dorsey: A Reinterpretation of an Iron Age Enclosure in South Armagh. *Proceedings of the Prehistoric Society* 59: 285–301.

Albarella, U.
  2007. The End of the Sheep Age: People and Animals in the Late Iron Age. In C. Haselgrove and T. Moore (eds.), *The Later Iron Age in Britain and Beyond*: 389–406. Oxford: Oxbow Books.

Alcock, S. E.
  2002. *Archaeologies of the Greek Past: Landscape, Monuments and Memories*. Cambridge: Cambridge University Press.

Aldhouse-Green, M.
2002. Any Old Iron! Symbolism and Ironworking in Iron Age Europe. In M. Aldhouse-Green and P. Webster (eds.), *Artefacts and Archaeology: Aspects of the Celtic and Roman World*: 8–19. Cardiff: University of Wales Press.

Aldrete, G. S.
2007. *Floods of the Tiber in Ancient Rome*. Baltimore: The Johns Hopkins University Press.

Alföldy, G.
1975. *Die römischen Inschriften von Tarraco*. Berlin: W. de Gruyter.

Allason-Jones, L.
2001. Material Culture and Identity. In S. James and M. Millett (eds.), *Britons and Romans: Advancing an Archaeological Agenda*: 19–25. York: Council for British Archaeology Research Report 125.

Allison, P.
1992. Artefact Assemblages: Not 'the Pompeii Premise'. In E. Nerring, R. Whitehouse, and J. Wilkins (eds.), *Papers on the Fourth Conference of Italian Archaeology*: 49–56. London: Accordia Research Centre.

Allison, P.
2004. *Pompeian Households: An Analysis of the Material Culture*. Los Angeles: Cotsen Institute of Archaeology at UCLA, Monograph 42.

Allison, P., Fairbairn A. S., Ellis, S. J. R., and Blackall, C. W.
2005. Extracting the Social Relevance of Artefact Distribution in Roman Military Forts. *Internet Archaeology* 17, available at http://intarch.ac.uk/journal/issue17/4/.

Ammerman, A.
1990. On the Origins of the Forum Romanum. *American Journal of Archaeology* 94: 627–45.

Anderson, J. C.
1997. *Roman Architecture and Society*. Baltimore: The John Hopkins University Press.

Anon.
1833. The Roman City of Silchester. *The Reading Mercury*, February 18, 1833.

Anon.
1854. Antiquities and Works of Art Exhibited. *The Archaeological Journal* 11: 57–62.

Anon.
1884. *History of the Decline and Fall of the British Empire*. Ye Leadenhalle Press Pamphlets. London: Field & Tuer.

Anthony, I. E.
1970. St. Michael's, St Albans, Excavations, 1966. *Hertfordshire Archaeology* 2: 51–61.

Aquilué Abadías, X.
2004. Arquitectura oficial. In X. Dupré Raventós (ed.), *Tarragona: Colonia Iulia Urbs Triumphalis Tarraco*: 41–53. Rome: 'L'Erma' di Bretschneider.

Arce, J.
1982. *El último siglo de la España romana*: 284–409. Madrid: Alianza Universidad.

Arce, J.
2002. Las ciudades. In R. Teja (ed.), *La Hispania del siglo IV: administración, economía, sociedad, cristianización*: 41–58. Bari: Edipuglia.

Arramond, J.-C. and Boudartchouk, J.-L.
2001. La destruction du temple. In J.-M. Pailler (ed.), *Tolosa: nouvelles recherches sur Toulouse et son territoire dans l'antiquité*: 443–5. Rome: École Française de Rome.

Asad, T.
1993. *Genealogies of Religion: Discipline and Reasons of Power in Christianity and Islam*. Baltimore: The Johns Hopkins University Press.

Ashby, T.
   1906. Excavations at Caerwent, Monmouthshire, on the Site of the Romano-British City of Venta Silurum, in the Year 1905. *Archaeologia* 60: 111–30.

Ashby, T., Hudd, A. E., and Martin, A. T.
   1904. Excavations at Caerwent, Monmouthshire, on the Site of the Romano-British City of Venta Silurum, in the Years 1901–1903. *Archaeologia* 59: 87–124.

Ashby, T., Hudd, A. E., and King, F.
   1909. Excavations at Caerwent, Monmouthshire, on the Site of the Romano-British City of Venta Silurum, in the Years 1907 and 1909. *Archaeologia* 61: 565–82.

Ashby, T., Hudd, A. E., and King, F.
   1910. Excavations at Caerwent, Monmouthshire, on the Site of the Romano-British City of Venta Silurum, in the Year 1908. *Archaeologia* 62: 1–20.

Ashwin, T.
   2000. Excavations at Harford Farm Caistor St. Edmund (Site 9794), 1990. In T. Ashwin and S. Bates (eds.), *Excavations on the Norwich Southern Bypass 1989–91, Part 1*. East Anglian Archaeology Report 91.

Atkin, M.
   1987. Excavations in Gloucester – An Interim Report. *Glevensis* 21: 7–17.

Atkinson, D.
   1930. Caistor Excavations, 1929. *Norfolk Archaeology* 24: 93–139.

Atkinson, D.
   1931. Caistor-by-Norwich. *Journal of Roman Studies* 21: 232–3.

Atkinson, D.
   1942. *Report on Excavations at Wroxeter (the Roman City of Viroconium) in the County of Salop, 1923–1927*. Oxford: Oxford University Press, for the Birmingham Archaeological Society.

Atkinson, M. and Preston, S. J.
   1998. The Late Iron Age and Roman Settlement at Elms Farm, Heybridge, Essex, Excavations 1993–5: An Interim Report. *Britannia* 29: 85–110.

Ayres, P.
   1997. *Classical Culture and the Idea of Rome in Eighteenth Century England*. Cambridge: Cambridge University Press.

Baccrabère, G.
   2001. Les thermes de la rue du Languedoc. In J.-M. Pailler (ed.), *Tolosa: nouvelles recherches sur Toulouse et son territoire dans l'antiquité: 424–5*. Rome: École Française de Rome.

Barber, A. J. and Collard, M.
   2000. Queen Elizabeth Road. In J. Wills (ed.), Archaeological Review No. 24 1999. *Transactions of the Bristol and Gloucestershire Archaeological Society* 118: 222.

Barber, B. and Bowsher, D.
   2000. *The Eastern Cemetery of Roman London: Excavations 1983–1990*. London: MoLAS, Monograph 4.

Barker, P., White, R., Pretty, K., Bird, H., and Corbishley, M.
   1997. *The Baths Basilica Wroxeter: Excavations 1966–90*. London: English Heritage.

Barndon, R.
   2004. A Discussion of Magic and Medicines in East African Iron Working: Actors and Artefacts in Technology. *Norwegian Archaeological Review* 37: 21–40.

Barrett, J. C.
   1988. Fields of Discourse. *Critique of Anthropology* 7(3): 5–16.

Barrett, J., Bradley, R., and Green, M.
   1991. *Landscape, Monuments and Society: The Prehistory of Cranborne Chase.* Cambridge: Cambridge University Press.

Bartholomew, P.
   1982. Fifth-Century Facts. *Britannia* 13: 261–70.

Bateman, N.
   1997. The London Amphitheatre: Excavations 1987–1996. *Britannia* 28: 51–86.

Bateman, N.
   1998. Public Buildings in Roman London: Some Contrasts. In B. Watson (ed.), *Roman London Recent Archaeological Work*: 47–57. Portsmouth, RI: Journal of Roman Archaeology Supplementary Series 24.

Bateman, N., Cowan, C., and Wroe-Brown, R.
   2008. *London's Roman amphitheatre: Guildhall Yard, City of London.* London: MoLAS, Monograph 35.

Bayard, D. and Massy, J. L.
   1983. *Amiens Romain: Samarobriva Ambianorum.* Amiens: Revue Archéologique de Picardie.

Bayard, D. and Piton, D.
   1979. Un bâtiment public du bas-empire à Amiens: 1973–1978, six ans de recherches au logis du roy. *Cahiers Archéologiques de Picardie* 6: 153–68.

Beard, D. and Cowan, C.
   1988. Excavations at 15–23 Southwark Street. *The London Archaeologist* 5(14): 375–81.

Beard, M. and Henderson, J.
   1995. *Classics: A Very Short Introduction.* Oxford: Oxford University Press.

Beaujard, B.
   2006. Les cités de la Gaule Méridionale du IIIe au VIIe s. *Gallia* 63: 11–23.

Bedon, R. (ed.).
   1996. *Les Villes de la Gaule Lyonnaise.* Limoges: PULIM, Caesarodunum 30.

Bell, T.
   2005. *The Religious Reuse of Roman Structures in Early Medieval England.* Oxford: Archaeopress, British Archaeological Reports British Series 390.

Bender, B.
   2001. Introduction. In B. Bender and M. Winer (eds.), *Contested Landscapes: Movement, Exile and Place*: 1–18. Oxford: Berg.

Bennett, P.
   1981. 68–69a Stour Street. *Archaeologia Cantiana* 97: 279–81.

Bennett, P.
   1988. No. 25 Watling Street. *Archaeologia Cantiana* 106: 129–30.

Bennett, P. and Nebiker, D.
   1989. No. 76 Castle Street. *Archaeologia Cantiana* 107: 283–6.

Bennett, P., Frere, S. S., and Stow, S.
   1982. *Excavations at Canterbury Castle.* Maidstone: Canterbury Archaeological Trust.

Bergstøl, J.
   2002. Iron Technology and Magic in Iron Age Norway. In B. S. Ottaway and E. C. Wager (eds.), *Metals and Society: Papers from a Session Held at the European Association of Archaeologists Sixth Annual Meeting in Lisbon 2000*: 77–82. Oxford: Archaeopress, British Archaeological Reports International Series 1061.

Bevan, B.
   1997. Bounding the Landscape: Place and Identity during the Yorkshire Wolds Iron Age. In A.

Gwilt and C. Haselgrove (eds.), *Reconstructing Iron Age Societies: New Approaches to the British Iron Age*: 181–91. Oxford: Oxbow Books.

Biddle, M.
1966. Excavations at Winchester, 1965: Fourth Interim Report. *The Antiquaries Journal* 46: 308–32.

Biddle, M.
1975. Excavations at Winchester, 1971: Tenth and Final Interim Report: Part II. *The Antiquaries Journal* 55: 295–337.

Biddle, M.
1984. *The Study of Winchester: Archaeology and History of a British Town*. London: The British Academy.

Biddle, M. and Kjølbye-Biddle, B.
2007. Winchester: From *Venta* to *Wintancæstir*. In L. Gilmour (ed.), *Pagans and Christians – From Antiquity to the Middle Ages: Papers in Honour of Martin Henig, Presented on the Occasion of His 65th Birthday*: 189–214. Oxford: Archaeopress, British Archaeological Reports International Series 1610.

Bidwell, P. T.
1979. *The Legionary Bath-House and Basilica and Forum at Exeter*. Exeter: Exeter City Council and the University of Exeter, Exeter Archaeology Reports, Volume I.

Binford, L. R.
1981. Behavioural Archaeology and the 'Pompeii Premise'. *Journal of Anthropological Research* 37(3): 195–208.

Birley, A. R.
2005. *The Government of Roman Britain*. Oxford: Oxford University Press.

Black, E. W.
1995. *Cursus Publicus: The Infrastructure of Government in Roman Britain*. Oxford: Tempus Reparatum, British Archaeological Reports British Series 241.

Black, J.
1985. *The British and the Grand Tour*. London: Croom Helm.

Blagg, T. F. C.
1980. Roman Pewter-Moulds. In C. Heighway and P. Garrod (eds.), Excavations at Numbers 1 and 30 Westgate Street, Gloucester: The Roman Levels: 103–5. *Britannia* 11: 73–114.

Blockley, K., Blockley, M., Blockley, P., Frere S. S., and Stow, S.
1995. *Excavations in the Marlowe Car Park and Surrounding Areas*. Canterbury: Canterbury Archaeological Trust, The Archaeology of Canterbury Monograph Series V(i).

Blockley, P.
1987. The Tannery. *Archaeologia Cantiana* 104: 314.

Blockley, P.
1989. Excavations at Riding Gate, Canterbury, 1986–87. *Archaeologia Cantiana* 107: 117–54.

Boman, H.
2003. *Movement in Space: An Architectural Analysis of Public Space in Archaic to Hellenistic Greece*. Göteborg: Department of Classical Archaeology and Ancient History.

Bomgardner, D. L.
2000. *The Story of the Roman Amphitheatre*. London: Routledge.

Bonnard, G. (ed.).
1945. *Le Journal de Gibbon à Lausanne 17 Août 1763–19 Avril 1764*. Lausanne: Librairie de l'Université.

Boon, G. C.
1974. *Silchester: The Roman Town of Calleva* (2nd ed.). Newton Abbott: David and Charles.

Booth, P.
    2001. The Roman Shrine at Westhawk Farm, Ashford: A Preliminary Account. *Archaeologia Cantiana* 121: 1–24.

Bouet, A.
    2003. *Les Thermes privés et publics en Gaule Narbonnaise*. Rome: École Française de Rome.

Bowden, W.
    2001. A New Urban Élite? Church Buildings and Church Building in Late-Antique Epirus. In L. Lavan (ed.), *Recent Research in Late Antique Urbanism*: 57–68. Portsmouth, RI: Journal of Roman Archaeology Supplementary Series 42.

Bowden, W. and Bescoby, D.
    2008. The plan of *Venta Icenorum* (Caistor-by-Norwich): Interpreting a New Geophysical Survey. *Journal of Roman Archaeology* 21: 324–34.

Bowersock, G. W.
    1976. Gibbon on Civil War and Rebellion in the Decline of the Roman Empire. *Daedalus* 105: 63–71.

Bowie, F.
    2000. *The Anthropology of Religion*. Oxford: Blackwell.

Bradley, R.
    1971. A Field Survey of the Chichester Entrenchments. In B. Cunliffe *Excavations at Fishbourne 1961–69*: 17–37. London: The Society of Antiquaries of London, Reports of the Research Committee Number 26.

Bradley, R.
    1975. Maumbury Rings, Dorchester: The Excavations of 1908–1913. *Archaeologia* 105: 1–97.

Bradley, R.
    2000. *An Archaeology of Natural Places*. London: Routledge.

Bradley, R.
    2002. *The Past in Prehistoric Societies*. London: Routledge.

Bradley, R. and Gordon, K.
    1988. Human Skulls from the River Thames, Their Dating and Significance. *Antiquity* 62: 503–9.

Branigan, K.
    1977. *Gatcombe Roman Villa*. Oxford, British Archaeological Reports British Series 44.

Braund, D.
    1996. *Ruling Roman Britain: Kings, Queens, Governors and Emperors from Julius Caesar to Agricola*. London: Routledge.

Breeze, A.
    2002. Does *Corieltavi* Mean 'Army of Many Rivers'? *The Antiquaries Journal* 82: 307–9.

Brewer, R. J.
    1990. Caerwent – Venta Silurum: A Civitas Capital. In B. C. Burnham and J. L. Davies (eds.), Conquest, Co-Existence and Change: Recent Work in Roman Wales. *Trivium* 25: 75–85.

Brewer, R. J.
    1993. Venta Silurum: A Civitas-Capital. In S. J. Greep (ed.), *Roman Towns: The Wheeler Inheritance: A Review of 50 Years' Research*: 56–65. York: Council for British Archaeology Research Report 93.

Brigham, T.
    1990. A Reassessment of the Second Basilica in London, AD 100–400. *Britannia* 21: 53–98.

Brigham, T.
    1992. Civic Centre Redevelopment: Forum and Basilica Reassessed. In G. Milne (ed.), *From Roman Basilica to Medieval Market: Archaeology in Action in the City of London*: 81–95. London: H.M.S.O.

Brock, E. P. L.
    1881. Proceedings of the Association. *Journal of the British Archaeological Association* 37: 90–1.

Bromwich, J.
    2003. *The Roman Remains of Northern and Eastern France*. London: Routledge.

Brooks, H.
    2006. Colchester before Colchester. In P. Ottaway (ed.), *A Victory Celebration: Papers on the Archaeology of Colchester and Late Iron Age-Roman Britain Presented to Philip Crummy*: 5–10. Colchester: Colchester Archaeological Trust.

Brown, A. (ed.).
    1995. *Roman Small Towns in Eastern England and Beyond*. Oxford: Oxbow Books.

Brown, D.
    1973. A Roman Pewter Hoard from Appleford, Berkshire. *Oxoniensia* 38: 184–206.

Brown, D.
    1976. Bronze and Pewter. In D. Strong and D. Brown (eds.), *Roman Crafts*: 25–41. London: Duckworth.

Brownley, M. W.
    1976. Gibbon: The Formation of Mind and Character. *Daedalus* 105: 13–25.

Bruce, J. C.
    1851. *The Roman Wall: A historical, topographical, and descriptive account of the barrier of the lower isthmus, extending from the Tyne to the Solway, deduced from numerous personal surveys*. London: J. R. Smith.

Brück, J.
    2007. Landscape Politics and Colonial Identities: Sir Richard Colt Hoare's Tour of Ireland, 1806. *Journal of Social Archaeology* 7: 224–49.

Bryant, S.
    2007. Central Places or Special Places? The Origins and Development of '*oppida*' in Hertfordshire. In C. Haselgrove and T. Moore (eds.), *The Later Iron Age in Britain and Beyond*: 62–80. Oxford: Oxbow Books.

Buckley, R.
    2000. *St. Nicholas Place, Leicester: An Archaeological Assessment of Excavations within the Footprint of the Roman Forum*. Leicester: University of Leicester Archaeology Services Report 2000/88.

Budd, P. and Taylor, T.
    1995. The Faerie Smith Meets the Bronze Industry: Magic versus Science in the Interpretation of Prehistoric Metal Making. *World Archaeology* 27: 133–43.

Burgers, A.
    2001. *The Water Supplies and Related Structures of Roman Britain*. Oxford: John and Erica Hedges, British Archaeological Reports British Series 324.

Burke, P.
    1976. Tradition and Experience: The Idea of Decline from Bruni to Gibbon. *Daedalus* 105: 137–52.

Burnham, B., Collis, J., Dobinson, C., Haselgrove, C., and Jones, M.
    2001. Themes for Urban Research, c 100 BC to AD 200. In S. James and M. Millett (eds.), *Britons and Romans: Advancing an Archaeological Agenda*: 67–76. York: Council for British Archaeology Research Report 125.

Burnham, B. and Wacher, J.
    1990. *The Small Towns of Roman Britain*. London: Batsford.

Burrow, J. W.
    1985. *Gibbon*. Oxford: Oxford University Press.

Bushe-Fox, J. P.
1914. *Second Report on the Excavations on the Site of the Roman Town at Wroxeter, Shropshire 1913*. London: The Society of Antiquaries of London, Reports of the Research Committee Number 2.

Bushe-Fox, J. P.
1916. *Third Report on the Excavations on the Site of the Roman Town at Wroxeter, Shropshire 1914*. London: The Society of Antiquaries of London, Reports of the Research Committee Number 4.

Busson, D.
1998. *Paris*. Paris: Fondation Maison des Sciences de l'Homme.

Cameron, A.
1993a. *The Mediterranean World in Late Antiquity AD 395–600*. London: Routledge.

Cameron, A.
1993b. *The Later Roman Empire AD 284–430*. London: Fontana Press.

Cameron, A.
2001. A response. In L. Lavan (ed.), *Recent Research in Late Antique Urbanism*: 238–9. Portsmouth, RI: Journal of Roman Archaeology Supplementary Series 42.

Camp, J.
1988. General Discussion on Water in the Cult. In R. Higg, N. Marinatos, and G. C. Nordquist (eds.), *Early Greek Cult Practice: Proceedings of the Fifth International Symposium at the Swedish Institute at Athens, 26–29 June, 1986*: 172. Stockholm: The Institute.

Cantino Wataghin, G.
1999. The Ideology of Urban Burials. In G. P. Brogiolo and B. Ward-Perkins (eds.), *The Idea and the Ideal of the Town between Late Antiquity and the Early Middle Ages*: 147–80. Leiden: Brill.

Cantino Wataghin, G.
2003. *Christian Topography in the Late Antique Town*. In L. Lavan and W. Bowden (eds.), *Theory and Practice in Late Antique Archaeology*: 224–56. Leiden: Brill.

Carter, H.
1972. *The Study of Urban Geography*. London: Edward Arnold.

Casal, L. A. and Gascó, C. A.
1993. The Roman Towns of the Levantine and Balearic Regions. In M. B. Galán (ed.), *The Hispano-Roman Town*: 84–107. Barcelona: Ámbit Servicios Editoriales.

Casey, E. S.
1993. *Getting Back into Place: Towards a Renewed Understanding of the Place World*. Bloomington: Indiana University Press.

Casey, E. S.
1996. How to Get from Space to Place in a Fairly Short Stretch of Time: Phenomenological Prolegomena. In S. Feld and K. H. Basso (eds.), *Senses of Place*: 13–52. Santa Fe: School of American Research Press.

Casey, P. J. (ed.).
1979. *The End of Roman Britain: Papers Arising from a Conference, Durham, 1978*. Oxford, British Archaeological Reports British Series 71.

Casey, P. J.
1989. A Votive Deposit from the River Tees at Piercebridge, County Durham. *Durham Archaeological Journal* 5: 37–42.

Casey, P. J.
1994. *Carausius and Allectus: The British Usurpers*. London: Batsford.

Casey, P. J.
2002. The Fourth Century and Beyond. In P. Salway (ed.), *The Roman Era. The British Isles: 55 BC–AD 410*: 75–104. Oxford: Oxford University Press.

Cepas Palanca, A.
1997. *Crisis y continuidad en la Hispania del siglo III*. Madrid: Conséjo superior de investigaciones cientfficas.

Champion, T.
1994. Socio-Economic Development in Eastern England in the First Millennium B.C. In K. Kristiansen and J. Jansen (eds.), *Europe in the First Millennium B.C.*: 125–44. Sheffield: J. R. Collis.

Chapman, J.
1997a. Landscapes in Flux and the Colonisation of Time. In J. Chapman and P. Dolukhanov (eds.), *Landscapes in Flux: Central and Eastern Europe in Antiquity*: 1–21. Oxford: Oxbow Books.

Chapman, J.
1997b. Places as Timemarks – The Social Construction of Prehistoric Landscapes in Eastern Hungary. In J. Chapman and P. Dolukhanov (eds.), *Landscapes in Flux: Central and Eastern Europe in Antiquity*: 137–61. Oxford: Oxbow Books.

Chavarría Arnau, A.
2004. Interpreting the Transformation of Late Roman Villas: The Case of *Hispania*. In N. Christie (ed.), *Landscapes of Change: Rural Evolutions in Late Antiquity and the Early Middle Ages*: 67–102. Aldershot: Ashgate.

Childe, V. G.
1950. The Urban Revolution. *Town Planning Review* 21: 3–17.

Christie, N.
2006. *From Constantine to Charlemagne: An Archaeology of Italy AD 300–800*. Aldershot: Ashgate.

Christie, N. and Loseby, S. T. (eds.).
1996. *Towns in Transition: Urban Evolution in Late Antiquity and the Early Middle Ages*. Aldershot: Scholar.

Churchill, W.
1941. *The Story of my Early Life: A Roving Commission*. New York: Charles Scribner's Sons.

Clarke, D. L.
1968. *Analytical Archaeology*. London: Methuen.

Clay, P. and Mellor, J. E.
1985. *Excavations in Bath Lane, Leicester*. Leicester: Leicestershire Museums Archaeological Report 10.

Clay, P. and Pollard, R.
1994. *Iron Age and Roman Occupation in the West Bridge Area, Leicester: Excavations 1962–1971*. Leicester: Leicester Museums Arts and Records Service.

Clifford, E. M.
1961. *Bagendon: A Belgic Oppidum. A Record of Excavations of 1954–56*. Cambridge: W. Heffer and Sons.

Coles, J.
2001. North European Bronzes, Rock Art and Wetlands: Looking for Context and Relations. A *Preliminary Study*. In B. A. Purdy (ed.), *Enduring Records: The Environmental and Cultural Heritage of Wetlands*: 148–57. Oxford: Oxbow Books.

Collingwood, R. G.
1946. *The Idea of History*. Oxford: Clarendon Press.

Collingwood, R. G. and Myres, J. N. L.
1936. *Roman Britain and the English Settlements*. Oxford: Clarendon Press.

Collingwood, R. G. and Richmond, I.
1969. *The Archaeology of Roman Britain*. London: Methuen.

Colyer, C. and Jones, M. J.
    1979. Excavations at Lincoln Second Interim Report in the Lower Town 1972–8. *The Antiquaries
    Journal* 59: 50–91.

Cool, H. E. M.
    2004. *The Roman Cemetery at Brough, Cumbria: Excavations 1966–67*. London: Society for the
    Promotion of Roman Studies, Britannia Monograph Series 21.

Cool, H. E. M.
    2006. *Eating and Drinking in Roman Britain*. Cambridge: Cambridge University Press.

Cool, H. E. M. and Baxter, M. J.
    2002. Exploring Romano-British Finds Assemblages. *Oxford Journal of Archaeology* 21: 365–80.

Cool, H. E. M., Lloyd-Morgan, G., and Hooley, A. D.
    1995. *Finds from the Fortress*. York: Council for British Archaeology for the York Archaeological
    Trust.

Cooper, N. J.
    1999. The Small Finds. In A. Connor and R. Buckley (eds.), *Roman and Medieval Occupation
    in Causeway Lane, Leicester*: 239–82. Leicester: School of Archaeological Studies, Leicester
    Archaeology Monographs 5.

Cooper, N. J.
    n.d. *Excavations at Blue Boar Lane, Leicester 1958*. Leicester: University of Leicester Archaeolog-
    ical Services, unpublished manuscript.

Cooper, N. J. and Buckley, R.
    2004. Recent, and not so Recent Work, in Roman Leicester (*Ratae Corieltauvorum*). In P. Bowman
    and P. Liddle (eds.), *Leicestershire Landscapes*: 51–70. Leicester: Leicestershire City Council.

Corder, P.
    1940. Excavations in the Forum of Verulamium (Insula XII) 1939. *The Antiquaries Journal* 20:
    500–3.

Cosgrove, D. E.
    1984. *Social Formation and Symbolic Landscape*. London: Croom Helm.

Cosh, S. R.
    2004. A Possible Date for the Silchester Roman 'Church'. *Britannia* 35: 229–33.

Cowan, C.
    1992. A Possible Mansio in Roman Southwark: Excavations at 15–23 Southwark Street, 1980–86.
    Transactions of the London and Middlesex Archaeological Society 43: 3–192.

Cowan, C., Seeley, F., Wardle, A., Westman, A. and Wheeler, L.
    2009. *Roman Southwark Settlement and Economy: Excavations in Southwark 1973–91*. London:
    MoLA, Monograph 42.

Cracknell, S. and Hingley, R., with Canti, M.
    1996. Hobditch Linear Earthworks: Survey and Excavation 1987. *Transactions of the Birmingham
    and Warwickshire Archaeology Society* 99: 47–56.

Craddock, P.
    1989. *Edward Gibbon, Luminous Historian, 1772–1794*. Baltimore: The Johns Hopkins University
    Press.

Crawford, M. H.
    1996. lex (2). In S. Hornblower and A. Spawforth (eds.), *The Oxford Classical Dictionary*: 849–53.
    Oxford: Oxford University Press.

Creighton, J.
    2000. *Coins and Power in Late Iron Age Britain*. Cambridge: Cambridge University Press.

Creighton, J.
    2001. The Iron Age–Roman Transition. In S. James and M. Millett (eds.), *Britons and Romans*:

Advancing an Archaeological Agenda: 4–11. York: Council for British Archaeology Research Report 125.

Creighton, J.
   2006. *Britannia: The Creation of a Roman Province*. London: Routledge.

Cresswell, T.
   2004. *Place: A Short Introduction*. Oxford: Blackwell.

Cripps, W.
   1898. Notes on the Roman Basilica at Cirencester, Lately Discovered by Wilfred J. Cripps, Esq., C.B. *Transactions of the Bristol and Gloucestershire Archaeological Society* 21: 70–8.

Croxford, B.
   2003. Iconoclasm in Roman Britain? *Britannia* 34: 81–96.

Crummy, N.
   1983. *The Roman Small Finds from Excavations in Colchester 1971–9*. Colchester: Colchester Archaeological Trust, Colchester Archaeology Report 2.

Crummy, N., Crummy, P., and Crossan, C.
   1993. *Excavations of Roman and Later Cemeteries, Churches and Monastic Sites in Colchester, 1971–88*. Colchester: Colchester Archaeological Trust, Colchester Archaeology Report 9.

Crummy, P.
   1980. The Temples of Roman Colchester. In W. Rodwell (ed.), *Temples, Churches and Religion in Roman Britain*: 243–84. Oxford, British Archaeological Reports British Series 77.

Crummy, P.
   1982. The Roman Theatre at Colchester. *Britannia* 13: 299–302.

Crummy, P.
   1984. *Excavations at Lion Walk, Balkerne Lane and Middleborough, Colchester, Essex*. Colchester: Colchester Archaeological Trust, Colchester Archaeology Report 3.

Crummy, P.
   1992. *Excavations at Culver Street, the Gilberd School and Other Sites in Colchester 1971–85*. Colchester: Colchester Archaeological Trust, Colchester Archaeology Report 6.

Crummy, P.
   1997. *City of Victory: The Story of Colchester – Britain's First Roman Town*. Colchester: Colchester Archaeological Trust.

Crummy, P.
   2008. The Roman Circus at Colchester. *Britannia* 39: 15–31.

Crummy, P., Benfield, S., Crummy, N., Rigby, V., and Shimmin, D.
   2007. *Stanway: An Élite Burial Site at Camulodunum*. London: Society for the Promotion of Roman Studies, Britannia Monograph Series 24.

Cunliffe, B.
   1984. *Danebury: An Iron Age Hillfort in Hampshire: Vol. 1–2, The Excavations, 1969–1978*. London: Council for British Archaeology Research Report 52.

Cunliffe, B.
   1988. Summary and Discussion. In B. Cunliffe (ed.), *The Temple of Sulis Minerva at Bath Volume 2: The Finds from the Sacred Spring*: 359–62. Oxford: Oxford University Committee for Archaeology.

Cunliffe, B.
   1992. Pits, Preconceptions and Propitiation in the British Iron Age. *Oxford Journal of Archaeology* 11: 69–83.

Cunliffe, B.
   1999. Sir Mortimer Wheeler. In T. Murray (ed.), *Encyclopaedia of Archaeology: The Great Archaeologists*: 371–83. Santa Barbara: ABC-CLIO.

Cunliffe, B.
  2000. *Roman Bath Discovered*. Stroud: Tempus.

Cunliffe, B.
  2004. Wessex Cowboys? *Oxford Journal of Archaeology* 23: 61–81.

Cunliffe, B.
  2005. *Iron Age Communities in Britain: An Account of England, Scotland and Wales from the Seventh Century BC until the Roman Conquest* (4th ed.). London: Routledge.

Darby, H. C.
  1973. The Age of the Improver: 1600–1800. In H. C. Darby (ed.), *A New Historical Geography of England*: 302–88. Cambridge: Cambridge University Press.

Dark, K.
  1993. Roman-Period Activity at Prehistoric Ritual Monuments in Britain and in the Armorican Peninsula. In E. Scott (ed.), *Theoretical Roman Archaeology First Conference Proceedings*: 133–46. Aldershot: Avebury.

Dark, K.
  1994. *Civitas to Kingdom: British Political Continuity, 300–800*. Leicester: Leicester University Press.

Darling, M. J. and Jones, M. J.
  1988. Early Settlement at Lincoln. *Britannia* 19: 1–57.

Darvill, T. and Gerrard, C.
  1994. *Cirencester: Town and Landscape*. Cirencester: Cotswold Archaeological Trust.

Darvill, T. and Timby, J.
  1986. Excavations at Saintbridge, Gloucester, 1981. *Transactions of the Bristol and Gloucestershire Archaeological Society* 104: 49–60.

Davies, J. A.
  1996. Where Eagles Dare: The Iron Age of Norfolk. *Proceedings of the Prehistoric Society* 62: 63–94.

Dawson, C.
  1934. Edward Gibbon. *Proceedings of the British Academy* 20: 159–80.

de Jersey, P.
  1996. *Celtic Coinage in Britain*. Princes Risborough: Shire Publications.

DeLaine, J.
  1999a. Benefactions and Urban Renewal: Bath Buildings in Roman Italy. In J. DeLaine and D. B. Johnston (eds.), *Roman Baths and Bathing*: 67–74. Portsmouth, RI: Journal of Roman Archaeology Supplementary Series 37.

DeLaine, J.
  1999b. Introduction: Bathing and Society. In J. DeLaine and D. B. Johnston (eds.), *Roman Baths and Bathing*: 7–16. Portsmouth, RI: Journal of Roman Archaeology Supplementary Series 37.

Derks, T.
  1998. *Gods, Temples and Ritual Practices. The Transformation of Religious Ideas and Values in Roman Gaul*. Amsterdam: Amsterdam University Press.

Díaz-Andreu, M.
  2002. Ethnic Identity/Ethnicity and Archaeology. In N. J. Smelser and P. B. Baltes (eds.), *International Encyclopaedia of the Social and Behavioural Sciences*: 4817–21. Oxford: Elsevier.

Dobney, K., Jacques, S., and Irving, B.
  1996. *Of Butchers and Breeds. Report on Vertebrate Remains from Various Sites in the City of Lincoln*. Oxford: Oxbow Books, Lincoln Archaeological Studies 5.

Dowden, K.
  1992. *Religion and the Romans*. London: Bristol Classical Press.

Down, A.
1978. *Chichester Excavations III*. Chichester: Phillimore.

Down, A.
1988. *Roman Chichester*. Chichester: Phillimore.

Down, A. and Magilton, J.
1993. *Chichester Excavations VIII*. Chichester: Phillimore.

Downey, R., King, A., and Soffe, G.
1979. *The Hayling Island Temple: Third Interim Report on the Excavation of the Iron Age and Roman Temple 1976–78*. London: R. R. Downey.

Driver, J. C., Rady, J., and Sparks, M.
1990. *Excavations in the Cathedral Precincts, 2 Linacre Gardens, 'Meister Omers' and St. Gabriel's Chapel*. Maidstone: Canterbury Archaeological Trust.

Drummond-Murray, J. and Thompson, P., with Cowan, C.
2002. *Settlement in Roman Southwark: Archaeological Excavations (1991–8) for the London Underground Limited Jubilee Line Extension Project*. London: MoLAS, Monograph 12.

Drury, P. J.
1984. The Temple of Claudius at Colchester Reconsidered. *Britannia* 15: 7–50.

Drury, P. J.
1988. *The Mansio and Other Sites in the South-East Sector of Caesaromagus*. London: Council for British Archaeology Research Report 75.

Dumasy, F.
2000. *Le théâtre d'Argentomagus (Saint-Marcel, Indre)*. Paris: Éditions de la Maison des Sciences de l'Homme.

Dungworth, D.
1998. Mystifying Roman Nails: *clavus annulis, defixiones* and *mintisi*. In C. Forcey, J. Hawthorne, and R. Witcher (eds.), *TRAC 97: Proceedings of the Seventh Annual Theoretical Roman Archaeology Conference*: 148–59. Oxford: Oxbow Books.

Dunnett, R.
1971. The Excavations of the Roman Theatre at Gosbecks. *Britannia* 2: 27–47.

Dunwoodie, L.
2004. *Pre-Boudican and Later Activity on the Site of the Forum: Excavations at 168 Fenchurch Street, City of London*. London: Museum of London Archaeology Service, Archaeology Studies Series 13.

Dupré Raventós, X.
2004. *Tarragona: Colonia Iulia Urbs Triumphalis Tarraco*. Rome: 'L'Erma' di Bretschneider.

Durrani, N.
2004. Tabard Square Excavations, Southwark. *Current Archaeology* 192: 540–7.

Dyson, S. L.
2006. *In Pursuit of Ancient Pasts: A History of Classical Archaeology in the Nineteenth and Twentieth Centuries*. New Haven: Yale University Press.

Dyson, T.
1978. Two Saxon Land Grants from Queenhithe. In J. Bird, H. Chapman, and J. Clark (eds.), *Collectanea Londiniensia: Studies in London Archaeology and History Presented to Ralph Merrifield*: 200–15. London: London and Middlesex Archaeological Society, Special Paper 2.

Edensor, T.
2000. Moving through the City. In D. Bell and A. Haddour (eds.), *City Visions*: 121–49. Harlow: Prentice Hall.

Edensor, T.
2005. *Industrial Ruins: Space, Aesthetics and Materiality*. Oxford: Berg.

Edmondson, J. C.
1996. Dynamic Arenas: Gladiatorial Presentation in the City of Rome and the Construction of Roman Society during the Early Empire. In W. J. Slater (ed.), *Roman Theatre and Society: E. Togo Salmon Papers I*: 69–112. Ann Arbor: University of Michigan Press.

Ellis, P.
1997. Pooling Resources – The Use of Water for Social Control in the Roman Empire. In K. Meadows, C. Lemke, and J. Heron (eds.), *TRAC 96: Proceedings of the Sixth Annual Theoretical Roman Archaeology Conference*: 144–50. Oxford: Oxbow Books.

Ellis, P. (ed.).
2000. *The Roman Baths and Macellum at Wroxeter: Excavations by Graham Webster 1955–85*. London: English Heritage.

Elton, H.
2006. The Transformation of Government under Diocletian and Constantine. In D. S. Potter (ed.), *A Companion to the Roman Empire*: 193–205. Oxford: Blackwell.

Esmonde Cleary, A. S.
1989. *The Ending of Roman Britain*. London: Batsford.

Esmonde Cleary, A. S.
2001. The Roman to Medieval Transition. In S. James and M. Millett (eds.), *Britons and Romans: Advancing an Archaeological Agenda*: 90–7. York: Council for British Archaeology Research Report 125.

Esmonde Cleary, A. S.
2004. Britain in the Fourth Century. In M. Todd (ed.), *A Companion to Roman Britain*: 409–27. Oxford: Blackwell.

Esmonde Cleary, A. S.
2005. Beating the Bounds: Ritual and the Articulation of Urban Space in Roman Britain. In A. Mac Mahon and J. Price (eds.), *Roman Working Lives and Urban Living*: 1–17. Oxford: Oxbow Books.

Evans, C.
1985. Tradition and the Cultural Landscape: An Archaeology of Place. *Archaeological Review from Cambridge* 4(1): 80–94.

Evans, J.
1993. Finds Synthesis. In P. J. Casey and J. L. Davies (eds.), *Excavations at Segontium (Caernarfon) Roman Fort, 1975–1979*: 80–1. London: Council for British Archaeology Research Report 90.

Farrell, J.
2001. *Latin Language and Latin Culture: From Ancient to Modern Times*. Cambridge: Cambridge University Press.

Faulkner, N.
1996. Verulamium: Interpreting Decline. *The Archaeological Journal* 153: 79–103.

Faulkner, N.
2000a. *The Decline and Fall of Roman Britain*. Stroud: Tempus.

Faulkner, N.
2000b. Change and Decline in Late Romano-British Towns. In T. R. Slater (ed.), *Towns in Decline AD 100–1600*: 25–50. Aldershot: Ashgate.

Faulkner, N.
2004. The Case for the Dark Ages. In R. Collins and J. Gerrard (eds.), *Debating Late Antiquity in Britain A.D. 300–700*: 5–12. Oxford: Archaeopress, British Archaeological Reports British Series 365.

Favro, D.
1996. *The Urban Image of Augustan Rome*. Cambridge: Cambridge University Press.

Feld, S.
1996. Waterfalls of Song: An Acousterology of Place Resounding in Bosavi, Papua New Guinea. In S. Feld and K. H. Basso (eds.), *Senses of Place*: 91–135. Santa Fe: School of American Research Press.

Fentress, J. and Wickham, C.
1992. *Social Memory*. Oxford: Blackwell.

Ferguson, J.
1970. *The Religion of the Roman Empire*. London: Thames and Hudson.

Field, N. and Parker Pearson, M.
2003. *Fiskerton: An Iron Age Timber Causeway with Iron Age and Roman Votive Offerings*. Oxford: Oxbow Books.

Fincham, G.
2002. *Landscapes of Imperialism: Roman and Native Interaction in the East Anglian Fenland*. Oxford: Archaeopress, British Archaeological Reports British Series 738.

Fincham, G.
2004. *Durobrivae: A Roman Town between Fenland and Upland*. Stroud: Tempus.

Finley, M. I.
1973. *The Ancient Economy*. Berkeley: University of California Press.

Fitts, R. L., Haselgrove, C. C., Lowther, P. C., and Willis, S. H.
1999. Melsonby Revisited: Survey and Excavation 1992–95 at the Site of Discovery of the 'Stanwick', North Yorkshire, Hoard of 1843. *Durham Archaeological Journal* 14–15: 1–52.

Fitzpatrick, A. P.
1984. The Deposition of La Tène Iron Age Metalwork in Watery Contexts in Southern England. In B. Cunliffe and D. Miles (eds.), *Aspects of the Iron Age in Central Southern Britain*: 178–90. Oxford: Oxford University Committee for Archaeology, Institute of Archaeology.

Foucault, M.
1970. *The Order of Things: An Archaeology of the Social Sciences*. London: Tavistock.

Fox, C. F.
1946. *A Find from the Early Iron Age from Llyn Cerrig Bach, Anglesey*. Cardiff: National Museum of Wales.

Fox, G. E. and St. John Hope, W. H.
1890. Excavations on the Site of the Roman City at Silchester, Hants. *Archaeologia* 52: 733–58.

Fox, G. E. and St. John Hope, W. H.
1893. Excavations on the Site of the Roman City at Silchester, Hants., in 1892. *Archaeologia* 53: 539–73.

Fox, G. E. and St. John Hope, W. H.
1894. Excavations on the Site of the Roman City of Silchester, Hants., in 1893. *Archaeologia* 54: 199–238.

France, N. E. and Gobel, B. M.
1985. *The Romano-British Temple at Harlow*. Harlow: West Essex Archaeological Group.

Freeman, P.
2007. *The Best Training-Ground for Archaeologists: Francis Haverfield and the Invention of Romano-British Archaeology*. Oxford: Oxbow Books.

Frere, S. S.
1967. *Britannia: A History of Roman Britain*. London: Routledge and Kegan Paul.

Frere, S. S.
1970. The Roman Theatre at Canterbury. *Britannia* 1: 83–113.

Frere, S. S.
1971. The Forum and Baths at Caistor-by-Norwich. *Britannia* 2: 1–26.

Frere, S. S.
　1975. The Silchester Church: The Excavation by Sir Ian Richmond in 1961. *Archaeologia* 105: 277–302.

Frere, S. S.
　1977. Roman Britain in 1976: Sites Explored. *Britannia* 8: 356–425.

Frere, S. S.
　1983. *Verulamium Excavations Vol. II.* London: The Society of Antiquaries of London, Reports of the Research Committee Number 41.

Frere, S. S.
　1984. Excavations at Dorchester on Thames, 1963. *The Archaeological Journal* 141: 91–174.

Frere, S. S. and Bennett, P.
　1987. *Canterbury Excavations: Intra- and Extra-Mural Sites, 1949–55 and 1980–84.* Maidstone: Canterbury Archaeological Trust.

Frere, S. S. and Stow, S.
　1983. *Excavations in the St. George's Street and Burgate Street Areas.* Maidstone: Canterbury Archaeological Trust.

Frezouls, E.
　1982. *Les Villes antiques de la France. 1, Belgique 1: Amiens, Beauvais, Grand, Metz.* Strasbourg: AECR.

Fulford, M.
　1979. Pottery Production and Trade at the End of Roman Britain: The Case against Continuity. In P. J. Casey (ed.), *The End of Roman Britain*: 120–32. Oxford, British Archaeological Reports British Series 71.

Fulford, M.
　1984. *Silchester Defences 1974–80.* London: Society for the Promotion of Roman Studies, Britannia Monograph Series 5.

Fulford, M.
　1989. *The Silchester Amphitheatre: Excavations of 1979–85.* London: Society for the Promotion of Roman Studies, Britannia Monograph Series 10.

Fulford, M.
　2001. Links with the Past: Pervasive 'Ritual' Behaviour in Roman Britain. *Britannia* 32: 199–218.

Fulford, M.
　2002. A Second Start: From the Defeat of Boudicca to the Third Century. In P. Salway (ed.), *The Roman Era. The British Isles: 55 BC–AD 410*: 39–73. Oxford: Oxford University Press.

Fulford, M. and Timby, J.
　2000. *Late Iron Age and Roman Silchester: Excavations on the Site of the Forum-Basilica 1977, 1980–86.* London: Society for the Promotion of Roman Studies, Britannia Monograph Series 15.

Fulford, M., Clarke, A., and Eckhardt, H.
　2006. *Life and Labour in Late Roman Silchester: Excavations in Insula IX since 1997.* London: Society for the Promotion of Roman Studies, Britannia Monograph Series 22.

Furet, F.
　1976. Civilization and Barbarism in Gibbon's History. *Daedalus* 105: 209–16.

Gale, J.
　2003. *Prehistoric Dorset.* Stroud: Tempus.

Gammon, A., Rudling, D., and Butler, C.
　2006. *Barcombe Roman Villa.* Brighton: University of Sussex.

Gansum, T.
　2004. Role the Bones – From Iron to Steel. *Norwegian Archaeological Review* 37: 41–57.

Gardner, A.
   2004. Introduction: Social Agency, Power, and Being Human. In A. Gardner (ed.), *Agency Uncovered: Archaeological Perspectives in Social Agency, Power and Being Human*: 1–15. London: UCL Press.

Gardner, A.
   2007. *Archaeology of Identity: Soldiers and Society in Later Roman Britain*. Walnut Creek, CA: Left Coast Press.

Ghosh, P.
   1997. The Conception of Gibbon's History. In R. McKitterick and R. Quinault (eds.), *Edward Gibbon and Empire*: 271–316. Cambridge: Cambridge University Press.

Gibbon, E.
   1966. *Memoirs of My Life* (edited by G. A. Bonnard). London: Nelson.

Gibbon, E.
   1994. *The History of the Decline and Fall of the Roman Empire* (edited by D. Womersley). London: Penguin Books. (Original work published 1776–1788)

Giblett, R.
   1996. *Postmodern Wetlands: Culture, History, Ecology*. Edinburgh: Edinburgh University Press.

Gibson, A. and Woods, A.
   1997. *Prehistoric Pottery for the Archaeologist* (2nd ed.). London: Leicester University Press.

Giddens, A.
   1984. *The Constitution of Society: Outline of the Theory of Structuration*. Cambridge: Polity Press.

Giles, M.
   2007. Making Metal and Forging Relations: Ironworking in the British Iron Age. *Oxford Journal of Archaeology* 26: 395–413.

Gilmour, B.
   2007. Sub-Roman or Saxon, Pagan or Christian: Who Was Buried in the Early Cemetery at St. Paul-in-the-Bail, Lincoln? In L. Gilmour (ed.), *Pagans and Christians – From Antiquity to the Middle Ages: Papers in Honour of Martin Henig, Presented on the Occasion of His 65th Birthday*: 229–56. Oxford: Archaeopress, British Archaeological Reports International Series 1610.

Gilmour, B. and Jones, M. J.
   1980. Lincoln, St. Paul-in-the-Bail. *Lincolnshire History and Archaeology* 15: 73–6.

Gosden, C. and Lock, G.
   1998. Prehistoric Histories. *World Archaeology* 30: 2–12.

Graddel, I.
   2002. *Emperor Worship and Roman Religion*. Oxford: Clarendon Press.

Grahame, M.
   1997. Towards a Theory of Roman Urbanism: Beyond Economics and Ideal-Types. In K. Meadows, C. Lemke, and J. Heron (eds.), *TRAC 96: Proceedings of the Sixth Annual Theoretical Roman Archaeology Conference*: 151–62. Oxford: Oxbow Books.

Granados, J. O.
   1995. Notes per a l'estudi de la Basílica i del conjunt episcopal paleocristia de Barcelona: Valoracio de la primera fase. In J. M. Gurt and N. Tena (eds.), *IV Reunió d'arqueología cristiana hispánica (Lisboa), Barcelona*: 121–32. Barcelona: Institut d'Estudis Catalans.

Graves, C. P.
   2000. *The Form and Fabric of Belief: An Archaeology of the Lay Experience of Religion in Medieval Norfolk and Devon*. Oxford: John and Erica Hedges, British Archaeological Reports British Series 311.

Green, H. J. M.
   1975. Roman Godmanchester. In W. Rodwell and T. Rowley (eds.), *The Small Towns of Roman Britain*: 183–210. Oxford, British Archaeological Reports British Series 15.

Green, M. J.
1986. *The Gods of the Celts*. Gloucester: Alan Sutton.

Greene, K.
2005. The Economy of Roman Britain: Representation and Historiography. In J. Bruhn, B. Croxford, and D. Grigoropoulos (eds.), *TRAC 2004: Proceedings of the Fourteenth Annual Theoretical Archaeology Conference Durham 2004*: 1–15. Oxford: Oxbow Books.

Gregory, T.
1991. Metal-Detecting on a Scheduled Ancient Monument. *Norfolk Archaeology* 41: 186–96.

Gros, P.
1996. *L'Architecture Romaine du début du IIIe siècle av. J.-C. à la fin du Haut-Empire I: Les monuments publics*. Paris: Les Monuments d'art et d'archéologie antiques.

Guest, P.
n.d. Report on the Excavations of the *Basilica* at Caerwent. Unpublished manuscript, University of Cardiff.

Gurney, D.
1986. A Romano-Celtic Temple at Caistor St. Edmund. In T. Gregory and D. Gurney (eds.), *Excavations at Thornham, Warham, Wighton and Caistor St. Edmund, Norfolk*: 37–54. East Anglian Archaeology Report 30.

Guyard, L.
2003. *Le college de France (Paris): du quartier gallo-romain au quartier Latin*. Paris: Éditions de la Maison des Sciences de l'Homme.

Guyon, J.
2006. Émergence et affirmation d'une topographie chrétienne dans les villes de la Gaule Méridionale. *Gallia* 63: 85–115.

Haaland, R.
1985. Iron Production, its Socio-Cultural Context and Ecological Implications. In R. Haaland and P. Shinnie (eds.), *African Iron-Working – Ancient and Traditional*: 50–72. Oslo: Norwegian University Press.

Hall, T.
2006. *Urban Geography* (3rd ed.). London: Routledge.

Halsall, G.
1996. Towns, Societies and Ideas: The Not-So-Strange Case of Late Roman and Early Merovingian Metz. In N. Christie and S. T. Loseby (eds.), *Towns in Transition*: 235–61. Hertfordshire: Scholar Press.

Hansen, M. F.
2003. *The Eloquence of Appropriation: Prolegomena to an Understanding of Spolia in Early Christian Rome*. Rome: L'Erma di Bretschneider.

Harris, J.
1993. The Background to the Code. In J. Harris and I. Wood (eds.), *The Theodosian Code*: 1–16. Ithaca, NY: Cornell University Press.

Haselgrove, C.
1983. Celtic Coins Found in Britain, 1977–82. *Institute of Archaeology Bulletin* 20: 107–54.

Haselgrove, C.
1987. *Iron Age Coinage in South-East England*. Oxford, British Archaeological Reports British Series 174.

Haselgrove, C.
1989. Celtic Coins Found in Britain, 1982–7. *Institute of Archaeology Bulletin* 26: 1–76.

Haselgrove, C.
1992. Warfare, Ritual and Society in Iron Age Wessex. *The Archaeological Journal* 149: 407–20.

Haselgrove, C.
1999. *The Iron Age*. In J. Hunter and I. Ralston (eds.), *The Archaeology of Britain*: 113–34. London: Routledge.

Haselgrove, C., Armit, I., Champion, T., Creighton, J., Gwilt, A., Hill, J. D., Hunter, F., and Woodward, A.
2001. *Understanding the British Iron Age: An Agenda for Action. A Report for the Iron Age Research Seminar and the Council of the Prehistoric Society.*Salisbury: Trust for Wessex Archaeology.

Haselgrove, C. and Hingley, R.
2006. Iron Deposition and Its Significance in Pre-Roman Britain. In G. Bataille and J.-P. Guillaumet (eds.), *Les dépôts métalliques au second âge du Fer en Europe tempérée: Actes de la table ronde des 12 et 14 octobre 2004 (Glux-en-Glenne – F-58)*: 147–63. Glux-en-Glenne: Bibracte, Centre archéologique européen.

Haselgrove, C. and Millett, M.
1997. Verlamion Reconsidered. In A. Gwilt and C. Haselgrove (eds.), *Reconstructing Iron Age Societies: New Approaches to the British Iron Age*: 282–96. Oxford: Oxbow Books.

Haselgrove, C. and Moore, T. (eds.).
2007a. *The Later Iron Age in Britain and Beyond*. Oxford: Oxbow Books.

Haselgrove, C. and Moore, T. (eds.).
2007b. New Narratives of the Later Iron Age. In C. Haselgrove and T. Moore (eds.), *The Later Iron Age in Britain and Beyond*: 1–15. Oxford: Oxbow Books.

Haselgrove, C., Turnbull, P., and Fitts, R. L.
1990. Stanwick, North Yorkshire, Part I: Recent Research and Previous Archaeological Investigations. *The Archaeological Journal* 147: 1–15.

Haselgrove, C. and Wigg-Wolf, D.
2005. Introduction. In C. Haselgrove and D. Wigg-Wolf (eds.), *Iron Age Coinage and Ritual Practices*: 9–22. Mainz am Rhein: Van Zabern.

Häussler, R.
1999. Architecture, Performance and Ritual: The Role of State Architecture in the Roman Empire. In P. Baker, C. Forcey, S. Jundi, and R. Witcher (eds.), *TRAC 98: Proceedings of the Eighth Annual Theoretical Roman Archaeology Conference*: 1–13. Oxford: Oxbow Books.

Haverfield, F.
1912. *The Romanization of Roman Britain*. Oxford: Clarendon Press.

Haverfield, F.
1913. *Ancient Town Planning*. Oxford: Clarendon Press.

Haverfield, F.
1924. *The Roman Occupation of Britain*. Oxford: Clarendon Press.

Hawkes, C. F. C. and Crummy, P.
1995. *Camulodunum 2*. Colchester: Colchester Archaeological Trust, Colchester Archaeology Report 11.

Hawkes, C. F. C. and Hull, M. R.
1947. *Camulodunum. First Report on the Excavation at Colchester 1930–1939*. London: The Society of the Antiquaries of London, Reports of the Research Committee Number 14.

Heard, K., Sheldon, H., and Thompson, P.
1990. *Mapping Roman Southwark. Antiquity* 64: 608–19.

Heather, P.
2006. *The Fall of the Roman Empire: A New History*. London: Pan.

Hebditch, M. and Mellor, J.
1973. The Forum and Basilica of Roman Leicester. *Britannia* 4: 1–83.

Heidegger, M.
1988. *Being and Time*. Oxford: Blackwell. (First English translation 1962)

Heighway, C. and Garrod, P.
1980. Excavations at Numbers 1 and 30 Westgate Street, Gloucester: The Roman Levels. *Britannia* 11: 73–114.

Heighway, C., Garrod, A. P., and Vince A. G.
1979. Excavations at 1 Westgate Street, Gloucester, 1975. *Medieval Archaeology* 23: 159–213.

Heijmans, M.
2004. *Arles durant l'antiquité tardive: de la duplex Arelas à l'urbs Genesii*. Rome: École Française de Rome.

Heijmans, M.
2006. La place des monuments publics du haut-empire dans les villes de la Gaule Méridionale durant l'antiquité tardive (IVe–VIe s.). *Gallia* 63: 25–41.

Henig, M.
1984. *Religion in Roman Britain*. London: Batsford.

Henig, M.
1998. The Temple as a Bacchium or Sacrarium in the Fourth Century. In J. Shepherd (ed.), *The Temple of Mithras, London: Excavations by W. F. Grimes and A. Williams at the Walbrook*: 230–2. London: English Heritage.

Herbert, E. W.
1993. *Iron, Gender and Power. Ritual Transformation in African Societies*. Bloomington: Indiana University Press.

Hill, C., Millett, M., and Blagg, T.
1980. *The Roman Riverside Wall and Monumental Arch in London: Excavations at Baynard's Castle, Upper Thames Street, London, 1974–76*. London: London and Middlesex Archaeological Society, Special Paper 3.

Hill, G. B. (ed.).
1900. *The Memoirs of the Life of Edward Gibbon with Various Observations and Excursions by Himself*. London: Methuen.

Hill, J. D.
1994. Why We Should Not Take the Data from Iron Age Settlements for Granted: Recent Studies of Intra-Settlement Patterning. In A. P. Fitzpatrick and E. L. Morris (eds.), *The Iron Age in Wessex*: 4–8. Salisbury: Trust for Wessex Archaeology.

Hill, J. D.
1995a. *Ritual and Rubbish in the Iron Age of Wessex: A Study on the Formation of a Specific Archaeological Record*. Oxford: Tempus Reparatum, British Archaeological Reports British Series 242.

Hill, J. D.
1995b. How Should We Understand Iron Age Societies and Hillforts? A Contextual Study from Southern Britain. In J. D. Hill and C. G. Cumberpatch (eds.), *Different Iron Ages: Studies on the Iron Age in Temperate Europe*: 45–66. Oxford: Tempus Reparatum, British Archaeological Reports International Series 602.

Hill, J. D.
2006. Are We Any Closer to Understanding How Later Iron Age Societies Worked (or Did Not Work)? In C. Haselgrove (ed.), *Les mutations de la fin de l'âge du Fer (Collection Bibracte 12/4)*: 169–79. Glux-en-Glenne: Centre archéologique européen.

Hill, J. D.
2007. The Dynamics of Social Change in Later Iron Age Eastern and South-Eastern England c. 300 BC–AD 43. In C. Haselgrove and T. Moore (eds.), *The Later Iron Age in Britain and Beyond*: 16–40. Oxford: Oxbow Books.

Hingley, R.
  1985. Location, Function and Status: A Romano-British 'Religious Complex' at the Noah's Ark
  Inn, Frilford (Oxfordshire). *Oxford Journal of Archaeology* 4: 201–14.

Hingley, R.
  1989. *Rural Settlement in Roman Britain*. London: Seaby.

Hingley, R.
  1997a. Resistance and Domination: Social Change in Roman Britain. In D. J. Mattingly (ed.),
  *Dialogues in Roman Imperialism: Power, Discourse and Discrepant Experiences in the Roman
  Empire*: 145–66. Portsmouth, RI: Journal of Roman Archaeology Supplementary Series 23.

Hingley, R.
  1997b. Iron, Ironworking and Regeneration: A Study of the Symbolic Meaning of Metalworking
  in Iron Age Britain. In A. Gwilt and C. Haselgrove (eds.), *Reconstructing Iron Age Societies:
  New Approaches to the British Iron Age*: 9–18. Oxford: Oxbow Books.

Hingley, R.
  1999. The Creation of Later Prehistoric Landscapes and the Context of the Reuse of Neolithic
  and Earlier Bronze Age Monuments in Britain and Ireland. In B. Bevan (ed.), *Northern
  Exposure: Interpretative Devolution and the Iron Ages in Britain*: 233–51. Leicester: School of
  Archaeological Studies, Leicester Archaeology Monographs 4.

Hingley, R.
  2000. *Roman Officers and English Gentlemen*. London: Routledge.

Hingley, R.
  2001. An Imperial Legacy: The Contribution of Classical Rome to the Character of the English. In
  R. Hingley (ed.), *Images of Rome: Perceptions of Ancient Rome in Europe and the United States
  in the Modern Age*: 145–65. Portsmouth, RI: Journal of Roman Archaeology Supplementary
  Series 44.

Hingley, R.
  2006a. Projecting Empire: The Mapping of Roman Britain. *Journal of Social Archaeology* 6:
  328–53.

Hingley, R.
  2006b. The Deposition of Iron Objects in Britain during the Later Prehistoric and Roman Periods:
  Contextual Analysis and the Significance of Iron. *Britannia* 37: 213–57.

Hingley, R.
  2008. *The Recovery of Roman Britain 1586 to 1906: A Colony So Fertile*. Oxford: Oxford University
  Press.

Hingley, R.
  2009. Esoteric Knowledge? Ancient Bronze Artefacts from Iron Age Contexts. *Proceedings of the
  Prehistoric Society* 75: 143–65.

Hingley, R. and Miles, D.
  2002. The Human Impact on the Landscape: Agriculture, Settlement, Industry, Infrastructure.
  In P. Salway (ed.), *The Roman Era. The British Isles: 55 BC–AD 410*: 141–71. Oxford: Oxford
  University Press.

Hingley, R. and Willis, S. (eds.).
  2007. *Roman Finds: Context and Theory*. Oxford: Oxbow Books.

Hirsch, E.
  1995. Landscape: Between Place and Space. In E. Hirsch and M. O'Hanlon (eds.), *The Anthropology of Landscape: Perspectives on Place and Space*: 1–30. Oxford: Clarendon Press.

Hobbes, T.
  1946 (1651). *Leviathan*. Oxford: Blackwell.

Hodder, I. R.
   1972. Locational Models and the Study of Romano-British Settlement. In D. L. Clarke (ed.),
   Models in Archaeology: 887–909. London: Methuen.

Hodder, I. R.
   1979. Pre-Roman and Romano-British Tribal Economies. In B. C. Burnham and H. B. Johnson
   (eds.), *Invasion and Response: The Case of Roman Britain*: 189–96. Oxford, British Archaeological Reports British Series 73.

Holbrook, N.
   1994. Corinium Dobunnorium; Roman Civitas Capital and Provincial Capital. In T. Darvill and
   C. Gerrard (eds.), *Cirencester: Town and Landscape*: 57–86. Cirencester: Cotswold Archaeological Trust.

Holbrook, N.
   1998. *Cirencester: The Roman Town Defences, Public-Buildings and Shops*. Cirencester: Cotswold
   Archaeological Trust.

Holbrook, N.
   2008. Cirencester and the Cotswolds: The Early Roman Evolution of a Town and Rural Landscape. *Journal of Roman Archaeology* 21: 305–23.

Holder, N. and Jamieson, D.
   2003. The Prehistory of the City of London: Myths and Methodologies. *The Archaeological Journal*
   160: 23–43.

Holland, L.A.
   1961. *Janus and the Bridge*. Rome: American Academy in Rome.

Holleymen, G.
   1937. Harrow Hill Excavations, 1936. *Sussex Archaeological Collections* 78: 230–5.

Hopkins, K.
   1978. Economic Growth and Towns in Classical Antiquity. In P. Abrams and E. A. Wrigley (eds.),
   Towns in Societies: Essays in Economic History and Historical Sociology: 35–77. Cambridge:
   Cambridge University Press.

Horne, P. and King, A. C.
   1980. Romano-Celtic Temples in Continental Europe: A Gazetteer of Those with Known Plans.
   In W. Rodwell (ed.), *Temples, Churches and Religion in Roman Britain*: 369–555. Oxford,
   British Archaeological Reports British Series 77.

Horsley, J.
   1974 (1732). *Britannia Romana: Or, the Roman Antiquities of Britain*. Newcastle upon Tyne:
   Graham.

Hull, M. R.
   1958. *Roman Colchester*. London: The Society of the Antiquaries of London, Reports of the
   Research Committee Number 20.

Hunt, D.
   1993. Christianising the Roman Empire: The Evidence of the Code. In J. Harris and I. Wood
   (eds.), *The Theodosian Code*: 143–58. Ithaca, NY: Cornell University Press.

Hunt, D.
   1998. The Church as a Public Institution. In A. Cameron and P. Garnsey (eds.), *The Cambridge
   History Volume 13: The Late Empire*, A.D. 337–425: 238–76. Cambridge: Cambridge University
   Press.

Hurst, H.
   1972. Excavations at Gloucester, 1968–1971: First Interim Report. *The Antiquaries Journal* 52:
   24–69.

Hurst, H.
   1999a. Topography and Identity in Glevum colonia. In H. Hurst (ed.), *The Coloniae of Roman*

Britain: New Studies and a Review: Papers of the Conference Held at Gloucester on 5–6 July,
1997: 113–35. Portsmouth, RI: Journal of Roman Archaeology Supplementary Series 36.

Hurst, H.
1999b. Civic Space at Glevum. In H. Hurst (ed.), *The Coloniae of Roman Britain: New Studies and*
a Review: Papers of the Conference Held at Gloucester on 5–6 July, 1997: 152–60. Portsmouth,
RI: Journal of Roman Archaeology Supplementary Series 36.

Hurst, H.
2005. Roman Cirencester and Gloucester Compared. *Oxford Journal of Archaeology* 24: 293–305.

Ingold, T.
1993. The Temporality of the Landscape. *World Archaeology* 25: 152–74.

Ingold, T.
2000. *The Perception of the Environment: Essays in Livelihood, Dwelling and Skill.* London:
Routledge.

Insoll, T.
2007. 'Natural' or 'Human' Spaces? Tallensi Sacred Groves and Shrines and Their Potential
Implications for Aspects of Northern European Prehistory and Phenomenological Interpretation. *Norwegian Archaeological Review* 40: 138–58.

James, H.
1984. Carmarthen (Moridunum). *Archaeology in Wales* 24: 51.

James, H.
2003. *Roman Carmarthen.* London: Society for the Promotion of Roman Studies.

James, S.
1988. The Fabricae: State Arms Factories of the Late Roman Empire. In J. C. Coulson (ed.),
Military Equipment and the Identity of Roman Soldiers: Proceedings of the Fourth Roman
Military Equipment Conference: 257–332. Oxford, British Archaeological Reports International
Series 394.

James, S.
1999. *The Atlantic Celt: Ancient People or Modern Invention?* London: British Museum Press.

Jarvis, P. A.
1986. The Early Pits of the Jewry Wall Site, Leicester. *Transactions of the Leicestershire Archaeo-*
logical and Historical Society 60: 7–15.

Johns, E. M.
1969. The Growth of Exeter from 1840 to the Present Day. In F. Barlow (ed.), *Exeter and its*
Region: 273–85. Exeter: University of Exeter.

Johnson, M.
2002. *Behind the Castle Gate: From the Middle Ages to the Renaissance.* London: Routledge.

Johnson, M.
2006. On the Nature of Theoretical Archaeology and Archaeological Theory. *Archaeological*
Dialogues 13: 117–32.

Johnson, M.
2007. *Ideas of Landscape.* Oxford: Blackwell.

Johnson, S.
1980. *Later Roman Britain.* London: Routledge.

Johnston, P. A.
1980. *Vergil's Agricultural Golden Age. A Study of the Georgics.* Leiden: Brill.

Jones, A. H. M.
1974. *The Roman Economy. Studies in Ancient Economic and Administrative History.* London:
Blackwell.

Jones, M. E.
1996. *The End of Roman Britain*. Ithaca, NY: Cornell University Press.

Jones, M. J.
1993. The Latter Days of Roman Lincoln. In A. Vince (ed.), *Pre-Viking Lindsey*: 14–28. Oxford: Oxbow Books, Lincoln Archaeological Studies 1.

Jones, M. J.
1999. Lincoln and the British Fora in Context. In H. Hurst (ed.), *The Coloniae of Roman Britain: New Studies and a Review: Papers of the Conference Held at Gloucester on 5–6 July, 1997*: 167–74. Portsmouth, RI: Journal of Roman Archaeology Supplementary Series 36.

Jones, M. J.
2002. *Roman Lincoln: Conquest, Colonia and Capital*. Stroud: Tempus.

Jones, M. J.
2003. The Colonia Era: Archaeological Account. In D. Stocker (ed.), *The City by the Pool: Assessing the Archaeology of the City of Lincoln*: 56–138. Oxford: Oxbow Books.

Jones, M. J. and Stocker, D.
2003. Settlement in the Lincoln Area in the Prehistoric Era: Archaeological Account. In D. Stocker (ed.), *The City by the Pool: Assessing the Archaeology of the City of Lincoln*: 19–33. Oxford: Oxbow Books.

Jones, R. and Robinson, D.
2004. The Making of an Élite House: The House of the Vestals at Pompeii. *Journal of Roman Archaeology* 17: 107–30.

Jones, S.
1997. *The Archaeology of Ethnicity: Constructing Identities in the Past and Present*. London: Routledge.

Jordan, D. P.
1971. *Gibbon and His Roman Empire*. Urbana: University of Illinois Press.

Jordan, D. P.
1976. Edward Gibbon: The Historian of the Roman Empire. *Daedalus* 105: 1–12.

Joyce, J. G.
1866. On the Excavations at Silchester. *Archaeologia* 40: 403–16.

Kamash, Z.
2008. What Lies Beneath? Perceptions of the Ontological Paradox of Water. *World Archaeology* 40: 223–37.

Keay, S.
1988. *Roman Spain*. Berkeley: University of California Press.

Keay, S.
1996. Tarraco in Late Antiquity. In N. Christie and S. T. Loseby (eds.), *Towns in Transition*: 18–44. Hertfordshire: Scholar Press.

Keay, S.
2003. Recent Archaeological Work in Roman Iberia (1990–2002). *Journal of Roman Studies* 93: 146–211.

Keen, L.
1977. Dorset Archaeology in 1977. *Dorset Natural History and Archaeology Society* 99: 120–6.

Kelly, C.
1997. A Grand Tour: Reading Gibbon's Decline and Fall. *Greece and Rome* 44: 39–58.

Kempe, A. J.
1838. Observations on the Map of the Roman Road exhibited February 2d, by Sir Henry Ellis, more especially in reference to the site of 'Calleva Atrebatum'. *Archaeologia* 27: 414–19.

Kent, J.
  1978. The London Area in the Late Iron Age: An Interpretation of the Earliest Coins. In J. Bird, H. Chapman, and J. Clark (eds.), *Collectanea Londiniensia: Studies in London Archaeology and History Presented to Ralph Merrifield*: 53–8. London: London and Middlesex Archaeological Society, Special Paper 2.

Kenyon, K. M.
  1935. The Roman Theatre at Verulamium, St Albans. *Archaeologia* 84: 213–61.

Kenyon, K. M.
  1938. Excavations at Viroconium, 1936–7. *Archaeologia* 88: 175–227.

Kenyon, K. M.
  1948. *Excavations at the Jewry Wall Site, Leicester*. London: The Society of Antiquaries of London, Reports of the Research Committee Number 15.

Kenyon, K. M.
  1959. *Excavations in Southwark 1945–7*. Guildford: Surrey Archaeological Society Research Papers 5.

Keynes, G. (ed.).
  1950. *The Library of Edward Gibbon: A Catalogue of his Books*. London: The Bibliographical Society.

King, A.
  1983. The Roman Church at Silchester Reconsidered. *Oxford Journal of Archaeology* 2: 225–37.

King, A.
  2004. *Yarford 2004 Interim Report*. University of Winchester, Archaeology Subject Group, available at www2.winchester.ac.uk/archaeology/current%20research/Quantocks/YAR /EXC/ YAR_EXC.htm.

King, A. and Soffe, G.
  2001. Internal Organisation and Deposition at the Iron Age Temple on Hayling Island, Hampshire. In J. Collis (ed.), *Society and Settlement in Iron Age Europe*: 111–24. Sheffield: J. R. Collis.

Kipling, R., Parker, D., and Cooper, L.
  2007. Leicester, Bath Lane, Merlin Works. *University of Leicester Archaeological Services News*, November 2007, 5–6.

Knapp, A. B. and Ashmore, W.
  1999. Archaeological Landscapes: Constructed, Conceptualised, Ideational. In W. Ashmore and A. B. Knapp (eds.), *Archaeologies of Landscape: Contemporary Perspectives*: 1–30. Oxford: Blackwell.

Knight, J.
  1967. Excavations at the Roman Town of Irchester, 1962–3. *The Archaeological Journal* 124: 100–28.

Knight, J.
  1996. Late Roman and Post-Roman Caerwent: Some Evidence from Metalwork. *Archaeologia Cambrensis* 145: 35–66.

Knight, J.
  2001. *Roman France: An Archaeological Field Guide*. Stroud: Tempus.

Krautheimer, R.
  1983. *Three Christian Capitals: Topography and Politics*. Berkeley: University of California Press.

Kulikowski, M.
  2004. *Late Roman Spain and its Cities*. Baltimore: The John Hopkins University Press.

Lambert, F.
  1916. Recent Roman Discoveries in London. *Archaeologia* 66: 225–74.

Laurence, R.
  1994. *Roman Pompeii: Space and Society*. London: Routledge.

Laurence, R.
  2000. The Image of the Roman City. *Cambridge Journal of Archaeology* 10: 346–8.

Laurence, R.
  2001. The Creation of Geography: An Interpretation of Roman Britain. In C. Adams and R. Laurence (eds.), *Travel and Geography in the Roman Empire*: 67–94. London: Routledge.

Lavan, L.
  1999. The Residences of Late Antique Governors: A Gazetteer. *Antiquité Tardive* 7: 135–64.

Lavan, L. (ed.).
  2001a. *Recent Research in Late Antique Urbanism*. Portsmouth, RI: Journal of Roman Archaeology Supplementary Series 42.

Lavan, L.
  2001b. A brief comment. In L. Lavan (ed.), *Recent Research in Late Antique Urbanism*: 243–5. Portsmouth, RI: Journal of Roman Archaeology Supplementary Series 42.

Lavan, L.
  2001c. The Praetoria of Civil Governors in Late Antiquity. In L. Lavan (ed.), *Recent Research in Late Antique Urbanism*: 39–56. Portsmouth, RI: Journal of Roman Archaeology Supplementary Series 42.

Lavan, L.
  2003a. Late Antique Urban Topography: From Architecture to Human Space. In L. Lavan and W. Bowden (eds.), *Theory and Practice in Late Antique Archaeology*: 171–95. Leiden: Brill.

Lavan, L.
  2003b. The Political Topography of the Late Antique City: Activity Spaces in Practice. In L. Lavan and W. Bowden (eds.), *Theory and Practice in Late Antique Archaeology*: 314–37. Leiden: Brill.

Lavan, L. and Bowden, W. (eds.).
  2003. *Theory and Practice in Late Antique Archaeology*. Leiden: Brill.

Lefebvre, H.
  1991. *The Production of Space*. Oxford: Blackwell.

Le Goff, J.
  1992. *History and Memory* (translated by Steven Rendall and Elizabeth Claman). New York: Columbia University Press.

Lemaire, T.
  1997. Archaeology between the Invention and Destruction of the Landscape. *Archaeological Dialogues* 4: 5–21.

Leone, A.
  2003. Topographies of Production in the Cities of Late Antique North Africa. In L. Lavan and W. Bowden (eds.), *Theory and Practice in Late Antique Archaeology*: 257–87. Leiden: Brill.

Leone, A.
  2007. *Changing Townscapes in North Africa from Late Antiquity to the Arab Conquest*. Bari: Edipuglia.

Lethbridge, T. C. and O'Reilly, M. M.
  1933. Archaeological Notes. *Proceedings of the Cambridge Antiquarian Society* 33: 164–7.

Lewis, M. J. T.
  1966. *Temples in Roman Britain*. Cambridge: Cambridge University Press.

Lewis, W. S. (ed.).
  1955. *Horace Walpole's Correspondence*. London: Oxford University Press.

Liebeschuetz, J. H. W. G.
  2000. *The Decline and Fall of the Roman City*. Oxford: Oxford University Press.

Liebeschuetz, J. H. W. G.
  2001. The Uses and Abuses of the Concept of Decline in Later Roman History or Was Gibbon

Politically Incorrect? In L. Lavan (ed.), *Recent Research in Late Antique Urbanism*: 233–45. Portsmouth, RI: Journal of Roman Archaeology Supplementary Series 42.

Lock, G., Gosden, C., Griffiths, D., and Daly, P.
2003. The Ridgeway and Vale Project: Excavations at Marcham/Frilford 2002. *South Midlands Archaeology* 33: 84–91.

Lock, G., Gosden, C., Griffiths, D., Daly, P., Trifkovic, V., and Marston, T.
2002. The Hillforts of the Ridgeway Project: Excavations at Marcham/Frilford 2001. *South Midlands Archaeology* 32: 69–83.

Lock, G., Gosden, C., and Daly, P.
2005. *Segsbury Camp: Excavations in 1996 and 1997 at an Iron Age Hillfort on the Oxfordshire Ridgeway*. Oxford: Oxford University School of Archaeology Monograph 61.

Loseby, S. T.
1996. Arles in Late Antiquity. In N. Christie and S. T. Loseby (eds.), *Towns in Transition*: 45–70. Hertfordshire: Scholar Press.

Lowther, A. W. G.
1937. Report on Excavations at Verulamium in 1934. *The Antiquaries Journal* 17: 28–55.

Lucas, G.
2005. *The Archaeology of Time*. Oxford: Routledge.

Luff, R.
1993. *Animal Bones from Excavations in Colchester, 1971–85*. Colchester: Colchester Archaeological Trust, Colchester Archaeology Report 12.

Lyle, M.
2002. *Canterbury: 2000 Years of History* (2nd ed.). Stroud: Tempus.

MacDonald, W. L.
1986. *The Architecture of the Roman Empire: Volume II. An Urban Appraisal*. New Haven: Yale University Press.

Mackreth, D. F.
1987. Roman Public Buildings. In J. Schofield and R. Leech (eds.), *Urban Archaeology in Britain*: 133–46. London: Council for British Archaeology Research Report 61.

Macphail, R.
1981. Soil and Botanical Studies of the "Dark Earth." In M. Jones and G. Dimbleby (eds.), *The Environment of Man: The Iron Age to the Anglo-Saxon Period*: 309–31. Oxford, British Archaeological Reports British Series 87.

Macphail, R.
1983. The Micromorphology of Dark Earth from Gloucester, London and Norwich: An Analysis of Urban Anthropogenic Deposits from the Late Roman to Early Medieval Periods in England. In P. Bullock and C. Murphy (eds.), *Soil Micromophology, Vol. 1: Techniques and Applications*: 245–52. Berkhamsted: A B Academic Publishers.

Magilton, J.
2003. The Defences of Roman Chichester. In P. Wilson (ed.), *The Archaeology of Roman Towns: Studies in Honour of John S. Wacher*: 156–67. Oxford: Oxbow Books.

Maltby, J. M.
1979. The Animal Bones. In C. M. Heighway, A. P. Garrod, and A. G. Vince (eds.), Excavations at 1 Westgate Street, Gloucester, 1975: 182–5. *Medieval Archaeology* 23: 159–213.

Manley, J. and Rudkin, D.
2005. A Pre-A.D. 43 Ditch at Fishbourne Roman Palace, Chichester. *Britannia* 36: 55–99.

Mann, J. C.
1996. *Britain and the Roman Empire*. Aldershot: Variorum.

Manning, W. H.

1972. Ironwork Hoards in Iron Age and Roman Britain. *Britannia* 3: 224–50.

Manning, W. H.

2003. The Defences at Caerwent. In P. Wilson (ed.), *The Archaeology of Roman Towns: Studies in Honour of John S. Wacher*: 168–83. Oxford: Oxbow Books.

Marsden, P.

1976. Two Roman Public Baths in London. *Transactions of the London and Middlesex Archaeological Society* 27: 1–70.

Marsden, P.

1980. *Roman London*. London: Thames and Hudson.

Marsden, P.

1987. *The Roman Forum Site in London: Discoveries before 1985*. London: H.M.S.O.

Marsh, G. and West, B.

1981. Skullduggery in Roman London. *Transactions of the London and Middlesex Archaeological Society* 32: 86–102.

Mason, D. J. P.

2001. *Roman Chester: City of the Eagles*. Stroud: Tempus.

Massey, D.

2005. *For Space*. London: Sage Publications.

Matthews, J.

1993. The Making of the Text. In J. Harris and I. Wood (eds.), *The Theodosian Code*: 19–44. Ithaca, NY: Cornell University Press.

Matthews, J.

1997. Gibbon and the Later Roman Empire: Causes and Circumstances. In R. McKitterick and R. Quinault (eds.), *Edward Gibbon and Empire*: 12–33. Cambridge: Cambridge University Press.

Matthews, J.

2000. *Laying Down the Law: A Study of the Theodosian Code*. New Haven: Yale University Press.

Mattingly, D. (ed.).

1997a. *Dialogues in Roman Imperialism: Power, Discourse and Discrepant Experiences in the Roman Empire*. Portsmouth, RI: Journal of Roman Archaeology Supplementary Series 23.

Mattingly, D.

1997b. Introduction: Dialogues of Power and Experience in the Roman Empire. In D. J. Mattingly (ed.), *Dialogues in Roman Imperialism: Power, Discourse and Discrepant Experiences in the Roman Empire*: 7–24. Portsmouth, RI: Journal of Roman Archaeology Supplementary Series 23.

Mattingly, D.

2004. Being Roman: Expressing Identity in a Provincial Setting. *Journal of Roman Archaeology* 17: 5–25.

Mattingly, D.

2006a. *An Imperial Procession: Britain in the Roman Empire*. London: Penguin Books.

Mattingly, D.

2006b. *The Imperial Economy*. In D. S. Potter (ed.), *A Companion to the Roman Empire*: 283–97. Oxford: Blackwell.

Mattingly, D. and Salmon, J. (eds.).

2000. *Economies beyond Agriculture in the Classical World*. London: Routledge.

Maurin, L. (ed.).

1992. *Villes et Agglomérations Urbaines Antiques du Sud-Ouest de la Gaule: Histoire et Archéologie*. Bordeaux: Fédération Aquitania.

McKitterick, R.

1997. Edward Gibbon and the Early Middle Ages in Eighteenth-Century Europe. In R. Mc-Kitterick and R. Quinault (eds.), *Edward Gibbon and Empire*: 162–89. Cambridge: Cambridge University Press.

McKitterick, R. and Quinault, R. (eds.).

1997a. *Edward Gibbon and Empire*. Cambridge: Cambridge University Press.

McKitterick, R. and Quinault, R.

1997b. Introduction. In R. McKitterick and R. Quinault (eds.), *Edward Gibbon and Empire*: 1–11. Cambridge: Cambridge University Press.

McWhirr, A.

1986. *Houses in Roman Cirencester*. Cirencester: Cirencester Excavation Committee.

Merrifield, R.

1987. *The Archaeology of Ritual and Magic*. London: Batsford.

Merrifield, R.

1995. Roman Metalwork from the Walbrook – Rubbish, Ritual or Redundancy? *Transactions of the London and Middlesex Archaeological Society* 46: 27–44.

Metzler, J., Méniel, P., and Gaeng, C.

2006. Oppida et espaces publics. In C. Haselgrove (ed.), *Les mutations de la fin de l'âge du Fer (Collection Bibracte 12/4)*: 201–24. Glux-en-Glenne: Centre archéologique européen.

Miles, D., Palmer, S., Lock, G., Gosden, C., and Cromarty, A. M.

2003. *Uffington White Horse and its Landscape: Investigations at White Horse Hill Uffington, 1989–95 and Tower Hill Ashbury, 1993–4*. Oxford: Oxford Archaeological Unit.

Millett, M.

1990. *The Romanization of Britain: An Essay in Archaeological Interpretation*. Cambridge: Cambridge University Press.

Millett, M.

1995. An Early Christian Community at Colchester? *The Archaeological Journal* 152: 451–4.

Millett, M.

2001. Approaches to Urban Societies. In S. James and M. Millett (eds.), *Britons and Romans: Advancing an Archaeological Agenda*: 59–66. York: Council for British Archaeology Research Report 125.

Mills, E. E.

1905. (Anon). *The Decline and Fall of the British Empire: a brief account of those causes which resulted in the destruction of our late ally, together with a comparison between the British and Roman Empires. Appointed for use in the National Schools of Japan. Tokio, 2005*, Oxford: Alden.

Milne, G.

1992. *From Roman Basilica to Medieval Market: Archaeology in Action in the City of London*. London: H.M.S.O.

Mitchell, S.

2007. *A History of the Later Roman Empire AD 284–641*. Oxford: Blackwell.

Moatti, C.

1989. *À la Recherche de la Rome Antique*. Découvertes Gallimard Archéologie.

Mommsen, T.

1864. *The History of Rome* (2nd ed., translated by W. P. Dickson). London: Richard Bentley.

Mommsen, T.

1996. *A History of Rome under the Emperors* (new English edited edition). London: Routledge.

Montagu-Puckle, F. H. G. and Niblett, R.

1983–1986. Observations on the South-East Side of the Basilica at Verulamium. *Hertfordshire Archaeology* 9: 178–82.

Monteil, M.
1999. *Nîmes antique et sa proche campagne: étude de topographie urbaine et périurbaine (fin VIe s. av. J.-C./VIe s. ap. J.-C.).* Lattes: CNRS.

Moore, T.
2006. *Iron Age Societies in the Severn-Cotswolds: Developing Narratives of Social and Landscape* (new English edited edition). Oxford: Archaeopress, British Archaeological Reports British Series 421.

Moore, T.
2007. Perceiving Communities: Exchange, Landscapes and Social Networks in the Later Iron Age of Western Britain. *Oxford Journal of Archaeology* 26: 79–102.

Morley, N.
2004. *Theories, Models and Concepts in Ancient History.* London: Routledge.

Morris, E.
2007. Making Magic: Later Prehistoric and Early Roman Salt Production in the Lincolnshire Fenland. In C. Haselgrove and T. Moore (eds.), *The Later Iron Age in Britain and Beyond*: 430–43. Oxford: Oxbow Books.

Morse, M.
2005. *How the Celts Came to Britain: Druids, Ancient Skulls and the Birth of Archaeology.* Stroud: Tempus.

Mould, Q.
2000. The Small Finds: Summary. In P. Ellis (ed.), *The Roman Baths and Macellum at Wroxeter: Excavations by Graham Webster 1955–85*: 108–21. London: English Heritage.

Mudd, A., Williams, R. J., and Lupton, A.
1999. *Excavations alongside Roman Ermin Street, Gloucestershire and Wiltshire: The Archaeology of the A419/A417 Swindon to Gloucester Road Scheme.* Oxford: Oxford Archaeological Unit.

Muir, R.
2000. *The New Reading the Landscape: Fieldwork in Landscape History.* Exeter: University of Exeter.

Munier, C.
1963. Concilia Galliae A. 314–A. 506. *Corpus Christianorum CXLVIII.*

Murray, T. (ed.).
1999. *Time and Archaeology.* London: Routledge.

Nardini, F.
1818. *Roma Antica.* Rome: Nella Stamperia de Romanis. (Original work published 1666)

Nash-Williams, V. E.
1930. Further Excavations at Caerwent, Monmouthshire, 1923–5. *Archaeologia* 80: 229–88.

Neal, D. S., Wardle, A., and Hunn, J.
1990. *Excavation on the Iron Age, Roman and Medieval Settlement at Gorhambury, St Albans.* London: Historic Buildings and Monuments Commission for England.

Niblett, R.
1999. *The Excavation of a Ceremonial Site at Folly Lane, Verulamium.* London: Society for the Promotion of Roman Studies, Britannia Monograph Series 14,.

Niblett, R.
2001. *Verulamium. The Roman City of St. Albans.* Stroud: Tempus.

Niblett, R.
2005a. Roman Verulamium. In R. Niblett and I. Thompson (eds.), *Alban's Buried Towns: An Assessment of St. Albans' Archaeology up to AD 1600*: 41–165. Oxford: Oxbow Books.

Niblett, R.
2005b. The Archaeological Assessment. In R. Niblett and I. Thompson (eds.), *Alban's Buried Towns: An Assessment of St Albans' Archaeology up to AD 1600*: 1–15. Oxford: Oxbow Books.

Niblett, R.
2006. From *Verlamion* to Verulamium. In P. Ottaway (ed.), *A Victory Celebration: Papers on the Archaeology of Colchester and Late Iron Age-Roman Britain Presented to Philip Crummy*: 19–26. Colchester: Colchester Archaeological Trust.

Niblett, R., with Manning, W. and Saunders, C.
2006. Verulamium: Excavations within the Roman Town 1986–1988. *Britannia* 37: 53–118.

Norton, J. E. (ed.).
1956. *The Letters of Edward Gibbon* (Vol. 2). London: Cassell.

O'Neil, H. and Grinsell, L. V.
1960. Gloucestershire Barrows. *Transactions of the Bristol and Gloucestershire Archaeological Society* 79: 5–149.

Olick, J. K. and Robbins, J.
1998. Social Memory Studies: From 'Collective Memory' to the Historical Sociology of Mnemonic Practice. *Annual Review of Sociology* 24: 105–40.

Ottaway, P.
1993. *Roman York*. London: Batsford.

Ottaway, P.
1999. York: The Study of a Late Roman Colonia. In H. Hurst (ed.), *The Coloniae of Roman Britain: New Studies and a Review: Papers of the Conference Held at Gloucester on 5–6 July, 1997*: 136–50. Portsmouth, RI: Journal of Roman Archaeology Supplementary Series 36.

Page, W.
1914. Celtic and Romano-British Hertfordshire. *The Victoria History of the County of Hertford*: 119–72. London: Constable and Company Limited.

Palmer-Brown, C.
1993. Significant New Dating Evidence for Linear Boundary Ditches. *Lincolnshire History and Archaeology* 28: 71–2.

Parslow, C. C.
1995. *Rediscovering Antiquity: Karl Weber and the Excavation of Herculaneum, Pompeii, and Stabiae*. Cambridge: Cambridge University Press.

Patterson, T.
1997. *Inventing Western Civilization*. New York: Monthly Review Press.

Penn, W. S.
1959. The Romano-British Settlement at Springhead: Excavations of Temple 1, Site C 1. *Archaeologia Cantiana* 73: 1–61.

Penn, W. S.
1960. Springhead: Temples 3 and 4. *Archaeologia Cantiana* 74: 113–40.

Penn, W. S.
1962. Temples 2 and 5. *Archaeologia Cantiana* 77: 110–32.

Perkins, P. and Nevett, L.
2000. Urbanism and Urbanisation in the Roman World. In J. Huskinson (ed.), *Experiencing Rome: Culture, Identity and Power in the Roman Empire*: 213–44. London: Routledge.

Perring, D.
1991a. Spatial Organisation and Social Change in Roman Towns. In J. Rich and A. Wallace-Hadrill (eds.), *City and Country in the Ancient World*: 273–93. London: Routledge.

Perring, D.
1991b. *Roman London*. London: Seaby.

Petch, D. F.
n.d. *Cottesford Place, Lincoln: A Roman Bath-Building*. Unpublished Excavation Report, City Museum, Lincoln.

Petts, D.
2003. *Christianity in Roman Britain*. Stroud: Tempus.

Phillips, D. and Heywood, B.
1995. *Excavations at York Minster Volume I: From Roman Fortress to Norman Cathedral*. London: H.M.S.O.

Philp, B.
1977. The Forum of Roman London: Excavations 1968–9. *Britannia* 8: 1–64.

Philpott, R.
1991. *Burial Practices in Roman Britain: A Survey of Grave Treatment and Furnishing A.D. 43–410*. Oxford: Tempus Reparatum, British Archaeology Reports British Series 291.

Pile, S.
2005. *Real Cities*. London: Sage Publications.

Pitts, L. F. and St. Joseph, J. K.
1985. *Inchtuthil: The Roman Legionary Fortress*. London: Society for the Promotion of Roman Studies, Britannia Monograph Series 6.

Pocock, J. G. A.
1999a. *Barbarism and Religion Vol. 1: The Enlightenment of Edward Gibbon, 1737–1764*. Cambridge: Cambridge University Press.

Pocock, J. G. A.
1999b. *Barbarism and Religion Vol. 2: Narratives of Civil Government*. Cambridge: Cambridge University Press.

Pocock, J. G. A.
2003. *Barbarism and Religion Vol. 3: The First Decline and Fall*. Cambridge: Cambridge University Press.

Pocock, J. G. A.
2005. *Barbarism and Religion Vol. 4: Barbarians, Savages and Empires*. Cambridge: Cambridge University Press.

Polanyi, K.
1957. The Economy as Institutional Process. In K. Polanyi and H. W. Pearson (eds.), *Trade and Market in the Early Empires*: 243–70. Glencoe, IL: The Free Press.

Porter, R.
1988. *Edward Gibbon: Making History*. London: Weidenfeld and Nicholson.

Potter, T. W.
1995. *Towns in Late Antiquity: Iol Caesarea and its Context*. Sheffield: University of Sheffield, Ian Sanders Memorial Committee.

Potter, T. W.
2002. The Transformation of Britain from 55 BC to AD 61. In P. Salway (ed.), *The Roman Era. The British Isles: 55 BC–AD 410*: 11–36. Oxford: Oxford University Press.

Poulton, R. and Scott, E.
1993. The Hoarding, Deposition and Use of Pewter in Roman Britain. In E. Scott (ed.), *Theoretical Roman Archaeology: First Conference Proceedings*: 115–32. Aldershot: Avebury.

Pretty, K.
1997. The Small Finds. In P. Barker, R. White, K. Pretty, H. Bird, and M. Corbishley (eds.), *The Baths Basilica Wroxeter: Excavations 1966–90*: 259–68. London: English Heritage.

Price, J.
2000. Report on Fragments from Two Glass Vessels. In M. Fulford and J. Timby (eds.), *Late Iron*

Age and Roman Silchester: Excavations on the Site of the Forum-Basilica 1977, 1980–86: 319–21. London: Society for the Promotion of Roman Studies, Britannia Monograph Series 15.

Pryor, F.
    2001. *The Flag Fen Basin: Archaeology and Environment of a Fenland Landscape*. Swindon: English Heritage.

Purcell, N.
    1996a. *Oppidum*. In S. Hornblower and A. Spawforth (eds.), *The Oxford Classical Dictionary*: 1069. Oxford: Oxford University Press.

Purcell, N.
    1996b. *Civitas*. In S. Hornblower and A. Spawforth (eds.), *The Oxford Classical Dictionary*: 335. Oxford: Oxford University Press.

Purcell, N.
    1996c. Rome and the Management of Water: Environment, Culture and Power. In G. Shipley and J. Salmon (eds.), *Human Landscapes in Classical Antiquity: Environment and Culture*: 180–212. London: Routledge.

Putnam, B.
    2007. *Roman Dorset*. Stroud: Tempus.

Qualmann, K. E., Rees, H., Scobie, G. D., and Whinney, R.
    2004. *Oram's Arbour: The Iron Age Enclosure at Winchester Volume 1: Investigations 1950–1999*. Winchester: Winchester Museums Service.

Quennell, P.
    1945. *Four Portraits: Studies of the Eighteenth Century*. London: Collins.

Quinault, R.
    1997. Winston Churchill and Gibbon. In R. McKitterick and R. Quinault (eds.), *Edward Gibbon and Empire*: 317–32. Cambridge: Cambridge University Press.

Rahtz, P. and Harris, L. G.
    1956–1957. The Temple Well and Other Buildings at Pagans Hill, Chew Stoke, North Somerset. *Somersetshire Archaeological and Natural History Society* 101–2: 15–51.

RCHME.
    1970. *Inventory of Historical Monuments in the County of Dorset Vol. 2 South-East Part 3*. London: H.M.S.O.

Reece, R.
    1980. Towns and Country: The End of Roman Britain. *World Archaeology* 12: 77–92.

Reece, R.
    1996. The Interpretation of Site Finds – A Review. In C. King and D. Wigg (eds.), *Coin Finds and Coin Use in the Roman World*: 341–55. Berlin: Gebr. Mann Verlag.

Reece, R.
    2003. The Siting of Roman *Corinium*. *Britannia* 34: 276–80.

Reid, A. and MacLean, R.
    1995. Symbolism and the Social Contexts of Iron Production in Karagwe. *World Archaeology* 27: 144–91.

Revell, L.
    1999. Constructing Romanitas: Roman Public Architecture and the Archaeology of Practice. In P. Baker, C. Forcey, S. Jundi, and R. Witcher (eds.), *TRAC 98: Proceedings of the Eighth Annual Theoretical Roman Archaeology Conference*: 52–8. Oxford: Oxbow Books.

Revell, L.
    2009. *Roman Imperialism and Local Identities*. Cambridge: Cambridge University Press.

Rhodes, J.
  1974. 96 Northgate Street. In H. Hurst (ed.), Excavations at Gloucester, 1971–1973: Second Interim
    Report. *The Antiquaries Journal* 54: 31–9.

Rich, J. W.
  2003. *Cassius Dio*. In S. Hornblower and A. Spawforth (eds.), *The Oxford Classical Dictionary*:
    299–300. Oxford: Oxford University Press.

Richards, D.
  2000. Iron-Working and Other Miscellaneous Metal-Working Residues. In M. Fulford and J.
    Timby (eds.), *Late Iron Age and Roman Silchester: Excavations on the Site of the Forum-
    Basilica 1977, 1980–86*: 421–2. London: Society for the Promotion of Roman Studies, Britannia
    Monograph Series 15.

Richmond, I. A.
  1963. *Roman Britain*. London: Jonathan Cape.

Rippon, S.
  2006. *Landscape, Community and Colonisation: The North Somerset Levels during the 1st to 2nd
    Millennia AD*. York: Council for British Archaeology Research Report 152.

Rivet, A. L. F.
  1958. *Town and Country in Roman Britain*. London: Hutchinson.

Rivet, A. L. F. and Smith, C.
  1979. *The Place-Names of Roman Britain*. London: Batsford.

Rodríguez Gutiérrez, O.
  2004. *El teatro romano de Itálica: estudio arqueoarquitectónico*. Madrid: Servicio de Publicaciones
    de la Universidad Autónoma de Madrid.

Rogers, A.
  2007. Beyond the Economic in the Roman Fenland: Reconsidering Land, Water, Hoards and
    Religion. In A. Fleming and R. Hingley (eds.), *The Making of the British Landscape: Fifty Years
    after Hoskins: Prehistoric and Roman Periods*: 113–30. Macclesfield: Windgather Press.

Rogers, A. and Hingley, R.
  2010. Edward Gibbon and Francis Haverfield: The Traditions of Imperial Decline. In M. Bradley
    (ed.), *Classics and Imperialism in the British Empire*: 189–209. Oxford: Oxford University Press.

Roskams, S.
  1991. The Dark Earth. In D. Perring and S. Roskams, with P. Allen (eds.), *Early Development of
    Roman London West of the Walbrook*: 64–5. London: Council for British Archaeology Research
    Report 70.

Roueché, C.
  1999. Looking for Late Antique Ceremonial: Ephesus and Aphrodisias. In H. Friesinger and F.
    Krinzinger (eds.), *100 Jarred Österreichische Forschungen in Ephesos*: 161–8. Vienna: Verlag der
    Österreichischen Akademie der Wissenschaften.

Rowsome, P.
  1998. The Development of the Town Plan of Early Roman London. In B. Watson (ed.), *Roman
    London Recent Archaeological Work*: 35–46. Portsmouth, RI: Journal of Roman Archaeology
    Supplementary Series 24.

Rowsome, P.
  1999. The Huggin Hill Baths and Bathing in London: Barometer of the Town's Changing Cir-
    cumstance? In J. DeLaine and D. B. Johnston (eds.), *Roman Baths and Bathing*: 263–77.
    Portsmouth, RI: Journal of Roman Archaeology Supplementary Series 37.

Rykwert, J.
  1976. *The Idea of a Town: The Anthropology of Urban Form in Rome, Italy and the Ancient World*.
    London: Faber and Faber.

Rykwert, J., Leach, N., and Tavernor, R. (trans.).
    1999. *Leon Battista Alberti: On the Art of Building in Ten Books*. Cambridge, MA: MIT Press.

Salway, P.
    1993. *The Oxford Illustrated History of Roman Britain*. Oxford: Oxford University Press.

Sankey, D.
    1998. Cathedrals, Granaries and Urban Utility in Late Roman London. In B. Watson (ed.), *Roman London Recent Archaeological Work*: 78–82. Portsmouth, RI: Journal of Roman Archaeology Supplementary Series 24.

Scheid, J.
    2003. *An Introduction to Roman Religion*. Edinburgh: Edinburgh University Press.

Schiavone, A.
    2000. *The End of the Past: Ancient Rome and the Modern West*. Cambridge, MA: Harvard University Press.

Schiffer, M. B.
    1985. Is There a 'Pompeii Premise' in Archaeology? *Journal of Anthropological Research* 41: 18–41.

Schnapp, A.
    1996. *The Discovery of the Past: The Origins of Archaeology*. London: British Museum Press.

Scott, B. G.
    1984. The Status of the Smith in Early Ireland. In B. G. Scott and H. Cleere (eds.), *The Crafts of the Blacksmith: Essays Presented to R. F. Tylecote at the 1984 Symposium of the UISPP Comité pour la Sidérurgie Ancienne*: 153–6. Belfast: UISPP Comité pour la Sidérurgie Ancienne.

Scott, E.
    1991. Animal and Infant Burials in Romano-British Villas: A Revitalisation Movement. In P. Garwood, D. Jennings, R. Skeates, and J. Toms (eds.), *Sacred and Profane: Proceedings of a Conference on Archaeology, Ritual and Religion, Oxford 1989*: 115–21. Oxford: Oxbow Books, Oxford University Research Committee for Archaeology Monograph 32.

Sear, F.
    1982. *Roman Architecture*. London: Batsford.

Seeck, O. (ed.)
    1876. *Notitia dignitatum: accedunt notitia urbis Constantinopolitanae et Laterculi provinciarum*. Berolini: Weidmann.

Semple, S.
    2004. Locations of Assembly in Early Anglo-Saxon England. In A. Pantos and S. Semple (eds.), *Assembly Places and Practices in Medieval Europe*: 135–54. Portland, OR: Four Courts Press.

Serjeantson, D.
    2000. The Bird Bones. In M. Fulford and J. Timby (eds.), *Late Iron Age and Roman Silchester: Excavations on the Site of the Forum-Basilica 1977, 1980–86*: 484–500. London: Society for the Promotion of Roman Studies, Britannia Monograph Series 15.

Sfameni, C.
    2004. *Residential Villas in Late Antique Italy: Continuity and Change*. In W. Bowden, L. Lavan, and C. Machado (eds.), *Recent Research on the Late Antique Countryside*: 335–75. Leiden: Brill.

Sharples, N.
    2010. *Social Relations in Later Prehistory: Wessex in the First Millennium BC*. Oxford: Oxford University Press.

Sheldon, H. L.
    1978. The 1972–4 Excavations: Their Contribution to Southwark's History. In J. Bird, A. H. Graham, H. L. Sheldon, and P. Townend (eds.), *Southwark Excavations 1972–4*: 11–49. London: London and Middlesex Archaeological Society and Surrey Archaeological Society, Joint Publication 1.

Shepherd, J.
  1998. *The Temple of Mithras, London: Excavations by W. F. Grimes and A. Williams at the Walbrook.* London: English Heritage.

Simonsen, K.
  1997. Modernity, Community or a Diversity of Ways of Life: A Discussion of Urban Everyday Life. In O. Källtorp, I. Elander, O. Erisson, and M. Franzén (eds.), *Cities in Transformation – Transformation in Cities: Social and Symbolic Change of Urban Space*: 162–83. Aldershot: Ashgate.

Simonsen, K.
  2003. The Embodied City: From Bodily Practice to Urban Life. In J. Öhman and K. Simonsen (eds.), *Voices from the North: New Trends in Nordic Human Geography*: 157–72. Aldershot: Ashgate.

Sirmond, J. and Pharr, C. (eds.).
  1969. *The Theodosian Code and Novels and the Sirmondian Constitutions.* Princeton, NJ: Princeton University Press.

Sjöberg, G.
  1965. *The Pre-Industrial City: Past and Present.* Glencoe, IL: The Free Press.

Smiles, S.
  1994. *The Image of Antiquity: Ancient Britain and the Romantic Imagination.* New Haven: Yale University Press.

Smith, K.
  2006. *Guides, Guards and Gifts to the Gods: Domesticated Dogs in the Art and Archaeology of Iron Age and Roman Britain.* Oxford: Archaeopress, British Archaeological Reports British Series 422.

Snelling, H.
  2006. The Human Remains. In M. Fulford, A. Clarke, and H. Eckhardt (eds.), *Life and Labour in Late Roman Silchester: Excavations in Insula IX since 1997*: 200–5. London: Society for the Promotion of Roman Studies Britannia Monograph Series 22.

Sparey Green, C.
  1986. Earthworks of Prehistoric or Early Roman Date in the Dorchester Area. *Proceedings of the Dorset Natural History and Archaeological Society* 108: 193–4.

Stambaugh, J. E.
  1978. The Functions of Roman Temples. *Aufstieg und Niedergang der Römischen Welt* II.16.1: 554–608.

Stead, P. M.
  2004. *Archaeological Excavation of Southernhay East Car Park Exeter.* Exeter: Exeter Archaeology Report 04.24.

Steane, K.
  2006. *The Archaeology of the Upper City and Adjacent Suburbs.* Oxford: Oxbow Books, Lincoln Archaeological Studies 3.

Stirling, L.
  2001. The East Baths and Their Industrial Re-Use in Late Antiquity: 1992 Excavations. In L. M. Stirling, D. J. Mattingly, and N. Ben Lazreg (eds.), *Leptiminus (Lamta) Report No. 2. The East Baths, Cemeteries, Kilns, Venus Mosaic, Site Museum and Other Studies*: 29–73. Portsmouth, RI: Journal of Roman Archaeology Supplementary Series 41.

St John Hope, W. H.
  1908. Excavations on the Site of the Roman City at Silchester, Hertfordshire in 1907. *Archaeologia* 61: 199–218.

Stocker, D.
  2003. The 'Colonia' Era – The Archaeological Agenda. An Introduction to the Research Agenda

Zone Entries. In D. Stocker (ed.), *The City by the Pool: Assessing the Archaeology of the City of Lincoln*: 138–40. Oxford: Oxbow Books.

Struck, M.

1997. Review of N. Crummy, P. Crummy and C. Crossan, Excavations of Roman and Later Cemeteries, Churches and Monastic Sites in Colchester, 1971–88. *Britannia* 28: 496–8.

Swan, V.

1980. *Pottery in Roman Britain* (3rd ed.). Aylesbury: Shire Publications.

Sweet, R.

2004. *Antiquaries: The Discovery of the Past in Eighteenth-Century Britain*. London and New York: Hambledon and London.

Swift, E.

2000. *The End of the Western Roman Empire: An Archaeological Investigation*. Stroud: Tempus.

Swift, E.

2003. *Roman Dress Accessories*. Princes Risborough: Shire Publications.

Tainter, J. A.

1988. *The Collapse of Complex Societies*. Cambridge: Cambridge University Press.

Taylor, J.

1997. Space and Place: Some Thoughts on Iron Age and Romano-British Landscapes. In A. Gwilt and C. Haselgrove (eds.), *Reconstructing Iron Age Societies: New Approaches to the British Iron Age*: 192–204. Oxford: Oxbow Books.

Taylor, J.

2001. Rural Society in Roman Britain. In S. James and M. Millett (eds.), *Britons and Romans: Advancing an Archaeological Agenda*: 46–59. York: Council for British Archaeology Research Report 125.

Tayor, J.

2007. *An Atlas of Roman Rural Settlement in England*. York: Council for British Archaeology Research Report 151.

Teague, S. C.

1988. Excavations at Market Street 1987–88. *Winchester Museums Service Newsletter* 2: 6–8.

Thébert, Y.

2003. *Thermes Romains d'Afrique du Nord et Leur Contexte Mediterranéan*. Rome: École Française de Rome.

Thomas, J.

1991. *Rethinking the Neolithic*. Cambridge: Cambridge University Press.

Thomas, J.

1993. The Politics of Vision and the Archaeologies of Landscape. In B. Bender (ed.), *Landscape: Politics and Perspectives*: 19–48. Providence: Berg.

Thomas, J.

1996. *Time, Culture and Identity: An Interpretative Archaeology*. London: Routledge.

Thompson, E. A.

1982. Zosimus 6.10.2 and the Letters of Honorius. *Classical Quarterly* 32: 445–62.

Thompson, I.

2005. Verlamion in the Late Pre-Roman Iron Age. In R. Niblett and I. Thompson (eds.), *Alban's Buried Towns: An Assessment of St Albans' Archaeology up to AD 1600*: 23–40. Oxford: Oxbow Books.

Thorpe, M.

1995. *Roman Architecture*. London: Bristol Classical Press.

Tilley, C.

1994. *A Phenomenology of Landscape: Places, Paths and Monuments*. Oxford: Berg.

Tilley, C.
2004. *The Materiality of Stone: Explorations in Landscape Phenomenology*. Oxford: Berg.

Timby, J. R.
1998. *Excavations at Kingscote and Wycomb, Gloucestershire*. Cirencester: Cotswold Archaeological Trust.

Timby, J. R.
1999. Pottery Supply to Gloucester Colonia. In H. Hurst (ed.), *The Coloniae of Roman Britain: New Studies and a Review: Papers of the Conference Held at Gloucester on 5–6 July, 1997*: 37–44. Portsmouth, RI: Journal of Roman Archaeology Supplementary Series 36.

Todd, M.
2004. The Rediscovery of Roman Britain. In M. Todd (ed.), *A Companion to Roman Britain*: 443–59. Oxford: Blackwell.

Tournaire, J., Büchsenschütz, O., Henderson, J., and Collis, J.
1982. Iron Age Coin Moulds from France. *Proceedings of the Prehistoric Society* 48: 417–35.

Trigger, B. C.
1990. Monumental Architecture: A Thermodynamic Explanation of Symbolic Behaviour. *World Archaeology* 22: 119–32.

Trow, S. D.
1988. Excavations at Ditches Hillfort, North Cerney, Gloucestershire, 1982–3. *Transactions of the Bristol and Gloucestershire Archaeological Society* 106: 19–85.

Trow, S. D.
1990. By the Northern Shores of Ocean: Some Observations on Acculturation Process at the Edge of the Roman World. In T. Blagg and M. Millett (eds.), *The Early Roman Empire in the West*: 103–18. Oxford: Oxbow Books.

Tyers, P.
1996. *Roman Pottery in Britain*. London: Batsford.

Tylecote, R. F.
1976. *The Prehistory of Metallurgy in the British Isles*. London: Institute of Metals.

Upex, S. G.
2001. The Roman Villa at Cotterstock, Northamptonshire. *Britannia* 32: 57–91.

Van Dyke, R. M. and Alcock, S. E.
2003. Archaeologies of Memory: An Introduction. In R. M. Van Dyke and S. E. Alcock (eds.), *Archaeologies of Memory*: 1–13. Oxford: Blackwell.

Vance, N.
1997. *The Victorians and Ancient Rome*. Oxford: Blackwell.

Wacher, J. S.
1959. Roman Britain in 1958: Leicester. *Journal of Roman Studies* 49: 113–15.

Wacher, J. S. (ed.).
1966. *The Civitas Capitals of Roman Britain*. Leicester: Leicester University Press.

Wacher, J. S.
1975. *The Towns of Roman Britain*. London: Batsford.

Wacher, J. S.
1995. *The Towns of Roman Britain* (2nd ed.). London: Batsford.

Wacher, J. S. and McWhirr, A.
1982. *Early Roman Occupation at Cirencester. Cirencester Excavations* 1. Cirencester: Cirencester Excavations Committee.

Wainwright, G. J.
1979. *Mount Pleasant, Dorset: Excavations, 1970–71: Incorporating an Account of Excavations*

undertaken at Woodhenge in 1970. London: The Society of Antiquaries of London, Reports for the Research Committee Number 37.

Wallace-Hadrill, A.
1991. Elites and Trade in the Roman Town. In J. Rich and A. Wallace-Hadrill (eds.), *City and Country in the Ancient World*: 241–72. London: Routledge.

Wallace-Hadrill, A.
1993. *Augustan Rome*. London: Bristol Classical Press.

Wardle, A.
1998. Roman London: Recent Finds and Research. In B. Watson (ed.), *Roman London Recent Archaeological Work*: 83–9. Portsmouth, RI: Journal of Roman Archaeology Supplementary Series 24.

Ward-Perkins, B.
1978. Luni – The Decline and Abandonment of a Roman Town. In H. McK. Blake, T. W. Potter, and D. B. Whitehouse (eds.), *Papers in Italian Archaeology I*: 313–21. Oxford, British Archaeological Reports International Series 41.

Ward-Perkins, B.
1981. Two Byzantine Houses at Luni. *Papers of the British School at Rome* 49: 91–8.

Ward-Perkins, B.
1984. *From Classical Antiquity to the Middle Ages: Urban Public Building in Northern and Central Italy, AD 300–850*. Oxford: Oxford University Press.

Ward-Perkins, B.
1998. The Cities. In A. Cameron and P. Garnsey (eds.), *The Cambridge History Volume 13: The Late Empire, A.D. 337–425*: 371–410. Cambridge: Cambridge University Press.

Ward-Perkins, B.
2005. *The Fall of Rome and the End of Civilization*. Oxford: Oxford University Press.

Ward-Perkins, J. B.
1981. *Roman Imperial Architecture*. Harmondsworth: Penguin Books.

Watts, D.
1991. *Christians and Pagans in Roman Britain*. London: Routledge.

Watts, D.
1998. *Religion in Late Roman Britain*. London: Routledge.

Webb, M.
2000. *The Churches and Catacombs of Early Christian Rome: A Comprehensive Guide*. Brighton: Sussex Academic Press.

Weber, M.
1958. *The City*. Glencoe, IL: The Free Press.

Webster, G.
1975. *The Cornovii*. London: Duckworth.

Webster, J.
1995. Sanctuaries and Sacred Places. In M. Green (ed.), *The Celtic World*: 441–64. London: Routledge.

Webster, J. and Cooper, N. (eds.).
1996. *Roman Imperialism: Post-Colonial Perspectives*. Leicester: Leicester School of Archaeological Studies, Leicester Archaeology Monographs 3.

Wedlake, W. J.
1982. *The Excavation of the Shrine of Apollo at Nettleton, Wiltshire, 1956–1971*. London: The Society of Antiquaries of London, Reports of the Research Committee Number 40.

Welch, K.
2003. A New View of the Origins of the Basilica: The Atrium Regium, Groecostasis and Roman Diplomacy. *Journal of Roman Archaeology* 16: 5–34.

Wheeler, R. E. M.
1943. *Maiden Castle, Dorset.* London: The Society of Antiquaries of London, Reports of the Research Committee Number 12.

Wheeler, R. E. M.
1966. *Civilizations of the Indus Valley and Beyond.* London: Thames and Hudson.

Wheeler, R. E. M. and Wheeler, T. V.
1936. *Verulamium: A Belgic and Two Roman Cities.* London: The Society of Antiquaries of London, Report of the Research Committee Number 11.

White, G. M.
1936. The Chichester Amphitheatre: Preliminary Excavation. *The Antiquaries Journal* 16: 149–59.

White, R.
1997. Appendix 11: List of Contexts, by Site and Phase, Division into Categories A, B, and C. In P. Barker, R. White, K. Pretty, H. Bird, and M. Corbishley (eds.), *The Baths Basilica Wroxeter: Excavations 1966–90*: 371–4. London: English Heritage.

White, R.
2000. Wroxeter and the Transformations of Late-Roman Urbanism. In T. R. Slater (ed.), *Towns in Decline AD 100–1600*: 96–119. Aldershot: Ashgate.

White, R.
2007. *Britannia Prima: Britain's Last Roman Province.* Stroud: Tempus.

White, R. and Barker, P.
1998. *Wroxeter: Life and Death of a Roman City.* Stroud: Tempus.

White, R. and Gaffney, V.
2003. Resolving the Paradox: The Work of the Wroxeter Hinterland Project. In P. Wilson (ed.), *The Archaeology of Roman Towns: Studies in Honour of John S. Wacher*: 221–32. Oxford: Oxbow Books.

Whyman, M. C.
2001. *Late Roman Britain in Transition, A.D. 300–500: A Ceramic Perspective from East Yorkshire.* Unpublished Ph.D. thesis, University of York.

Wickenden, N. P.
1992. *The Temple and Other Sites in the North-East Sector of Caesaromagus.* London: Chelmsford Archaeological Trust Report 9 and Council for British Archaeology Research Report 75.

Wickham, C.
2005. *Framing the Early Middle Ages: Europe and the Mediterranean 400–800.* Oxford: Oxford University Press.

Wightman, E.
1985. *Gallia Belgica.* London: Batsford.

Wilkes, J. J.
1996. Introduction. In P. Johnson (ed.), *Architecture in Roman Britain*: 1–5. London: Council for British Archaeology Research Report 94.

Williams, H. M. R.
1998. The Ancient Monument in Romano-British Ritual Practices. In C. Forcey, J. Hawthorne, and R. Witcher (eds.), *TRAC 97: Proceedings of the Seventh Annual Theoretical Roman Archaeology Conference*: 71–86. Oxford: Oxbow Books.

Williams, H. M. R.
2006. *Death and Memory in Early Medieval Britain.* Cambridge: Cambridge University Press.

Williams, T.
    1993. *Public Buildings in the South-West Quarter of Roman London. The Archaeology of Roman London Volume 3*. London: Council for British Archaeology Research Report 88.

Williams, T.
    2003. Water and the Roman City: Life in Roman London. In P. Wilson (ed.), *The Archaeology of Roman Towns: Studies in Honour of John S. Wacher*: 242–50. Oxford: Oxbow Books.

Willis, S.
    2007a. Roman Towns, Roman Landscapes: The Cultural Terrain of Town and Country in the Roman Period. In A. Fleming and R. Hingley (eds.), *The Making of the British Landscape: Fifty Years after Hoskins: Prehistoric and Roman Periods*: 143–64. Macclesfield: Windgather Press.

Willis, S.
    2007b. Sea, Coast, Estuary, Land and Culture in Britain during the Iron Age. In C. Haselgrove and T. Moore (eds.), *The Later Iron Age in Britain and Beyond*: 107–29. Oxford: Oxbow Books.

Willis, S. and Hingley, R.
    2007. Roman Finds: Context and Theory. In R. Hingley and S. Willis (eds.), *Roman Finds: Context and Theory*: 2–17. Oxford: Oxbow Books.

Wilmott, T., Garner, D., and Ainsworth, S.
    2006. The Roman Amphitheatre at Chester: An Interim Account. *English Heritage Historical Review* 1: 7–23.

Wilson, D. R.
    1970. Roman Britain in 1969: Sites Explored. *Britannia* 1: 269–305.

Wilson, D. R.
    1975. Roman Britain in 1974: Sites Explored. *Britannia* 6: 221–83.

Witcher, R.
    1998. Roman Roads: Phenomenological Perspectives on Roads in the Landscape. In C. Forcey, J. Hawthorne, and R. Witcher (eds.), *TRAC 97: Proceedings of the Seventh Annual Theoretical Roman Archaeology Conference Nottingham 1997*: 60–70. Oxford: Oxbow Books.

Womersley, D.
    1988. *The Transformation of the Decline and Fall of the Roman Empire*. Cambridge: Cambridge University Press.

Womersley, D.
    1994. Introduction. In E. Gibbon (ed.), *The History of the Decline and Fall of the Roman Empire*: xi–cvi. London: Penguin Books.

Womersley, D. (ed.)
    1997. *Edward Gibbon: Bicentenary Essays*. Oxford: Voltaire Foundation.

Womersley, D.
    2002. *Gibbon and the 'Watchmen of the Holy City': The Historian and His Reputation 1776–1815*. Oxford: Clarendon Press.

Wood, I.
    2004. *The Final Phase*. In M. Todd (ed.), *A Companion to Roman Britain*: 428–42. Oxford: Blackwell.

Woodward, A.
    1992. *Shrines and Sacrifice*. London: Batsford/English Heritage.

Woodward, A. and Leach, P.
    1993. *The Uley Shrines: Excavations of a Ritual Complex on West Hill, Uley, Gloucestershire, 1977–9*. London: English Heritage.

Woodward, P. and Woodward, A.
    2004. Dedicating the Town: Urban Foundation Deposits in Roman Britain. *World Archaeology* 36: 68–86.

Woodward, P. J., Davies, S. M., and Graham, A. H.
  1993. *Excavations at Greyhound Yard, Dorchester 1981–4.* Dorchester: Dorset Natural History and Archaeology Society.

Woolf, G.
  1993. Rethinking the Oppida. *Oxford Journal of Archaeology* 12: 223–34.

Woolf, G.
  1998. *Becoming Roman: the Origins of Provisional Civilisation in Gaul.* Cambridge: Cambridge University Press.

Woolf, V.
  1943. The Historian and 'The Gibbon'. In V. Woolf (ed.), *The Death of the Moth and Other Essays*: 55–63. London: Hogarth Press.

Wright, T.
  1872. *Uriconium: A Historical Account of the Ancient City.* London: Longmans, Green and Co.

Yegül, F.
  1992. *Baths and Bathing in Classical Antiquity.* Cambridge, MA: MIT Press.

Yoffee, N. and Cowgill, G. L.
  1988. *The Collapse of Ancient States and Civilizations.* Tucson: University of Arizona Press.

Yule, B.
  1990. The 'Dark Earth' and Late Roman London. *Antiquity* 64: 620–8.

Yule, B.
  2005. *A Prestigious Roman Building Complex on the Southwark Waterfront: Excavations at Winchester Palace, London, 1983–90.* London: MoLAS, Monograph 23.

Zanker, P.
  1989. *The Power of Images in the Age of Augustus.* Ann Arbor: University of Michigan Press.

Zanker, P.
  2000. The City as Symbol: Rome and the Creation of an Urban Image. In E. Fentress (ed.), *Romanisation and the City: Location, Transformation and Failures. Proceedings of a Conference Held at the American Academy in Rome to Celebrate the 50th Anniversary of the Excavations at Cosa, 14th–16th May, 1998*: 25–41. Portsmouth, RI: Journal of Roman Archaeology Supplementary Series 38.

Zant, J. M.
  1993. *The Brooks, Winchester, 1987–88. The Roman Structural Remains.* Winchester: Winchester Museums Service Archaeology Report 2.

Index

Page numbers in italics are figures; with 't' are tables.

Lightning Source UK Ltd.
Milton Keynes UK
UKOW07f1611061215

264156UK00005B/246/P